Strange Bedfellows

POLITICS AND CULTURE IN MODERN AMERICA

Series Editors: Margot Canaday, Glenda Gilmore,
Michael Kazin, Stephen Pitti, Thomas J. Sugrue

Volumes in the series narrate and analyze political and social change
in the broadest dimensions from 1865 to the present, including ideas
about the ways people have sought and wielded power in the public
sphere and the language and institutions of politics at all levels—local,
national, and transnational. The series is motivated by a desire to reverse
the fragmentation of modern U.S. history and to encourage synthetic
perspectives on social movements and the state, on gender, race, and labor,
and on intellectual history and popular culture.

STRANGE BEDFELLOWS

Marriage in the Age of Women's Liberation

Alison Lefkovitz

PENN

UNIVERSITY OF PENNSYLVANIA PRESS

PHILADELPHIA

Published by
University of Pennsylvania Press
Philadelphia, Pennsylvania 19104-4112
www.upenn.edu/pennpress

Printed in the United States of America
on acid-free paper

10 9 8 7 6 5 4 3 2 1

Library of Congress Cataloging-in-Publication Data
Names: Lefkovitz, Alison, author.
Title: Strange bedfellows: marriage in the age of women's liberation / Alison Lefkovitz.
Other titles: Politics and culture in modern America.
Description: 1st edition. | Philadelphia: University of Pennsylvania Press,
    [2018] | Series: Politics and culture in modern America | Includes
    bibliographical references and index.
Identifiers: LCCN 2017046028 | ISBN 9780812250152 (hardcover: alk. paper)
Subjects: LCSH: Marriage—United States—History—20th century. |
    Marriage—United States—History—20th century—Public opinion. | Domestic
    relations—United States—History—20th century. | Marriage law—United
    States—History—20th century. | Women's rights—United
    States—History—20th century. | Sex role—United States—History—20th
    century. | Public opinion—United States.
Classification: LCC HQ535 .L36 2018 | DDC 306.810973—dc23
LC record available at https://lccn.loc.gov/2017046028

CONTENTS

In the inaugural issue of *Ms. Magazine*, the feminist activist Judy Syfers proclaimed that she "would like a wife."[1] But her desire was not sexual or emotional. Instead, she offered a deeply felt and wry critique of the state of marriage in modern America. After all, she said, only a wife could provide her with certain comforts like working for wages, taking care of children, keeping the house clean, preparing meals, having sex with her, and much more. Syfers concluded with a rhetorical flourish: "My God, who *wouldn't* want a wife?"[2] A few pages away in this same issue, Johnnie Tillmon, the president of the National Welfare Rights Organization, critiqued not only the Aid to Families with Dependent Children program but also marriage. She proclaimed that all women were domestic slaves, and even marriage provided wan protection or pay for this labor.

Outside of the pages of *Ms.*, other Americans debated marriage. Divorced men's rights activist Charles Metz, for example, opened his own book-long manifesto on marriage reform in 1968 with a triumphant recognition that "noise is swelling from hundreds of thousands of divorced male victims. God help us to swell this noise, still a whimper, into a roar of indignation that will be felt in every court and legislative body in this Union of States and their Federal Government."[3] Phyllis Schlafly, similarly, decried the Equal Rights Amendment for its potential danger to the institution of marriage broadly and to wives in particular. The Immigration and Naturalization Service (INS) identified sham unions as one of the main threats to the nation's borders. Gay men and lesbians, meanwhile, dressed in drag to try to win marriage licenses from oblivious bureaucrats and then went to local newspapers to call attention to their exclusion from marriage.

In other words, a broad array of Americans identified marriage as a problem in the 1960s and 1970s, and the subsequent changes to marriage law at the local and federal levels constituted a legal revolution. But legislators and courts instituted these changes unevenly to ameliorate the problems they identified as the most dangerous, rather than give activists exactly what they had asked for. These new policies replaced the more blatant gender and racial inequalities that courts and legislatures had stripped out of the law during the civil rights revolution. Like law and order campaigns and the War on Drugs, the legal revolution in marriage at once instituted formal legal equality and also created new forms of political inequality that historians—like most Americans—have yet to fully understand.

The difficulty began with the legal foundations of marriage. Half a century after the long struggle for votes for women had secured an amendment to the nation's founding document, wives and husbands were still sharply distinguished not only in popular culture and private life but also in law. State laws nationwide obliged wives to perform nearly all of the homemaking tasks that Syfers catalogued in *Ms.*; wives' unpaid labor in the home still belonged to their husbands in practice and in law.[4] Indeed, laws in every state entitled husbands to their wives' bodies. Until legislators began to recognize the existence of rape in marriage in the late 1970s, state law defined rape as the violent act whereby a man forced a woman *who was not his wife* to have sexual intercourse. A man could legally force his wife to have sex. Although technically, either spouse could win a divorce based on fault for his or her partner's sexual indiscretion, only a wife lost the right to alimony and marital property when her husband won a divorce for her infidelity.[5]

Yet husbands had their own gendered obligations to fulfill, characterized above all by the duty to support their wives and children. Though a wife had to bring her case to court, the government enforced a husband's financial duties as spouses entered and left a marriage.[6] Many men faced harsh ramifications for failing to fulfill these breadwinning obligations ranging from court orders to jail sentences. Of course, there were limits to the breadwinner-homemaker political economy. Even at its peak, only some couples managed to live up to these roles. The family wage that enabled some wives to work from home eluded many in the working class. Not all men and women were punished for failing to fulfill these obligations. Nonetheless, for over a century, the roles of breadwinner and homemaker had not only defined what couples privately hoped to practice but had also shaped public policy. This particular system of gendered obligations was codified alongside the rise of separate spheres, justified higher wages for men, and eventually was enshrined in federal welfare programs from Social Security to Aid to Dependent Children.[7]

Beginning in the 1960s, a feminist revival worked to dismantle this system.[8] Feminists questioned and then assaulted the institution of marriage and the gendered roles within it.[9] Different feminists advocated for different ideas ranging from the total destruction of the institution to more cosmetic changes. Liberal feminists had the greatest success at reforming the law, but even among them, two different concepts of equality rivaled one another. One was what I call *expansionist*—it sought to keep the protections that wives enjoyed by extending them to husbands as well. Wives could take care of their husbands just as husbands had traditionally taken care of wives. The other concept of equality was *individualist*—it sought to make wives' roles equal to husbands' financially and in law by compensating women for their household labor at the point of divorce, retirement, or widowhood. Neither spouse would have to take care of the other over time. Both visions of equality had some significant though mitigated effects on marriage law, which changed but without fully accounting for the vast gender difference that persisted within the home and in terms of jobs, income, and wealth.

Feminists' redefining of the marriage relationship led husbands to question their roles as well. Many husbands increasingly resented their support obligations as wives began rethinking their roles as homemakers.[10] Most husbands were not well organized, but many nonetheless backed away from breadwinning obligations en masse in the 1970s. Other husbands, like Charles Metz, founded divorced men's groups that sued or lobbied to free men of these obligations. And though these groups were not the most effectively organized of activist bodies, their claims seemed to resonate with state legislatures and courts who limited men's support obligations.

Feminists and divorced husband groups' questioning of the marriage relationship also coincided with welfare, immigration, and gay marriage activists' rising demands that lawmakers treat their families equitably. While their specific goals and who they counted as a family varied, all three of these emerging social movements asked the government to provide the same legal recognition and financial support that "traditional" families received. This diverse array of advocates on the left also made use of the changing legal ground, new resources, and new strategies forged by the civil rights and feminist movements to make demands such as extending gender-neutral obligations to all families or decoupling benefits from family relationships entirely. The resources and strategies had their limits, however. While the feminist movement won a moderated victory in the form of greater legal equality between husbands and wives, these activists gained even less.

While feminists, divorced men's groups, welfare rights activists, gay liberationists, and immigration reformers attacked husbands' and wives' traditional obligations, breadwinning and homemaking also crumbled from within. A range of pressures weighed on the institution of marriage, but financial concerns prompted by deindustrialization were among the most anguishing ones. More husbands found it increasingly difficult to get jobs offering a family wage; financial distress also seemed to spur the growing number of women working outside the home.[11] Though everyday Americans were not necessarily aware of the coming collapse of the postwar economic boom, they certainly understood their own inability to earn a family wage. Even as a diverse array of activists challenged the old marriage regime, many husbands and wives were already necessarily reorganizing their own marriages, "on the ground," on an individual basis across the United States.

The federal structure of the American legal and political system profoundly shaped the outcomes of this marriage revolution. In particular, the strand of liberal feminism that advocated for an expansionist approach to equality had significant success at the federal level. The Supreme Court and Congress preserved wives' rights by making them gender-neutral. But the protection of gender-neutral breadwinner and homemaker obligations on the federal level had more destructive effects on women on welfare, their partners, immigrant spouses, and gay and lesbian couples.

Individualist feminists won a more moderated victory on the state level than expansionist feminists had at the federal level. Many state legislatures passed laws that gave modest financial compensation to some wives for their household labor, but they also scaled back men's breadwinning obligations. Together these two changes helped produce what legal scholar Mary Anne Case has termed a "thin" definition of marriage—legally, husbands and wives owed each other few duties.[12] Ultimately the ideas circulating at the state level had a larger impact on husbands' and wives' lives than did the Supreme Court or Congress, both of which ignored or did not notice the state-level disintegration of marital duty. The federal government had the power to influence state marriage law, just as it did in other state programs through block grants and other means. In other words, the federal government's striking failure to recognize the changes occurring at the state level was not inevitable.[13]

Understanding the changes to breadwinning and homemaking policies and the varied effects of those changes on differently situated people sheds light on a number of trends in postwar U.S. history. First, feminists were not the only actors affecting marriage law—a revolt by male breadwinners also had momentous effects on state law. Therefore even gender-neutral law left gendered inequalities in the family in place. This story also brings into sharper focus one of the key developments in the late twentieth century history of gender, the feminization of poverty. Under the new marriage law regime, most white women and most women of color increasingly faced similar fates. Policies premised on the breadwinner-homemaker division of labor had long sought to protect white women from the vagaries of the market, but most women of color had been left out of this bargain from the beginning. By the mid-1990s, very few women retained these protections, and even middle-class white women found themselves solely responsible for the household as many women of color had long been.[14]

Furthermore, this story also helps to explain the New Right's rise to power.[15] The fracturing of the breadwinner-homemaker household in law first allowed conservatives to displace some anger about the economic downturn onto feminists. Conservatives then made simultaneous moral and economic claims against the aspirations not only of feminists, but also of welfare rights activists, immigrants, and gay men and lesbians.

Finally this story also helps to explain how liberal reforms coexisted with the persistence of inequality for the poor, people of color, and the LGBTQ community. Stripping marriage of its thick gender obligations benefited only the most privileged. For example, poor women did not receive the compensation for their household labor that wealthier divorced women did; poor men could not as easily escape their breadwinning responsibilities as middle-class men could. Gay men and lesbians did not win the legal right to form a household until decades after marriage lost most of its gendered properties.

In the nineteenth century Americans struck a bargain that marriage and family would provide a social safety net, and we have continued to rely on this idea of family even as other countries have transferred that care over to the state. Increasingly now, marriage does not provide this in practice or in law. The greatest burdens for providing care for the vulnerable have fallen on women, the poor, and other disadvantaged Americans. This disjuncture between the social safety net we still think marriage provides and the vast gaps in marriage's coverage is an unfinished revolution.

*   *   *

The book unfolds in two parts. The first section recounts how lawmakers removed gender from marriage law. It begins by detailing challenges to the institution of marriage from liberal feminists and radical marriage dissenters in the 1960s and '70s. Despite disagreements between feminist reformers and marriage dissenters, the expansionist vision of legal equality nonetheless transformed marriage law at the federal level. It then deals with divorce law at the state level and the implementation of individualist legal equality. Liberal feminists and men's rights activists successfully pushed legislators to dismantle both a wife's right to perpetual support and a husband's right to his wife's household and sexual labor.[16]

The book's second section explains why the extraordinary achievements of this revolution in marriage were nonetheless circumscribed. Feminists' success in stripping gender distinctions out of marriage legally and culturally at first seemed to open up new political possibilities for the ordering of family life, but others worked with equal vigor to limit the scope of social change. Fears that feminism would lead to the decline of the middle-class family defeated the Equal Rights Amendment. Despite fierce organizing by welfare rights activists, state and federal governments tried to compel women on welfare into financial dependence on their sexual partners through substitute father laws. The Immigration and Naturalization Service and Congress became opposed to a citizen's right to extend his or her citizenship to a spouse and employed several strategies to prevent spouses from becoming dependent on the state. On the other hand, legislators and bureaucrats punitively enforced an extreme model of individual responsibility onto gay couples. In the midst of increasingly audible voices against gay marriage, courts deliberately broke up homosexual households through housing, welfare, and child custody policies.

The book concludes with an extended meditation on the pivotal year of 1996, when the impulses embedded in 1970s debates over welfare, immigration, and gay marriage policy all came to fruition in the form of powerful rewritings of federal policy. The Clinton administration's welfare reform in the 1990s once again allowed states to relentlessly impose "thick" breadwinning obligations on men in order to avoid granting welfare payments to families with dependent children. The INS also began enforcing citizens' financial responsibility for their former spouses and barred the poor from marrying noncitizens. And, in the same year, Congress passed the Defense of Marriage Act to prevent same-sex couples from taking advantage of any federal household benefits whatsoever. Some of this policymaking intersected in Congress; for example, a large percentage of the savings achieved by welfare reform came from purging permanent residents—some of them immigrant spouses—from the welfare rolls. Other legislation did not intersect explicitly but still reflected a cohesive, if twisted, underlying logic. Like the reforms of the 1960s and 1970s, those of the 1990s heightened distinctions based on class. Marriage for the poor imposed obligations; marriage for the privileged protected individual property rights. Thus were gender, family, and economics rewritten in late twentieth-century America.

CHAPTER 1

The Problem of Marriage
in the Age of Women's Liberation

In the 1960s and '70s, marriage emerged as a fundamental problem in American life. Immediately following one disruptive and momentous demographic change in American life—the Baby Boom—yet another began. Couples married less often, later in life, and split up more frequently. Wives worked outside the home more regularly; husbands served as the sole breadwinner less frequently. In the midst of these fundamentally reordering trends, two distinct but overlapping groups sought significant interventions in the law and practice of marriage. First, liberal feminists criticized the rigidity of traditional gender roles in marriage; they claimed that society's assumption that women would become dependent housewives created gender inequality in education, employment, and the law. At the same time, marriage dissenters (made up of cohabiters, gay liberation activists, and radical feminists) rejected the institution as irreparable.

Both groups condemned marriage for the constraints it placed on women (and sometimes men) but otherwise had very different concepts of the problem. Liberal feminists believed that the breadwinner-homemaker model of the home could persist as long as men had the same right to receive the Social Security, alimony, and other dependence benefits that wives had. So long as husbands could be homemakers and vice versa, a division of labor with robust but different expectations for each spouse could remain. The impulse behind this was expansionist—the benefits of marriage could be made gender-neutral and thus accessible to husbands and wives. In a sense, liberal feminists made use of what critic Isaiah Berlin has defined as a positive concept of liberty. They wanted wives to have the "freedom to" choose to be homemakers or breadwinners without the "external forces" of culture and law confining women to a traditional homemaking role. Marriage dissenters seemingly made use of Berlin's definition of a negative concept of liberty, arguing that marriage itself necessarily oppressed people.[1] Marriage dissenters sought "freedom from" marriage and the homemaker/breadwinner roles it imposed.

Both groups had a significant impact on American practice and ideology. Marriage dissenters particularly modeled a new kind of household, and increasingly Americans quit marrying altogether. But only liberal feminists effected significant legal change on the federal level. In the midst of enacting a broader gender revolution, the federal government and particularly the Supreme Court had to determine how to apply formal equality to family law. They embraced liberal feminists' expansive definition of equality by making "thick" spousal support benefits—child support, Social Security survivor, military dependency, alimony, and other benefits—available regardless of gender.[2] In doing so, the Supreme Court fundamentally altered marriage law at the federal level and the legal rights of women overall.

State of the Union

Critiques of marriage as an institution that repressed men and women emerged with the founding of the United States. The Revolution itself led lawmakers to loosen divorce law because men and women's confinement to marriage seemed to contradict the very freedom that the Revolution had ushered in.[3] Thereafter, marriage continued to evolve in the new nation. Decades later, the nineteenth-century woman's movement, which grew out of the abolitionist movement, claimed that wives' legal status resembled that of slaves.[4] As historian Amy Dru Stanley has explained, "to [feminists'] way of thinking, [marriage] was the question of contract that logically followed abolition, for it distilled the inequality of the sexes and the continuing ownership of persons."[5] These attacks justified the first significant blows to coverture: more expansive married women's property acts and the "earning" statutes, which gave wives the legal status to control their own property and wages earned outside the home.[6] Free love philosophers from the Civil War–era also rejected traditional marriage for treating women as property.[7] The suffrage generation of American feminists continued to condemn the system of coverture, and in particular objected to American women's disenfranchisement and loss of citizenship upon marriage to a foreigner.[8] At the same time, Americans also began reformulating the purpose of marriage: feminists of the 1910s hoped to make marriage a partnership centered on mutual satisfaction.[9] Nonetheless, even this ideal of partnership did not yet demand formal equality between the men and women within it: men remained the primary providers and wives their dependents.[10]

Over the course of the twentieth century, political questions about marriage remained even as the practice of marriage transformed significantly. Women had fewer children, married at later ages, increasingly worked for wages while they were married, and divorced more often. In 1933, the birth rate was a mere 18.4 births per 1,000 women. The birth rate spiked at 25.3 during the Baby Boom, but following the legalization of birth control for married couples in 1965, the rate sank to 17.8 by 1967.[11] A later age of first marriage accompanied the lower birth rate. The age of first marriage for women increased from 24.2 to 26.1 from 1960 to 1980. The divorce rate also boomed. In the long view, the divorce rate ballooned from 1.6 per 1,000 marriages in 1920 to 5.2 per 1,000 marriages in 1980.[12] Colloquially, one of every two marriages ended in divorce in 1980.[13] The rise of divorce also pointed to another demographic change—the growing number of single-parent families in the late twentieth century. The number of women maintaining families (the vast majority of single-parent families) sank as low as 9.4 percent of all families by 1950. In 1975, however, the number jumped up to 13 percent and to 15.9 percent in 1983.[14] Moreover not all single mothers were divorced. The number of never-married mothers also increased in this time period, marking one of many changes introduced by the sexual revolution.[15]

Wives also increasingly worked outside the home during the late twentieth century. Elizabeth Waldman, the senior economist in the Office of Employment and Unemployment Analysis in the Bureau of Labor Statistics in 1983, identified the 1970s as the decade when "a million women were added to the labor force in every year but one."[16] In 1900, approximately 5.3 million women worked for wages compared to 23.7 million men. By 1970, 30.6 million women worked for wages compared to 50 million men.[17] In 1980, women made up 43 percent of the paid workforce.[18] The rate of married women working outside the home skyrocketed from 30.5 percent in 1960 to 49.8 percent in 1980.[19] Women who worked for wages still had children. Among ever-married women in 1978, women in the paid workforce had an average of 2.7 children while women not in the paid workforce had an average of 3.2 children.[20]

The cause of this increase of women in the paid workforce is widely disputed, but certainly economic forces played an important role in this process. Since the nineteenth century, the promise of a family wage for breadwinners had led many Americans to hope that their children could go to school and that women could focus on the unpaid labor of caring for the home.[21] However, only middle-class and elite families enjoyed high wages for men, and working-class women (and children) often served in the paid labor market to supplement blue-collar men's low wages.[22] During the Depression and World War II, married middle-class women increasingly entered the paid labor market to make up for lost male wages from economic catastrophe or military service respectively.[23] Many women shifted back into the home after World War II, and more families managed a breadwinner-homemaker arrangement due to the strength of unions, GI Bill provisions for housing and education, and a booming economy.[24] The combination of deindustrialization and inflation by the early 1970s, however, seemed to ring a death knell for the temporary triumph of the family wage for blue-collar families. Moreover, even the middle-class families that had formerly counted on the family wage found it increasingly difficult to sustain a wife's full-time commitment to unpaid labor.[25] For blue-collar families, this meant the loss of a newly won prize; for middle-class families, this represented a tremendous break from the generations-long tradition of breadwinner-homemaker households.

Women's entrance into paid labor was one of the most monumental social changes in twentieth-century America, but it generally did not decrease wives' workload in the household. In the mid-1960s, sociologist Joann Vanek discovered that working mothers worked eighty hours per week on average, compared to sixty-five hours for fathers.[26] These numbers persisted despite significant changes in household technology and the sweep of women into the labor market. Electricity, indoor plumbing, refrigeration, washing machines, vacuums, and more were sold to wives as means of eliminating household labor, but these new household technologies only heightened expectations for cleanliness and the amount of time a mother should spend with her children.[27] Even in the midst of these changes, many women recognized this conundrum. For instance, when sociologist Helena Znaniecka Lopata conducted a survey of suburban housewives for the *Chicago Tribune*, one interviewee acknowledged that household technology had changed immensely since her grandmother's era, but that she was nonetheless busier than her grandmother had been. She then clarified that the modern housewife's life was "not harder physically, but more nerve-wracking than grandma's" because "we've become slaves to our appliances."[28] Another woman was less existential. As she explained, the modern conveniences were helpful but did not compensate for the loss of household help that her grandmother had enjoyed.[29] Women who worked outside the home faced a double day alongside these heightened expectations. When sociologist Arlie Hochschild published *The Second Shift* in 1989, twenty years after Vanek conducted her study, she estimated that the average woman worked an extra month per year compared to her husband.[30]

Such significant changes to the practice of marriage in the midst of legal stasis seemed to change the questions even to be asked about marriage at the dawn of the second-wave feminist movement. If fewer women married, would marriage even be a concern for women in the future? If married women all worked, would there be such distinct roles for men and women in marriage even if the law still dictated it? Nonetheless it was clear that marriage had not gone away for women or for men. Even though the divorce rate spiked, so did the remarriage rate. In 1980, married-couple families made up 80 percent of the population, only a small downtick from the 84 percent of 1940.[31] While the working rates of married women seemed inevitably to overwhelm the number of traditional housewives, only half of married women had entered the workforce even as late as 1980 (compared to 80.9 percent of men).[32] In 1960, the trajectory to our modern-day family was hardly obvious. The sociologist Lopata had asked hundreds of women what they expected for their daughters' generation, and very few anticipated that their own daughters would not be housewives. Even in 1983, when Ruth Schwartz Cowan published one of the definitive histories of household labor, she acknowledged that full-time housewives were on the decline but still noted that "more people spend their days in this 'peculiar' form of labor than in either of the two more 'standard' forms—blue-collar or white-collar work."[33] Therefore marriage—and the homemaker within it—remained an institution to wrestle with even in the era of women's liberation.

And Americans did wrestle with marriage as soon as second-wave feminism emerged. President John F. Kennedy appointed Eleanor Roosevelt, Attorney General Robert F. Kennedy, Assistant Secretary of Labor Esther Peterson, and dozens of other luminaries to serve on the President's Commission on the Status of Women (PCSW), which produced a report just a few months before freelance journalist Betty Friedan published *The Feminine Mystique* in 1963.[34] The two texts became classics, shaping a generation of feminist thought and action. Both stressed the urgent need to improve women's opportunities in education, employment, and citizenship. Notably, both gave expression to the rising belief that gender inequality in the public sphere was insurmountable while gender differentiation in marriage persisted.

The assigned mission of the PCSW was to assess "the position of women and the functions they perform in the home, in the economy, in the society."[35] In addition to making recommendations for widely available and affordable daycare, improved education for women, and equal pay for equal work, the final report *American Women* also contained several suggestions for dealing with discrimination inside of and stemming from marriage.[36] *American Women*'s authors recommended laws that equalized "the civil capacity of married women and married men . . . through the elimination of legal restrictions on the rights of married women to contract, convey, or own real or personal property, to engage in business, to act as surety or fiduciary, to receive and control their own earnings, and to dispose of their own property by will."[37]

Betty Friedan's 1963 book *The Feminine Mystique* introduced her own variation on the critique of marriage, which liberal feminists built on for the rest of the decade. At its heart, the book argued that even as career opportunities and citizenship rights for women expanded in the postwar period, marriage determined the ways in which women could act. Friedan saw the assumption that women should and would become dependent housewives as central to every other problem of gender they encountered.[38] Beyond producing neurotic women, the mystique also limited women's educational and employment opportunities since schools and employers believed that women would quickly quit their jobs to become homemakers. Friedan argued that shedding the feminine mystique did "not mean, of course, that she must divorce her husband, abandon her children, give up her home."[39] Instead Friedan demanded maternity leaves, daycare, and more to allow wives to work.[40]

Though these two critiques were published independently, their authors—Friedan and members of the PCSW—converged quickly. Members of the commission such as black civil rights legal expert Pauli Murray and former National Bar Association president Marguerite Rawalt eventually helped found the National Organization for Women (NOW) with Friedan in 1966, a response in part to the lack of enforcement of Title VII of the Civil Rights Act.[41] NOW endorsed the Equal Rights Amendment (ERA) in 1967 and just three years later won a congressional hearing by picketing the Senate.[42] There—and in the congressional debates and legal battles that followed—ERA proponents' testimony reiterated that, to make men and women equal, legislators had to reform the laws ordering the public and private spheres alike.[43]

This is not to say there were not differing viewpoints among feminists, and black feminists particularly offered a distinctive perspective. Leaders among these black liberal feminists, such as the Chicago-based organization National Alliance of Black Feminists (NABF), argued that black women faced unique problems in regards to marriage. NABF was an offshoot of the National Black Feminist Organization (NBFO). NBFO was established in 1973, and within a year had a thousand members. In 1976, NBFO folded, but its foundering spawned both the Combahee River Collective and NABF. NABF lasted until 1982 but never gained a widespread member base despite its national reach. Membership peaked at 152 paying members, and even as a chapter of the NBFO, the organization only had about 300 members on its mailing list.[44] Nonetheless, the organization attracted a great deal of media attention.

Most obviously, black feminists saw the persistence of anti-miscegenation laws as a unique and persistent problem. Though *Perez v. Sharp* and reform in individual states had worn away at the ubiquity of interracial marriage bans, the persistence of such laws in sixteen states served as a constant reminder of continued inequality.[45] Therefore black feminists of course saw *Loving v. Virginia*, which legalized interracial marriage, as a triumph over racial supremacy. But *Loving* did not entirely resolve the question of interracial relationships. For example, Brenda Eichelberger, the president and founder of NABF and the ex-wife of a white man herself, cited marriage between black men and white women as "a thorn in the side of black women" because there were "so many fewer black men than black women to begin with."[46]

Similarly, some black feminists worried about the shared sources of racism and patriarchy. For black members of the PCSW, reforming marriage was as necessary for racial equality as it was for gender equality.[47] Black feminists saw that the same problems marriage posed for white women affected black women even more direly. For example, one religious activist and ERA proponent explained that patriarchy stemmed from the same origins as racism: "Black men have accepted without questions the patriarchal structures of the White society as normative for the Black community. . . . How can a Black minister preach in a way which advocates St. Paul's dictum concerning women while ignoring or repudiating his dictum concerning slaves?"[48] To this activist, this meant that black women depended all the more on the Equal Rights Amendment to change marriage.

Nonetheless NABF and similar organizations paid more attention to the political economy of black marriages than they did interracial marriage or patriarchy. This was in keeping with what we already know about the priorities of most black activists during this time, who saw interracial sex and marriage as low on the issues of concern to the black community.[49] Instead, the focus on the political economy of marriage reflected the demographic realities of African American women as a whole—few black women were engaged in interracial relationships, but many black women struggled to support families within the framework dictated by a breadwinner-homemaker model. Employers rarely paid black men a family wage. This had deep historical origins, dating back to the era when women hoped to become homemakers following the Civil War but could seldom afford it.[50] According to black feminist luminary Pauli Murray, "the black female has experienced neither the 'protections' which the opponents of the Equal Rights Amendment are so zealous to preserve nor the idealizations of 'womanhood' and 'motherhood' which the society includes in its mythology."[51] Therefore some twentieth-century black women fully embraced homemaking. For example, a group titled the Consultation on Ethnic Minority Involvement in the Equal Rights Amendment argued that black women should be empowered to stay in the home. Eichelberger did not dismiss this solution outright. NABF literature explained that some members of the black community opposed the ERA because they felt that "its passage would . . . preclude Black women from finally assuming their rightful place in the home."[52] For these women, homemaking was not the problem; the way in which it was offered unevenly was.

More commonly, black feminist groups made damning critiques of men's monopoly on a living wage. Prominent black feminists ranging from Pauli Murray to Aileen Hernandez argued that black women should not have to depend on a breadwinner or even a two-income household.[53] Increasingly it seemed black women were delaying marriage, divorcing, or never marrying. The 1970 census indicated that women headed 27 percent of African American families, compared to 22 percent in 1960 and 17 percent in 1950. By comparison, women headed only 9 percent of white families in 1970.[54] NABF argued that black women's low wages were not high enough to support a family even though many black women did. The assumption that their wages were supplementary to their husbands' was impoverishing black women who headed households.[55] NABF president Eichelberger argued that because "more and more women of all races must work to help support themselves and their families," a feminist "realizes she cannot afford to continue in the work force and not receive equality with men."[56] Thus black activists began to demand that women get enough to raise their own families rather than assume women were dependents of men.[57]

Despite some key differences, white and black liberal feminists coalesced around the Equal Rights Amendment as a solution that could eliminate all gender problems, including marriage, in one fell swoop.[58] The National Woman's Party, a minority organization among former suffragists, first presented the ERA to Congress in 1923 in order to give men and women formal legal equality.[59] At that time, critics argued it was a measure that benefited only elite women to the detriment of working women and homemakers who needed gender-based protective legislation. The ERA failed to pass both houses during the twenties and for nearly half a century thereafter, rarely making it past committee to the floor. In the late 1960s, however, several organizations began pushing more concertedly for its passage, including especially the newly forged National Organization for Women.

Demands for the ERA gained traction in Congress in the wake of the renewed attention to women's rights, and Michigan representative Martha Griffiths and Indiana senator Birch Bayh headed an effort to pass the ERA in the House and Senate respectively.[60] A subcommittee of the House Committee on the Judiciary held hearings from March 24 to April 5, 1971, and the Senate Subcommittee on Constitutional Amendments of the Committee on the Judiciary did so in May of 1970. National and state legislators, representatives from women's groups like NOW and the National Federation of Business and Professional Women's Clubs, labor organizations such as the American Federation of Labor and Congress of Industrial Organizations (AFL-CIO) and the Communications Workers of America, and scholars and writers testified in both hearings. A few months later, in September of 1970, Democratic senator from North Carolina Sam Ervin organized an additional set of hearings to get at the effect the ERA would have on the "constitutional system and the various merited rights and exemptions upon women."[61] Ervin was a fierce opponent of civil rights legislation throughout his career but was more famous for opposing Senator Joseph McCarthy. In 1973, he would lead the charge in the Watergate hearings. In the interim he became an early leader of the anti-ERA movement. For Ervin, his gender beliefs were of a piece with his opposition to civil rights since he believed in the benevolent pursuit of "natural" hierarchies.[62] Ervin invited a higher concentration of ERA opponents to testify at this later set of hearings.

The real stakes of the amendment were not always clear in these hearings and the debate that followed, but the ERA did provide a venue through which various parties hashed out their hopes for the future of gender, family, and the political economy. A host of ERA advocates at the hearings argued that in order to effect real legal equality, the Equal Rights Amendment had to enter the home and establish equality there as well as in the public sphere.[63] New York representative Bella Abzug and Michigan representative Martha Griffiths asserted that family law restricted a wife's right to engage in business, determine her domicile, choose her last name, contract, manage property, make use of certain grounds for divorce, access entitlements such as the GI Bill and Social Security, and be tried by a jury of her peers.[64] Dr. Bernice Sandler, of the Women's Equity Action League, and Brenda Feigen Fasteau, the legislative vice president of NOW, argued that women were not admitted to graduate and professional programs because universities assumed women would marry, have children, and then leave the work world.[65] Similarly, Pauli Murray, who had crafted the concept of Jane Crow, testified that women spent only a small portion of their lives raising children, but lost the opportunity to sway public policy for their entire lives.[66] Marguerite Rawalt testified on behalf of the Women's Bar Association that married women's unequal status had persisted because most women had good husbands. Those who did not marry decent men, Rawalt concluded, heretofore had no organized lobby.[67] But such blatant inequality in the law would be unconstitutional under the ERA.

The call to change marriage law struck at ERA opponents' deepest fears. ERA opponents, who were in the minority at the hearings and in Congress, argued that the ERA would inflict real damage on traditional marriage laws. Harvard law professor Paul Freund had written the definitive legal statement on the Equal Rights Amendment in 1945.[68] In 1970, he still critiqued the ERA for undermining divorce laws that made "a husband liable for the support of his wife."[69] Similarly Republican representative Charles Wiggins of California, Democratic representative Emanuel Celler of New York, and Democratic senator Sam Ervin of North Carolina all warned that the ERA would eliminate the system that held men responsible for the support of their families.[70] In light of this critique, Wiggins introduced an amendment in the House of Representatives that made an exception for any law "which reasonably promotes the health and safety of the people" in part because "domestic relations laws in the several States could be reduced to a shambles."[71] In tandem with Wiggins's efforts in the House, Senator Ervin tried to preserve men's thick legal breadwinning obligations with Amendment No. 1068, the first of several amendments Ervin proposed to the ERA. Ervin intended the amendment to ensure that the law would still "impose upon husbands the primary responsibility to provide homes and livelihoods for their wives and children, and make them criminally responsible to society and civilly responsible to their wives if they fail to perform this primary responsibility."[72] The ERA would deprive women of support and comfort, he alleged.[73]

In their direct response to these criticisms, liberal feminists argued that women's expectation of support was not at risk. Alimony and child support had traditionally been based on a woman's and children's dependence on the male head of household. In most states, men alone had the thick legal obligation to be breadwinners—an obligation enforced mostly at the point of divorce through fault divorce statutes and support orders. A husband who did not support his family could lose in a fault divorce proceeding through grounds of nonsupport, desertion, or cruelty.[74] Even after divorce it was still a husband's duty to support his blameless wife, and that blameless wife's privilege to be dependent on her husband. As of 1968, thirty-one states and Washington, DC, explicitly allowed alimony only for wives, and even the states that did not specify who could receive alimony did not grant it to husbands.[75]

Husbands who failed to fulfill these thick duties of support could face harsh ramifications, including prison. Every state other than Missouri affirmed the legality of imprisoning a husband for being in contempt of an alimony or child support order in the postwar period.[76] For example, in Cook County in Illinois, men could be imprisoned in special "Alimony Rows" for failing to pay their alimony or child support. Other prisoners referred to these men as "baby starvers."[77] As late as the 1960s, hundreds of men were imprisoned every week according to the *Tribune*.[78] New York allowed imprisonment for six months for a default larger than $500 in 1951; jail sentences for a default of less than $500 was limited to three months.[79] The prospect of jail shaped how men and women privately negotiated a husband's obligations. Clearly not all men who defaulted on alimony or child support payments went to jail, but press coverage of Alimony Row and famous inhabitants kept the threat of it alive.[80] Wives threatened to send their husbands to Alimony Row or begged county officials to let husbands out, according to their private negotiations and needs.

Of course, courts did not enforce these thick breadwinning and homemaking duties against all couples equally. White middle-class women were more likely to be found worthy of wifely privileges than poor women of any race. While women did the vast majority of the housework no matter their class status, many working-class wives worked outside the home as well. Courts less frequently credited these working-class wives as homemakers deserving of support. In addition, public policy had historically discouraged black women from being homemakers.[81] Similarly not all men had to live up to their breadwinning duties. Wives made use of nonsupport as grounds for divorce much less frequently than cruelty or desertion. A wealthy white woman could convince a judge that her husband had failed to support her much more easily than the wife of a laborer, black or white. Finally, alimony was reserved only for some; at its peak, about 25 percent of divorced women received it in the postwar period.[82] Nonetheless this was a significant increase from the late nineteenth century, when only 9.3 percent of women received alimony. Also long-married women more often received alimony in the postwar era; Lenore Weitzman concluded that 46 percent of California women married more than fifteen years received alimony.[83] Certainly wealthier white women were again more likely to profit from the breadwinner-homemaker model.[84]

Feminists conceded that, because these means of enforcing breadwinning targeted men, they necessarily had to be reworked under the Equal Rights Amendment. Nonetheless, ERA proponents suggested that alimony and child support could be given to spouses in need or with custody without regard to gender.[85]

In other words, ERA supporters endorsed what I've termed an expansionist interpretation of the amendment—as making either spouse obligated to be a breadwinner for his or her partner through a simple substitution of "spouse" for "wife" in state laws. The idea that protections for women could be extended to men was almost as old as legal protectionism itself. As part of her contribution to the Brandeis brief in *Muller v. Oregon*, Elizabeth Brandeis hoped that protective labor laws for women and children could be an "opening wedge" that would eventually help all workers. She characterized the strategy as "fight[ing] the battle behind women's petticoats."[86] ERA supporters in the early 1970s had rather unequivocally rejected protective labor legislation, but they saw no problem in making need a gender-neutral category. They wanted to allow women the "freedom to be," in Berlin's formulation, either homemakers or breadwinners.[87] As opposed to the accusations of opponents at the time and even some historians since, liberal feminists did not reject the possibility of breadwinning in a feminist world.[88]

Proponents endorsed the expansionist vision of the ERA in congressional hearings. For example, Myra Ruth Harmon, the national president of the Federation of Business and Professional Women's Clubs, rejected alimony that was only given to wives but testified in Senate hearings that the "continued support of one spouse by the other after divorce or separation, if based on actual economic dependency or relative ability to provide family support, would not be prohibited by this Amendment. Here the criterion is not sex but economic need."[89] The Unitarian Universalist Women's Federation, an organization with seventeen thousand members, praised the ERA in part because women who did not need alimony would not be granted it; men who did would.[90] Edith M. Parkey, the founder of the Central Cincinnati Chapter of Federally Employed Women, dismissed fears that "in some mysterious way, strong family life would be destroyed" by the ERA. Instead alimony would be available according to need rather than gender.[91]

In congressional debate too, supporters argued that the basic premise of a division of labor between the breadwinner and homemaker would not be altered. Indiana senator Birch Bayh, a sponsor of the ERA in the Senate, argued that "as far as alimony and children and dower rights and all other rights are concerned, what we are suggesting is that, rather than wipe out all these rights, we are going to say to a woman and to a man that each will be treated equally under the law, . . . that if a father and husband has certain rights, a wife and mother should have the same rights" and vice versa.[92] Bella Abzug, in the House, elaborated that judges could award men alimony. Marriage would

Figure 1. Senators Birch Bayh, Martha Griffiths, Sam Ervin, and Marlow Cook after the Equal Rights Amendment passed in the Senate. Courtesy of the Associated Press.

retain traditional forms of dependency, shedding only the gender categories that defined who was dependent and who was not.

Congress as a whole seemed reassured by the expansionist possibility of the female breadwinner enough to pass the ERA without amendments. Ervin's Amendment No. 1068 failed 14 yeas to 77 nays, and the Wiggins amendment, House Joint Resolution 208, failed 87 ayes to 265 nays. The ERA passed on March 22, 1972, and read "Equality of rights under the law shall not be denied or abridged by the United States or by any State on account of sex. The Congress shall have the power to enforce, by appropriate legislation, the provisions of this article." By the time the amendment passed, a broad coalition of liberal feminist groups had rallied behind it. Eventually, a host of new organizations mushroomed up locally and nationally to ensure its passage. The fight for the ERA absorbed a significant portion of liberal feminists' resources until its defeat in 1982.

Expansionist Gender Equality in the Courts

The initial effects of liberal feminists' expansionist demands had transformative effects on marriage law even while the ERA remained in limbo. Marriage laws remained on the books, but courts began to apply expansionist gender equality to their provisions. The states with equal rights amendments in their state constitutions began acting as laboratories for formal equality with thick obligations intact. Pennsylvania's state equal rights amendment was instructive. In 1973, the Pennsylvania Supreme Court ruled in *Henderson v. Henderson* that since the law granted support after separation only to women, that the statute "must fall in light of the Equality of Rights Amendment to the Pennsylvania Constitution."[93] The court, however, noted that laws that specified "the party [wife or husband]" were acceptable under the Pennsylvania ERA and urged the legislature to pass such a bill. They elaborated in *Wiegand v. Wiegand* later that year that counsel fees, alimony, and costs could be granted to a needy spouse so long as either husband or wife was eligible.[94] The Pennsylvania legislature quickly substituted the word "spouse" for "wife" in its statutes.[95] Pennsylvania had followed the path that ERA proponents had anticipated in the congressional hearings on the ERA.

Other states followed suit, and a few courts began notoriously granting alimony to dependent men. For instance, in the 1977 Florida case *Pfohl v. Pfohl*, Margaret Pfohl was ordered to pay her husband, Roger, a large lump sum ($30,000) and $5,000 in monthly alimony for the next year and a half. The appellate court concluded that Roger Pfohl indeed deserved alimony just as a needy wife would based on the circumstances of their marriage. Roger Pfohl married independently wealthy Margaret Pfohl in 1966, and he continued his job as a toy salesman until Margaret pressured him to quit his job two years later. After nine total years of marriage, and after Florida passed a new no-fault statute that allowed the distribution of alimony to either dependent party, Margaret kicked Roger out of their home. At this point the trial court awarded Roger the aforementioned alimony. Margaret appealed, but the appellate court mused that, "in some marriages . . . the wife is the sole support of the family unit with the husband fulfilling some non-economic role. It is in these non-traditional type marriages where the question of alimony for the husband may arise."[96] The court concluded that, like a wife, Roger became financially dependent on his spouse when she asked him to give up his career. By 1976, even without a national or state ERA, thirty-one states allowed alimony awards to either spouse.[97] The legal system replaced the distinction between men and women with a distinction between needy spouses and not needy spouses.

An even more revolutionary implementation of expansionist equality came through a series of Supreme Court decisions that applied the equal protection clause to the category of gender. Ruth Bader Ginsburg used a strategy first formulated by Pauli Murray in the 1963 President's Commission on the Status of Women report to link race and women's oppression to challenge sex discrimination with the Fourteenth Amendment.[98] The first successful step in this direction was the 1971 case *Reed v. Reed*, which overturned an Idaho law that favored male relatives as the executors of wills. Other rulings invalidated laws that, for example, prevented spouses from testifying against one another.[99] Like state courts, the highest court also extended the category of "dependent" to men as well as women, which stripped homemaker and breadwinner of their gender norms while keeping thick obligations intact. Beginning in 1973, the Supreme Court began to use the Fourteenth Amendment to break down state sponsorship of a husband's exclusive obligation to support his wife with the cases *Frontiero v. Richardson* (1973), *Weinberger v. Wiesenfeld* (1975), and *Califano v. Goldfarb* (1977). These cases formed the backbone of Ruth Bader Ginsburg's American Civil Liberties Union project to bring strict scrutiny to the category of sex after the ERA had passed but prior to its ultimately unsuccessful ratification.[100]

It may seem ironic that Ginsburg selected a slate of cases that highlighted the ways in which men suffered from gender difference in the law, but Ginsburg deliberately chose an incremental path that illustrated how "double-edged" gender discrimination was.[101] She selected cases that showed how men and women alike suffered from laws that originated from coverture precepts—a husband had the unique burden of supporting his dependent wife, but the government looked askance at a wife who supported her husband.[102] Ginsburg did not challenge the idea that one spouse would support the other, but she did question the assumption that women could not be caretakers of dependent men. In other words, Ginsburg pursued the promise of the "opening wedge" that Elizabeth Brandeis had first imagined in 1908 to give husbands dependence benefits. Ginsburg initially tackled these issues with *Frontiero v. Richardson*, which challenged a statute that automatically provided married male military personnel with medical, dental, and housing allowances for their wives.[103] But the husband of a married female military member only received the additional benefits if she provided three-quarters of her household's income.

Sharron Frontiero, a lieutenant in the U.S. Air Force whose husband did not meet the military standards for being financially dependent, asserted that it was unfair for her to have to demonstrate her husband's dependence when male military members did not. She also objected to the fact that the wives of soldiers received the benefit even when they earned their own substantive incomes.[104] The policy showed the extent to which the husband's obligation to support his wife had infiltrated the state's entitlement system.[105] To Ginsburg and Frontiero's delight, the court concluded that classifications based on sex were suspect.[106] Though the military could have eliminated the benefit entirely, it instead extended dependency benefits to all spouses irrespective of their income or gender. This set a precedent for how the Supreme Court would rule on other similar cases: the right to provide for dependent spouses would be extended to wives.

Ginsburg also sought expansionist equality in *Weinberger v. Wiesenfeld*, which granted Social Security survivor benefits traditionally given only to widows to widowers as well. Prior to *Weinberger*, Social Security excluded widowers from the survivor benefit on the assumption that widowers would be breadwinners.[107] Paula Wiesenfeld, however, earned a much higher income as a high school math teacher than her husband, Stephen, did in his computer consulting business. Tragically, Paula died in childbirth leaving Stephen to care for their child alone. Stephen sued for the same survivor benefit a wife would receive so he could care for their infant son.[108] Using *Frontiero*, the court concluded that the distinction was based on unconstitutional assumptions "that male workers' earnings are vital to their families' support, while female workers' earnings do not significantly contribute to families' support."[109] Similarly the Supreme Court ruled in *Califano v. Goldfarb* that providing survivor benefits to an elderly widower only if he was receiving at least half his support from his wife constituted discrimination against female wage earners. The court determined that giving breadwinner benefits only to husbands was inconsistent with contemporary reality.[110] *Weinberger* and *Califano* both extended the right to be a breadwinner to wives.

In the 1978 case *Orr v. Orr*, the Supreme Court granted wives the right and obligation to financially support one's dependent spouse.[111] In 1974, William and Lillian Orr divorced, and Lillian Orr was awarded over $1,200 a month in alimony. Two and a half years later, Lillian Orr took William Orr to court to recover nearly $6,000 in unpaid alimony. William Orr contended that Alabama alimony statutes were unconstitutional since only husbands had to provide alimony to their former wives.[112] He hoped to escape paying alimony entirely. The court did reject the "old notion" that men alone were legally obligated to be breadwinners, but this was not enough to overturn William Orr's thick obligation to support his wife.[113] Instead the court concluded that alimony was constitutional as long as needy husbands received it as well. This was also a cheaper fix than the ones the justices had made in *Frontiero, Weinberger*, and *Califano*: "needy males could be helped along with needy females with little if any additional burden on the State."[114] In an aside, the ruling clarified that William Orr was not relieved of his duty since Alabama could simply extend the obligation to wives of dependent men. Alabama did, and so William Orr achieved an ambiguous objective. He still owed Lillian Orr alimony, but she would have had to support him as well in the event that he had been financially dependent on her when they divorced.

In 1981 the Supreme Court also severed a husband's control over a household's finances. In 1974, Joan Feenstra filed child molestation charges against her husband, Harold. Harold Feenstra hired a lawyer named Karl J. Kirchberg to defend him against these charges. In order to pay Kirchberg, Harold posted their co-owned home as security on a promissory note. Mr. Feenstra was able to do so without Ms. Feenstra's knowledge or consent because Louisiana's "head and master" laws gave a husband the exclusive power to dispose of joint property. Ms. Feenstra later dropped her charges, and Mr. Feenstra left the state. Ms. Feenstra discovered the mortgage on her home when Kirchberg began foreclosure proceedings in 1976. Ms. Feenstra's counterclaim targeted not only Kirchberg, but also the state's head and master laws. By the time the case made it to the Supreme Court, Louisiana had already passed a statute that gave spouses equal rights to dispose of this property. Nonetheless, Mr. Feenstra's contract was still at issue, having been entered into before the statute passed. In 1981, the Supreme Court overthrew a husband's unilateral control over property jointly owned with a wife on the basis that head and master laws violated the equal protection clause.[115] Homemakers were no longer hostages to breadwinners' financial decisions.

With these cases, the gendered distinctions between breadwinners and homemakers were ostensibly eliminated. The Supreme Court ruled that wives had the same right to be financially responsible for husbands as husbands did for wives; moreover, wives and husbands equally could make their own financial decisions. These few cases represented a substantial portion of the case law that made gender a suspect category. At the same time, the concept of dependence remained in place even if it had been stripped of its gendered properties. Women like Sharon Frontiero, Paula Weinberger, and Sharon Orr could all continue to reap the benefits of state entitlements for dependent husbands. Theory had changed much; practice had changed little. In fact, the courts had not questioned the underlying gendered assumptions that defined the concept of dependence, and the result was an expansionist version of gender equality.

Radical Solutions and Marriage Abstention

As NOW members, ERA proponents, Congress, and the Supreme Court labored to implement an expansionist vision of equality in marriage, radical feminists, members of the counterculture, and gay liberationists voiced more comprehensive critiques of the institution. All these radical dissenters argued that no amount of reform could save the irredeemably flawed institution of marriage, which had been sustained only by a myth of love.[116] By the late twentieth century, these marriage abstainers had grown skeptical of love's existence, uncertain whether it could survive in an institution like marriage, or hostile toward it as a means of oppressing women. All people needed to be freed *from* marriage instead of the freedom *to* marry that positive liberty reformers had embraced.

Radical feminists largely disputed liberal feminists' belief that marriage could be reformed.[117] Groups such as the Chicago Women's Liberation Union

(CWLU) and the Redstockings emerged out of the New Left in 1967 and 1968 respectively, soon after the formation of NOW in 1966. CWLU was much more Marxist in orientation than the Redstockings, but many radical feminist groups agreed that women only married because love operated as a false consciousness to support a patriarchal political economy. Shulamith Firestone, a founding member of New York Radical Women, the Redstockings, and the New York Radical Feminists, identified love as "the pivot of women's oppression" even more than childbearing because it masked and legitimated women's unpaid labor in the home.[118] Radical feminists drew on Friedrich Engels to protest that a woman's household work neither earned a wage nor entitled her to medical leave, unemployment, minimum wages, and other protections that benefited most workers.[119]

Free household labor, radical feminists believed, shored up the patriarchy. First, women's unpaid labor in the home—temporary, in conjunction with paid work, or permanent—kept individual women financially and emotionally dependent on men. Firestone argued that a woman exchanged love for emotional security, emotional identity (since she did not work or contribute to society otherwise), and economic class security.[120] Kate Millett, in the groundbreaking essay "Sexual Politics," compared the household economy to other precapitalist systems of domination in that they depended on bartering sex for food.[121] And like the oppressors in these older systems, men profited from subjugating women.[122] Betsy Warrior argued that without women, men would have to perform household drudgery themselves or hire someone to do it for them.[123] Pat Mainardi, a member of the Redstockings, probably wrote the most famous anti-housework diatribe in 1968 with her essay "The Politics of Housework." In it she provided "translations" for the excuses men provided when they did not wish to help women in the home. Her tone vacillated between hilarious and heartbreaking. She characterized the benefit of unpaid labor in the home to men most simply. Speaking in the voice of a husband, she wrote, "Oppression is built into the system and I, as the white American male, receive the benefits of this system."[124]

Women's roles in the home also shored up capitalism by providing free productive and reproductive labor, producing consumption, falling in and out of the market according to labor needs, and keeping wages low. Radical feminist academics like Firestone, Marlene Dixon, Rae André, Ann Oakley, and many others explained that women produced new workers by physically birthing children and socializing them into being workers.[125] Feminist organizations outside the United States, like the Italian group Wages for Housework, helped

American feminists hone these arguments. The Power of Women Collective, a British group that often collaborated with radical feminists throughout Europe, critiqued a society that encouraged women to have children "for 'love'" when in fact society only wanted those children to become future workers and consumers.[126] Women also maintained the conditions under which men could work outside the home by cooking, cleaning, laundering, and otherwise providing the daily services men needed to return to work each day. As Dixon understood it, the housewife's reproductive labor allowed her husband to spend the vast majority of each day at the workplace rather than procuring the basic necessities to sustain his own life.[127] Wages for Housework cofounder, Mariarosa Dalla Costa, expanded—families left men available for full-time direct exploitation by capital.[128] Housewives also provided men the psychological strength they needed to withstand an alienating work environment.[129]

Women's work in the home also absorbed the inefficiencies of capitalism by generating consumption and providing low-wage labor power on a casual basis. At the 1968 women's liberation conference at Camp Hastings in Lake Villa, Illinois, one workshop discussed the way families were necessary to "build domestic markets." One participant, Laurel Limpus, argued that department store ads aimed at brides conditioned women to see marriage as a time to amass the broad range of consumer goods available for home and family.[130] Dixon saw housewives as the temporary bandage to a system that vastly overproduced. Housewives absorbed the waste of capitalism.[131] Women's unpaid work in the home also enabled capital to shift laborers into and out of the market as needed, which kept wages low. Women in the home acted as a "reserve army of temporary labor" in Karen Sacks's interpretation.[132] Women worked and then returned home according to the needs of capital.[133] Firestone characterized women as "exceedingly useful and cheap as a transient, often highly skilled labor supply."[134] The Wages for Housework Committee in Los Angeles, an offshoot of the Italian organization, allied itself with immigrant laborers because it saw both immigrants and housewives as contingent labor for local factories.[135]

Radical feminists also believed that women's unpaid labor brought wages down for everyone. Sheila Cronan, a founder of the New York group The Feminists, argued that the battle against employment discrimination was doomed so long as women worked for nothing inside the home.[136] Rae André saw women as part of a larger workforce that included mostly women and racial minorities. This "pool of cheap labor" worked in deeply unsatisfying and low-waged jobs because an even larger pool of housewives could potentially take their jobs. The Wages for Housework Committee in Los Angeles identified industrial, medical, agricultural, and clerical positions as particularly low paid because women lacked the energy to organize for better working conditions.[137] Juliet Mitchell, the prominent writer of *Psychoanalysis and Feminism*, saw women's inability to organize as stemming from "unskilled, uncreative, service jobs that can be regarded as 'extensions' of their expressive familial role."[138] The benefits of marriage accrued to husbands and capitalists, not women.

Though radical feminists agreed that marriage oppressed women, they diverged when it came to providing a solution for the family's oppression of women. Many international feminists, most obviously the various branches of the Wages for Housework organization, supported wages for housewives' work in the home. They saw this strategy as undermining both patriarchy and capitalism. Dalla Costa particularly saw wages for housework as capable of collectivizing women's struggle since housework was "the only work that we all have in common."[139] The international prostitution movement identified sex as work for which women should get paid.[140]

But other radical feminists, international and otherwise, argued that only communal kitchens and universal daycare would free women from the patriarchal system.[141] Oakley believed that wages for housework would perpetuate the private and isolated conditions of women's labor.[142] Perhaps the most vivid critique of wages for housework came in the 1983 film *Born in Flames*. *Born in Flames* is set in the near future and recounts a fictional socialist utopia. In this socialist utopia, a fringe Women's Liberation Army (WLA) demands an end to rape, to economic inequality, and to exclusion from positions of power in the government. The WLA dismisses wages for housework as an attempt to buy off the revolution. The film ends with the group righteously blowing up the World Trade Center's radio tower in order to prevent the president's call for wages for housework from going out into the world.[143]

Though few Americans ever read these thinkers, much less adopted radical feminists' critique of capitalism, some ordinary American women did share the radical perspective that women should be paid for their work in the home. The need to compensate homemakers, and a fair means of doing so, was debated among the men and women who entered an essay contest on "A Practical Program to Achieve Economic Justice for Homemakers." The contest was hosted by Babson College, public relations pioneer Edward Louis Bernays, and his wife, Doris Bernays. It was advertised in a myriad of media platforms in 1978, ranging from *McCall's* to the *Des Moines Tribune* to KXOK radio station in St. Louis.[144] From across the country, men and women, as couples and alone, politicians, academics, and feminist organizers responded in the thousands. The various solutions proposed can tell us a great deal about the revolutionary debates about property distribution among ordinary women. When an Indianapolis woman very forcefully asserted that her housework contributed more to her family than paid work would, for example, she saw her contribution as an uncompensated monetary contribution rather than a cultural, spiritual, or social one. Gardening, canning, freezing, and foregoing gasoline and work clothes all saved her family more money than her presumably paltry wages would contribute.[145] The problem to this housewife was only that none of this labor was acknowledged legally or financially.

The men and women who entered this contest proposed a few predominant models of remuneration, though the terms of compensation were hardly straightforward or set in stone. The authors of some entries endorsed a business partnership model. Spiritually this was far from the position of the radical feminists, except that both groups saw an unacknowledged value in women's labor. The business partnership model contest entrants wanted the government to consider a couple a corporation, and they wanted both partners to share equally in the assets of the marriage.[146] One woman called for the homemaker to "be treated as a full partner of her income-receiving husband" whereby she would receive half of his assets and salary.[147] More radical entries criticized this notion. The problem with treating marriages as a business partnership was that the wives of rich men made more than the wives of poorer men, even if the work was essentially the same. A woman from New Jersey, for example, suggested that "the high school drop-out and the woman with the PhD are doing identical jobs at home, perhaps the high school drop out is a better housekeeper. Should the high school drop-out earn more money as a home maker?"[148] For this woman, the PhD candidate with inferior homemaking skills had an obvious advantage over the more skilled high school dropout who presumably received less in any partnership scheme.

Other contestants preferred a model that quantified how much work went into keeping a home rather than how much money a husband made; in essence they called for wages for housework despite all the trouble that wages presented. One frequent proposal based the compensation scale on the number of children a woman took care of, which could equalize working-class and more elite women.[149] Even here, though, some housewives grew angry at the prospect of being paid the same for working hard as another mother who set her children in front of a television set all day. Another entry—from a man—

recommended that judges evaluate "a homemaker's prowess as a cook, dispensing wholesome, good-tasting foods. Judge her in the 'reasonable' cleanliness of her home, her participation in civic & community affairs, the love and respect she gives & receives from her family."[150]

Many entries assumed wives would become their husbands' employees. In Lima, Ohio, one man recommended that husbands pay all the taxes employers always paid, including Social Security, income tax, and state and local taxes for their wives.[151] A Miami, Florida, woman suggested that a 10 percent deduction from a husband's paycheck should be given directly to his wife.[152] A Maine woman suggested 25 percent.[153] In each theoretical case, it was clear that part of a husband's salary would belong to and be controlled by wives, but also that they would be compensated at a rate that was less than half of what their husbands earned. The differential "payment" for poor wives and rich wives also remained since poor men made too little to compensate women sufficiently.[154] Being treated as an employee under these proposals was also a problem because women were perhaps more rather than less dependent on their husbands when their husbands were literally their employers. Don and Kitty Kovar worried that like any employee, homemakers could be fired, disciplined, and relegated to certain tasks.[155] Overall, radical feminists may not have convinced these contestants that they should abandon marriage, but certainly the concept that wives provided uncompensated labor infiltrated American cultural consciousness more than we might expect. But radical feminists and the ordinary women they influenced were not alone in turning away from marriage.

Much as radical feminists' rejected marriage, young couples loosely affiliated with the counterculture, straight and gay alike, demanded freedom from marriage.[156] Their solution was not wages, but instead to cohabit either individually or in communes. This trend rattled a number of psychologists, sociologists, and journalists who started interviewing straight cohabiters to figure out why they rejected marriage. Above all, these experts concluded, cohabiters viewed marriage as a failed institution. Their interviews and surveys, many taken from 1968 to 1974, produced a picture of disenchantment with many of the facets considered intrinsic to marriage: sexual exclusivity, permanence, and a strict gendered division of labor. All of these, cohabiters believed, prevented the realization of genuine love between men and women.[157]

Family experts attributed the increasing attraction of cohabitation to a fear of commitment caused by anything from their parents' unhappy marriages to the Vietnam War. Marvin Mitchelson, the lawyer who later famously won a palimony case against the actor Lee Marvin in California, noted that the young had noticed that formal marriage had not "worked for their predecessors."[158] One study participant in a *Journal of Marriage and the Family* report admitted, "'I hardly know anybody who is happily married.'"[159] Alternatively Carl Danziger, a young sociologist studying cohabitation, pointed particularly to a changing economy, which demanded extensive vocational or secondary education before a worker could be secure in his or her career.[160] A Manhattan psychiatrist attributed the tendency to cohabit to the uncertainty of young men facing the draft. Avoiding war had potentially reordered the life cycle enough that continuing one's education and cohabiting seemed a more secure strategy than marriage.[161]

The cohabiting couples themselves saw living together without marriage as a means to restore love. For example, a couple in Boston believed that cohabiting was superior to marriage because "it is the legal tie . . . that is the subtle influence in making a marriage go sour."[162] Other couples reported to Mitchelson that they worked harder in cohabitation because living together without marriage meant you could not take the relationship for granted.[163] If the relationship were to break up, couples also felt free to pursue love in new venues, without the stigma or emotional scars that divorce imposed. Mervyn Cadwallader, a sociology professor, suggested that a flexible contract would prevent couples that "grew disenchanted with their life together" from having "to go through the destructive agonies of divorce, and carry about the stigma of marital failure, like the mark of Cain on their foreheads." Cadwallader instead advocated allowing former couples to seek romance elsewhere.[164] Cohabitation was a new strategy for achieving an old ideal.

Some cohabiters lived together to challenge the gender roles marriage imposed on women.[165] Such was the case for Linda LeClair, the famous Barnard coed who created a national scandal by cohabiting with her boyfriend, Peter Behr.[166] Many other couples reported to experts that cohabitation would prevent a traditional division of labor.[167] A woman interviewed by the *New York Times* said, "You know, someone did a test of American wives, and it turned out that they saw their husbands as breadwinners, fathers, companions and lovers, in that order. It ought to be reversed!"[168] Danziger also reported that couples rejected marriage so that they could think of themselves as equal partners rather than as breadwinners and homemakers.[169] Sociologist Roy Ald reported that one woman explained that she did not want to marry her partner because she would then feel obligated to quit school and get a job to help his career. Instead she wanted to concentrate on finishing her own degree.[170]

Commune members also hoped to escape traditional marriage roles and obligations. Certainly not all communes, or members of communes, refused to marry. In fact, many couples joined communes in an attempt to "save" their marriages.[171] But many others rejected the premise of traditional marriage. For example thirty-two middle-class urban communes studied in Chicago in the 1970s, which averaged only 7.6 members each, rejected traditional marriage and traditional monogamy for encouraging "possessive" and "patriarchal" values.[172] Similarly members of the Twin Oaks Commune in Virginia believed that many couples married either because it was the most readily available way to have sex or because women felt financial pressure to do so.[173] At Downhill Farm in the Alleghenies, founder Jud Jerome noted that prior to joining the commune, his wife's life had become one of "housekeeping and childcare and perpetual shopping" while he himself had "contracted the endemic disease of American males—the association of personal worth with annual income."[174] Without marriage, these couples hoped to treat one another as equal, independent individuals who could love one another freely.

Cohabiting couples more easily dispensed with men than women's traditional obligations in practice. Many cohabiters struggled to determine who would do household labor, pay the bills, and more. Mitchelson, the lawyer who famously won actor Lee Marvin's live-in partner some of the benefits of marriage, explained that some cohabiters broke up because they fell into old roles: "'If I wanted to iron his shirts and cook his meals, I would have gotten married,' a disillusioned live-in woman complains. 'If I wanted to be told when to get home every night, I would have taken on a wife,' the indignant man sneers."[175] As Mitchelson indicated, the reality of living without gender prescriptions was difficult: couples often disagreed to what extent they wished to shed gendered obligations and even more often disagreed about what this would mean.

Cohabitation did not help women escape the obligation to perform most, if not all, of the household labor. Eleanor Macklin reported that many couples shared chores like shopping and laundry, but that women still cooked and cleaned.[176] Nick Stinnett, a professor of human development, interviewed a couple who had hoped to shed the gendered division of labor in the home, only to find themselves unsuccessful in doing so.[177] Over time she almost involuntarily found herself doing the "cooking, cleaning, shopping and laundry, while he worked on the house, cars, and yard."[178] Similarly, Ald noted that many women did not want to discuss housekeeping at all, which he suspected was because they thought revealing the actual division of labor would reveal their relationships as less coequal than they aspired to be.[179] Though Twin Oaks Commune in Virginia and many urban communes encouraged a more egalitarian division of labor—sometimes, as in the case of the San Francisco commune Harrad West, by hiring an outside housekeeper—most traditional corporate communes did not.[180] Quantitative data seemed to confirm these impressions. Though Danziger noted that the ability of couples to create an egalitarian division of household labor varied, his study estimated 70 percent of the cohabiting couples he interviewed had divided household labor according to traditional gender roles.[181]

On the other hand, some men embraced cohabitation over marriage precisely because they did not have to be breadwinners for their girlfriends, who nonetheless still provided free domestic labor. The *New York Times* interviewed a man who was searching for a woman to cohabit with after two unsuccessful living arrangements. The man noted that he sought a partner who "can 'clean a fork.'"[182] Ald made note of a man who circulated through girlfriends who would perform household duties: his ex-partners included a woman who was an excellent homemaker and a woman who was a proficient typist.[183] Another interviewee was inspired by a friend's cohabiting girlfriend who "play[ed] housemother." His friend's gambit inspired him to move out of the dorm and find a girl who would provide the services—presumably laundry, cooking, and similar chores—that the dormitory had formerly provided.[184]

Many of these cohabiting men did not support their female partners financially. Danziger noted that 60 percent of the couples he studied equally shared financial obligations even when women did the vast majority of domestic chores and men earned more.[185] In other words, what women received in exchange for cleaning forks, doing laundry, and typing term papers was scant. This hybrid of a gendered division of labor and equal financial obligations frustrated many cohabiting women. A cohabiter named Enise queried "Why shouldn't he clean up? We both go to classes, have studying to do. We share the expenses for the place."[186] Another woman had the same complaint: "Helen explained that problems concerning money, in her relationship with Frank, came from two sources. She feels that Frank has failed to live up to the bargain they had made with respect to household responsibilities; and the fact that she contributed more financially than he did made the situation even worse. According to Helen, '. . . whenever it's his turn to cook he wants to use "our" money to go out to eat.' "[187] Helen was frustrated to discover that relieving her partner of his duty to support her did not relieve her of any of the household duties they had negotiated. Some men on communes escaped the obligation to be breadwinners by dispensing with earning entirely.[188]

Many gay men and lesbians had voiced these ideas about replacing marriage with love and sexual freedom much earlier than this generation of cohabiters.[189] Their early critiques of marriage operated on two levels. First, gay men and lesbians increasingly refrained from marrying heterosexual partners and leading a double life, opting instead for thinking about marriage through the metaphor of the closet. In a 1962 edition of *ONE*, journalist Paul Britton asked his readers if they had ever met a homosexual who had managed to stay married. He explained "if you have, I'm sure I don't have to tell you here you have the true sick homosexual—and for real!"[190] Britton believed that homosexual men were who they were. If they married, they either betrayed their authentic selves or betrayed their wives when they gave in to their true homosexual desires. The double life had no meaning for Britton; only the closet did.[191] For the most part, though, the gay press took it for granted that homosexuals should not marry straight spouses. They had already turned to the issue of gay marriage.

Though certainly some members of the gay and lesbian community embraced gay marriage, which I will discuss in the last chapter, most homophile activists did not want to embrace a repressive institution that heterosexuals astutely seemed to be rejecting. In 1959, *ONE* journalist Hermann Stoessell explained that "the twentieth century heterosexual . . . [is] abandoning marriage, at least of the 'til death do us part' variety. Should we pick up the remnants of a system he is casting off?"[192] Stoessel believed that homosexual men hoped to marry only out of jealousy, possessiveness, and a perverse belief that humans could merge with each other.[193] To other gay men and lesbians, the prescribed inequality in marriage was a threat. In 1953, E. B. Saunders wrote an article in *ONE* posing the question of whether gay marriage was a good idea. He posited that the year was 2053 and that after homosexuality had gained widespread acceptance, gay marriage confined "deviates" with premarital sex bans and the regulation of breadwinners just like in straight marriage.[194] Therefore Saunders believed that homosexuality should remain a deviant practice, outside of both marriage *and* the realm of "acceptable behavior," in order for it to remain free.

As gay liberation supplanted the homophile movement a half generation later, activists continued to reject the institution of marriage. Jim Kepner, originally a frequent contributor to *ONE*, wrote in the more commercial gay publication the *Advocate* that it was a symbol of the homosexual community's strength that couples rejected marriage, or "that straightjacket." Kepner then quoted Marnie Jacobs, who also argued, "'now that a few heterosexuals are beginning to throw off their chains, the homosexuals come in demanding an equal share of the old slavery. How crazy can we get?'"[195] Pat Arrowsmith, a British lesbian activist and peace promoter, famously married to claim an inheritance left to her under her father's condition that she take a husband. Arrowsmith told the British press that making a mockery of marriage was part of her plan, since it was such a problematic institution.[196] In other words, many gay liberationists saw straight cohabiters as allies in overthrowing a marital regime that inhibited the free expression of love and sexuality.

Other gay liberationist critics rejected marriage as uniquely contrary to gay couples' interests. One journalist indicated that biological gender difference held marriages together, while it was an alliance of interest and temperament that united gay couples.[197] Because of this difference, and the inability to have children, gay couples therefore could not and should not try to recreate heterosexual marriage.[198] Similarly, a social scientist who opposed gay marriage explained in an interview with the *Advocate* that gay relationships would always differ for several reasons, including the way that men and women were socialized to play breadwinner and homemaker roles within a marriage. Gay and lesbian couples could not rely on these set roles where "you sew, and shop and take care of the children, and I work in the garden and fix the car."[199] Lesbians particularly identified themselves as benefiting from rejecting marriage. Liza Cowan, who regularly wrote for *DYKE* magazine, identified housework as a pervasive problem among feminists, citing Pat Mainardi as the inspirational pioneer of this critique. But for Cowan, housework itself was not the problem. Instead it was "men, not housework, that oppresses women."[200] Cowan complimented lesbians for creating lesbian-only spaces and issued a call to push further in designing spaces where women would be comfortable. These would serve as a counterpoint not only to prisons, supermarkets, and schools, but also marriage itself.

Others suggested that gay men and lesbians offered insights into love that would help heterosexuals break down the institution of marriage. They could be "pioneers for society."[201] In his "Gay Manifesto," Students for a Democratic Society member and gay liberationist Carl Wittman declared that gay marriages would have all the trouble of the "fraught, oppressive institution" of traditional marriage. He encouraged gay and straight couples alike to walk away from it.[202] Martha Shelley, a member of the early lesbian political organization Daughters of Bilitis, also saw marriage as a confining institution that no longer offered any social good. She both attributed the desire of gay men and lesbians to marry as a "form of Uncle-Tomism" and compared the concept of permanent bliss in marriage to the equally unrealistic concept of love at first sight. Shelley speculated that marriage was no longer necessary with the demise of a religious agrarian society that relied on marriage to distribute property.[203] Marriage was a trap, but gay men and lesbians believed they could guide society to a new path.

While these marriage dissenters did not have the effects on law that liberal feminists had, their model became increasingly common in practice. Many more couples cohabited than ever had before, and the rate of never-married couples expanded immensely.[204] But as the struggles among radical feminists, cohabiters, and gay liberationists indicate, the decision to cohabit did not necessarily diminish women's heavier burden of providing the majority of household labor or create absolute freedom.

*   *   *

In the first decade of the revived feminist movement, marriage occupied a significant place in the ideology and strategies of feminists. Liberal feminists believed that marriage limited the opportunities of all women by making education and careers less accessible. They saw an equal rights amendment as a means of making marriage compatible with gender equality. For most ERA proponents at this time, however, this meant expansionist equality. The breadwinner-homemaker model of the home could persist as long as men had the same right to receive Social Security, alimony, and other dependence benefits that wives had. Radical feminists, cohabiters, and gay liberationists disagreed. They saw no way in which marriage could be saved.

Liberal feminists' expansionist definition of equality remained the dominant interpretation of the Equal Rights Amendment once the debate reached Congress and then the Supreme Court. Via a slate of groundbreaking cases, the Supreme Court acknowledged that any spouse, regardless of gender, could be a breadwinner for his or her spouse. Members of the federal government— from the Supreme Court to congressional supporters of the ERA—expected this to benefit men and women alike. On the federal level, it did. But eventually, state legislators would enact a significantly different though equally revolutionary set of changes to marriage law. State legislatures and courts largely dispensed with husbands' and wives' traditional thick breadwinning and homemaking obligations.

CHAPTER 2

The End of Breadwinning and Homemaking

In the late 1970s, bureaucrats in the state government of Illinois solicited the Family Research Center at Sangamon State University to conduct an independent study of child support in the state. Family expert and sociologist Walter D. Johnson took the project on and surveyed seven different counties' marriage and divorce laws. He uncovered alarming rates of child support noncompliance. In 1965, only 21 percent of men fully ignored their child support orders, but just eleven years later, 69 percent of men failed to pay any of their court-ordered child support.[1] Johnson also compared these numbers to an unidentified county in Wisconsin, where similar declines had taken place. Johnson argued, default "sets in much earlier and has progressed much faster in 1970 than it did in 1965 or 1955."[2] Such a shift indicated a massive sea change in less than a decade. Why had fathers so suddenly stopped meeting their obligations to provide for their children? Such a drastic drop emerged because many divorced men were in full-scale revolt against thick breadwinning obligations. This prompted feminists to search for different solutions to the problem of marriage than the ones settled on by the Supreme Court and Congress.

Though the Supreme Court and Congress had declared that men and women alike could be breadwinners according to an expansionist definition of gender equality, many state legislatures and courts were beginning to envision an entirely different notion of equality based on freedom from the obligations of marital responsibilities for women and men.

This was in part based on the persistence of coverture in state law, the gendered system that enforced men's roles as husbands and women's roles as wives. Though generations of activists had successfully fought to have many of the tenets of coverture eliminated, beginning with married women's property acts in the nineteenth century, wives retained some of their traditional obligations even into the 1960s. Wives owed their husbands household labor including childcare, housework, work in a family business, and any improvements they made to household property. Wives also provided husbands unlimited and exclusive sexual access. A woman had no legal recourse if her husband raped her, and women who cheated on their husbands could lose custody of their children and alimony. Men also had their own legal roles within this system, characterized above all by their thick obligation to provide financially for their wives and children.[3] Even after divorce it was still a husband's duty to support his blameless wife, and that blameless wife's privilege to be dependent on her husband.

As the postwar era ended, state legislatures began to rethink these gendered roles. Through the passage of no-fault divorce statutes, state equal rights amendments, the acknowledgement of homemaker contributions in the distribution of household property, and rehabilitative alimony, states ensured that husbands and wives owed each other fewer and more temporary duties. Instead of the expansionist formal equality strategy that the Supreme Court had implemented in cases ranging from *Frontiero* to *Orr*, which made the roles of breadwinner or homemaker available to men and women, the bulk of the states vastly limited the obligations associated with both of these roles. By the mid-1980s, state legislators were taking an individualist, even neoliberal, approach to family obligations.

Multiple parties endorsed and benefited from these changes. In Illinois, which this chapter uses as a case study, ex-husbands and their sympathetic legal allies politicized older grumblings about breadwinning. Alimony had served as the most notorious physical manifestation of a husband's duty to financially support his wife—to serve as breadwinner. Most likely few divorced husbands had ever appreciated paying alimony. But as household labor seemed less arduous and the women's movement erupted in the early 1960s, divorced men in Illinois and throughout the country formed groups—such as the American Divorce Association for Men and America's Society of Divorced Men—to lobby legislators to eliminate alimony laws. They found sympathy among judges, bureaucrats, and legislators.

Meanwhile, however, feminist organizations such as the National Organization for Women, Housewives for ERA, and the Illinois Coalition of Women Against Rape proposed an alternative individualist notion of formal equality, which could make the regime of no-fault divorce fairer to women. As no-fault divorce made expansionist equality ineffective, these groups began to integrate critiques of the household economy into their agenda. They demanded a share of the household property—in the form of real estate, savings, stocks, pensions, and more—*in exchange for* household labor. Husbands' sexual entitlement to their wives remained, but this largely fell too with the passage of a more expansive rape law.

These feminist groups recast some traditional wives' rights as earned and fought for new ones.[4] But they did so defensively as a breadwinners' revolt shifted divorce law under wives' feet, which did not yield the most progressive results in the end. If these groups endorsed the radical assumption that household labor had economic value, they also overlooked or accepted the ways in which only the most privileged women could reap the benefits of the new laws. Even with radical understandings of women's unpaid labor, these feminists shared men's rights activists' embrace of negative liberty. In the end, state legislatures failed to create free-market families fully stripped of thick gendered obligations. Most wives continued to perform household labor for free. A distinction between marital rape and rape persisted. Maintenance remained a potential—albeit temporary and gender neutral—breadwinner obligation. The household had entered a middle ground. It was neither market based nor a refuge from market values.

Illinois was somewhat late to implement these innovations compared to other states. In fact, beginning with California's no-fault divorce law of 1969, twenty states had already implemented some change to alimony and marriage law. It was also unusual in implementing changes to men's and women's obligations in the same set of legislation, which allows us to see how legislators' weighed both parties' concerns. Nonetheless the laws Illinois implemented were representative of what occurred in many other states both before and after Illinois's actions. State legislators constructed an individualist gender equality that made concessions to wives, favored husbands, and never fully divested the family of gendered assumptions.

The Rejection of Breadwinning

No matter whether a court ordered alimony, child support, or another property decision, divorced women and men alike faced weaker financial standing after a marital split.[5] As one journalist estimated in the 1970s, monthly expenses for a divorced couple could go up as much as $523 a month when additional rent, home maintenance, utilities, clothing for a working wife, furniture, food, car insurance for a single woman, transportation, household items, and day care costs were all factored in.[6] For many husbands, the majority even, this was the cost of a failed marriage. But for those involved in an incipient breadwinners' revolt, they saw themselves not as victims of a failed marriage but as victims of their wives—and the judges, lawyers, and lawmakers standing behind their wives. Tension over breadwinning and homemaking roles led the federal and state governments to diverge on their approach to breadwinning. Though Robert Self has skillfully shown that a postwar consensus on the importance of male breadwinning continued to shape federal policy into the 1970s and beyond, Serena Mayeri has also beautifully illustrated that the successful Supreme Court fight for women's employment rights nonetheless "undercut the male breadwinner/female homemaker model as a basis for public policy."[7] But less tension existed on the state level. Changes to state marriage law began to weaken breadwinner and homemaker roles even further.

The weight of legal and cultural pressure behind men's breadwinning obligations in divorce proceedings prompted a breadwinners' revolt in the 1960s. This was not only a cultural phenomenon, and the revolt—alongside changes in the economy and the unintended consequences of other legal innovations—contributed to the end of breadwinning.[8] Critiquing breadwinning was a venerable postwar genre, perhaps best encapsulated by *Playboy Magazine*'s article "Miss Gold-Digger of 1953" in its inaugural issue. It advocated avoiding marriage altogether because "mercenary" wives would "stay home afternoons and let the ex-hubby pay the bills."[9] *Playboy*'s readers perceived their [ex-] wives as drains on family resources, rather than essential helpmeets to their husbands. The reference to an ex-wife lounging about in the afternoon alluded to a postwar labor problem. At least some husbands had grown skeptical about the household labor their wives performed. Household labor had not been eliminated, as housewives well knew, but it increasingly appeared that way.[10] Ronald Reagan, who would later be the first governor to sign reform marriage laws in 1969, helped perpetuate the notion that housework involved no work in ads for General Electric. After Ronald praised her dinner in the ad, his wife, Nancy Reagan, said: "well it's the easiest meal to make: my electrical servants do everything."[11] Sociologist Helena Znaniecka Lopata tested the assumption that women's work had little value in a late-1950s questionnaire she conducted on behalf of the *Chicago Tribune*.[12] She prompted her interviewees by stating that "Many husbands seem to feel that women are poorly organized." She then asked women if their own husbands considered women in the home poorly

organized, and many wives disclosed that their husbands were smug and crit-
ical about their wives' housework.[13]

Breadwinning critics particularly felt that women could and ought to earn
their own livings. In 1963, *Chicago Tribune* columnist George T. Horback
argued that, given women's new equality, independence, and capability of self-
support, imprisoning "a man for failing to continue alimony payments for an
ex-wife after she is earning her own living and sometimes drawing a higher
salary is completely ridiculous."[14] In 1974, an Illinois appellate court agreed,
arguing that "the emancipation of women socially and economically has led
courts to criticize the general rule that a husband is responsible for maintaining his wife at a standard of living to which she became accustomed during
marriage."[15] Another *Tribune* columnist referred to alimony as "lifetime 'rep-
arations'" to healthy ex-wives.[16] Even many wives agreed. An anonymous divorcee told one reporter that she didn't believe in alimony because doing so
made men slaves and women kept women.[17] A 1974 survey by Virginia Slims
indicated that 66 percent of women disapproved of alimony in cases where the
ex-wife could earn her own decent income.[18]

In contrast to these modern wives who could easily earn their own livings,
critics increasingly argued that husbands could not afford to support their
families. Critics of all backgrounds repeatedly invoked men's financial woes
in the face of alimony obligations. The *Playboy* article cited specific cases in
which judges ordered husbands to pay alimony they could not afford or that
even exceeded their income. In 1973, a prominent Chicago lawyer bemoaned
courts' disinterest in safeguarding men's financial stability.[19] A divorced men's
group leader explained that "you're taking the same dollars and trying to
make them stretch" to pay for "two stoves instead of one; two pots instead of
one" and more.[20]

It is difficult to say whether an individual man objected to support payments because he could not afford them or simply because he did not wish to
pay for support. Husbands indeed felt the pinch of finding employment that
provided a family wage. The GI Bill, unionization, and a booming postwar
economy had temporarily allowed a widespread realization of the family
wage, but the subsequent economic slowdown certainly reduced the number
of breadwinning jobs available. It was also true that more husbands—and
therefore more less wealthy men—paid alimony than they used to. Certainly
the leap in the rate of husbands who paid alimony from 9 percent to 25 percent indicated that more middle-class men had support obligations in the
postwar period than at the turn of the century.[21] But the quarter of men

ordered to pay alimony were nonetheless much more likely to be better off financially than most other husbands, and objections that men were not able to afford to pay child support were more frequently true than objections that men could not afford alimony.[22] As the postwar economy and new technology accelerated husbands' discontent with breadwinning, individual men increasingly revolted against what they perceived as unjust obligations to be breadwinners. These men did not yet act collectively, but their individual actions had a substantive cumulative effect. Nor did these men distinguish between their obligations as husbands and their obligations as fathers. This fit the concept of breadwinning during this time; husbands were supposed to care for all the dependents in their household. Even judges and legal scholars often thought of "alimony as one element in a financial package."[23] Finally, this revolt took place when husbands still had significant control over their households' wealth. A husband alone had the right to dispose of the household income as he saw fit. A husband owned all the household property in seventeen states and Washington DC, so long as his name was on the title. The rest of the states distributed property according to equitable distribution, meaning that judges could but often did not distribute household property to wives when their husbands' names alone were on the title.[24] Only in the eight community property states did husbands and wives split household property equally.[25]

One of the main means for a husband to minimize his thick support obligation was to negotiate a divorce settlement in his favor. Most divorces were resolved at the settlement stage throughout the postwar period. A 1965 national survey of nearly six hundred judges indicated that 94 percent believed they intervened in less than 10 percent of marital settlement agreements.[26] A homemaking wife's inability to afford a good lawyer therefore was a huge disadvantage.[27] Other wives settled for less in the hopes that something was better than nothing. One separated wife readily admitted that she could not support her child on a five-dollar weekly support payment even though she also brought in sewing, occasionally worked outside the home, and lived with her father. But she rejected the judge's suggestion that her ex-husband pay ten dollars a week because she feared that such a high order would prompt him to stop paying child support entirely.[28] This wife accepted six dollars a week instead. Another woman who realized that default or a later adjustment of her alimony rate was a possibility sought out a lump-sum payment instead. She stated in her complaint for divorce that her husband squandered his money.[29] This wife thereafter owned the property bestowed to her in her settlement rather than rely on her husband to continue to pay out alimony. This is not to say that divorce law did not matter, but many men and women negotiated for settlements within the flexible bounds set out by divorce law.[30]

Other husbands used "head and master" laws that gave them exclusive control over the family's finances to hide family property from wives, their lawyers, and judges. A husband who sold a family car, property, stocks, and more in the months just prior to a divorce decree could put any joint property well beyond his wife's reach by hiding the money with a friend or family member.[31] This happened so frequently that it became common for wives to beg judges for an injunction so that their husbands would not dispose of the property a couple shared while a divorce was in process. One Chicago woman asked the judge to stop her husband from selling a tavern the couple owned together.[32] Another woman, who suffered from a degenerative disorder that left her dependent on crutches, feared that her husband would sell income-yielding property that the two owned out of her reach in Arizona. This wife, who had provided the down payment for the property, depended on income from the property to provide for her extensive medical expenses.[33] Even with these measures available to them, many wives discovered that "diligent" husbands could hide property from courts.[34]

Husbands also simply ignored court orders. Although men with alimony orders were, on the whole, wealthier than the average man, about 30 percent of men with court orders in 1978 never paid any of their alimony order. Another 30 percent paid part; only 41 percent paid the full amount ordered by the court.[35] One popular method to avoid payments was to leave the state, since the courts had limited means of imposing or enforcing alimony and child support orders across jurisdictions. For example, in 1946, a wife reported that her husband had threatened to move himself and all his property to Florida.[36] In fact, *Playboy* endorsed this particular method, and real men did in fact follow such advice. Despite the adoption of a Uniform Reciprocal Enforcement and Support Act by all fifty states in the 1960s, a wife had to know the location of her former husband. Even if she did, nearly half of judges found the system only moderately effective.[37] When husbands fled before a divorce was final, judges reserved the question of alimony and child support until the husbands were found. Case files indicated that husbands almost never were.[38]

And some men refused to pay child support. Alarming national census numbers in 1978 indicated that only 49 percent of women received their full court-ordered child support payment. Nearly a third of women received none of the court-ordered child support.[39] That children in some states fared even more poorly, as indicated by Walter Johnson's study of Illinois in the 1960s, therefore, should not entirely surprise us.[40]

Husbands Campaign for Marriage Reform

As husbands and wives continued to tangle over divorce settlements throughout the postwar period, divorced men gained new allies, including judges, prison bureaucrats, men's rights interest groups, and eventually legislators. With these new allies, rather than simply fight an individual alimony or child support order, some newly politicized ex-husbands were emboldened to reform marriage law itself.

In Illinois, husbands' first allies were judges, who shared some of the same poor opinions of wives that husbands expressed and allotted alimony awards accordingly.[41] In 1968, for example, Judge Daniel A. Covelli testified before the Illinois legislature that he disliked permanent alimony and rarely granted it.[42] Nor were Illinois judges alone. Judge Harvis DuVal of Florida was hostile toward alimony on the grounds that it was so unfair to husbands that many were forced to leave town to default on their payments.[43] By 1975, critics noted that "increasingly fudges [*sic*] are awarding the divorced woman alimony for only two or three years so she may make the needed adjustment—complete education or training—to be able to support herself."[44]

Judges were both wary of and sympathetic to fathers when it came to child support. Most judges surveyed in 1976 indicated that ordering child support was an impossible situation. Seventy-three percent of judges believed that many fathers were in fact trying to cast responsibility for their children onto public assistance. One judge emphasized that he tried to award the children enough so that a father would "have enough of his earnings to go to his employment to earn the money in the first place."[45] He saw much greater hardship in intermittent rather than small payments. In spite of this skepticism, judges increasingly perpetuated fathers' ability to cast away thick responsibility for their children. Late in the postwar period, the justices on the U.S. Supreme Court lent understandable sympathy toward fathers in *Zablocki v. Redhail*. On the basis of the right to marry established in *Loving v. Virginia*, the court overturned a Wisconsin statute that did not allow a man to marry if he were in arrears on his child support.[46] Wisconsin restored marriage rights for these men but lost a tool in its child support enforcement arsenal.

In fact, judges' sympathy toward fathers seemed to increase after the mid-1960s. The guidelines judges established for reasonable child support actually declined from 1965 to 1975. In his state-funded study, Walter D. Johnson noted, "in spite of the rise in incomes and cost of living, a comparison of similar benchmarks . . . developed ten years apart indicate that current guidelines for support provide substantially lower awards than their earlier counterparts."[47] In 1965, a survey of national judges recommended a man with a weekly income of $50 should pay $12.50 a week for child support for one child. In 1975, a survey of Illinois judges recommended a man with the same income pay $8.50 a week for child support for one child.[48] In other words, similar groups of judges recommended less for child support in 1975 than they had in 1965.

The result of this sympathy was a further burden on mothers and often less support for children. Overall, judges self-reported that 20 to 50 percent of a father's income was allocated to child support, depending on the number of children. Only one judge, out of one hundred, had ever allocated more than 50 percent of a father's income, no matter how many children were involved. In 1969, the President Nixon–appointed group Citizens' Advisory Council on the Status of Women stated, "fathers by and large are contributing less than half the support of the children in a divided family."[49] While judges were aware of the increasing rates of default, only 12 percent had some measure in place to take note when fathers did not pay out child support.[50] Though the majority of judges found this unacceptable, in practice the custodial parent's only resort was to initiate contempt proceedings. In most cases, judges acknowledged that children did not receive support above what they would receive on public assistance. Even worse, judges often did not even allocate child support to children of color. While 71 percent of white women received child support, only 44 percent of Latina women and 29 percent of black women did.[51] Of course, the partners of Latina and black women were more likely to be poor, but so were Latina and black women themselves. Without support from husbands, Latino/a and black children were also more likely to be poor.

Bureaucrats at Cook County jail also became skeptical about breadwinning. Indeed, one of the first casualties of the breadwinning revolt in Illinois was Alimony Row, where formerly the county had jailed some husbands who defaulted on alimony or child support. By 1966, Cook County jail mainstreamed the prisoners in Alimony Row with the rest of the population in light of its dwindling numbers.[52] In Cook County, the clerk for the Department of Corrections reported that the number of men jailed for failure to pay alimony began to drop sharply from "hundreds" to only four or five a week by the mid-1970s.[53] A judge who presided over alimony contempt cases confirmed that only ten men hoped to be freed for Christmas in 1976, which had been a holiday tradition in the early 1960s. Men continued to go to jail for being in arrears on alimony and child support, but seemingly less frequently.[54] Cook County's turn away from Alimony Row left a symbolic if not literal gap in the enforcement of alimony and child support orders.

Organized men's rights activist groups were other allies for divorced men in their revolt against breadwinning. The first divorced men's groups originated in California in 1960, where community property laws had long given California wives the right to half of their households' property.[55] Illinois's local critics began organizing independently into groups inspired, they claimed, by feminist organizations like NOW in the late 1960s and early 1970s.[56] These groups focused on divorced men's strained circumstances and alimony's perpetual nature.[57] Charles Metz, the founder of America's Society of Divorced Men (ASDM) believed that many divorced men were "the unwitting stooges of conniving women, incompetent and equally conniving lawyers, and acquiescent judges" based on the status of alimony, custody, and lawyer fee decisions in the United States.[58] Charles Metz saw himself as representative of his club members. He and his first wife had divorced in the mid-1950s. Rather than pay child support, Metz chose to go to jail for eight years.[59] Metz remarried but remained angry about the divorce. He published a "guide and primer" to help divorced men navigate the "Divorce Racket" in the late 1960s.[60] It recommended sixteen reforms, including abolishing alimony, ending the practice of husbands paying their wives' divorce lawyers, and granting fathers custody when it was in the best interests of the child.

Three years after the book came out, Metz founded ASDM in Elgin, Illinois, in part to help individual men negotiate their own divorces.[61] ASDM consulted with 1,200 men about their divorces in 1969 and 1970 and charged forty dollars per consultation.[62] They identified forty other groups as possible men's rights–based divorce reform groups, and some members went on to form other organizations.[63] To highlight their expertise, the group bragged that none of their officers paid alimony or child support, seemingly to attract men hoping to overthrow men's obligation to provide for their children.[64]

Metz argued that the best chance men had for legal change was to take a cue from the civil rights movement and lobby their state legislatures and courts as blocs of votes.[65] Metz urged divorced men to learn from the civil rights movement that "picketing embarrasses courts as much as it does City

Figure 2. Like Charles Metz and members of ASDM, protesters in New York in 1966 opposed alimony and the practice of sending alimony defaulters to prison. Courtesy of the Associated Press.

Hall—especially when the picketers are clean-shaven, and wearing neckties and business suits."[66] This endorsement reflected divorced men's groups' simultaneous indebtedness to and advantages over civil rights groups. Certainly the strategic methodology of the civil rights movement was something that ASDM hoped to adopt, much as other groups inspired by the civil rights revolution had. Moreover some divorced men's groups did ally with African Americans briefly on some issues—including opposing an Illinois bill that proposed to test persons wishing to marry for genetic diseases such as Sickle Cell Anemia, Tay-Sachs disease, and thalassemia.[67] Other times, divorced men's activists positioned their actions as helping black men alongside white.[68]

Nonetheless, ASDM exploited its advantages over traditional civil rights movement groups and expressed little interest in their goals. Metz's endorsement of respectability while protesting tacitly acknowledged the advantages that ASDM would have as a group that was most visibly white. Though ASDM did not record demographic information about its numbers, it does seem that most members were probably white based on the photographs that do exist. Moreover, Elgin, Illinois, was a suburb of Chicago and in 1960 the population was only 1.2 percent African American, with no other ethnic minorities to speak of.[69] Most divorced men's groups in Illinois similarly seemed interested in civil rights only strategically. Consistently, divorced men's groups were hostile to core civil rights issues such as affirmative action.[70] Metz and other activists likely pursued civil rights–inspired strategies because they saw the language of oppression and the organizing strategies as potentially effective.

ASDM conducted a two-pronged campaign against the state of Illinois for its part in divorced men's alleged oppression. First, in 1971, Metz filed a class-action lawsuit against the governor of Illinois and various members of the Illinois bureaucracy to prevent state officials from enforcing divorce law on the basis that it was discriminatory toward men.[71] Metz recounted his usual host of complaints, including that wives were favored for custody, visitation rights for fathers were not enforced, and orders of protection were nearly always directed against men. In addition, he objected to the whole practice around alimony, including the lack of guidelines for how alimony was awarded, how it could be refuted or mitigated, or how much should be awarded. Moreover, temporary alimony awarded while a divorce was pending could not be appealed. And above all, Metz noted, "male litigants are frequently jailed for failure to pay alimony or support."[72] Metz claimed that intimidated men faced such a disadvantage that they agreed to unfair settlements.[73] He argued that marriage law "appear[ed] on its face to be fair and equal," but was faithfully applied against men's interests.[74] His council claimed that this violated equal protection and inflicted "immediate and irreparable injury."[75]

ASDM ultimately lost its case that divorce orders discriminated against men. The state bitingly critiqued ASDM for not representing the class it claimed to represent, misidentifying the governor and executive branch as the perpetrators of the harm, and not presenting a suitable remedy.[76] The only remedy the state could imagine was for all state agencies to enjoin all divorce cases until new statutes could be written. The court, including future Supreme Court justice John Paul Stevens, found every aspect of the suit problematic. The justices particularly disputed ASDM's claim to represent all divorced men in Illinois: "the interests of all divorced men are obviously not the same. For example, many divorced men are required by their decrees to pay alimony. Many others are not. Some have obligations to support their minor children, others do not."[77] Above all, the ruling concluded that ASDM would be better served by pursuing the proper defendants.

Once Metz's case failed, ASDM directed its anti-breadwinning message more exclusively to the Illinois legislature.[78] The concept of men's rights was not new to legislators; Illinois legislator Richard Elrod (D) had introduced a series of men's equality bills in 1969.[79] ASDM and other men's rights groups had reached out to the Illinois legislature directly nearly from their inception, sending letters, pamphlets, and op-eds directly to targeted legislators.[80] By the early 1970s, they had a tentative seat at the table as experts on marriage law. In 1974, they testified before the Divorce Lawyers Practices Committee in Springfield. After Metz's death, the new president of ASDM, Frank Kohler, suggested to the legislative committee that once a spouse gained custody of his or her children, "the other spouse should remain completely out of the picture from then on." This meant neither child support nor visitation for fathers since Kohler highlighted that a second husband would be better able to take care of his new family without interference from the biological father.[81] Kohler carried on Metz's legacy here, since Metz had endorsed the end of all child support after a mother remarried as one of his sixteen legal reforms. Metz's rationale was that filial love was unsustainable with visitations alone: "love, my friends, is a nasty old *matter of proximity*."[82] According to Metz, children ceased to love or belong to their fathers once they stopped living with them.[83] Though obviously not all fathers seeking divorce rights wanted to relinquish their rights as fathers, ASDM leaders did.

The Chicago-based American Divorce Association for Men (ADAM), which had about 2,000 members in 1972, shared ASDM's anti-alimony approach and worldview.[84] They characterized men as "divorced victims" and railed against Alimony Row.[85] Instead of the tactics of the civil rights movement, ADAM more readily appropriated feminists' strategies and sold divorce reform as part of women's liberation. ADAM president Louis Filzcer asserted that "with alimony, the wife is maintained as a vegetable."[86] Harvey Bass, an attorney for ADAM, reported to the *Chicago Tribune* that he defined women's liberation as the elimination of alimony.[87] ADAM also targeted Illinois courts and the legislature. The group engaged in actions like "pop power" and "Thankless Day" rallies in the Civic Center Plaza.[88] In 1973, ADAM publicly announced its support for ratification of the ERA in Illinois with the hope that the ERA would extend alimony, child support, pension rights, and other benefits to men as Congress had suggested.[89] As late as September 1990, ADAM was still demanding that the ERA be adopted.[90] ADAM also participated in the hearings with the Divorce Lawyers Practices Committee in Springfield in 1974 and published a pamphlet that it sent to state legislators that endorsed a no-fault divorce bill like California's. ADAM

believed that a tax should replace jail sentences and alimony should be eliminated for women capable of work.[91]

ASDM, ADAM, and other men's rights activists initially hoped that the
Illinois legislature would pass no-fault divorce as a more immediate solution
to alimony than the ERA. In 1971, ADAM believed that instituting no-fault
divorce would stop "the clear violation of men's rights under the Fifth and
Eighth Amendments to the Constitution and the 1964 Civil Rights Act."[92]
Though ADAM in particular would recant its support for no-fault by 1975 as
adulterous wives in other states won marital property, men's rights groups
were initially promiscuous in their strategies to destroy the thick obligations
of breadwinning.[93]

Thus eliminating a wife's permanent entitlement to her husband's support
was one of the inspirations for no-fault divorce. If fault divorce laws held that
a couple must fulfill certain basic expectations in a marriage, there were no
violations under no-fault laws. A marriage dissolved not when the judge decided that the spouse had violated the marriage contract, but instead when
one member or both decided not to be married anymore. California legislators voted for the nation's first no-fault divorce law in 1969.[94] No-fault then
spread across the country like wild fire, passing in the majority of states within
a few years. One definite cause of the rush to no-fault divorce was the increasingly common practice of collusion between husbands and wives. Certainly
many legislators and the American Bar Association were concerned that husbands and wives plotting to evade strict fault divorce laws could undermine
faith in the rule of law. But anti-alimony sentiment also inspired some of its
support in California and elsewhere.[95]

The mechanisms for no-fault to undermine the expectation for alimony
were twofold. First, wives could no longer negotiate alimony from husbands
who were not legally at fault but who wanted their wives to collude with them
to get a divorce. Advocates of no-fault repeatedly evoked wives' use of blackmail to win alimony from husbands who wanted a divorce but whose wives
had not committed any fault under fault divorce statutes. Legal experts affiliated with NOW acknowledged that fault divorce equipped dependent spouses
with leverage in negotiations for a better financial settlement.[96] Policy maker
and law professor Herma Hill Kay, who served on the California Governor's
Commission on the Family that introduced no-fault reform, explicitly identified the elimination of blackmail as one of the goals of divorce reform.[97]

Second, legislators simply paired anti-alimony measures with no-fault divorce on the assumption that alimony had been a punishment no longer ap-

propriate to no-fault divorce.[98] When Washington, DC, held hearings on its own no-fault bill in 1975, Harvey L. Zuckman, a legal expert on the Uniform Marriage and Divorce Act, testified that the no-fault divorce law would prevent judges from using alimony as a punishment for the husband's misconduct.[99] Instead, it should only be awarded in cases of extreme economic need. In fact, anti-alimony sentiment was a hallmark of no-fault's passage in California in 1969. In hearings in 1964, one of the inspirations for no-fault was women's unfair advantage in divorce proceedings.[100] Then five years later, when articulating the need for the new divorce law to the legislators who eventually ushered it in, policy makers cited only three inspirations: a more equitable division of property, a reduction in accusations, and the introduction of a partnership model of marriage.[101]

These nods to equitable division of property and partnership models perhaps intended to suggest feminist influence, but legislators betrayed their sympathy to husbands when the new law retained the understanding that "the husband is head of the family."[102] Moreover, since California was a community property state, wives already received half of a household's property at divorce; perhaps some lawmakers sought to reduce what wives received. Kay confirmed later that formal gender equality was not a goal of the marriage reformers in the 1960s, but neither was the disadvantage of women.[103] Instead, according to Kay, judges interpreted the laws in ways that privileged men after no-fault divorce was enacted. California husbands expected more reasonable alimony awards.[104]

California's innovation in divorce law and its effects on alimony were well-known to divorced men's activists and the press. A divorced men's activist in Illinois cited the new California law as an inspiration for the rest of the country, including his former state of Minnesota.[105] The national press declared the new law as ushering in "fewer and fewer requests for alimony, or 'spousal support,' on the part of women."[106] Written into the novel California law was the new understanding that alimony was only appropriate in the case of need, rather than as an assumed reward for innocence—and need would come to be defined narrowly.[107] Making alimony a temporary measure was an additional crucial aspect of alimony reform in the new California law and its copycats.

Feminists Protest Unequal Impact of Divorce Reform

Most feminists greeted no-fault divorce not with enthusiasm but instead with a damning critique: no-fault divorce would eliminate men's thick coverture-based obligations, but not women's. In 1974, Elizabeth Coxe Spaulding, a NOW officer, explained that women were losing alimony because of divorce reform, but the law still assumed that women's labor in the home belonged to their husbands. According to Spaulding, being a homemaker was no longer possible because laws increased the ex-wife's "obligation to provide support without giving her property rights during the marriage or recompense in the divorce settlement."[108] Radical feminist Sheila Cronan echoed this sentiment: "Given the existence of marriage and the fact the women work for no pay but with the expectation of security—that is, that their husbands will continue to 'support' them—divorce is against the interests of women. Many of us have suspected this for some time because of the eagerness with which men have taken up the cause of divorce reform (i.e., making it easier to get one)."[109] While NOW endorsed opening employment to women workers, NOW also believed that working outside the home should be a woman's choice. In fact, by 1979, NOW complained that few remembered that it had been feminists who "opposed the new dissolution laws as premature in a society that had failed to provide either equal opportunity or encouragement for women to achieve and maintain skills to be self-supporting."[110] Feminists feared that breadwinning would die, but homemaking would live on.

State-level divorce reform threatened to unsettle the expansionist gender equality that the Supreme Court had seemingly established in its series of revolutionary 1970s decisions, including *Frontiero v. Richardson* (1973), *Weinberger v. Wiesenfeld* (1975), and *Califino v. Goldfarb* (1977). These decisions did not accommodate the increasingly shaky ground on which homemakers' benefits rested in state legislatures. No-fault divorce threatened to gut dependent homemaker benefits without disrupting homemaker obligations. Illinois feminists pointed to cases like *Debrey v. Debrey* as evidence that wives still owed husbands their household labor.[111] In 1971, James LeRoy Debrey appealed a divorce ruling that granted his former wife, Nancy June Debrey, the marital home and shares of stocks on the grounds that the ruling violated his property rights. An Illinois appeals court restored the house and stocks to James because, under common law, a husband had a right to his wife's labor. The court held, "There is no evidence that any money, property or *service beyond the duties imposed by the marital relationship* contributed in any way towards the acquisition or improvement of this property."[112] The appeals court relied on a special equities clause of the 1875 Husband and Wife Act that stated that a wife would not gain ownership of household wealth in exchange for "labor performed for her minor children or husband."[113] Notably the 1875 law had granted a wife a right to wages for work earned outside the home for the first time but explicitly excluded any work she did inside the home.[114] For the next several years, appellate courts in Illinois cited *Debrey* to transfer property back to husbands.[115] According to Illinois courts, the value of a wife's homemaking services belonged entirely to her husband.

The gender-neutral dependency route also left a husband's sexual rights intact. In the early 1970s, Illinois law defined rape as a sexual assault by a man who was not the woman's husband. By definition, husbands could not rape their wives.[116] Although first-wave feminists critiqued the marital rape exception in the mid-nineteenth century, Illinois courts and statutes alike held a husband's sexual rights sacrosanct.[117] The cumulative effect of the marital rape exception in Illinois and forty-nine other states was stunning. The Coalition to Reform the Sex Offense Laws, a group of thirty different religious, legal, and feminist organizations, estimated that husbands raped six hundred thousand wives each year. Other statistics indicated that women who faced other forms of domestic violence had a 30 percent chance of also being sexually assaulted by their husbands.[118]

Feminists found the marital exception in rape law appalling. In a 1977 report, *The Legal Status of Homemakers in Illinois*, the authors noted that the exception applied even when the parties were separated or divorced.[119] A feminist homemakers' organization highlighted cases that revealed the twisted logic of the laws, including one in Ohio where a husband and his friend kidnapped, raped, and attempted to murder the husband's estranged wife. Only the friend faced rape charges, though both the friend and husband were charged with kidnapping, attempted murder, and felonious assault.[120] U.S. congresswoman Martha Griffiths (D-MI), a sponsor of the ERA, observed that the practical difficulties of determining marital rape while a couple lived together seemed insurmountable. A wife could not prove she had not consented, and Griffiths hoped only to expand battery laws.[121]

The uneven benefits of marriage reform were particularly destructive because many women continued to live as homemakers even after divorce reform had altered state laws. A whole generation of older divorced women—dubbed displaced homemakers—had to try to enter the job market without skills, experience, or property after late-life divorces. For example, one Kentucky homemaker, whose husband had divorced her after twenty-five years, had never worked. She feared "that the only answer would be suicide." She explained, "I am so scared. I'm 48 and have three grown daughters."[122] This homemaker was not alone in her despair; thoughts of suicide came up not infrequently in the "forum" section of displaced homemaker newsletters. Such desperation inspired many liberal feminists to look for new solutions.

Debrey, marital rape exceptions, and the fate of displaced homemakers convinced Illinois feminists that expansionist gender equality alone could not bring women equality.[123] Instead, they began to draw on the logic of the President's Commission on the Status of Women, Margaret Mead, the National Conference of Commissioners on Uniform State Laws, Housewives for ERA, and radical feminists to create a new vision of equality rooted in the home. They argued that homemakers' dependence on their husbands was based on the fiction that housework had no value, when instead women's household labor was very valuable indeed.[124]

Failure to pay wives for their household labor, according to feminists, created problems for all women. First, even career women were likely to drop out of the workforce temporarily to care for children. This disrupted their climb up the professional ladder and payment into pensions and social security.[125] Second, feminists blamed the problem of low wages for women on the problem of unpaid labor in the home. Michigan representative Martha Griffiths believed that "if women's work is not valued in the home, it has a low value outside the home."[126] Women were underpaid as waitresses, secretaries, nurses, and day care workers precisely because some women performed this labor for free. Therefore the means of eliminating dependence for either sex was to recognize housework as work either through the federal Equal Rights Amendment, through the courts, or through state statutes. To achieve true equality, women's separate sphere—the literal work of keeping the home—had to be acknowledged in the law as having monetary value. Liberal feminists rearticulated the meaning of equality, shifting its essence from expansionist equality to equal independence by giving monetary compensation for housework in the form of a share of household property (real estate, stocks, pensions, and more).

Liberal feminists drew on social theorists who had already presented the need to compensate housewives monetarily. The President's Commission on the Status of Women had recommended a legal understanding of marriage as a partnership.[127] The PCSW argued that this should be accomplished by giving each spouse "a legally defined substantial right in the earnings of the other, in the real and personal property acquired through those earnings, and in their management."[128] In other words, the household should be treated as a business, with women's contribution to this business as highly valued as men's. This legal strategy would invest women's labor in the home with value, recognizing women's work as work.[129] Clare Booth Luce extended the business metaphor by using the language of "severance pay" in a 1967 *McCall's* article.[130]

The significantly more staid National Conference of Commissioners on Uniform State Laws also endorsed a model that would recognize the fiscal value of housework. The nonpartisan organization of lawyers, judges, and other legal experts was founded in 1892 in order to recommend laws that would prevent disjuncture between different states' policies. In 1965, the organization began research on the possibility of no-fault divorce with the financial sponsorship of the Ford Foundation and the United States Department of Health, Education, and Welfare. The American Bar Association joined the research via a liaison committee in 1967. Herma Hill Kay—who had helped usher no-fault divorce in California—served on the committee as well. In 1970, the organization wrote a model law, the Uniform Marriage and Divorce Act.[131] The members of the commission endorsed the end of alimony, but in important ways they also echoed the PCSW report.[132] The model law recommended that marital property be divided according to the contribution of each spouse to its acquisition and maintenance, specifically including the contribution of a spouse as a homemaker. The innovation was inspired at least in part by the desire to mitigate the ill effects that alimony reform would have: one committee member particularly worried about the fate of young innocent wives once no-fault divorce transformed the traditional distribution of property and support.[133] As the report's prefatory note suggested, "the distribution of property upon the termination of a marriage should be treated, as nearly as possible, like the distribution of assets incident to the dissolution of a partnership."[134] If the PCSW made these suggestions on the federal level, the Uniform Marriage and Divorce Act, sought to intervene in domestic law through state statutes.[135]

Similarly, in a 1971 *Yale Law Journal* assessment of the impact of the ERA on law, Professor Thomas I. Emerson and several law students—Barbara A. Brown, Gail Falk, and Ann E. Freedman—also argued that women's labor should be given monetary value. Emerson, Brown, Falk, and Freedman acknowledged that under the ERA, laws that held only husbands responsible for alimony and child support would be unconstitutional. But the authors also insisted that judges must consider financial contributions and household labor as equivalent contributions. Rather than decreasing the child support payments men owed to their wives, Emerson and his students argued that acknowledging nonmonetary contributions could forestall the need for mathematically equal contributions.[136] The effect of making homemaking and breadwinning equal contributions was to invest women's labor with monetary value.

One organization that particularly focused on the monetary value of wives' labor in the home was Housewives for ERA, or HERA, later recast as the Homemakers' Equal Rights Association (named after the goddess Hera). Jo Anne Budde began the organization in Illinois in 1973. Conventional wisdom would have it that Budde—a white homemaker involved in the church and concerned about the effects of the ERA on housewives—would have staunchly opposed the ERA.[137] This description, in fact, closely resembles the amendment's preeminent opponent, Phyllis Schlafly, who claimed to represent the forgotten housewife. Budde, however, rejected Schlafly's stewardship of housewives. Nor was Budde alone. Her successor as HERA president was Anne Follis, a self-proclaimed homemaker, minister's wife, Christian, and author of *I'm Not a Women's Libber But. . . .*[138]

Though HERA did not retain membership numbers, the organization was moderately sized—large enough to have branches in Florida, New Jersey, Virginia, Oklahoma, and a few other states. As with ASDM, it is difficult to say what the racial makeup of the group was, but from pictures, the group seemed largely composed of white women. HERA was also recognized in the wider feminist community as a significant player. Senator Nancy Kassebaum presented the keynote at HERA's annual convention in 1979, and Follis presented alongside famous feminists like Gloria Steinem and Midge Costanza at another event.[139] But it was still small enough for its officers to worry that the other major feminist organizations considered HERA "rinky dink."[140]

The mission of the organization was literally in its name—to pass the ERA—but the spirit behind its support of the amendment originated from disgust with a legal system that regarded the wife as the "property of her husband." The ERA would recognize "the homemaker's non-monetary contribution to the family welfare as being of equal value to that of the wage earner." HERA called for a "full legal partnership for homemakers, as well as recognition, in government, business, and all areas of society, of the value of work done in the home."[141] Budde demanded the acknowledgment of the value of homemaking via financial, rather than cultural or emotional, compensation.

Having wives' housework recognized as labor would also set homemakers free from their husbands' power. Budde believed that the traditional expectation that a wife should use her feminine wiles to procure her own basic needs was the most degrading situation a woman could find herself in.[142] It was also insecure.[143] With the economic security offered by compensation for housework, HERA believed that women could choose homemaking without sacrificing their independence. Like men's rights activists, feminists in Illinois endorsed formal gender equality in the home but defined gender equality differently.

HERA's agenda soon extended beyond the ERA as progress on ratification stuttered. The organization believed other measures could also provide homemakers with compensation for their household labor. For instance, its officers sought to have one half of a husband's salary recognized as compensation for the homemakers' unpaid wages.[144] HERA also endorsed incremental measures including IRAs for homemakers, reform of inheritance laws, and access to disability coverage for housewives.[145] NOW eventually introduced some of these reforms to Congress.[146] Finally HERA also called for divorce reform: "Divorce laws must recognize the homemaker's contribution; they don't now! When dividing up property acquired during a marriage, courts should take into account each party's financial contribution to the acquisition of that property, including the contribution of the spouse as homemaker."[147] Similarly, the Pennsylvania branch of HERA published a booklet on marriage rights to advocate for the passage of the uniform marriage act in Pennsylvania. HERA wanted legislative change while it waited for the ERA.

Like ADAM and ASDM, HERA took its case to the Illinois legislature. In 1974, HERA president Budde testified before the Illinois House Human Resources Committee hearing on the Equal Rights Amendment. After establishing her status as a housewife, mother, and PTA member, she presented the *Debrey* case as evidence of the need to replace the common law concept of marriage with the "recognition of marriage as a partnership between husband and wife."[148] HERA members also made pilgrimages to Springfield a few times a year, days they called "Hostage Day" or "Roses Day."[149] Board members gladhanded and corresponded with state legislators such as Betty Lou Reed, Adeline Geo-Karris, and Ronald Greisheimer, among many others.[150] They issued regular press releases to put media pressure on legislators.[151] Some board members also campaigned for individual legislators who had supported the cause.[152]

Wives also found allies in judges who interpreted state equal rights

Figure 3. Members of the Homemakers' Equal Rights Association (HERA)
met with Governor James Thompson of Illinois in 1982. Courtesy of the
Women and Leadership Archives, Loyola University Chicago.

amendments as yielding compensation for women's unpaid labor. As the
1970s proceeded, courts in many states began recognizing housework as work
in property divisions, childcare payments, and alimony settlements on the
basis of state ERAs.[153] Some states with equal rights amendments recognized
women's household labor first in child support hearings.[154] In the Pennsylvania case *Green v. Freiheit*, presiding judge Murphy ruled that because of the
state ERA, both parents must share the duty of support but added that "this is
not, of course, to suggest that a mother who is keeping a house and caring for
her children must secure the services of a baby sitter and seek employment in
order to contribute to the children's financial support."[155] Mothers simply provided a different form of support. Judges in states from Washington to Texas
made similar rulings that mothers' caretaking constituted an equal monetary
contribution.[156]

Judges granting childcare monetary value in these cases laid the ground-
work for granting housework value in property settlements as well. In the
1975 case *DiFlorido v. DiFlorido*, a wife had been granted some property in-

cluding items she had inherited from her mother and some household goods. Her husband appealed, arguing that her mother's property constituted marital property and, because he was the sole provider, all the household goods belonged to him. But the Pennsylvania Supreme Court ruled that women's labor constituted a nonmonetary contribution to the acquisition or maintenance of property: "we can not accept an approach that would base ownership of household items on proof of funding alone, since to do so . . . would fail to acknowledge the equally important and often substantial nonmonetary contributions made by either spouse."[157] Judges in Pennsylvania, Maryland, Texas, Washington, and other states interpreted their state ERAs as granting homemakers' work monetary value.

These rulings in several states set precedents for other states and promised a national solution if the federal ERA passed. Feminist legal experts in Pennsylvania interpreted court decisions optimistically, conveying to their sisters in Illinois and other states that state ERA decisions had provided a legal basis for recognizing "the dependent spouse's right to support and a fair division of the economic fruits of the marriage."[158] They titled an article on their analysis, "State ERAs Are Working." The recognition of women's labor in Pennsylvania was particularly vital since Pennsylvania historically had only allowed temporary alimony.[159] Similarly, legal scholar Judith Avner hoped to use precedents from other states to convince Connecticut courts that the state ERA granted wives compensation for their unpaid labor. These rulings represented a valuable precedent to many feminists, indicating that the ERA would be interpreted in such a way as to achieve equality for all women. But of course, the necessary thirty-eight states never ratified the ERA. During the stalemate that lasted throughout the 1970s and until 1982, ERA advocates focused on state legislatures as their remaining hope.

The Illinois Legislature Implements Divorce Reform

The Illinois legislature turned to a new no-fault divorce law in the midst of a failing ERA campaign, and in some respects both men's rights activists and feminists' agendas were on the table. Although new divorce bills introduced to the Illinois legislature in the mid-1970s were the first serious contenders since the 1875 law to propose reform to the marriage law, they still faced serious opposition. Antagonism to the bills emerged in part because of the power of the Catholic Church in the Illinois, but legislators also commonly voiced their unwillingness to sacrifice men's traditional sexual or property privileges.

Some legislators—and even ADAM—opposed no-fault divorce in 1976 because they imagined it would bestow alimony on unworthy women. These legislators tried to amend a preliminary no-fault divorce bill to deny cheating wives alimony.[160] Democratic House member and sponsor of the bill George Sangmeister explained the purpose of one amendment was to allow the judge to take into consideration whether a wife had "a gigolo living with her"; if she did, the judge would "not have to award alimony."[161] Republican representative Harry D. Leinenweber urged his colleagues to pass the amendment if they supported no-fault divorce, saying it would be the only way to calm opponents of the no-fault bill who worried about husbands who would have to pay alimony to cheating wives.[162] Illinois Republican representative Ronald Griesheimer tried to pass another amendment that prohibited alimony in childless marriages lasting less than five years in order to prevent "the situation where you get a shakedown marriage."[163] Despite these amendments, this no-fault divorce bill failed in 1976.

In 1977, legislators introduced the most significant bill yet in that it brought all of these activists' demands together by explicitly curbing alimony and introducing a clause that monetarily recognized a wife's household labor. First, though the bill retained fault grounds for divorce, fault could *not* be considered in property distribution or child custody.[164] This deliberate half step toward a no-fault divorce law brought on board the support of the influential Catholic Church officials who worried that divorce rates would rise with no-fault divorce.[165] Second, the bill would also usher in an equitable distribution of property system that acknowledged wives' labor to replace the common law system based on a husband's ownership of his wife's labor. The bill required the court to "divide marital property . . . in just proportions considering all relevant factors, including . . . the contribution of a spouse as a homemaker or to the family unit."[166] Property distribution could include compensation for unpaid household labor.

Third, the bill also dispensed with the term alimony, replacing it with "maintenance" instead. This change was not cosmetic. Maintenance was distributed without considering fault *or* gender, but it also diverged from alimony in that it was considered strictly temporary and driven by need. The proposed Marriage and Dissolution of Marriage Act provided maintenance *only* if the spouse lacked property and could not support him- or herself with employment.[167] Moreover, the length of time maintenance was provided was based on the financial resources of the party seeking maintenance, the time needed to acquire enough education or training to find work, the standard of living during the marriage, the length of the marriage, and the age and health of both spouses. The bill considered maintenance a tactic of last resort and tried to provide property "in lieu of maintenance" in order to "preclude future claims to maintenance."[168] Husbands or wives received it only for a short time while they got back on their feet. It clearly echoed the language in the California no-fault divorce law that had so drastically cut back alimony.

In effect, the last two provisions offered moderated versions of both anti-breadwinner activists' and homemakers' demands. One provision gave a housewife property rights to some of the household's wealth in recognition of her household labor. The other provision dismantled the expectation that men would serve as breadwinners; either men or women could be ordered to support dependent spouses, but only temporarily in extreme circumstances.

The competing motives for supporting the bill, and its predecessor bills, emerged in Illinois House debate. Some legislators called attention to the aid the bill would provide to housewives. Illinois Republican representative (and NOW member) Susan Catania celebrated the recognition of the contribution of the homemaker in the bill. She thought it would particularly provide security for a wife who had the "misfortune to be cast out by her husband after several years of serving with no monetary reimbursement."[169] Even Griesheimer, the Republican representing the Thirty-First District who had proposed banning alimony, argued that the 1875 clause that gave husbands possession of their wives' labor in the home should be struck down because housewives had no legal right to that property under Illinois law.[170]

The Illinois legislature's support for a new marriage bill that granted housewives compensation for their work could have suggested a feminist victory alone, but anti-breadwinning advocates clearly had their hand in the legislation as well. Some critics absolutely opposed homemakers' compensation. Senator Stearney claimed that by granting wives household property the bill would "[destroy] the concept of private ownership of property."[171] The new ADAM president opposed this bill for "giv[ing] the wife 'homemaking' pay, and creat[ing] a community property concept which takes away one's individually owned property purchased during the marriage and makes it 'marital property.' "[172] The bill, they believed, would circumvent the Illinois courts' refusal in *Debrey* to acknowledge women's labor in the home.

Legislators assuaged these concerns in part by reassuring those sympathetic to husbands' property rights that the compensation for housework would be modest. As the House discussed the 1977 marriage and dissolution bill, Democratic representative Roland "Tip" Tipsword worried that the bill conceptualized a wife as a "a partner in a partnership owning partnership property."[173] He thought this provision could lead to husbands losing too much property to their wives in a divorce. Democratic representative Alan Greiman responded, the courts would "look at the contribution of the spouse into the acquisition of that property . . . and I suspect that if one party had nothing to do with the contribution . . . even though that party might be a homemaker, the interest would be minimal."[174] The word "minimal" was telling. Tipsword queried further whether there was a possibility that a homemaker could be awarded part or all of the partnership property. Greiman again reassured Tipsword that what the partner could get would be a "minimal kind of interest," and certainly not enough of a share to control a husband's business. Later in the debate, Democratic representative Aaron Jaffe clarified to the doubtful that the bill did "not create community property."[175] Jaffe's reassurance was necessary and effective. Griesheimer, who had opposed alimony in the 1976 bill, had the most explicit explanation of what the 1977 bill would enact. He noted that the homemaker provisions were "at best lip service to the concept of the judge looking into the status of the homemaker."[176] He believed that even with consideration of the contribution of the spouse as homemaker, "a woman whose husband places all the property in his name will wind up with nothing except one-half of the marital home."[177]

If the award of a homemakers' entitlement was so controversial that even its own supporters declared it a mere token, the Illinois legislature barely noted the transformation of permanent alimony into temporary maintenance. What was unremarked upon was how rare and temporary maintenance would be. The commissioners of the act explained they had written the law "to encourage the court to provide for the financial needs of the spouses by property disposition rather than by an award of maintenance."[178] The only concern raised about the transition was the possibility that cheating wives might get maintenance.[179] One last attempt to retain the sexual exclusivity wives legally owed their husbands in Illinois failed. With the new law, wives were in fact free of the unique obligation not to cheat. But maintenance was reserved for special cases. After a great deal of debate and negotiation, the bill became the 1977 Marriage and Dissolution of Marriage Act.

The voting record in the passage of the 1977 Marriage and Dissolution of Marriage Act suggested the role of legislators sympathetic to husbands. Of the ninety-seven Illinois lawmakers who voted in favor of divorce reforms, twenty-five had voted repeatedly against the Equal Rights Amendment. Some of these legislators possibly had women's rights in mind when voting for the new marriage laws even if they believed the ERA went too far, but most seemed opposed to any controversial women's rights policies as a whole. For example on House Bill 333, which determined whether state funds could be used to fund abortions for public aid recipients, twenty of these legislators opposed the use, one legislator voted in favor of continuing to use state funds for abortions, and the rest voted either present or absent. This group of twenty-five legislators seemingly voted for the new marriage law at least in part because the value of what women would win through homemaker entitlements was small.[180] Abbreviated alimony obligations were perhaps an unspoken bonus.

In Illinois, the legal changes to breadwinner and homemaker duties withstood challenges. After the Illinois Marriage and Dissolution of Marriage Act took effect in 1978, Joseph Kujawinski filed a class action lawsuit asserting that the new law violated his property rights. As Joseph Kujawinski understood it, "if I own property and some legislators come along and tell me I no longer own it, that is a violation of the Constitution."[181] This was an argument that ASDM founder Charles Metz had made in his book in 1965 and that ADAM had argued in its opposition to the new law in 1977.[182] By the end of the year, the Illinois Supreme Court ruled against Joseph Kujawinski. The court argued that "by giving both spouses an interest in 'marital property' upon dissolution of marriage, the legislature sought to award economic credit in the distribution of property for indirect or domestic contributions to the accumulation of property."[183] In other words, the previous divorce law had deprived women of their property—the real value of their labor—rather than vice versa. Some women's housework suddenly had some financial value in divorce courts. Women outside of Illinois also gained property via homemaker entitlements in most states.[184] By 1981, judges recognized the homemaker's contribution in more than half of property distribution cases.[185] By 1990, the U.S. Bureau of the Census had determined that 30 percent of all divorced women received marital property, a significant number.

Nonetheless, it was clear that homemaker entitlements neither compensated women well nor did they benefit all women. Some studies indicated that fewer wives received property awards in 1990 than before; 30 percent was a decline rather than an increase.[186] Most women did not get to share their family's most valuable asset—the long-term earning potential of a husband's advanced degree.[187] Poor women did not benefit at all from these laws since a household had to reach a certain threshold of wealth for a housewife to share in it. If a family had little or no property, housewives received little or nothing. Lenore Weitzman determined in her study of Los Angeles couples that half of all households owned "less than $20,000 in assets."[188] Similarly, the vast majority of women—85 percent—did not receive alimony or maintenance in recognition of their household labor. We cannot pretend that this was because they did not perform household labor. Women continued to perform the lion's share of household labor throughout this period.[189] Some wives did not benefit even when they were in middle-class households. Courts often compensated years of unpaid labor only with a car title or perhaps half the marital home.[190] One homemaking woman with three kids—including one child with epilepsy—was married fifteen years to a husband earning $30,000 a year. At their divorce, she settled for $150 a week in child support and a claim on two years of his pension when it became vested.[191] True to Representative Greiman's word, Illinois women in 1985 did not gain an interest in their husbands' businesses.[192] Even women who directly contributed to a husband's business could end up with very little. One woman, who was married only a short time but contributed significantly to a family real estate business, received only a 1978 Buick, half the wedding gifts, a stereo, and her grandmother's table in their divorce.[193]

Similarly, wives who worked for wages rarely benefited from laws that compensated wives for their household labor. Seemingly most wage-earning women did not ask for compensation for their second shift, but those who did faced "tests" to determine that they had truly contributed as a homemaker. For instance, in 1988 in Illinois, an appellate court overturned a circuit court's decision to grant Jane Elizabeth Tatham, a veterinarian's assistant and horse trainer, approximately $16,000 in recognition of her contribution as a wage earner *and* a homemaker. The appellate court reasoned that the wife had failed to show that she did more housework than her husband. Both Jane and her husband, Jonathan, acknowledged that Jane Tatham had worked full-time without wages for six months on her family's farm early in the marriage and moreover that she took care of her stepchildren alongside her biological children. Where Tatham and her husband diverged was how much household labor she otherwise performed. He claimed that a weekly cleaning lady, his occasional care for their daughter, the help of the older children, travel, and eating in restaurants made Jane's labor scant or unnecessary. The burden was on Jane to make her case, and the court was not convinced.[194]

Refusing to grant additional compensation for wage-earning wives' double contributions belied the concept that these were earned benefits. Though a "test" like the one imposed on Jane Tatham may seem fair, courts at other times treated equitable distribution as a matter of need rather than of recognizing homemakers' contributions. For instance, a "test" was not applied to men who had lower income than their wives and still received alimony and maintenance following *Orr v. Orr*.[195] Statistically we cannot assume that these men did the majority of the housework since very few men did during this time.[196]

Moreover, with the passage of divorce reform, alimony became a rare and temporary measure for Illinois wives. In interpreting the act for its readership, the *Chicago Tribune* reported, "the new law also requires the judge, for the first time, to determine an ex-wife's ability to support herself before setting alimony."[197] Later the newspaper again noted that judges gauged alimony to a specific time period to allow a homemaker time to find employment.[198] One judge told reporters that he was "firm in forcing women to work. 'Sometimes [the women] find it suddenly opens a new world.'"[199] An Illinois attorney reported that judges were getting much stricter about women working: "they really quiz spouses on their work ability."[200] Divorce reform deliberately shuffled divorced wives into paid employment, and judges were skeptical when wives could not find it.

Across the country, other state legislatures enacted similar changes to alimony laws by making them temporary and rare, even when wives struggled to find work.[201] In California, the nation's first no-fault state, spousal support payments decreased from ninety-nine dollars a month under fault to sixty-one dollars a month under no-fault.[202] Most significantly, the "median time period for spouse support" in California was only two years by 1982 rather than the lifelong benefit it had been previously.[203] Similarly, a lawyer noted in 1973 that alimony payments in Florida had shrunk in terms of "amount and duration than they [had been] even five years ago."[204] Nationally, the rate of women receiving alimony was already down to 14 percent in 1976 from its postwar peak of 25 percent, which is largely where the rate has remained.[205] If it seems less than monumental to see the alimony rate decline only 10 percent because of this revolt against breadwinning, over two million women did not receive alimony in 1990 who statistically would have in the postwar period. Of the approximately three million women who did receive alimony or maintenance in 1990, nearly all received a temporary rather than permanent award.[206] In Illinois, the change was even more drastic. According to one account in 1981, maintenance was awarded in less than 5 per cent of all divorce

Table 1. Divorce Reform State-by-State

State	Rehabilitative Alimony	Homemaker Entitlement	State	Rehabilitative Alimony	Homemaker Entitlement
Alabama	1986	—	Montana	1983	1981
Alaska	1986	1982	Nebraska	—	1981
Arizona	1973	1973	Nevada	1978	1979
Arkansas	1979	1982	New Hampshire	1983	1968
California	1970	1982	New Jersey	—	1974
Colorado	1973	1973	New Mexico	1976	1978
Connecticut	1973	1981	New York	1983	1977
Delaware	1974	1979	North Carolina	—	1981
Florida	1971	1974	North Dakota	1986	1981
Georgia	1982	1979	Ohio	1974	1974
Hawaii	1985	1981	Oklahoma	1976	—
Idaho	1980	1982	Oregon	1983	1982
Illinois	1978	1978	Pennsylvania	1980	1974
Indiana	1986	1980	Rhode Island	1986	1985
Iowa	1980	1980	South Carolina	1987	1982
Kansas	1985	1999	South Dakota	1987	1978
Kentucky	1972	1972	Tennessee	1983	1991
Louisiana	1987	1983	Texas	1998	1975
Maine	1981	1972	Utah	—	1976
Maryland	1980	1980	Vermont	1986	1988
Massachusetts	1988	1974	Virginia	1994	1982
Michigan	1989	—	Washington	1986	1961
Minnesota	1983	1978	West Virginia	1986	1983
Mississippi	1993	1988	Wisconsin	1981	1981
Missouri	1973	1969	Wyoming	—	1977

By the mid-1980s, most other states had instituted temporary or rehabilitative alimony and homemakers' entitlements. I based this table on statutes when possible, when these concepts began to be cited in case law, and on law review literature. The Nebraska date is based only on a table in Doris Freed and Henry Foster Jr., "Divorce in the Fifty States: An Overview," *Family Law Quarterly* 14 (Winter 1981): 229–84. Texas had no alimony until 1998; when it instituted it in 1998, it was rehabilitative alimony only. In 1999, Kansas first granted money for household labor in a domestic partnership case (*Pepper v. Greer,* 1999 Kan. App. Unpub. LEXIS 70). For more information on the content of this table, see Ariz. Rev. Stat. Ann. § 25-319 (1976); Cal. Civ. Code § 4801 (West Supp. 1986); Colo. Rev. Stat. § 14-10-114 (1973 and Supp. 1985); Conn. Gen. Stat. Ann. § 46b-82 (West 1986); Del. Code Ann. tit. 13, § 1511 (1974); Fla. Stat. § 61.08 (1984 and Supp. 1986); Ga. Code Ann. § 19-6-1 (1982); Haw. Rev. Stat. § 580-47 (1985); Idaho Code § 32-705 (1983); Ill. Ann. Stat. chap. 40, para. 504 (Smith-Hurd Supp. 1986); Ind. Code Ann. § 31-1-11.5-11 (Supp. 1986); Iowa Code § 598.21 (Supp. 1987); Ky. Rev. Stat. Ann. § 403.200 (Michie/Bobbs-Merrill 1981); La. Civ. Code Ann. art. 160 (West Supp. 1987); Me. Rev. Stat. Ann. tit. 19, § 721 (1981); Md. Fam. Law Code Ann. § 11-106 (1984); Minn. Stat. Ann. § 518.552 (West Supp. 1987); Mo. Ann. Stat. § 452.335 (Vernon 1986); Mont. Code Ann. § 40-4-203 (1985); N.H. Rev. Stat. Ann. § 458.19 (Supp. 1986); N.Y. Dom. Rel. Law § 236 (McKinney's 1986); Or. Rev. Stat. § 107.105 (1984); Pa. Stat. Ann. tit. 23, § 501 (Purdon Supp. 1986); Tenn. Code Ann. § 36-5-101 (1984); Vt. Stat. Ann. tit. 15, § 752 (Supp. 1986); Wash. Rev. Code Ann. § 26.09.090 (1986); W. Va. Code § 48-2-16 (1986); Wis. Stat. § 767.26 (1981). Kansas limits awards of alimony to 121 months. Kan. Stat. Ann. § 60-1606 (Supp. 1986); David H. Kelsey and Patrick P. Fry, "The Relationship Between Permanent and Rehabilitative Alimony," *Journal of the American Academy of Matrimonial Lawyers* 4 (1988): 1–8. Ohio implemented its version of the Uniform Marriage and Divorce Act, Senate Bill 348/Substitute House Bill 233, in 1974.

Several other states implemented or clarified the bounds for temporary alimony via case law; in Alaska, see *Carlson v. Carlson*, 722 P.2d 222 (1986); in Connecticut, see *Stern v. Stern*, 165 Conn. 190, 332 A.2d 78 (1973); in Arkansas, see *Hatcher v. Hatcher*, 265 Ark. 681, 580 S.W.2d 475 (1979); in Florida, see *Kahn v. Kahn*, 78 So. 2d 367 (1955); in Iowa, see Rosemary Shaw Sackett and Cheryl K. Munyon, "Alimony: A Retreat from Traditional Concepts of Spousal Support," 35 *Drake Law Review* (1985–86): 297–321; in Maryland, see *Coleman v. Maryland*, 37 Md. App. 322 (1977); in Mississippi, rehabilitative alimony was allowed if the judge specified a reason for the termination date as seen in Charles Galloway, "Family Law—Rehabilitative Alimony—An Answer to Mississippi's Inconsistent Treatment of Durational Alimony," *Mississippi Law Journal* 65 (1995–96): 187–204; in New Jersey, see *Turner v. Turner*, 158 N.J. Super. 313, 386 A. 2d1280 (1978); in North Dakota, see *Bagan v. Bagan*, 382 N.W.2d 645 (1986); in Oklahoma, see *Johnson v. Johnson*, 1983 OK 117, 674 P.2d 539 (1983); in Rhode Island, see *Stevenson v. Stevenson*, 511 A.2d 961 (1986); in South Carolina, see *Toler v. Toler*, 292 S.C. 374, 356 S.E.2d 429 (1987); in South Dakota, see *Tesch v. Tesch*, 399 N.W. 2d 880 (1987). See also Martin A. Rosen, "Indiana's Alimony Confusion," *Indiana Law Journal* 45 (1969–70): 595–605; Kelsey and Fry, "Relationship Between Permanent and Rehabilitative Alimony," 1–8; Freed and Walker, "Family Law in the Fifty States," 417–571; Camille W. Cook, "Family Law: Surveying Fifteen Years of Change in Alabama," *Alabama Law Review* 36 (Winter 1985): 419–71; Barbara J. Torrez, "Arizona Property Division upon Marital Division," *Arizona State Law Journal* 1979 (1979): 411–37; Gordon W. Hawthorne, "Family Law—Divorce—Constitutionality of Arkansas Property Settlement and Alimony Statutes. *McNew v. McNew*, 262 Ark. 567, 559 S.W. 2d 155," *University of Arkansas at Little Rock Law Journal* 123 (1979): 123–34; Sandra R. Scott, "A Survey of Florida Alimony Since Passage of the 1971 Dissolution of Marriage Act," *University of Florida Law Review* 28 (1975–76): 763–86; James H. Siesky, "Domestic Relations: Guidelines for the Award of Permanent and Rehabilitative Alimony Under the 1971 Dissolution of Marriage Act," *Stetson Intramural Law Review* 5 (1975): 101–4; Rosemary Shaw Sackett and Cheryl K. Munyon, "Alimony: A Retreat from Traditional Concepts of Spousal Support," *Drake Law Review* 35 (1985–86): 297–321; Kathleen Bilbe, "Permanent Alimony: Wife's Earning Capacity Not Considered," *Southern University Law Review* 266 (1976–77): 266–77; Galloway, "Family Law" 187–204; Linda Bailiff Marshall, "Rehabilitative Alimony: An Old Wolf in New Clothes," *New York University Review of Law and Social Change* 13 (1984–85): 667–93; *Johnson v. Steel Incorporated*, 94 Nev. 483; 581 P.2d 860 (1978); William M. Rubenstein, "New Jersey Law—'Rehabilitative Alimony' as a Tool for the Encouragement of Spousal Self-Support—Is There Life After Arnold?—*Arnold v. Arnold*, 167 N.J. Super. 478, 401 A.2d 261 (App. Div. 1979)," *Western New England Law Review* 3 (1980–81): 127–43; Robert E. McGraw, Gloria Sterin and Joseph Davis, "Case Study in Divorce Law Reform and Its Aftermath," *Journal of Family Law* 20 (1981–82): 443–88; Robert G. Spector, "Support Alimony: The Uncertain State of the Law," *Oklahoma Law Review* 44 (1991): 585–634; Patrick M. Coyne, "History of Alimony in Pennsylvania," *Duquesne Law Review* 28(1989–90): 709–26; Brenda L. Storey, "Surveying the Alimony Landscape," *Family Advocate* 25 (2002–3): 10–13; James W. Paulsen, "The History of Alimony in Texas and the New 'Spousal Maintenance' Statute," *Texas Journal of Women and the Law* 7 (1997–98): 151–59; Michael D. Smith, "Family Law—The Duration of the Alimony Obligation in Wyoming: Longer than We Both Shall Live—*Oedekoven v. Oedekoven* [notes]," *Land and Water Law Review* 383 (1998): 383–98; *Coby v. Coby*, 489 So. 2d 597 (1986); *Carlson v. Carlson*, 722 P.2d 222 (1986); *In re. Marriage of Bukaty*, 180 Cal. App. 3d 143, 225 Cal. Rptr. 492 (1986); *McCann v. McCann*, 191 Conn. 447, 464 A.2d 825 (1983); *Weiman v. Weiman*, 188 Conn. 232, 449 A.2d 151 (1982); *Scoville v. Scoville*, 179 Conn. 277, 426 A.2d 271 (1979); *Gordon v. Gordon*, 26 Mass. App. Ct. 973; 528 N.E.2d 876 (1988); *Krause v. Krause*, 177 Mich. App. 184; 441 N.W.2d 66 (1989); *Armstrong v. Armstrong*, 618 So. 2d 1278 (1993); *Poague v. Poague*, 579 S.W.2d 822 (1979); *Henry v. Henry*, NH 525 A.2d 267 (1987); *Altman v. Altman*, 101 94 Nev. 483; 581 P.2d 860 (1978); *Lewis v. Lewis*, 106 N.M. 105; 739 P.2d 974 (1987); *McClure v. McClure*, 90 N.M. 23; 1976-NMSC-042; 559 P.2d 400 (1976); *Taylor v. Taylor*, 122 A.D. 2d 134, 504 N.Y.S. 2d 698 (1986); Virginia Statute in 1994 chap. 518, Senate Bill 481; 994 Va. ALS 518; 1994 Va. Acts 518; 1994 Va. Ch. 518; 1994 Va. SB 481; *Bibighaus v. Bibighaus*, 66 Del. 281 (Ct. Common Pleas, Delaware Cnty. 1979); *McArthur v. McArthur*, 256 Ga. 762; 353 S.E.2d 486 (1987); *In. re. the Marriage of McDowell*, 244 N.W.2d 238 (1976); *In re. the Marriage of Lattig*, 318 N.W.2d 811 (1982); Me. Rev. Stat. Ann. tit. 19, § 722-A; *Stevens v. Stevens* 390 A.2d 1074 (1978); *Cheatham v. Cheatham* 537 So. 2d 435 (1988); *Claunch v. Claunch*, 525 S.W.2d 788 (1975); N.C. Gen. Stat. § 50-20 (2015), *General Statutes of North Carolina* (Charlottesville, VA: Matthew Bender and Co., Inc., 2014), chap. 50; *In the Matter of Marriage of Jenks*, 294 Ore. 236; 656 P. 2d 286 (1982); *Rochefort v. Rochefort*, 494 A.2d 92, (1985); *Kittelson v. Kittelson*, 272 N.W.2d 86 (1978); Tenn. Code Ann. § 36-4-121(c) (1991) as seen in *Wade v. Wade*, 897 S.W.2d 702 (1994); *Klein v. Klein*, No. 86-274, 150 Vt. 466; 555 A.2d 382 (1988); "Notice from Wyn Somers 862-7689," September 19, 1977, box 1, folder NOW: Lexington Area, Mariwyn Somers Papers, Schlesinger Library on the History of Women in America, Radcliffe Institute, Harvard University; Judith I. Avner, "Using the Connecticut Equal Rights Amendment at Divorce to Protect Homemakers' Contributions to the Acquisition of Marital Property," *University of Bridgeport Law Review* 4 (1982–83): 265–81; *Patterson v. Patterson*, 167 W. Va. 1; 277 S.E.2d 709 (1981). (But then *Patterson* was overruled in 1983, in the case *LaRue v. LaRue*, 172 W. Va. 158; 304 S.E.2d 312 [1983]).

settlements.[207] By 1982, even the once-hopeful HERA warned its members that "homemakers need be even more wary of relying on mythical legal protection of their role by the courts."[208]

In other words, less than a decade after the U.S. Supreme Court reconsidered the premise of alimony in *Orr v. Orr* in 1978, few states still offered lifelong alimony to women or men. The Supreme Court had not questioned alimony, breadwinning, or dependence, while men's activists and even feminists had already embraced the individualist model of formal equality in order to shed the thick gendered imperatives that the household had been built on.

Most unexpectedly, many critics believed that no-fault divorce and its rejection of women's dependence produced further decreases in child support awards.[209] A California study indicated that child support payments declined from seventy-five dollars a month to sixty-one dollars a month in the first decade of no-fault divorce. Moreover, awards were only distributed to 89 percent of women after no-fault arrived in California, down from 94.4 percent.[210] California seemed on trend, if a bit ahead of the curve. A study funded by the state of Illinois and conducted by the Center for Policy Study reported that between 1978 and 1985, "the real value of child support orders declined by 25 percent."[211]

These plummeting numbers for child support did not go without notice even in the Illinois legislature, but attempts to correct inadequate child support provisions ran into repeated hurdles. Early on in the divorce reform era, Congress had scant interest in helping women who were not on welfare retrieve missing child support payments from negligent fathers. Congress rejected bills that made failing to make child support payments a federal crime, that gave mothers who were not on welfare access to the IRS or Social Security Locating Service, and that took liens on federal benefits for non-welfare fathers.[212] Congress in these few cases trumpeted concerns about privacy. Garnishing wages and putting a lien on property were strategies directed exclusively against the fathers of children on welfare. State officials failed to pick up the federal government's slack. In 1968, only fourteen states allowed a lien on a husband's property for failure to provide child support, and only fourteen other states garnished wages.[213]

The federal government slowly began paying more attention to fathers who defaulted on child support beginning in 1975. The 1975 Child Support Act both increased the federal presence in procuring child support and aimed to include non-welfare fathers who neglected to provide support. The legislation required states to set up child support enforcement agencies, locate absent parents, and collect payments from parents.[214] But still the federal government only began to talk about universally garnishing wages in the 1980s.[215] In 1983, the Health and Human Services secretary, Margaret Heckler, called for "states to garnish the paychecks and intercept state tax refunds of all delinquent parents, whether or not the parent with custody is on welfare."[216] Heckler found allies in Congress, including the Congressional Caucus on Women's Issues. In 1984, Congress passed the bill, which penalized states that failed to garnish wages and to put liens on property or wages.[217] In 1988, the Family Support Act required each state to establish paternity for a certain proportion of their clients and to institute wage withholding from fathers.[218]

Nonetheless, states still had power to tinker with how much child support fathers owed. For instance, in 1984, the Illinois legislature proposed an amendment to a new marriage and divorce law that both allowed the Department of Public Aid to access a father's Social Security number and that established a guideline that at least 20 percent of the noncustodial parent's net income should go to child support.[219] Even state legislators who supported the measure wrangled over the available deductions counted in calculating net incomes—the bill included previous support orders but not private debts. Legislators still wanted to protect men from unduly large child support payments.[220] While its sponsors used the anti-welfare sentiment in the room to successfully push the bill through in 1984, a backlash drove the new law's supporters to expand the available deductions in 1985, effectively lowering support obligations.[221] Critics of the bill nonetheless protested that the men's rights group Fathers Fight for Rights had not weighed in on the new bill and recommended overturning child support guidelines entirely.[222] Comparing these Illinois guidelines to the informal ones in place in 1965 and 1975 shows us that a 1985 father paid less than fathers in 1975 and 1965 when we take inflation into account, and less in real dollars than in 1965. A father of one earning $50 a week paid $10 in 1985; he would have paid only $8.50 a week in 1975 and $12.50 in 1965.[223]

After a divorce, men fared better than women. By the 1980s, this was clear to feminist scholars. Lenore Weitzman claimed that in the first year after divorce, women experienced a 73 percent loss in standard of living compared to men's 42 percent gain.[224] Later studies indicated that more accurate results were significantly less stark: men's standard of living declined by 10 percent compared to women's 30 percent decline.[225] Nonetheless, men still suffered less than women. Sociologist Arlie Hochschild suggested that most divorced men still earned a family wage but chose to "no longer 'redistribute' it to their children or the ex-wife who care[d] for them."[226] In the pages of the *New York University Law Review and Social Change*, Linda Bailiff Marshall called rehabilitative alimony an "old wolf in new clothes."[227] The new order led prominent legal feminist experts such as Martha Fineman and Lenore Weitzman to deplore the "illusion of equality" promised but never realized by divorce reform.[228] Divorce reform had almost fully undermined the idea that men should support their wives or even their children.

Shortly after divorce reform passed, wives won another difficult and mitigated victory when they made progress in criminalizing marital rape. A 1979 court case indicated that Illinois courts were skeptical about the existence of marital rape even in the most extreme cases. One Downer's Grove woman accused her ex-husband of forcing entry into her home through a basement window, throwing her to the ground, and attempting to rape her. The ex-wife's attorney called the case "Illinois' first case in which a man was tried for 'trying to rape his wife.'" But it was a civil suit since rape of one's former wife was not a criminal offense. The judge dismissed the rape charge, saying, "there is reasonable doubt. It is his word against hers." The judge charged the husband sixty-five dollars for violating an injunction against entering her home after a long history of domestic abuse.[229]

The Illinois legislature also confronted the problem of marital rape for the first time in 1979. Senator Robert Mitchler fruitlessly brought it up in a debate over child custody in abuse cases. Mitchler stated, "it's amazed me, the number of wives that are battered, the number of wives that are actually raped and beaten by their husbands, but under the State of Illinois that's not a crime" due to the legal definition of rape in the state.[230] After being chastised for not confining his remarks to the bill at hand, Mitchler nonetheless called for funds to start a program to combat marital rape.[231] The Senate introduced bills in both 1979 and 1981 that the Illinois Coalition of Women Against Rape, alongside other organizations, helped draft.[232] Democratic sponsor Earlean Collins, the first African American woman elected to the Illinois Senate, wanted to protect women whose husbands "come into the house at will and simply because he has to pay child support in some cases . . . forces the woman to have sexual intercourses with him against her will."[233] Under the force of objections in the legislature, the bill was amended to make spousal rape a lesser crime than nonmarital rape. A sexual assault on a wife would only qualify as rape if the spouses were separated or if divorce proceedings had been initiated. Its sponsor admitted the bill was "not all what the bill started out to be" but was "a step in the right direction."[234] The bill passed in the Senate, but stalled in committee in the House in both 1979 and 1981.

The Illinois legislature only revisited the issue of spousal rape in May of 1983 under a bill intended to consolidate and make a whole series of sexual assault crimes gender-neutral. Some House members were still skeptical, however, with Representative Friedrich objecting to the part of the bill that, he claimed, could "involve even a fondling. If a husband, however, clumsily wishes to make up by forcing a hugging on his wife, he can be guilty of criminal sexual abuse."[235] Friedrich asked, appalled, "Have we gone that far?"[236] The sponsor of the bill deflected Friedrich's critique, explaining that the language of the bill had been tightened.[237] The newly elected Kathleen Wojcik also defended the rights of husbands to conjugal relations with their wives. She explained that she voted for the overall bill reluctantly because she did "not believe that once you take the marriage bond that a wife can claim rape."[238] Many senators also opposed criminalizing marital rape. One queried about the potential hypothetical situation where a wife threatened to accuse her husband of rape unless he gave her a great deal of the marital property. Despite one of the bill's sponsor's assurance that the bill would lead to very few prosecutions because of the restrictions put on it, Senator Philip declared, "if this doesn't leave a man at a disadvantage, I don't know what does. Now, you've got everything you've worked for all your life and you many [sic] not be wrong, she may be wrong, you know, and she files the complaint on rape, they got you. And you're going to have to give in and give her everything you've worked for your whole entire life."[239]

These objections ensured that marital rape was criminalized by the legislature in 1984 with serious limitations. Senator John D'Arco, a Democrat from Chicago, told opponents of the criminalization of marital rape that they valued a man's right to his personal property over a woman's right to her bodily integrity. D'Arco conceded wives might use the charge to negotiate a divorce settlement, but argued, "what happens if a husband does, in fact, rape his wife? What recourse does the wife have under the present law? She has none."[240] D'Arco's moral claim at last outweighed those of his opponents. Nonetheless the legislature imposed serious limitations on the bill. Perpetrators of marital rape faced a lesser penalty for spousal rape and could only be prosecuted if the parties were separated, a weapon was involved, the accused caused great bodily harm, or there had been a pattern of domestic violence prior to the incident. The legislature justified these limits on marital rape as "a compromise with the Illinois State Bar Association."[241] By the time this bill was introduced, similar laws were in effect in Oregon, Washington, Nebraska, Kansas, New Jersey, and Michigan, but only seventy spouse rape charges had gone to trial.[242] The criminalization of marital rape was rarely prosecuted. In 1994, the U.S. Supreme Court overturned a woman's requirement to notify her husband prior to an abortion in part because marital rape remained a pressing concern.[243]

*   *   *

Activist husbands, feminists, legislators, and judges all acted to dismantle men's and women's thick legal obligations in marriage in the 1970s and 1980s. Significant gendered aspects—especially the wife's double day, a married husband's right to sex with his wife, and a newly divorced wife's right to temporary support—remained in the law. Nonetheless, this action imperfectly dismantled two of the most fundamental elements of coverture that remained in the postwar period—a wife's right to her husband's support and her husband's ownership of her sexual and household labor. But subsequent political debate showed that the role of activist husbands and their allies was much less visible than that of feminists, who bore the brunt of the blame for these changes. Even worse, only middle-class husbands and wives profited from even these mitigated victories. Men and women on welfare, immigrants, and gay and lesbian couples continued to face legal pressure to perform traditional breadwinner and homemaker roles.

CHAPTER 3

Blaming Feminism for the Fragile Family

Since the spread of market relations, wage labor, and industrialization, Americans had viewed cooking, cleaning, and childcare as the physical manifestations of a wife and mother's love—and consequently as not even work at all. Feminists rejected the idea that women should work for love and made some progress toward compensating household labor via divorce reform laws. Nonetheless they identified a national ERA as the key to this reform. But opponents were able to defeat the ERA. Certainly, as historians have shown, moral objections were a fundamental aspect of the opposition to the ERA. But concerns relating to the political economy also proliferated.[1] Indeed during the ERA battle, this fusion was neither strategic nor conceptual. It was literal. In addition to equal employment and affirmative action, ERA proposals to compensate housework—through wages, alimony, property, or social security— raised a simultaneous moral and fiscal crisis for the ERA's opponents: that women must be paid to do care work.

To convincingly pose this as a threat, ERA opponents first performed a monumental bait and switch as they predicted that the passage of the ERA would destroy breadwinning even after men's breadwinning obligations were already vastly reduced in practice (from deindustrialization) and in law (via divorce reform). In other words, anti-feminists accused feminists of seeking to end the homemaker and breadwinner roles that had always been out of reach, had already been lost, or would quickly be dismantled through divorce reform laws.

Due to this ignorance—or denial—it followed easily that anti-ERA activists also opposed feminists' solutions to the loss of breadwinning. They saw the expansion of homemaker entitlements in the form of marital property rights, Social Security, and more as competition rather than a wan replacement for traditional breadwinning. Instead anti-feminists argued that all of these solutions raised the tax burden and put the traditional family at risk. Opponents alleged that families would either become poor or at best be regulated like poor families. The ERA's detractors believed that while the state's financial protection was necessary to preserve the white middle-class family, feminism had made the state increasingly hostile. Implied in this fear was the assumption that the family was a fundamentally weak and tenuous institution. The question remained: what made traditional families so vulnerable?

At its heart, what made the family seem so fragile was a deep class anxiety rooted in the political economy of the 1970s. Many anti-feminists were in fact new to the middle-class. As such, they were perhaps members of the first generation in their family to be able to afford for a wife to stay at home, along with other markers of midcentury middle-class living. As they observed the failing family wage, inflation, and deindustrialization around them, they feared that the hard-won gains made during the early postwar years would be lost in the late postwar era. Conservative politicians knew that economic anxieties were pervasive among all Americans, even those who did not share their Cold War, pro-business, conservative Christian worldview. By shifting the blame for the decline of breadwinning from deindustrialization to feminists and the ERA, these politicians did several layers of work. They both capitalized on economic anxieties and deflected attention away from the actual causes of those anxieties. They stopped feminist activism while appearing, superficially, to be championing the working class. They infused fiscal arguments with moral meaning, and vice versa.

Feminists Destroyed the Fragile Family

In the wake of technological advancements and second-wave feminism, some ex-husbands and sympathetic lawmakers began a movement to overturn men's thick obligation to serve as breadwinners. Of course, not all men served as breadwinners for their families, even as this expectation peaked in the postwar period. Nonetheless, divorced men throughout the country stopped paying support and sometimes formed men's rights groups to lobby lawmakers to eliminate alimony laws. They found ready allies in judges, legislators, and bureaucrats. By 1970, new divorce laws began to undermine alimony, undoing men's traditional obligations to provide for their financial dependents.

But many ordinary Americans did not note the injury already done to men's legal obligation to provide for their families and instead identified the ERA as the real threat to breadwinning. The ratification process for the ERA went much less smoothly in state legislatures than it had in Congress. After its passage, the swelling of anti-ERA sentiment among ordinary citizens led some organizers to found new anti-feminist organizations. Longtime anti-Communist political activist Phyllis Schlafly founded the most famous of these organizations with STOP ERA and the Eagle Forum in September 1972 and November 1975 respectively. Schlafly thereafter functioned as the public face of the movement.[2] The Eagle Forum had sixty thousand members by 1982.[3] Smaller organizations proliferated as well. For instance, Mormon activist Jacquie Davison founded Happiness of Womanhood in 1972 for members of the Church of Latter Day Saints, and ten thousand women joined the organization.[4]

Such dissent held sway with state legislators much more than it had in Congress. After 1974, the rate of approval for the ERA in state legislatures slowed significantly. States that were expected to pass the ERA easily, including Illinois, failed to do so.[5] Moreover, five states rescinded their approval of the ERA, beginning with Tennessee in April of 1974. By 1978, only thirty-five of the necessary thirty-eight states had ratified the ERA, and the amendment failed by its October 1982 deadline. The Eagle Forum and STOP ERA's vision of equality was so terrifying it not only helped defeat the ERA, but it also shored up the conservative movement with newcomers fearing for their own families' futures. Anti-ERA critiques in part gained traction with the passage of further feminist congressional legislation. An array of other laws that quickly followed the passage of the ERA made many of the issues presented in congressional debate—equity in pay, education, and credit—less relevant.[6] Though each of these had uncertain applications and even less certain effectiveness, they all drained some of the urgency away from more traditional claims for the ERA.[7] Critics, however, notably did not track the equally momentous changes to marriage and divorce laws that accompanied these public sphere changes. Therefore opponents of the ERA, through artifice or ignorance, justified their position by presenting an evolving set of public policies and a static set of marriage laws.

Opponents repeatedly warned that the Equal Rights Amendment would bring about the end of the thick breadwinning obligation. Many studies of these new conservative organizations illuminate the ways in which ERA opponents feared the elimination of husbands' duties toward their wives. The right feared a lack of obligation in many areas of life, but this was an explicitly dangerous one.[8] But studies so far have not acknowledged that these obligations were largely already gone for most men. ERA advocates' proposals sought to distribute marital obligations more equally in light of the loss of breadwinning, but opponents operated as if those obligations were still in place. Nor did they acknowledge that even at their peak these laws only protected a minority of women. They argued that courts would use the ERA to eliminate all husbands' obligations. This central misrepresentation—presumably conceit by some; misunderstanding by others—led opponents to repeatedly decry the ERA as an amendment that would eliminate the already-lost obligation of breadwinning.

Opponents' assertion that the ERA would undermine breadwinning was an effective tactic. Many of these claims emerged early on when it was not yet clear what changes the California adoption of no-fault divorce had wrought. These claims also obscured the reality that a mere 25 percent of wives had ever received alimony even prior to divorce reform. William E. Dunham was the typical early opponent of the ERA, the author of a series of diatribes against abortion, the Occupational Health and Safety Administration (OSHA), socialized medicine, and more produced by the John Birch Society.[9] In 1972, Dunham tied men's breadwinning obligations to their wives directly to the survival of humankind: "To enable women to do these things and thereby make the existence and development of the race possible, these State laws impose upon husbands the primary responsibility to provide homes and livelihoods for their wives and children, and make them criminally responsible to society and civilly responsible to their wives if they fail to perform this primary responsibility."[10] The ERA, Dunham believed, would end this. At this point, no-fault was a mere two years old and not yet implemented in all states. In 1974, STOP ERA stated that older women in particular would lose their right to support and a home under ERA.[11] Similarly, the small Illinois organization ERA Opposed published a pamphlet that promised that wives would lose all the laws that required husbands to provide financial support.[12] The Mormon Church identified a danger of the ERA as the possibility that, rather than make wives equally responsible for husbands, "passage of the ERA could eliminate all legal responsibility for both spouses."[13] These early claims drew on the ambiguous outcome of divorce reform laws.

But claims that the ERA would eliminate breadwinning continued on through the decade, even as divorce reform increasingly eradicated nonsupport as a grounds for divorce and reduced alimony to a rare and short-term benefit. In October of 1977, well after many states had passed no-fault divorce and hemmed in traditional alimony, the Texas group the Association of Women Who Want to Be Women (Association of the W's) declared that it believed in the right of the husband to be a provider and the right of the wife to be a full-time homemaker.[14] Similarly in 1977, STOP ERA still cited Thomas Emerson's 1971 *Yale Law Journal* article to predict that the ERA "would take away women's family support rights" even though the article came out prior to *Reed v. Reed*, the Equal Employment Opportunity Act of 1972, the Higher Education Act, the Equal Credit Opportunity Act of 1974, and nearly all the no-fault divorce laws that undermined men's breadwinner obligations.[15] In 1981, Schlafly still published anti-ERA pieces in her newsletter that claimed that the ERA would eliminate "the traditional family concept of husband as breadwinner and wife as homemaker."[16] In another pamphlet published after Reagan signed the Economic Recovery Act in 1981, STOP ERA promised that the ERA would "eliminate the husband's primary duty to support his wife and children."[17]

Activist husbands and sympathetic lawmakers did not receive the blame because they operated under the radar in fifty distinct political systems. Many women did not know of the new laws until they reached divorce court.[18] Even the U.S. Supreme Court—when it considered *Orr v. Orr*—did not acknowledge that the right to alimony they had extended to men barely existed in many states. The media largely ignored or were ignorant of these changes and the benefits they held for divorced men. And so it was easy for ERA opponents both to deny that the deathblow to breadwinning had already occurred and to suggest that feminism must be stopped so that it did not end breadwinning in the future. On the other hand, ERA opponents did pay attention to the action taken by groups like the National Organization for Women, Homemakers' Equal Rights Association, the Women's Equity Action League, displaced homemakers organizations, and every other feminist organization wrestling to create homemakers' entitlements on the basis of women's labor in the home. It was a strategy ERA opponents also deployed in the battle over protective labor legislation. Long after courts had invalidated protective labor laws, ERA opponents continued to oppose feminism for abrogating labor protection for women.[19]

Opponents' claim that the ERA would end breadwinning took advantage of feminists' wildly diverging dreams about the possibilities of the ERA. Anti-ERA activists contrasted a false future with breadwinner obligations still in place with whichever future feminist proposal most scared them (or most suited their case). This did not lead to a coherent set of predictions. Oftentimes one opponent would assume the preservation of some aspect of the old order while another would assume it would disappear. Nonetheless, a distinct logic tied all of these predictions together. To anti-feminists, the family was a profound but weak institution shored up in the tumult of deindustrialization only by the exclusivity of the government's entitlements to traditional families.

According to ERA opponents, monetarily compensating housewives was economically untenable for all but the wealthy and had the potential for economic and moral disaster. Paying women for their work through Social Security or other measures was not only immoral; it was also impractical. Opponents saw feminists' arguments that women's work would count toward the support of the family as false promises or, at best, an inferior proposition to the breadwinning provisions ostensibly still in place. In the long term, the expense of homemakers' new entitlements would force most women into the workforce and destroy the family. Even if the state retained each spouse's obligations to one another and granted women's work in the home the same status as work outside the home, the new obligations would compromise the family itself by ending the privacy and respect bestowed on "traditional" families. While the coalition between fiscal and cultural conservatives has frequently been seen as simply strategic, fears about compensating homemaking represented a genuine convergence of these concerns.

According to ERA opponents, one program that the ERA's recognition of housewives threatened to transform was Social Security. Social Security paid housewives a small benefit on the basis of her dependence on her husband—a dependent's benefit. This benefit was modest because it was designed to supplement her husband's Social Security income.[20] The ERA's supporters argued that the ERA would grant an independent payment on the basis of housewives' labor in the home. Feminists had a double rationale for replacing the dependent benefit with a larger benefit that wives would earn through their household labor—a homemaker's entitlement. First it would protect impoverished widows who had to get by on the smaller Social Security benefits that were designed to be only a supplement to their husbands' full benefits. When a husband lived, the combination of his and her benefits could sustain a household. But if he were to die, her smaller supplement was insufficient for maintaining her.[21] Second, as the laws currently stood, divorced women—including some who had been married up to twenty years until legislators reduced it to ten years—received no dependent homemaker Social Security benefit at all.[22]

But, appropriating feminists' own struggle with the puzzle of paying for housework, ERA opponents argued that buying into Social Security meant figuring out how to finance the new entitlements. In one scenario, ERA opponents suggested that giving a wife Social Security would reduce a family's overall Social Security benefits. They speculated that a couple would evenly divide only a husband's Social Security benefit much like couples did for a private pension in some divorce settlements.[23] One opponent gauged that this would produce "a 19% cut to the traditional family."[24] This opponent's use of the word "traditional" ignored the plight of widows, suggesting like other ERA opponents that financing a homemaker's entitlement would only benefit broken homes.[25]

In another scenario where housewives received independent Social Security benefits, opponents argued that families would have to pay more into the Social Security system to earn two full benefits. Literature circulated by the Mormon Church cited expert Sylvia Porter, a feminist ERA advocate and Social Security expert, as proof that the ERA would grant homemakers an independent Social Security benefit equal to that of their working husbands.[26] How much this would cost was unclear. Nancy J. Rider, a Mormon homemaker from Ohio, gauged the cost at $800 a year per family.[27] Phyllis Schlafly (who had already argued via the Eagle Forum that families would lose an entire benefit) did her own calculations of the costs of a full entitlement benefit. She estimated that, if Social Security assumed that a homemaker's earnings would be $12,000 a year, the Social Security administration would assess an 8 percent self-employment tax on her. This would mean a homemaker owed the federal government $960 a year to earn the premium. According to Schlafly, "the average guy, pinched by inflation, would say, 'Honey, you'll have to get out and get your own job and pay your own tax.'"[28] Rider and Schlafly identified the additional cost of recognizing this labor as unaffordable for working- and middle-class families. Therefore husbands would have to take on a second or third job or force their wives to take on work outside the home.[29] One contestant in the Babson-Bernays competition, which asked American citizens across the country how to achieve economic justice for homemakers, argued that any sort of compensation for housewives would overwhelm the millions of men already barely bringing home a family wage. This contestant asked whether "a wife who is a homemaker [would] become a privilege for the better-off?"[30] Homemaking would become an inaccessible service for most families.

Opponents also argued that the ERA would discredit laws that forced husbands to support their wives after a divorce. Even though courts had been interpreting homemaking as unpaid work in terms of divorce settlements and child support awards, ERA opponents identified this solution as temporary. Opponents claimed that under the ERA, a woman's contribution must make up 50 percent of the total income of all families. They doubted courts' premise that housework represented an "equal," that is 50 percent, contribution to the household. ERA opponents cited 50 percent as often as possible. STOP ERA threatened that the "ERA will impose on women the equal (50%) financial obligation to support their spouses (under criminal penalties, just like husbands). ERA will impose on mothers the equal (50%) financial obligation for the financial support of their infant and minor children."[31] The Happiness of Womanhood newsletter translated equal to mean 50 percent.[32] The Eagle Forum worried that under ERA "a husband and wife must each pay equal (50%) family financial support."[33]

To ERA opponents, the expectation of a 50 percent contribution doomed women because women's work in the home was not worth as much as men's work outside the home. Some contestants in the Babson-Bernays essay contest brought up the value of homemaking repeatedly. These contestants did not see household labor as unpaid. Instead they argued that housewives got more back in the form of goods and services than they gave in labor. Jennifer Baker of Kentucky argued that it was a "misconception that housewives don't get paid."[34] They were compensated in the form of shelter, food, and clothing. Baker felt that the labor conditions were good—she had breaks. She asked whether husbands who did housework to help their wives would also be compensated, whether lazy housewives would receive the same benefits as conscientious ones, and whether wives without many children did much in the home at all given modern conveniences ranging from polyester to dishwashers.[35] To Baker, women were more than sufficiently compensated by their husbands for doing a job that was not worth nearly what feminists claimed it was, and certainly not equal to their husbands' labor. C. F. Berry more succinctly suggested that husbands bill their wives for room and board, mowing the lawn, medical expenses, and other goods and services they supplied.[36]

Opponents believed that women's household labor would be worth even less if the ERA made federal day care compulsory. ERA skeptics argued that many courts considered housework valuable only when the housewife had childcare responsibilities. ERA opponents believed that day care centers would eliminate this category: all women could support themselves when there was universal childcare. One anti-ERA brochure argued that after the ERA made husbands and wives equally responsible for family support, "the next step will

Figure 4. STOP ERA produced this image to stoke fears that women would be responsible for both household labor and providing 50 percent of the household's income. Courtesy of Abraham Lincoln Presidential Library and Museum.

be to agitate for government-operated child care centers. Then even a mother of small children may no longer be considered 'unable' to support herself and would lose the right of support from her husband."[37] Once day care was available to all women, according to STOP ERA, the monetary worth of women's work in the home would drop, and women would have to work outside the home to continue to contribute equally to the family economy.[38] This meant that women's work qualified as work enough to thrust the family into the market, but not enough to secure women from having to leave her homemaking career once day care was widely available.[39]

ERA opponents thus flip-flopped between praising the invaluable, irreplaceable work of the housewife, on one hand, and dismissing such labor as fairly worthless, on the other. This was an explicit flip of feminists' own questions about underpaid working-class housewives: how much housework would make women's contribution in the home equal to men's monetary contribution? The implicit threat was that in many families—even those of full-time housewives—housework would never be equal. In the interpretation of one of the cofounders of the Anti-Women's Liberation League (AWLL), a wife must become a "joint breadwinner" with her husband because housework could not be considered equal.[40]

To some extent, ERA opponents argued that equal contributions in the household would be impossible even for women working outside the home. An editorial in the *St. Louis Globe* laid bare the relationship between the political economy of the home and wages in a diatribe against the ERA: "The husband and wife would be equally responsible for support of their family, and although the wife's role as homemaker may be considered, what of the non-worker or low wage-earner who does little housework?"[41] To the *Globe*, even working women did not contribute equally if they had low-wage jobs. Since much of women's work outside the home remained poorly-paid, the ERA posed an impossible task for women. Nor was the *Globe* alone. Republican congressman John G. Schmitz, a John Birch Society member and an eventual presidential candidate for the American Independent Party, also worried that women could not compete with men economically.[42] He argued that, given women's household obligations, wives would lack the time to get their work skills up to snuff. Pink-collar wages and the double day conspired against women, who could not hope to ever match the contributions their husbands made to the household economy.

At other points ERA opponents argued that the amendment would lead to housewives facing competition from their husbands. Compensating household labor, according to anti-ERA activists, would make it appealing to some men. The worst of these men would then force women out of the home and into the workforce. Illinois STOP ERA argued the amendment would require any principal wage earner to support any spouse, no matter his or her gender. The organization stated "if [a wife] had a lazy husband who did not want to work, and if she was a conscientious woman who took a job to feed herself and the children, then she would by law be the 'principal wage-earning spouse' and would acquire the legal obligation to support her children and lazy husband."[43] Syndicated columnist Jenkin Lloyd Jones questioned whether men had any support obligation under ERA: "after all, if she has a right to sit around home looking at soap operas, why shouldn't he?"[44] In a worst-case scenario, one North Carolina woman worried to her congressman that husbands would take over homemaking as wives went overseas to fight in the military.[45]

Anti-ERA activists also argued that husbands could usurp mothers' roles after a divorce. Phyllis Schlafly feared the breakdown of the custom of giving women custody, because she believed that children provided comfort to a traumatized wife.[46] Though this qualm seemed at first to refer to a mother's emotional experience after divorce, Phyllis Schlalfly was actually referring to a wife's economic well-being after divorce: she clarified "the custody of the children is what enables her to secure a reasonably fair divorce settlement from her husband, who usually has the income-producing job."[47] Rosemary Thompson, an Illinois officer of the Eagle Forum, objected to a real-life case where a father won custody. She reported that a Washington, DC, judge awarded custody to a husband but reserved her disgust for the judge's order that the mother pay $200 monthly child support payments.[48] Rather than retaining the status—and livelihood—of homemakers, compensating household labor would make the job appealing to husbands.

According to ERA opponents, men could count on women to be breadwinners if for no other reason than that they could physically enforce payment. A resolution issued by a relatively small anti-feminist group, Operation Wake-Up, declared, "we do not wish to pay alimony to someone who outweighs us by forty pounds thereby making unnecessary the collection of arrears by the Friend of the Court."[49] ERA opponents thus reversed the feminist insight that men sometimes used violence to enforce the traditional gendered order. According to Operation Wake-Up, men were not afraid to resort to violence to upend the traditional gendered order either, and this time it would be encouraged by the state. Men could not be counted on to do their duty to their wives or their children, with or without equality.

These fears were inspired in part by a deep skepticism about men and their generosity toward their families.[50] Most famously, Schlafly believed that, unlike women, men had no natural instinct to care for their families. Schlafly added that men took care of their families only because they knew the consequences of defying the enforceable marriage contract.[51] According to Schlafly, "every man has known when he got married that he was taking on the obliga-tion to support his wife and children."[52] Harvard law professor and anti-ERA activist Paul Freund also saw men as eager to abandon their responsibilities to their families, and New York University professor Warren T. Farrell had warned ERA supporters that "men should eagerly look forward to the day when they can enjoy free sex and not have to pay for it. The husband will no longer be 'saddled with the tremendous guilt feelings' when he leaves his wife with nothing after she has given him her best years."[53] And perhaps most simply, Sam Ervin argued that in his many years as a lawyer, perhaps a simple country one, he saw many women who married "sorry husbands and d[id] need protection from ornery men."[54] When pushed, Phyllis Schlafly echoed Charles Metz when she said that divorce drove love for sons and daughters out the window. Courts alone enforced the duty to support children.[55] ERA oppo-nents believed that men not only did not love their wives; they also did not love their kids.

In sum, through the very act of granting homemaker rights, opponents believed that the ERA threatened to put homemaking literally out of business. And they used market language to argue this. Several ERA opponents char-acterized homemaking as a business venture for wives that would fail in the feminist political economy. As the Mormon Church argued, "Women already married who prefer to remain home and bear children would . . . be giving up their own earning power."[56] Similarly Phyllis Schlafly saw the ERA as posing danger to homemakers' livelihoods: "Children are a woman's best security." Schlafly believed that "'the family gives the woman the physical, financial and emotional security of the home for all her life,'" thereby eliding the domestic violence, male un- and underemployment, widowhood, and divorce that many wives faced in their domestic lives.[57] Professor Arthur E. Ryman Jr., of the Drake University School of Law, argued that if the ERA were ratified, it would degrade the homemaker's supposed financial security.[58]

If feminists believed that divorce law had already forced homemaking women into the workforce, opponents argued that only the passage of the ERA could have this effect. By denying that thick breadwinning obligations had already been vastly reduced, anti-ERA activists could scare voters with a vision of the future that they did not realize they were already living in. They argued that paying for homemaking entitlements in addition to providing support to wives did not make economic sense—which made it easy to reject an Equal Rights Amendment that they saw as including other troubling changes to the traditional gender order. Such concerns created a big tent.

Class Anxieties

ERA opponents did not limit their fears to the fiscal ramifications of the amendment; they also identified a range of cultural side effects that resulted from these fiscal hardships. These emerged at least in part from an intense sense of class anxiety—of a fear that the hard-won gains made during the postwar era would be lost in the 1970s as elites just got further ahead. The class anxieties that converged with anti-gender equality sentiment emerged from rising inflation, a failing family wage, and a dwindling sense of class status. Natasha Zaretsky and Robert Self especially have discussed the conflu-ence of these three converging circumstances with fears about the future of the American family.[59] Members of the white middle class saw their social position as increasingly perilous, and they displaced these fears onto the ERA.[60] Doing so allowed them to rope in other conservative manifestations of moral and financial anxiety, including critiques of affirmative action, abortion policy, and school integration.

ERA opponents were often vague about the class status of a family that they claimed the ERA would harm. In this, ERA opponents took a careful cue from silent majority politics, the Richard M. Nixon administration's short-hand for serving Americans who opposed the massive social and legal changes of the 1960s. Like the Nixon administration, ERA opponents also blurred the lines between the competing interests of working- and middle-class Ameri-cans while ostensibly speaking for both groups.[61] Sometimes anti-ERA activ-ists defined the families who would be hurt by the ERA as middle-class Americans; other times as working-class Americans. Therefore, while ERA opponents pointed to the fiscal problems cited above, they also evoked other markers of class that would depreciate for families. By threatening a family's ability to have a breadwinner-homemaker family structure, the ERA, oppo-nents argued, attacked the class status of the silent majority.

The 1970s recession, marked by high unemployment and inflation, truly was endangering the hard-won economic gains of the postwar for many fam-ilies.[62] Men's chances of procuring a breadwinning position materially de-creased during this time period.[63] By the 1970s the prospect of a family wage was increasingly shaky. This difficulty in part inspired some husbands to re-volt against breadwinning in the first place. But the momentousness of this transition—especially for families that had only a generation ago won the privilege of a breadwinning-homemaking household—affected many more families than the numbers in men's divorce reform or anti-ERA groups would suggest.

ERA opponents claimed that forcing the silent majority of women to work would endanger wives and their families' carefully won class status. ERA opponents saw a bleak version of the job market for most wives and their families once the ERA forced these women into the workforce. STOP ERA quoted Jean Noble, from the National Council of Negro Women, who identified the ERA as tough on black women. Noble reminded her audience that black women in particular worked in the service industry and would presumably continue to do jobs involving "liftin' and totin'."[64] A woman who saw Ellie Smeal on the *Phil Donahue Show* imagined that most women would face unsatisfying jobs as general office workers, grocery checkout girls, or typists.[65] Another anonymous writer accused the pro-ERA congressman Willis Whichard of being "the retainer of a few ambitious women who'd like to have help from the federal government every time they want a job or promotion. . . . These women, of course, are not the ones who would be sent into combat or the ones who would man, I mean woman, the day-care centers."[66] This anonymous critic also believed that with the ERA, women would have a choice of menial jobs.

Those menial jobs would deprive housewives of the few benefits of women's work in the home, particularly the emotional satisfaction and ability to control their own time. Margaret Mead, who opposed the ERA even if she supported a wage structure for homemaking, evoked the examples of women's roles in the Soviet Union and on the kibbutz in Israel. She complained that women there did everyone's laundry instead of their own, explaining that women there were "beginning to say if I've got to do laundry I'd rather do it for love."[67] According to other ERA opponents, private household labor at least had affective benefits. Congressman John G. Schmitz commented, "What a boost for the Department of Health, Education and Welfare's proposed system of State Nurseries, when all those mothers are forced to take jobs (many of them, no doubt, as employees of the State Nurseries, where they will engage in collective child-rearing according to directives from Washington!)."[68] Women would have the same jobs—caring for children—but now they would have federal bosses that directed them how to do them. The celebrated hallmarks of women's work in the home would be gone.

ERA opponents were also skeptical that once women worked outside the home men would take on a share of the housework, pointing out that the ERA could not actually enforce this. A flier titled "The Power of Suggestion: How

Easily Are You Fooled?" challenged readers: "And who will do the home chores? You guess."[69] The organization Women Who Want to Be Women argued that American women would face the same fate as Russian women who, according to the *Los Angeles Times*, worked "sweeping the streets, bricklaying, loading cargo ships, collecting garbage, building dams, digging ditches and mining coal . . . then she must spend at least 50% of her off-work time shopping and cooking. She can expect little help from her husband."[70] Similarly Senator Sam Ervin (D-NC) argued that none of the feminist utopias—he named Sweden in particular—had actually generated a system where men truly shared the housework.[71] ERA opponents even adopted language that already haunted feminists, indicating at a STOP ERA workshop in Springfield, Illinois, that working would only burden women with a double day.[72] All women would be overworked. ERA opponents also noted that employed mothers would be too busy to supervise children and thereby encourage delinquency, drug use, sexual activity, and more.[73]

Anti-ERA activists suggested that the ERA's transformations would make families resemble the most "deviant" family of all—the black family. Historian Robert Self has shown that defending breadwinner families was a means of evoking race without doing so explicitly.[74] But ERA opponents did not always camouflage these racial fears. One accusation was that the ERA would blur the line between white and black families via racial integration. *Moody Monthly* ran an article by Rosemary Thompson accusing the ERA of enabling racial integration: "the government would be authorized to involve itself in total physical and mental health of all children, their social development and nutrition by means of socio-economic *racially balanced* day care centers for youngsters."[75] Other opponents saw a precedent in the federal government's previous actions, and particularly compared the prospect of the ERA to bussing.[76]

Moreover, the repeated evocation of lazy husbands seemed keyed to evoke the matriarchal family so strongly imprinted on the public zeitgeist by Daniel Patrick Moynihan in his study *The Negro Family*. Commonly known as the Moynihan Report, it stated simply: "A fundamental fact of Negro American family life is the often reversed roles of husband and wife."[77] As seen above, ERA opponents predicted this same pathology for white families under ERA, but some critics made the predicted resemblance clear. For instance, the Colorado League of Housewives circulated an interview with a Labor Department official and a divorced men's activist. In the interview, he advocated the repeal of the sex provision of the 1964 Civil Rights Act because "if males are to the head of their families, they must be given the first opportunities for vocational preparation and for job opportunities." He then specifically evoked the Moynihan Report, suggesting that the ERA would emasculate white men as racism had emasculated black men.[78] With women working, "lazy" men at home doing little to no work, and children unsupervised, the traditional family would quickly decay into the welfare family.

Lazy men winning the homemaker role over worthy women also carried all the apparent threats of affirmative action.[79] ERA opponents imagined that husbands and wives would now compete for the role of unwaged homemaker. In their minds, "opening" housework to men was just as upsetting as opening white-dominated jobs to nonwhites. Phyllis Schlafly actually suggested that Congress could build an automatic triggering device like the one in section 4 of the Voting Rights Act, which automatically instituted remedies if registration fell below fifty percent of the voting-age population.[80] Schlafly imagined that if judges gave custody of children to less than half of the men in any state, then "those states would be automatically disabled from establishing or enforcing their own child-custody laws; or, if less than 50 percent of ex-wives were paying alimony to their ex-husbands, those states would be automatically disabled from establishing or enforcing their own alimony laws."[81] Schlafly used conservative hostility to the Voting Rights Act to stir up opposition to the ERA. She invoked a world in which, whether married or divorced, women were not guaranteed their traditional jobs as homemakers. Instead men had the advantage in a brave new world of equal homemaking privileges.

Anti-ERA activists also lumped their hostility to abortion and birth control into their opposition to the amendment. In their view, the ERA would lead to treating all families like welfare families (that is, dominating and controlling them). It would also make it possible for the government to try to limit the number of children a family had, much as they attempted—unsuccessfully the right claimed—with welfare families.[82] Thus while ERA opponents seemed to support punishing welfare recipients or limiting the number of children they had, they disapproved of any such imagined limitations on their own families. In their view, the ERA was a means of literally depriving traditional families of children. Like with bussing, limiting family size unfairly cost the white majority.[83] Congressman John Schmitz blamed feminists for sacrificing family itself, with the ultimate cost paid only by the white majority. After criticizing the prototypical feminist for refusing to stem immigration or the fertility of women on welfare, he went on to castigate one particular witness testifying on behalf of the ERA for taking "aim at the great middle-class Silenced Majority." " 'This group must limit their families to 2.1 (children) per family,' she told a House Committee, since it is 'the non-poor (79%) who have 68% of the babies,' " reported Schmitz. "Thus the group having proportionately fewer children, and better able to care for those they have, become the illogical but ideologically understandable target of her outrage," he concluded.[84] Opponents' perception of themselves as the victims of gross violations of reproductive rights reversed any version of reality, but the threat was effective. They convinced many that the ERA would strike traditional families where it hurt the most.

In the end, opponents claimed that the ERA threatened to degrade the status of many middle-class women, and their families would degrade with them. These prospects deeply frightened ERA opponents. Working demeaned wives, making them exhausted and undervalued. Being treated like welfare mothers was even worse, however, as it implied that otherwise traditional white women were as irresponsible as the black women who stereotypically received welfare. In both cases, the implications of the loss of a traditional household would affect children and the family itself. Traditional homemaking could not survive government interference, and the traditional family could not survive without homemakers.

If opponents cast "traditional" families as the ERA's losers, they also identified two sets of ostensible elites—wealthy women and the homosexual family—as its winners. Some ERA opponents claimed only elite women wanted the ERA because it would shore up their own already-healthy incomes. Margaret Mead claimed that only middle-class white women supported the amendment to the detriment of black and white working women.[85] Mead was shaped by the earlier, 1920s-era debate about the ERA, in which the ERA was pitted against protective labor legislation for women, but she was not alone. Reflecting the successful mobilization of class anxieties to oppose the ERA, one woman, writing to Senator Sam Ervin, claimed that all the women she knew who hoped to gain employment rights through the ERA lived in "$65 thousand and way up homes."[86] She argued that simply learning to live on their husbands' salaries, rather than filling existential gaps with material goods, would help these women spiritually and protect homemakers.[87] Another letter writer from Raleigh, North Carolina, feared, "the women in favor of ERA are educated women that can do paper work and sit behind desks, they are not women that work in mills through out N.C. or who are waitresses, or maids or any other tasks that keep this great civilization of ours going."[88] Similarly, one couple from Freeport, Illinois, claimed that only women with college degrees wanted the ERA.[89]

Professional women's employment was having a dramatic effect on household income during this time. By 1983, the median weekly income for a one-earner family was $354 but $646 for dual-earner families.[90] Of course, we cannot assume that all the one-earner families involved a male breadwinner supporting a female homemaker. Single-parent households, most of which were headed by women, increased dramatically during this time period. Presumably, woman-headed households reduced the average income of single-earner families. Nonetheless two-income families clearly made gains over one-income families—including those with a breadwinner-homemaker makeup. This reversed the pattern that had previously marked a working wife as "a family's badge of lower-class status."[91] Increasingly the families with the highest incomes had two earners rather than one: "From March 1950 to March 1970, the overall percentage of husband-wife families with wife in the paid labor force has risen from some 25 per cent to 40 per cent. In the $10,000-and-over income bracket, the increase was from 2 per cent to 50 per cent."[92] A family's income had the potential to change dramatically during this era, almost solely depending on whether the household had two earners or not.

Such income differentials were visible at the time. A journalist for the *Family News and Features* asked its readers if they had "been noticing lately that your next-door neighbor has acquired a color TV set, a new car and is refurnishing his home?" The article suggested, perhaps the neighbor had been lucky on the stock market, won the lottery, received an inheritance, "or his wife may have gone back to work. In all likelihood, the last alternative fits the bill (or, foots the bill, if you prefer)." Keeping up with the Joneses had an all-new set of rules as wives' financial contribution helped some families shift to or stay in the middle class.[93] Therefore the incomes of two-earner families began to diverge sharply from the incomes of breadwinner-only families.

Critics also claimed that gay and lesbian couples would win the right to marry while the silent majority of wives would lose homemaking privileges. These critics characterized the ERA as taking privileges from traditional couples—and particularly women—and giving them to gay and lesbian couples. The elevation of gay families was a boogeyman that opponents highlighted in order to make the loss of "traditional" family dominance even more galling. Most succinctly, the *Phyllis Schlafly Report* and the Illinois Small Businessmen's Association both argued that only gay men and lesbians would profit from the ERA.[94] Similarly, a STOP ERA pamphlet warned "pregnant, ill, poor, minority, or disadvantaged" women that ERA propaganda would not help women but instead would take their rights and give them to homosexuals.[95] The small San Francisco–based AWLL believed the ERA took away rights for men and women while giving marriage and adoption rights to gay couples.[96]

As other historians have argued, conservatives believed that the ERA would grant homosexual couples the right to marry after gay couples' Fourteenth Amendment claims seemed to fail.[97] Courts, perhaps following ERA proponents' cues, rejected the claims that the Fourteenth Amendment granted homosexuals the right to marry. For instance, Richard Baker initiated the first gay marriage case with James McConnell in Minnesota on the basis of the Fourteenth Amendment in 1971. The case made it all the way to the U.S. Supreme Court but was dismissed for want of a significant legal question.[98] Therefore the Minnesota Supreme Court's ruling—that what the couple proposed was not a marriage—stood. Similarly, Richard Adams tried to claim his Australian partner, Anthony Corbett Sullivan, as his dependent in order to give Sullivan American citizenship after procuring a marriage license from a Colorado clerk. Again courts refused to recognize the license.[99]

ERA opponents insisted that the rulings in these cases would violate the Constitution if the amendment were ratified. This was most strikingly apparent in Senator Sam Ervin's introduction of an amendment to the ERA before it left Congress. As discussed in Chapter 1, Ervin had initiated a set of hearings on the ERA to highlight how it would injure women, but he also tried to prevent the possibility that the ERA would legalize gay marriage. His amendment stated, "this article shall not apply to any law prohibiting sexual activity between persons of the same sex or the marriage of persons of the same sex."[100] Ervin believed that barring marriages between two men or two women constituted sex discrimination under an ERA.[101] Congress rejected the amendment, not because its members embraced gay marriage, but because they saw Ervin's fears as an example of inauthentic grandstanding.

Other ERA opponents agreed with Ervin that the amendment would legalize gay marriage. They saw ERA proponents' arguments that gay men and lesbians were excluded equally from gay marriage as the sort of faulty reasoning recently overturned in *Loving v. Virginia*. As the Illinois Eagle Forum argued, "A Supreme Court decision overturned laws forbidding interracial marriages, even though the laws apply equally to blacks and whites. This same ruling will apply to homosexual marriages."[102] In a pamphlet, the Mormon Church cited the January 1973 *Yale Law Journal* to argue that the ERA would necessarily legitimize gay marriage.[103] State representative William G. Batchelder argued during the ratification process in the Ohio legislature that *Loving v. Virginia* provided a clear parallel to any statute prohibiting marriage on the basis of sex.[104] His fellow Ohio legislators disagreed and ratified the amendment. But lawmakers in Florida allegedly cited the danger of homosexual marriage as a reason not to ratify the amendment.[105]

ERA opponents also argued that homosexual couples could adopt children once the state sanctioned gay marriage. One small anti-ERA group, the League of Housewives, speculated: "And if these couples 'marry,' will they not be eligible to adopt children, as are normal married couples?" To prove the point, the pamphlet pointed to a gay Minnesota couple whose applications to several adoption agencies were still pending.[106] Another pamphlet from ERA Illinois made use of Pat Buchanan's assertion that the amendment would immediately yield a constitutional right to adopt.[107] Even Illinois state representative Betty J. Hoxsey jumped in, warning the Illinois Moral Majority that gay couples might adopt children under the ERA.[108] In their view, gay marriage represented a moral challenge to traditional values, and children adopted into a gay family promised the acceptance of deviant lifestyles by the very young.

On the surface, the competition from gay families was simply moral competition. The Eagle Forum declared, "We support the family as the basic unit of society, with certain rights and responsibilities, including . . . the right to defend the institution of the family by according certain rights to husbands and wives that are not given to those choosing immoral lifestyles."[109] The Eagle Forum felt that reserving rights to the traditional family was the only way to ensure the preservation of the traditional family form. The Texas group the Association of Women Who Want to be Women agreed: "WE BELIEVE . . . that families form the building blocks of a prosperous and stable society, and we endorse the Biblical family structure, including . . . the right of families to be given by law certain protections and privileges not granted to those choosing other lifestyles."[110] ERA opponents experienced any concession to gay rights as a visceral reversal to the moral order.

ERA opponents also argued that gay couples posed a fiscal threat to silent majority families. Ervin introduced the theme of fiscal competition early in the debate about the Equal Rights Amendment. He offered the hypothetical of a gay marriage solemnized by Rev. Troy Perry, the Los Angeles founder of the Metropolitan Community Church already known for officiating at gay weddings: "[He] performs a marriage ceremony between two men, one of whom let's say, is a movie star, makes a lot of money. They live together as man and wife for 4 years, during which the movie star makes several million dollars. Then they break up and the one who was performing the wifely function comes to court and he says we were married. This is a community property State and I want my half of the income which you earned in the 4 years of our marriage. A woman could claim that half and I have a right to claim that half."[111] Divorce would reveal the rights and obligations of gay spouses, according to Ervin, and among those would be wifely privileges for gay men. Ervin rejected the idea that a "wife" could be a man. In Ervin's view, it should be biological femaleness, not household labor, that earned a "wife's" privileges. But it is also notable that Ervin selected the most elite gay man he could imagine—a Hollywood star. Implicit in this choice was the suggestion that the silent majority of wives would lose their homemaker privileges, but elite gay househusbands would not.[112]

ERA opponents also argued that traditional families would lose if the government extended tax and inheritance privileges to gay men and lesbians. Schlafly's various outlets spoke as one on this. The Illinois Eagle Forum worried that tax and inheritance rights "allowed normal married couples will also be allowed homosexuals."[113] For Phyllis Schlafly, the ERA not only legalized gay marriage but also gave gay couples the right to file joint income tax returns.[114] STOP ERA was angered that the ERA would "permit such 'couples' . . . to get tax and homestead benefits [then] given to husbands and wives."[115] It was outrageous because it implied that "deviant" couples were the equivalent of "normal" couples, at least as far as tax law was concerned. Psychologist Robin Smith referred to the tax breaks and the other financials boons of marriage as a "bounty" society paid couples for reproduction; gay marriage threatened to extend that bounty to gay couples without the same services rendered.[116] In a debate on gay marriage hosted out of WGBH radio station in Boston, the opponent of gay marriage asked the advocate whether "the concept of a legal marriage for the homosexual is nothing more than an excuse to secure for that individual certain tax and property advantages."[117] In other words, some of the ERA opponents that generally opposed taxation as a government burden on free individuals supported higher taxes for gay families. As taxes pressed on families more and more amid rising inflation, ERA opponents were concerned that gay and lesbian families would strain the federal government's resources even further by drawing their own tax and homestead benefits. Gay couples represented the same kinds of threats as welfare mothers or any other deviant group that drew on the federal government's resources.

The Political Ramifications of Equality

These ideas about the danger the ERA posed to families quickly infiltrated national politics. At first, both parties officially supported the ERA. In 1972, the ERA was widely endorsed by Republicans. It had a prominent position in the 1972 Republican platform. On April 14, 1972, then-governor Ronald Reagan identified the ERA as "morally unassailable."[118] One speaker at a Young Republicans' meeting in 1976 cited poll numbers showing Republican women supporting the ERA by a three to one margin.[119] Ronald Reagan's own daughter Maureen Reagan testified before the Republican Platform Committee Hearing on June 14, 1976. She urged the committee to keep the ERA in the Republican platform.[120] Maureen Reagan explained, if a breadwinner were to refuse "to put food on the table, a roof over the family . . . or clothes on the back of those members, the only option is divorce or separation where support becomes the arbitrary possession of the court without the legal understanding that when one adult in a family (male or female) works and the other works at home (male or female) they are both working and earning whatever that family accumulates."[121] Maureen Reagan cast the ERA as entirely consistent with Republican values. Such arguments proved compelling enough in 1976 to include the ERA in the Republican Party platform again.

But by 1976, Ronald Reagan and many other Republicans had changed their stance on the ERA. On August 13, 1975, Ronald Reagan went on the radio at seven o'clock in the morning to present a short program entitled "Equal Rights Amendment—Con." After conceding the need to award jobs and education on the basis of merit and not sex, Reagan asserted that he still did not like the ERA because it "would take away laws that were passed especially to make sure that women were not put upon by men. Divorce laws, for example. Child support laws."[122] Like many anti-ERA organizations, Reagan ignored the fact that divorce laws, child support laws, and protective labor legislation had already been drastically reduced from their robust midcentury versions. In fact, he had signed into law the first no fault divorce regime—with the first significant reduction in alimony—as governor of California. Though Reagan also cited the draft and private restrooms as other possible costs of the ERA, he circled back to family rights. He endorsed legislation "to correct inequalities and, indeed, to insure that women who choose to be housewives and full-time mothers are protected."[123]

In 1978, Congress debated the possibility of extending the deadline for the Equal Rights Amendment's ratification from 1979 to 1982. Certainly some of its opponents maintained the same objections. Sam Ervin had already retired, but he remained a prominent anti-ERA figure even as a private citizen. He composed a diatribe for the House Judiciary Committee, which Schlafly reprinted in the *Phyllis Schlafly Report* in July of 1978. In it he asserted, "the distinction between what the advocates of ERA say they seek and what ERA, if ratified, would actually do is as wide of the gulf which yawns between Lazarus in Abraham's bosom and Dives in hell."[124] What Ervin argued was that the ERA would lead to the elimination of laws that held men responsible for the financial care of their wives and children, women's inclusion in the draft, and gay marriage. And if his sense that the ERA would introduce a gender-neutral draft and gay marriage may have been correct, the laws that held men responsible for their wives were already a slim shadow of what had been.

But the ERA had gained new opponents, and not only Ronald Reagan. For example, Indiana University law professor William A. Stanmeyer testified to the Subcommittee on Civil and Constitutional Rights that he supported the ERA when Congress initially passed it, but that additional reading and reflection had caused him to change his mind. He cited—like Ervin, Schlafly, and many others—homosexual marriage, the draft, and the desire for the "certain exemptions and privileges for women and some additional burdens on men— for example, in matters of family support."[125] When pressed by Representative Elizabeth Holtzman, the extension's cosponsor, to name a state in which a husband's obligation to support his wife had been struck down, he could not do so. But he did accurately argue that a wife only maintained her right to support if she could not support herself.[126] Stanmeyer, like most ERA opponents, attributed the loss of breadwinner obligations to the Equal Rights Amendment, rather than to no-fault divorce and other divorce reform.

Some newly elected congressmen and women also opposed the ERA. For instance, Mr. Eldon Rudd, a Republican congressman from Arizona first elected in 1977, also evoked marriage and the family to oppose the extension. Rudd explained, "Section 2 of the proposed amendment opens the door to a Federal Government takeover of all matters dealing with marriage, divorce, child raising, child support, and so forth, by requiring Congress to pass all legislation considered necessary to implement total equality of the sexes."[127] Similarly Thomas Kindness, a Republican representative elected in 1974, queried his fellow representatives whether they could imagine regulating marriage, divorce, probate, insurance, and more.[128] Dave Treen joined the Senate in 1973. In congressional debate, he voiced his concerns regarding abortion and the military, but also he worried "about the effect of ERA on the historical rights of States to lawfully enact statutes which establish differing obligations and responsibilities on husband and wife and mother and father."[129] Though Treen believed that distinctions based on a marital or parental relationship did not violate the Constitution, he feared that the Supreme Court would strike down any distinction based on biology. After some vacillation, he opposed the extension, which passed only under a simple majority rather than the two-thirds majority the original ERA had passed by.[130]

By the 1980 election, the ERA had not only been purged from the Republican Party platform but also many of its local and national supporters had also been ejected from positions of power. Most obviously Reagan won over President Carter. But three of the most prominent national ERA supporters—Senate sponsor Birch Bayh; Representative Elizabeth Holtzman, the sponsor of the ERA extension bill; and outspoken advocate Representative Bella Abzug—lost their seats in 1980, 1980, and 1976 respectively. Though all three supported a broad liberal agenda, and several other senators lost alongside Bayh and Holtzman in 1980, all three seemed to have particular trouble with their positions on women's rights.[131] The Eagle Forum certainly claimed success for ERA supporters' national losses. Two sponsors of the federal childcare legislation, Walter Mondale and John Brademas, also lost their elections.[132] Moreover, the Eagle Forum paid particular attention to the three women running for spots in the Senate and took great satisfaction in that only the anti-ERA candidate, Paula Hawkins, was elected. Overall, of the thirty-three members of the House to lose in the 1980 elections, twenty-six voted aye on whether to extend the deadline for the ERA.[133] In addition to these prominent national politicians, ERA opponents on the local level also won their elections. The Eagle Forum claimed credit for the success of two anti-ERA legislators in Illinois, two state senators in Florida, four state legislators and a governor in North Carolina, four state senators in South Carolina, and four state legislators in Oklahoma.[134]

It is impossible to say definitively whether gender politics caused these victories. Even Schlafly, while gloating about her own role in Reagan's victory, conceded that probably the economy or foreign affairs were a significant causal factor in Carter losing the election.[135] Nonetheless, questions of family were clearly not divorced from the economic and global questions in play at the election. The struggle over the ERA helped point some women to one party or the other in 1980, as exemplified in one woman's correspondence

with the retired but still respected Senator Sam Ervin.[136] Though most corre-
spondents simply expressed their veneration for Ervin, this thirty-one-year-
old Colorado housewife turned to Ervin to ease her transition from one side
of the political spectrum to the other. "Mrs. Shay" Buckley wrote a letter to
Ervin in 1975 explaining that she had read some anti-ERA material distributed by the League of Housewives at her stepdaughter's school. The literature
cited Ervin, and it explained that the ERA threatened women with going to
war, being subject to searches by male police officers, and losing the "right not
to work" because, it warned, "if ERA is passed you may not choose to stay in
your home you will be forced to supply half the family support, or all of it, if
you are a better wage earner than your spouse."[137] Also Buckley feared that the
ERA would grant gay and lesbian couples the right to marry and adopt. Such
possibilities inspired Buckley to, as she said, get "up on my soap-box begging
people to write their State Rep. and tell him not to pass E.R.A."[138]

But Buckley considered herself an open-minded person, and when she
discovered that the League of Women Voters supported the measure, she decided to inquire of the league why it did not oppose the changes she so feared.
Buckley was stunned when the League of Women Voters told her that the
fliers she had received had misinformed her: they were full of "alarmist tactics.
Scare tactics. They had heard the John Birch Society was behind this material.
It's propaganda!" Discovering that the anti-ERA rhetoric might have misrep-
resented the ERA made her "bubble burst and [her] soap box collapse." Buckley clearly felt uneasy affiliating herself with the John Birch Society over the
League of Women Voters. For counsel, Buckley turned not to her own senator
or the *Denver Capital*, but instead to Sam Ervin, the authority cited in the
League of Housewives literature. She asked him whether women would lose
their right to stay home, to privacy, and more. Was the material propaganda?
Did the John Birch Society put it out? Sam Ervin had retired at this point and
wrote only a short reply. He explained only that he did oppose the ERA and
included a copy of one of the statements he had made when it was being debated in the Senate in 1972.[139] Presumably this statement, like all of Ervin's
public discourses on the ERA, confirmed many if not all of Buckley's fears
about the ERA. Though it is difficult to know how Buckley received Sam Ervin's brief reassurances, it is easy to imagine that Ervin was the means of making Buckley comfortable with affiliating herself with a group like the John
Birch Society over the League of Women Voters.

By 1981, even the legal premise behind homemakers' entitlements was
somewhat insecure. When the Supreme Court heard the case of *McCarty v.*

McCarty, its makeup had not changed drastically from the court that ruled in *Orr*. But Justices Blackmun, Marshall, Stevens, and White, who had all concurred with the preservation of alimony by extending it to men, rejected the claim that homemakers earned a portion of their husbands' income. *McCarty* was immediately preceded by and stemmed from the Supreme Court's decision in *Rostker v. Goldberg* to allow an all-male draft. In *Rostker*, the majority ruled that women did not have an obligation to serve because women would damage the US military.[140] The next day, the Supreme Court justices cited *Rostker's* evocation of national security to rule against Mrs. McCarty's claim that a military pension constituted community property.[141] The majority feared that it would hurt the military's recruitment efforts in the all-volunteer era if soldiers knew their wives could eventually share their pensions. This meant that McCarty did not get to share her ex-husband's pension as she would every other form of property under California's community property law.

In this, the Supreme Court disagreed even with judges in a state as conservative as Texas. For instance, Agnes Boone was a West German citizen who met her husband while he was deployed there in the military. Boone reported that her husband was controlling, even trying to prevent her from learning English. Then in 1977 he suddenly filed for divorce in Texas. The court there granted the divorce but also gave Boone 25 percent of her husband's pension in the divorce settlement.[142] In the late 1970s, 65 percent of Texas wives won a portion of their husband's retirement annuity.[143] Whereas Texas had seen a well-paid pension as a significant asset in a household's wealth, the Supreme Court saw it as a soldier's sole property. Phyllis Schlafly saw the pension this way too. For Schlafly, the draft registration case was a triumph for women because it retained their protected status.[144] Congress's action a year later restored a portion of military pensions to some divorced wives, but the Supreme Court had not confirmed state courts' assertion that women's labor in the home had value.[145]

When Reagan spoke of the Republican platform purged of the ERA in 1980, he characterized it as a compromise. He explained: there were "two groups on opposite sides. One wanted a definite plank in the platform opposing the amendment; the other, of course, wanted one supporting it. I believe we were very successful in getting a plank that emphasized our concern with equal rights for women without getting into the matter of whether this would be done by an amendment."[146] Reagan's compromise contributed to his victory for the presidency. Just a year later, as time ran out on ratifying the ERA, he echoed Schlafly and suggested that the ERA offered "an opportunity for mischief-making, not on the part of women, but on the part of men who would seek to take advantage of it for their own benefit."[147] Reagan offered instead modest substitute legislation, including an executive order establishing the Task Force on Legal Equity for Women and the Fifty States Project.[148] Both these "investigatory" initiatives reproduced much of what feminist groups had already created in the 1970s—simple catalogs of the ways in which the law distinguished between men and women. *Ms. Magazine*, alongside Congressman Don Edwards, characterized these task forces as giving cover to state legislators to reject the ERA without raising the ire of ordinary women.[149]

*   *   *

Under the ERA, opponents believed, only the privileged would receive the benefits of marriage. Because of these fears, the fight for the ERA was vicious. A great deal was at stake for both sides: a fundamental revolution in marriage and the family and a substantial disruption of the political economy. Opponents cast enough doubt on the outcome of the ERA that many Americans believed that new entitlements for homemakers particularly threatened the survival of the families of the silent majority. The men and women who joined the Reagan coalition staunchly believed that class status was too high a cost to pay for formal gender equality.

ERA opponents had tapped into an effective strategy of fusing moral ruin with fiscal doom. It was one that conservatives would use in other policy battles. Even as ERA opponents raised the specter of expanded moral and financial rights for feminists and queer families, other conservatives fought attempts by welfare rights, immigration, and gay liberation activists to expand the marriage revolution using the same strategy. These three groups of activists sought their own expansive set of marriage rights only to be thwarted with claims that those rights would be expensive affronts to the nation's morals.

CHAPTER 4

Race, Welfare, and Marriage Regulation

Poor women fought to have the value of their own household labor recognized and demanded welfare reform. This was a much more arduous process than it was for the wives who lobbied state legislatures for homemaker entitlements. Welfare had always been designed to provide for women with children who were not married, but it did so selectively. State legislatures were free to pass laws to distinguish between the deserving and undeserving poor however they saw fit based on a suitable home amendment to Social Security in 1939.[1] Widows, as opposed to deserted or single mothers, were the most likely to receive benefits. For decades, women and their children had been purged from—or more likely, never added to—the welfare rolls on the basis of the mother's supposed inability to provide a suitable home.

In 1961, the United States Department of Health, Education, and Welfare (HEW) adopted the Flemming Ruling—an amendment named after HEW Secretary Arthur Flemming—which made it more difficult to remove women and children from the welfare rolls on the basis of a suitable home clause.[2] With the elimination of this traditional means of keeping welfare costs low, many state legislatures rushed to pass new "substitute father" or "man in the house" laws that ostensibly held a man financially responsible for the children of any woman he had sex with. These substitute fathers inherited new thick breadwinning obligations regardless of whether they were married to these women or had fathered these children. Under the authority of these state laws, social workers had the ability to expel a woman and her children from the welfare rolls so that the mother's boyfriend could begin to take responsibility for their financial well-being. Since these women were not married, states sought to impose quasi-husbands on them.

Welfare rights activists fought the government's attempts to confine women to marriage whenever possible. In 1968, women on welfare won a major victory when the Supreme Court overturned substitute father laws in *King v. Smith*. Welfare activists also demanded financial compensation for all women's household labor in the form of a minimum income.[3] But welfare rights activists' victories only strengthened a backlash against welfare. While President Richard Nixon's proposed Family Assistance Plan (FAP) appeared to meet activists' demands for a minimum income, it also contained restrictive disciplinary actions against men. Congress members from both parties tried to resurrect the letter and then the spirit of the substitute father laws through FAP. When Congress failed to pass the bill in both 1970 and 1972, only some of FAP's disciplinary innovations lived on in later bills

The welfare policies targeting men did double work. The laws aimed to constrain men's past, present, and future sexuality, whether reproductive or not, to marriage or marriage-like institutions. Meanwhile, they also cast fiscal responsibility for dependent women and children onto the poorest men. While legislatures protected divorced men's privacy, the fathers of children on welfare faced punitive measures to get them to pay child support. Often these were the men least able to do so. This did not mean that women thrived in the new welfare climate. In fact, after the Flemming Ruling in 1961, welfare policy targeted working-class women and men as a unit, pitting them against one another or using punitive measures against men as a means of "solving" the problem of dependent women and children. Since the Progressive Era, poor men had been criminalized for failing to serve as breadwinners in traditional households, but welfare bureaucrats faced a new era with dwindling marriage rates and a deindustrializing economy that threatened to destroy the family wage.[4] The loss of substitute father laws and the eventual failure of Nixon's Family Assistance Plan meant that states could only use a few components of their legal arsenal to impose the problems of the dependence of women on welfare on men. But legislators on the federal and state levels never gave up trying to innovate new ways of doing so.

The evolution of welfare and, in particular, the provisions governing men's place in the family, also illuminate the racial limits of the marital revolution. Most women on welfare were white.[5] But in practice these exclusionary policies for welfare families were most often directed at people of color, especially in states in the South such as Alabama.[6] For instance, in a sample of seven counties in Alabama, 97 percent of the women and children dropped from welfare rolls under substitute father laws were black.[7] Therefore many of these policy innovations drew on the long tradition of government actors interfering with black marriages. Even as no-fault divorce began to free most husbands from their thick breadwinning obligations toward their dependents, the welfare system continued to push the sexual partners of black women on welfare and the fathers of black children on welfare to act as breadwinners. When race was ostensibly eased out of the legal system, bureaucrats still instituted more punitive policies against welfare fathers than non-welfare fathers. Moreover, what feminists won—financial compensation for housewives' work in the home—was never granted to women on welfare. The household labor monetized for more privileged divorcees remained a symbol of dependence for Aid to Families with Dependent Children (AFDC) recipients, especially for black women on welfare. The failure to gain the same rights for women on welfare as for women with other means of support highlights the modesty of feminists' gains. The compensation for women's work in the home never transcended the small property settlements given by privileged ex-husbands to their wives.

Regulating Race and Marriage

Marriage has been identified as a crucial site of racial struggle ever since the arrival of African slaves on American shores. Slaveholders barred slaves from formal marriage relations, outlawed interracial marriage, wielded the specter of family separation as a weapon against unruly slaves, and justified slavery in terms of patriarchy. One of abolitionists' most potent weapons was to criticize the lack of patriarchal power slaves wielded as fathers and husbands.[8] Long after emancipation, interracial marriage bans and the selective punishment of extramarital sex continued to be a source of power over African Americans.[9] Many scholars have shown that welfare authorities more often deprived black women of welfare, custody of their children, and their reproductive freedom because of bureaucrats' and politicians' beliefs about black women's irredeemable sexual "deviance" outside the institution of marriage.[10] Marriage policy also targeted black men's sexuality.[11]

The role of black labor in the United States further complicates the history of marriage and race. Following the Civil War, many freed slaves sought to establish breadwinner-homemaker households. But this did not suit the labor needs of former slave masters, and policies attempted to direct black women into the job market as domestics.[12] One of the most effective means of doing so was to deny black men a family wage. This pattern held into the twentieth century; in most black families, two incomes were necessary to sustain the household. Black families joined the Great Migration in hopes of finding better pay. Even in the North, however, family wage jobs proved elusive, and black men were the first to be laid off when they did gain them.[13]

From 1939 until 1961, many black women were excluded from Aid to Dependent Children (ADC), AFDC's predecessor, via a clause that allowed states to bar mothers who did not provide a "suitable home" for their children.[14] Throughout this time period states adopted narrow definitions of a suitable home to protect themselves from what they perceived as an onslaught of women and children clamoring for aid.[15] For example, in 1960, Louisiana passed a law that retroactively removed from the welfare rolls any child whose mother had ever had an illegitimate child after being certified for ADC. In July of that year, the state dropped 22,501 children, of whom over 20,000 were black, from the state's welfare rolls on the basis of their mothers' perceived sexual indiscretions. The sudden withdrawal of benefits, as well as the difficulty in getting them reinstated even if the mother could prove she had offered a suitable home for her family, led many mothers to lose custody of their children.[16] This seismic loss of benefits prompted a national and international outcry and helped bring attention to the problem of poverty in America.

As the public, politicians, activists, and social scientists began studying poverty in the 1960s, the exclusion of the "undeserving" from welfare benefits began to lose favor.[17] HEW Secretary Arthur S. Flemming helped lead the way. Flemming had been the first director of the School of Public Affairs at American University before Franklin Roosevelt appointed him as a Republican member of the U.S. Civil Service Commission in 1939.[18] Eisenhower then appointed Flemming as the third director of HEW in 1958, and soon thereafter Flemming began to formulate a way to circumvent suitable home clauses.

The "Flemming Ruling," as Flemming's solution to the problem of suitable home clauses came to be known, eliminated the cost-saving appeal of the suitable homes clauses. HEW asserted that since the purpose of ADC was to help children, measures that punished children were unacceptable. Instead state agencies should focus on "the effects on children of the environment in which they are living" and mandated that services "be directed toward affording the children maximum protection and strengthening their family life."[19] Most importantly, HEW ruled that states could not deny a child aid on the basis that the home situation was unsuitable without either taking steps to improve the family situation or removing the child from the home. Both measures were costly, which in effect eliminated the fiscal advantage of ruling a home unsuitable. In 1961, amendments to the Social Security Act formally instituted HEW's Flemming Ruling. In doing so, Congress removed the option of shedding "undesirable" welfare recipients through suitable home clauses, stating that "grants to States would not be available if the State terminated assistance to children determined to be unsuitable unless the State made other provision for the children affected."[20] The enforcement options, however, were profoundly limited; HEW's only recourse to violations of this law literally or in spirit was to withdraw all federal funding from a state.

Less than two years after Congress formally instituted the Flemming Ruling, George Wallace was elected to his first term as governor of Alabama and appointed Ruben K. King as commissioner of the Alabama State Department of Pensions and Security.[21] King had attended law school with Wallace's brother but had no background in social work. Because Alabama now had a suitable home law rendered illegal by the Flemming Ruling, Wallace ordered King to "work on the AFDC problem."[22] King instituted a study of Aid to Families with Dependent Children in Alabama, which "led to the adoption and promulgation of the 'substitute parent' policy."[23] Though the first substitute parent law was passed in 1947, the subsequent flood of "substitute father" or "man in the house" laws passed in nineteen states and Washington, DC, allowed state governments like Alabama's to circumvent the Flemming Ruling. They did so by holding a man who had sex with a welfare recipient ostensibly responsible for the care of that welfare recipient and her children.[24] Therefore, states could remove welfare recipients from the rolls without having to place the child in a state facility or other suitable home.[25] The infamous Alabama regulation defined a man as a "substitute parent" "(1) if 'he lives in the home with the child's natural or adoptive mother for the purpose of cohabitation'; or (2) if 'he visits [the home] frequently for the purpose of cohabiting with the child's natural or adoptive mother'; or (3) if 'he does not frequent the home but cohabits with the child's natural or adoptive mother elsewhere.' "[26]

Ruben King's concept of cohabitation is probably clear from his broad definition. It is not difficult to interpret the meaning of "cohabit" when it refers not only to living in the home but also to visiting the home to "cohabit." Alabama AFDC officials were even less likely to couch their intentions in a euphemism. They interpreted "cohabitation" to mean "that the man and woman have 'frequent' or 'continuing' sexual relations."[27] King himself indicated that "if a man enjoys the privileges of a parent, then he should have the responsibility of a parent." As he put it, "the question is . . . does the man have the privileges of a husband?"[28] For King, sex was exclusively the "privilege" of a married man. The implicit meaning behind cohabitation was clear to social workers and welfare recipients as well. One caseworker explained her approach: "since the women 'don't exactly know what cohabitation means,' she would ask them, 'Do you have sexual intercourse?' or 'Do you have sex relations with . . . ?'" In one case, an investigating lawyer reported that "the kids were asked whether their mother was sleeping around."[29]

The application of the substitute father law also varied by social worker and according to who the client was.[30] Not surprisingly, Alabama state officials particularly targeted black women.[31] The Center of Social Welfare Policy and Law discovered that 182 of 184 families cut off in one Alabama county under the substitute parent law were black.[32] The numbers were similar in a broader study tracing seven representative counties over thirty months between 1964 and 1966: 97 percent of the 498 cases closed under substitute father laws dropped black children from the welfare rolls.[33] Alabama also gave social workers broad discretion in implementing substitute father laws by using an elastic understanding of "frequent or continuing." In practice, AFDC officials interpreted "frequent" or "continuing" as ranging from having "sex at least once a week" to "once every six months." No matter what, a pregnancy or baby under six months of age was sufficient evidence of a substitute father.[34]

The substitute father regulations were a blatant means of purging putatively immoral women and their children—particularly black women and children—from the welfare rolls without having to bear the cost of placing these children in more "suitable" home environments. In Alabama alone, 16,000 children were denied financial assistance during the mid-1960s.[35] An additional 6,400 applications were rejected outright.[36] Experts speculated that nationally, the numbers amounted to nearly 400,000.[37] Alabama justified the cut in part by showing that "the average payment per family per month immediately before the regulation was promulgated was $48.15 per family or $11.69 per recipient. In January 1967, two and one half years later, the payment was $52.68 per family or $12.72 per recipient."[38] According to state officials, it would cost $645,000 and the salaries of several additional caseworkers to restore services to all the families cut from the rolls.[39] Justice William Brennan later succinctly characterized the policy as giving "more milk to some children by giving none to others."[40] Since the children purged from the welfare rolls were usually black, a disproportionate number of white children benefited from a disproportionate number of black children's loss.

The social workers who kicked black women and children off the welfare rolls also defended their decisions by appealing to men's breadwinning duties. Katie B. Shaw and Nan C. Murphy, both of whom were county directors of Aid to Dependent Children in Alabama in the 1960s, admitted that social workers mostly interfered with the relationships of black men and women. When pressed by lawyers for the civil rights group Center on Social Welfare Policy and Law about her own exclusive attention to the boyfriends of black women, Murphy sounded a familiar refrain: "You're from the North and can't really understand our problem." The difficulty, according to these social workers, was black men's unwillingness to support the women they slept with. Shaw explained, her clients "want our help in getting rid of the men who live off their welfare checks. . . . They really do. Many times I tell them, 'You shouldn't go with Mr. Jones or Mr. Washington because he's no good,' and they appreciate it." Shaw saw her clients as misguided, but ultimately good, and herself as their helper and benefactor. The real villains, in her eyes, were boyfriends like Jones and Washington, men who took advantage of women on welfare and of the welfare system. Ultimately Murphy accused men of living off their girlfriends' welfare benefits to avoid real work. She explained, "these men who see our recipients just won't work. The feds tell us the unemployment rate in my county is seventy-five percent. Now, you know, if a man wants to work, there's a job for him."[41] For Murphy, all black men could and should fulfill their breadwinner roles to support women and children.

Nonetheless, the strategy of using a substitute father law to circumvent the Flemming Ruling tells us as much about ideology as it does about finances. Alabama was certainly interested in withholding welfare payments from those black women who had sex and bore children who subsequently needed aid. But Alabama's attention to working-class black fathers also represented genuine beliefs about the role of men in families. As a radical welfare rights advocate argued, "Behind the cohabitation ruling is the preposterous assumption that, because a man and a woman sleep together, the man should also keep any number of children the woman might have by other men—i.e. he is supposed to pay for her sexual services."[42] Alabama linked men's sexual activity to the thick responsibilities of fatherhood, even when that sexuality had not produced a child. It punished sex, rather than the failure to support one's dependents. It punished the failure to marry, and Alabama articulated this complaint explicitly. A 1968 Alabama brief to the Supreme Court argued that cohabitation would not "help a deserted mother, widow, or unwed poor mother or affluent mother, get a husband."[43] Similarly, Mary Lee Stapp, the Department of Pensions and Security lawyer for the state of Alabama, snapped in a private meeting, "Why don't they get married? We don't have the money to support all those children."[44] King claimed that Alabama was interested in child support rather than morality, but he also contended that any mother could "give up her pleasure" to get benefits back.[45] The policy revealed Alabama policy makers' beliefs about the immorality of extramarital sex for women and men alike.[46]

Welfare recipients did not always agree that sex should only take place within a marriage or that men should have to or would care for the children of their sexual partners. Sylvester Smith, a welfare recipient and the plaintiff in *King v. Smith*, was a thirty-four-year-old African American widow caring for four children and one grandchild. Smith had been widowed at the age of twenty-three when her husband died "in a fight over a woman." Smith filed for welfare benefits, and her monthly allowance for her three toddlers was forty-five dollars a month.[47] She later had a fourth child with a man who shortly thereafter left their small town of Tyler, Alabama. After this, she received a benefit for all four children. Sometime in the next decade, she developed a sexual relationship with William E. Williams, a married father of nine. Williams and his wife both worked to support their own children, but he nonetheless would on occasion scrape together four or five dollars a month to help Smith.[48]

In 1966 Smith lost the bulk of the welfare income she had been receiving. First, her thirteen-year-old daughter, Ida Elizabeth, had a child and was subsequently dropped from the welfare rolls. Smith wrote a letter to President Lyndon B. Johnson fruitlessly objecting; Smith now had a smaller monthly welfare benefit to hold her larger family together. A few months later, Smith secured work as a night-shift cook and waitress in Selma for twenty dollars a week. The job and its accompanying move to Selma prompted two significant changes. First, Smith lost more of her welfare benefit in recognition of her new wages; Alabama now contributed only twenty-nine dollars a month to the family compared to the sixty-seven dollars Smith received prior to the birth of her grandchild and her new job. Second, a less tolerant caseworker replaced Smith's original caseworker, who had ignored Smith's relationship with Williams. When the new caseworker, Jacquelyn Stancil, learned of Williams's continued visits to Smith in Selma via "a little bird," she ended aid to Smith's family under the substitute father clause. Had Smith applied to be reinstated, she would have had to inform the state she was no longer seeing Williams and had her claim corroborated by two "law-enforcement officials, ministers, neighbors, [or] grocers."[49] Smith disaggregated financial support

Figure 5. The *New York Times* published this photograph of Sylvester Smith with her children, grandchildren, and a nephew in its coverage of *King v. Smith*. Courtesy of George Tames/The New York Times/Redux.

and sex when she complained, "As long as I'm not having no more kids for you to support, why should you bother me?" She then added, "I'm gonna make a relationship with somebody. . . . If God had intended for me to be a nun, I'd be a nun."[50] Smith also rejected the idea that boyfriends should pay for their girlfriends' families and alleged that many men did not even take care of their own children.[51]

The 1974 film *Claudine*, produced by the minority-owned company Third World Films, fictionalized Smith's objections to social workers' efforts to impose sexual propriety. In the film, Diahann Carroll plays the title figure—a mother of six on welfare. Notably, this was a significantly larger number of children than Smith had in real life, and much larger than the 3.0 children in the average AFDC recipient family in 1969.[52] But in other ways Claudine's experience was like Smith's. Claudine secretly works as a maid in a white suburb. While she is at her job, she meets James Earl Jones's character, Roop. The two begin a relationship, which Claudine's social worker, Miss Kabak, quickly finds out about. In one of her visits, Miss Kabak begins her inspection by asking Claudine if she has been working. Despite having been employed for much longer than she was in a relationship, Claudine is able to easily conceal this fact. But Miss Kabak is much more persistent in regards to Claudine's love life. She reports that she knows Claudine is seeing a man. Then Claudine echoes Smith almost literally, objecting, "What am I, a damn nun?" Smith's refusal to marry made her a target for Alabama despite these objections. Substitute father laws, in other words, used sex to coerce poor black women and men into a legal relationship resembling marriage when the state could not force them into official marriages. The laws, moreover, attempted to impose thick breadwinner obligations on men. Instead of fostering marriages with breadwinning men, however, these laws made sex a potentially dangerous engagement for women.

Smith decided to challenge being kicked off the welfare rolls. Smith first turned to local organizers. She chose to contact "some civil-rights workers who had won a reputation around Selma for talking tough to welfare-department functionaries."[53] One of these civil rights workers, the Lawyers Constitutional Defense Committee lawyer Donald Jellinek, then passed the case on to the Columbia University Center on Social Welfare Policy and Law attorney Martin Garbus.[54] The Center on Social Welfare Policy and Law saw the case as part of a civil rights southern strategy to "examine the deficiencies in the welfare system."[55]

Garbus pursued *King v. Smith* in part due to the stark numbers indicating black children disproportionately bore the brunt of the substitute father laws in the South and beyond.[56] Other southern states suggested similar outcomes, and states like Georgia explicitly admitted to targeting black mothers on welfare.[57] Garbus believed that these laws were used in similar ways in the North. But he passed over other possible substitute father cases, including one in Michigan that was certainly "racially discriminatory," because he thought they would have been more difficult to prove to a northern court.[58] The Smith complaint to the U.S. District Court in Alabama was that the substitute father regulation "was conceived to deny aid to blacks, and that it had that effect."[59] The Alabama federal district court ruled in favor of Smith but did not accept the claim that the case was "a civil rights matter."[60] Instead the court emphasized that the equal protection clause could be used to protect all needy children's right to aid.

Garbus, who had left the Center on Social Welfare Policy and Law by this point, shifted his reasoning to claim that substitute father laws infringed on a welfare recipient's right to privacy, that recipients deserved a hearing before their benefits were withdrawn, and that the needy had a right to welfare aid.[61] The Center on Social Welfare and Policy and Law, on the other hand, focused its amicus brief on the problem that no other state agency in Alabama treated substitute fathers as legally liable for the care of those children barred from welfare payments.[62] These laws did not consider whether a substitute father supported the children purged from the rolls.[63] Instead they defined substitute fathers as "men who are not in fact natural or adoptive parents, who have no legal responsibility to support the children in the family, and who have not in fact assumed the responsibility to give support," including men who had "no relationship to the children, . . . [did] not live in the house or aid or guide the children in any way—or even know the children."[64] Such definitions denied assistance to "needy children."[65] The victims of the regulation of men by welfare authorities were ultimately not men, but instead children and women.

The Supreme Court ruled the substitute parent laws unconstitutional in 1968 on the basis that substitute father laws hoisted thick marital responsibilities on any man who slept with a woman receiving welfare but failed to enforce them. The court ruled "Alabama's substitute father regulation, as written and as applied in this case, requires the disqualification of otherwise eligible dependent children if their mother 'cohabits' with a man who is not obligated by Alabama law to support the children. . . . In denying AFDC assistance to appellees on the basis of this invalid regulation, Alabama has breached its federally imposed obligation to furnish 'aid to families with dependent children.' "[66]

King v. Smith vastly expanded the right of thousands of poor children to receive public assistance. Some estimates suggested *King* "allowed at least 100,000 families to get welfare benefits—people who previously would not have applied for aid or would have been dropped."[67] Nonetheless welfare rights activists had to expend significant effort to enforce it. Soon after the ruling, Michigan's director of social services pledged "to stand fast in refusing aid to children whose mothers are having extramarital relations."[68] One newspaper report also noted, "investigations are still conducted."[69] As of 1970, two years after *King v. Smith*, fifteen states still purged women and children from the welfare rolls under substitute parent laws.[70] Moreover, many states still used " 'man-in-the-house' budgeting rules, which included the income of unrelated cohabitors in the resource base of the unit when determining grant amounts."[71]

Welfare rights organizations pushed back whenever it seemed *King* was being violated through consciousness-raising and legal action. They published welfare rights handbooks and other pamphlets to educate recipients about what social workers could legally do. The National Welfare Rights Organization warned its members: "under the United States Supreme Court Case *Smith v. King*, and under new regulations passed by H.E.W., the welfare department cannot deny, cut off, or reduce welfare aid because you are going with someone."[72] Despite the grassroots organizing, other court cases were necessary to protect the rights in *King*. First, *Goldberg v. Kelly* established the right to a hearing before a woman lost a welfare benefit. This transformed the benefit into something closer to a right and removed some of social workers' vast discretion to decide whether to kick a woman off the rolls.[73] The right to a hearing was an essential mechanism in ensuring that *King* had teeth. Then in 1970, the Supreme Court ruled in *Lewis v. Martin* against budgeting rules that deducted part of a welfare benefit on the basis of the presence of a substitute father. The court explained that after *King*, social workers could not assume children had access to support from a mother's boyfriend and then reduce a benefit. The decision stated, "any lesser duty of support might merely be a device for lowering welfare benefits without guaranteeing that the child would regularly receive the income on which the reduction is based."[74] The court drew on its *King* ruling to conclude that the budgeting rules thus violated children's right to welfare.[75]

Some clients still faced questions and lost benefits even after these

Supreme Court decisions.[76] Home visits certainly continued.[77] AFDC recipient Barbara James felt that the visits raised "questions concerning personal relationships, beliefs and behavior," which she found "unnecessary for a determination of continuing eligibility." She refused to allow a social worker entrance into her home, which then disqualified her for the AFDC benefit. She then sued the New York City Department of Social Services to regain her benefit under the objection that such visits constituted an unreasonable search under the Fourth Amendment. The case made it to the Supreme Court as *Wyman v. James*, where the justices indeed hedged AFDC recipients' privacy rights.[78] In his ruling Justice Blackmun distinguished between a search by police and a search to ensure that a dependent child indeed received the AFDC benefit. Even here, however, Blackmun conceded that recipients should be informed of home visits ahead of time. Visits should not take place after normal office hours or involve forcible entry or snooping.[79] Of course, once a social worker entered a household, it was difficult to prevent him or her from snooping. Nonetheless, even with significant hedging of recipients' privacy rights via *Wyman*, *King* and *Lewis* marked major obstacles in lawmakers' attempts to limit dependency among black mothers.

Welfare Warriors on Marriage

For many welfare rights activists, the right to live above the poverty line had nothing to do with black men. Or at least they believed that it *should not* have anything to do with black men. Women on welfare, many of whom were not content with *King* and *Lewis* alone, fought for even broader rights through the welfare rights movement. Foremost among these welfare rights organizations was the National Welfare Rights Organization (NWRO), which had an expansive membership and broad support from the civil rights movement. George Wiley, a former professor, left his post as associate director of the Congress of Racial Equality in 1966 to begin the Poverty Rights Action Center (PRAC). The next year PRAC, envisioned as an organization to combat poverty, met with over sixty local welfare rights organizations to form NWRO. NWRO folded in 1975, but at its peak, it had over thirty thousand members. Casual participation in the movement was even broader, reaching nearly one hundred thousand women. It was led mostly by African American women.[80] Welfare rights activists critiqued the government's promotion of the breadwinner-homemaker household.

Instead of providing basic rights, activists argued with palpable frustration, society derided poor women for not being able to keep a man.[81] NWRO asserted that society saw sex as a permanent commitment between a man and a woman, but that black women were responsible for making the men they had sex with stay. Those women who failed to do so were deviant, as were the families they led. As one woman explained, "a woman with children is not simply a woman with children but an incomplete family."[82] French radical feminist and AFDC critic Andre Leo made a similar point in an essay on the American welfare system when she claimed that the prize for women's ability to "win" a man was becoming a housewife and mother.[83] Johnnie Tillmon, a later president of NWRO, was the most explicit: "if you don't have a man to pay for everything, particularly if you have kids, then . . . you've 'failed' as a woman, because you've failed to attract and keep a man. There's something wrong with you."[84]

But welfare rights activists saw separation and divorce as inevitable and even sometimes economically advantageous. Poverty led many men to leave their families. Wiley, the first president of NWRO, told the *Chicago Defender*, "the failure to be able to provide for your family when that's what society expects of you is an assault on your manhood. . . . So it's a natural reaction, when things get too tough to bug out."[85] A fellow at the Brookings Institute, Leonard Goodwin, attributed desertion and illegitimacy to poverty, saying that men who could not afford to take care of their families deserted their children or never married in the first place.[86] One letter writer told a welfare rights organization that her husband would leave town and then demand money to get back home.[87]

Poverty also led many women to end relationships.[88] One informant told Carol Stack, the author of *All Our Kin*, that her relatives discouraged her from getting married: her mother "knows that it be money getting away from her. . . . I'd have my husband to look after."[89] Ultimately, Stack believed that if a husband were unemployed, he could not possibly compete with other kin.[90] Celestine Ware was affiliated with the feminist, civil rights, and more loosely the welfare rights movements, and she pointed out that husbands could present additional financial hardships rather than restore the breadwinning relationship. She reported that "poor black males complain of being told to 'Get out! And don't bring your ass back here until you've got a job!' "[91]

Welfare rights advocates also argued that welfare policies themselves forced many men out of the house. Tillmon, the president of NWRO after Wiley, explained that "in half the states there really can't be men around because AFDC says if there is an 'able-bodied' man around, then you can't be on welfare. If the kids are going to eat, and the man can't get a job, then he's got to go. So his kids can eat."[92] Addie Garel, the president of a local welfare union on Chicago's South Side explained that wives asked husbands to leave because they would be "better without [them].' "[93] The Chicago Welfare Rights Organization (CWRO) went so far as to compare welfare policies to "genocide," because such policies forced poor black men to "leave their families when they cannot support them."[94] Racism in the labor market and welfare policies together reached into the black family and snatched out fathers and husbands.

Even though marriage failed to provide financial stability to poor couples, it nonetheless justified lower wages for women. One welfare rights activist noted that welfare was a better option than working for poverty-level wages: "even if a woman does get a job, she's likely to get more money on ADC than from work outside her home. She will also have problems finding and paying for baby-sitters or day care." Working for such low wages would make any woman "realize why so many ADC mothers stay home": "Now she has two full-time jobs, and only one for pay! Her life will be a continual round of backbreaking labor with hardly any time for leisure or the enjoyment of her children. And all that for poverty-level wages."[95] One woman taking classes for welfare mothers was "unemployed due to the fact that the salary that she received along with her husband's was not sufficient to pay for day care, rent, clothing and food, therefore Mrs. quit her job to remain home with her children."[96] Betsy Warrior, a welfare rights advocate, explained, "whether the money a mother receives is doled out by a husband or a paternalistic welfare department makes little difference. Both are degrading, and many women prefer welfare to a husband."[97]

The lack of formal marriage did not preclude economic entanglements, however, and boyfriends did sometimes provide essential stopgaps for impoverished mothers. The reality of the job market and her husband's desertion forced another woman onto welfare, which she then supplemented with help from a boyfriend. Though she said "she would work 3 jobs to get off welfare," she instead "went to the public assistance office and they provided her with emergency food and paid 3 months back rent on the apartment she was then living in." Even so, her boyfriend's help was still essential to her survival: "she says she could not make it without her boyfriend."[98] Carol Stack also had examples of informal aid provided by boyfriends or fathers when women were on welfare. Fathers who found it "impossible . . . to assume financial duties as parents" were still expected to help out with a hospital bill "or by bringing milk and diapers to the mother after the birth of the child."[99] Welfare and aid from friends together were necessary to ensure the survival of working-class women and their children after marriage had failed.

Welfare rights activists argued the solution to poverty was not marriage but first fair employment prospects and pay for women. Keeping a man should not be necessary for women to sustain their own families much as liberal black feminists had argued.[100] Welfare rights activists issued a series of demands to make this possible. First they demanded decent wages for all women, but particularly women of color who were more likely to earn insufficient incomes and head their own households. The Hull House Welfare Rights Organization noted that cuts to welfare were "racist to the core" since "Black and Latin workers [were] forced on welfare in greater numbers because of racist firing and hiring practices."[101] Jessie Muril Williams, in a letter to Alabama senator James Allen, tried to articulate the difficultly of making ends meet for domestic workers who often headed their households: "The cost of living keep climbing higher and higher, even a penny box of matches have gone up to two cents a box. Do you have any idea what it is like to work 5 days a week from 7:00 a.m. till 5:30 in the afternoon for $25.00 dollars a week with no fringe benefits at all; with 5 children to feed and clothe?"[102] Sylvester Smith, who made huge strides with the case *King v. Smith*, clearly made so little as a waitress that she still qualified for extensive aid under Alabama law. Similarly, the fictional Claudine in the film *Claudine* could not make ends meet with her maid job.

Second, welfare rights activists also demanded adequate day care. Poor women's low wage problem was compounded by the cost and scarcity of day care. The Task Force on Public Aid noted that "in Chicago there are only 4600 places in day care centers and over 144,000 children who need them," and the Hull House Welfare Rights Organization observed that six million mothers competed for spots in day cares that could only ever serve 12 percent of their children.[103] Women with young children were especially vulnerable. Operation COPE, a Washington, DC, organization sponsored by the National Council of Negro Women that aimed at helping women on welfare get back on their feet, provided aid to one woman with a fourteen-month-old daughter who was "unemployed because she [did] not have a babysitter": "COPE should also seek to find day care services for her child so that she will be able to find a job and/or pursue courses which will lead her to a career in accounting."[104] The situation was even worse since there were restrictions on founding day cares to such an extent that even some churches did not always qualify to open one.[105]

Third, activists demanded equitable recognition of poor women's home-making. Welfare rights activists often argued that there was a double standard between white women's and black women's work in the home. Double standards between white women and black women—and critiques of them—dated back to Reconstruction.[106] The critiques took on new meaning as black women fought for and even gained access to welfare. Welfare rights advocate Andre Leo explained, "a social worker next to me at work said, 'These women have no pride. Why don't they go out and work instead of getting handouts from ADC?' That same social worker's mother never 'worked.'"[107] Leo noted that a divorced woman forced onto welfare did the same household labor as before her divorce but had become "bad, lazy, and a leech" for accepting welfare funds to do so. This sort of critique implied to welfare recipients that "there are two kinds of housewives, the 'good' ones and the 'bad' ones. The 'good' ones do the same work as she does but they are still living with a man who 'provides' them with their needs from *his* pay from *his* work. The 'bad' ones are those who are not living with or being paid for by *a man* and so the state replaces him in the form of an ADC check ('The Man')."[108] Johnnie Tillmon, the president of NWRO, made a similar point when she argued that "If you're a society lady from Scarsdale and you spend all your time sitting on your prosperity paring your nails, well, that's okay. Women aren't supposed to work. They're supposed to be married. But if you don't have a man to pay for everything, particularly if you have kids, then everything changes."[109] Similarly, in a document put together by the Campaign for Adequate Welfare Reform Now, issued out of Washington, DC, in 1971, one objection to proposed welfare reform was the mandate that women on welfare would work. A welfare mother explained that she did not want someone else to raise her child but to nonetheless be held personally responsible for her child's behavior.[110]

The blacklisted Hollywood screenwriter of *Claudine* adapted these famous critiques of a double standard for his script as well. When Claudine's social worker, Miss Kabak, insists she must know if Claudine is sleeping with someone and receiving something in return, Claudine asks if Miss Kabak is sleeping with someone. When Miss Kabak wants to deduct the value of what Claudine's boyfriend gives her, Claudine compares $2.15 worth of beer her boyfriend brought to the wine that Miss Kabak presumably drank on her dates. When Miss Kabak asks if that's all she receives, Claudine asks her, "How much do you get?" Later in the film, Claudine compares welfare to marriage

Figure 6. Johnnie Tillmon, president of the National Welfare Rights Organization, made the case that all women's household labor was undervalued in "Welfare Is a Women's Issue." Courtesy of Wisconsin Historical Society, WHS-8771.

again, but makes it clear that welfare is the worst possible kind of marriage. In a monologue, she explains: "I am married. I'm married to the welfare man. That's my husband. He makes me beg for them pennies. Starvation money. If I can't feed my kids, that's child neglect. If I go out and get myself a little job on the side and don't tell him, then I'm cheating. If I stay at home, then I'm lazy. You can't win. Mr. Welfare—that is the nosiest husband in the world. Ooo Mr. welfare, I'd do anything to divorce that bastard." If married women escaped the stigma of working at home, then they also benefited from the possibility of kind husbands. The state—the Man in the parlance of so many pamphlets—proved to be a much harsher husband than many men.

Fourth, welfare rights activists demanded access to the new entitlements feminists were winning in recognition of their homemaking labor. Welfare rights activists insisted that welfare mothers needed displaced homemaker privileges—traditionally defined as education and other training benefits for homemakers who had lost access to a family wage through death or divorce—as much as any other homemakers. Alexis Herman, in her keynote address on ERA and Ethnic Minority Women for the Consultation on Ethnic Minority Involvement in the Equal Rights Amendment, raised the issue of "women who have been on welfare most of their lives and lose that assistance when their children reach 16, 17 or 18 years of age. Would they, too, be displaced because they no longer have a limited income and would the definition of displaced homemaker be wrought to include that population as well?" Eventually, a House bill did include women who had been on welfare, but Herman noted it "was not an easy debate to have."[111]

Finally welfare rights advocates endorsed a minimum income law to give women the choice to stay home and a guarantee that underpaid women would not starve. They demanded a welfare floor of either $5,500 or $6,500 a year for a family of four and developed financial tables that encouraged employment without forcing recipients to work. According to NWRO president Tillmon, paying women for their unwaged work in the home would solve the problems of welfare mothers and housewives alike: "If I were President, I would solve this so-called welfare crisis in a minute and go a long way toward liberating every woman. I'd just issue a proclamation that women's work is real work. In other words, I'd start paying women a living wage for doing the work we are already doing child raising and housekeeping. And the welfare crisis would be over. Just like that. Housewives would be getting wages, too—a legally determined percentage of their husband's salary—instead of having to ask for an account for money they already earned."[112] The Chicago Welfare Rights Organization deployed the national organization's strategy locally: "We are asking that this country END the WAR and BEGIN to SUBSIDIZE LIFE instead of death. NWRO's Guaranteed Adequate Income Plan is designed to provide every family with an adequate income."[113] The CWRO in this instance pegged the minimum income at $5,500.

By making these demands to ensure the financial viability of the female-headed household, welfare rights activists turned the notorious Moynihan Report on its head. The Moynihan Report famously argued that black women had too much power in the home, which emasculated black men. Daniel Patrick Moynihan, an assistant secretary in the Department of Labor at the time, first identified declining marriage rates and increasing numbers of divorces and illegitimate births as a problem. Moynihan then explained that all of these conditions had turned the African American community "into a matriarchal structure which, because it is so out of line with the rest of American society, seriously retards the progress of the group as a whole, and imposes a crushing burden on the Negro male and, in consequence, on a great many Negro women as well."[114] Though Moynihan professed to offer no solutions, he did admit, "a national effort towards the problems of Negro Americans must be directed towards the question of family structure. The object should be to strengthen the Negro family so as to enable it to raise and support its members as do other families."[115] As Lee Rainwater and William L. Yancy have argued, Moynihan's solution to ending poverty was to restore men's patriarchal power over wives and children in the home through improved employment.[116] Moynihan's argument became so widespread that, in addition to becoming a cornerstone of Johnson's War on Poverty, it was echoed by factions of the Black Power Movement.[117] But like black liberal feminist organizations, welfare rights activists believed that the key to helping not only the black community, but all families, was to strengthen women's economic and cultural power. Marriage presented no solution; its monopoly in American culture should be ended.

The Family Assistance Plan

The defeat of the substitute father laws inspired some lawmakers to search for new strategies to make black men responsible for black children, which perverted the National Welfare Rights Organization's dream of a minimum income. Daniel Patrick Moynihan, now head of the Urban Affairs Council, prepared a minimum income program called the Family Assistance Plan for the Nixon administration in 1969.[118] FAP was notable for its attempt to implement a very low—lower than most AFDC benefits at the time—guaranteed annual income, accompanied by new stricter work requirements. Nixon's FAP guaranteed only $1,600 annually for a family of four as compared to the NWRO's demand for "$5,500 or Fight!"[119] Nixon's plan nonetheless created an uneasy alliance between liberals, who sought a guaranteed annual income, and conservatives, who wanted more punitive treatment of welfare recipients. Liberal congressmen and women envisioned FAP as a mechanism to fortify a father's legitimate place in the family with the AFDC-Unemployed Parent benefit. Conservatives, on the other hand, wanted to use FAP to restore the morality and financial logic that ruled welfare before the Flemming Ruling and *King v. Smith*. Such widely diverging goals led to FAP's eventual defeat.

In this era, liberals in Congress agreed with welfare rights activists that policy was driving un- or underemployed fathers out of the house.[120] Congressman Wilbur Mills (D-AK) argued before Congress that AFDC "encourages family breakup": "Do not think for 1 minute that it has not made a contribution to many, many fathers leaving their families in order that the family could eat and have clothing to wear. Yes. Take my word for it."[121] Wisconsin representative John William Byrnes (R-WI) did the math and concluded the same thing. For a man earning minimum wage and facing the costs of working, his family got more through welfare.[122] Even Nixon pointed to welfare as "economic pressure to split apart."[123]

On the other hand, conservatives saw a post-*King* world in which *male* dependence was actively encouraged by AFDC policies. Daniel Patrick Moynihan described a "vast dependent population of female-headed families, and a shadow population made up of the presumably absent fathers" living on welfare.[124] Conservative critics who imagined a shadow population of boyfriends who were dependent on women who received welfare saw this situation as financially and morally untenable. Stanford scholar Roger Freeman testified before the Senate Finance Committee that many fathers of welfare recipients "prefer to move in with another AFDC mother and live off her grant, at least for 9 or 10 months, when his own child is born and he swaps girlfriends with another man," a situation Freeman thought possible only because "man in the home" laws were "forbidden by the Dept. of HEW and the courts, leaving welfare rolls wide open."[125] Freeman also argued in congressional hearings that traditionally a man tried to avoid getting his girlfriend pregnant, but that his caution would disappear "if he knows that he not only will not have to accept financial responsibility but that a child will enable her to get a dependable monthly income from the government."[126] Russell B. Long (D-LA), the chairman of the Senate Finance Committee and the son of Huey Long, queried, "why should [a father] give up his freedom and accept the burdens that go with marriage and the status of a husband if the result is going to be a large loss of overall income?"[127] John Peter O'Brien, the supervisor of Milwaukee's Department of Public Welfare referred to these men as "weekenders" who "on the surface desert their family, come back for weekend visits, but . . . let the taxpayers of the U.S. Government support their children instead of doing the supporting themselves."[128] Rather than selflessly leaving for the sake of his family under unfair welfare regulations, as liberals believed, welfare critics argued that untrustworthy men saw welfare as an incentive to have children and then escape their thick breadwinning obligations.

For conservatives in Congress, the men who were allowed to slither away from their responsibilities because of *King* were again conspicuously black. Freeman immediately followed his discussion of fathers swapping welfare girlfriends with an addendum that such a situation "explains to a large extent the appalling break-down among low-income Negro families."[129] He then noted that half of welfare families were black and casually cited Moynihan, who had already famously raised the specter of the black matriarch in 1965, for confirmation. Moynihan had not turned his attention away from the African American family by the early 1970s. In his own account of "the vast dependent population," he noted, "the racial and ethnic imbalance of the dependent population became unmistakable." He then attributed "the intensity of racial conflict" in the 1969 New York mayoral election to a welfare family's ability to earn an "income at least equal to and probably that of the average New York family."[130] Thus ideas about race certainly still inflected conservatives' approach to welfare reform.

FAP's bumpy trajectory began in the House, which tried to address the issue of the absent father through legislation that would provide financial support to preserve the two-parent household. In the House version of FAP, one of the major innovations of the bill was to extend the AFDC-Unemployed Parent benefit, which had been passed in twenty-three states over the course of the 1960s, to all states.[131] The benefit, also known as AFDC-U, supplemented families whose father earned less than $2,000 a year working fewer than thirty-five hours a week.[132] Advocates of the AFDC-U benefit envisioned it as the necessary bridge between underemployment and the idealized patriarchal family structure. FAP would extend this benefit to families with fathers to all states, enshrining it in federal law.

Along with federally establishing this benefit, however, FAP would impose strict federal penalties on fathers who left despite provisions that enabled them to stay with their families in the midst of unemployment. Once they offered financial incentives for underemployed fathers to stay with their families, congressmen and women identified any father who left as simply unwilling to support his family. Such a decision seemed morally inexcusable, and Congress arranged to punish these men. These penalties included significant liens against a father's federal entitlements, ranging from veteran benefits to tax refunds to social security. FAP could also impose a fine of up to $1,000.[133] The legislation would moreover make desertion a federal crime punishable with jail time. Elliot L. Richardson, the secretary of HEW, extolled FAP for "provisions for fulfilling a Federal plan against a deserting father."[134]

Freeman testified: "About two million fathers have left the families they spawned to the tender care of AFDC and most of them contribute nothing. . . . Parental failure to support should be made a federal offense—because federal money is involved." Such penalties were supposed to hold men responsible for their children when they had the means to do so but left their families anyway.

Such penalties were intended to reduce childbearing. Some FAP supporters resisted any coyness in the first place, stating outright, "when you establish to their satisfaction that the long arm of this Government can reach out and get them and make them pay to support those families, we might be able to make some of these fathers interested in family planning as well as some of these mothers."[135] Similarly Wilbur Mills, who earlier lamented the way AFDC broke up families, claimed the provision holding men responsible to the federal government for their children's welfare debt acted "as a brake upon parental desertion and births out of wedlock, two of the most significant problems that plague the present AFDC program."[136] Moynihan too called for "a sharp curtailment of the freedom now by and large enjoyed by low-income groups to produce children they cannot support."[137]

The system also enlisted welfare recipients to punish their deserting partners. The laws "would require . . . mothers to cooperate in locating a deserting spouse, or be subject to losing all benefits."[138] In addition to their cooperation locating former spouses, applicant mothers were " 'expected' to bring a support action."[139] To enable all women to do so, the national government proposed founding "regional blood labs to establish paternity."[140] Women who did not identify and then prosecute their former husbands could lose the benefits. FAP advocates also endorsed this tactic even though some critics objected that pressing charges posed a threat to "women from errant husbands or ex-husbands for divulging to the authorities their husbands' addresses."[141] Such regulations would potentially purge women from welfare rolls through their relationships with men. These rules were certainly punitive, but the House at least acknowledged the reality of employment opportunities for black and white men alike when it made AFDC-U available to all families.

Though FAP passed in the House with 140 Democrats and 103 Republicans supporting and 84 Democrats and 71 Republicans against, it got stalled in the Senate Finance Committee in the summer of 1970.[142] Committee senators worried that with AFDC-U, fathers would have an incentive to turn down work that they were offered or that men who worked part time would bring home more cash with the benefit than a man who worked full time. The senators worked out elaborate schemes on behalf of fathers whereby they would only accept part-time work or would make significant efforts to get fired in order to retain their benefit.[143]

To accommodate the Senate Finance Committee's fears that fathers would turn down work, the administration dropped the AFDC-U benefit in its revision while retaining the new penalties against fathers.[144] Critics speculated that with the elimination of AFDC-U and any matching federal funds, the twenty-three states that did offer AFDC-U would also drop the benefit.[145] The administration did not drop the liens against federal entitlements, however. The elimination of AFDC-U meant that the strict penalties against fathers who left no longer met the original putative purpose of keeping underemployed fathers in the home. Instead, the measures against fathers operated only to punish and control underemployed men. Despite the revisions, the Senate Finance Committee never sent FAP to the Senate, and it was deferred to the Ninety-Second Congress.

After scrapping the AFDC-U benefit and keeping penalties against poor fathers, the Senate Finance Committee attempted to restore substitute father laws through a Social Security amendment, which made the committee members' objectives for retaining the liens and other penalties unmistakable.[146] When challenged to explain how such a rule could be restored in light of the Supreme Court ruling in *King v. Smith*, Senator Russell Long "brushed aside any constitutional questions that might be involved" and stated, "it's not what you do, it's the way you do it."[147] Long, who thought of himself as a populist, like his father Huey Long, was crucial in defeating liberal hopes for FAP. He had already taken a particularly obstructive position by pressuring the administration to strip the AFDC-U benefit from FAP and helping prevent FAP from reaching a vote on the Senate floor.[148] To secure a second generation of substitute father laws, moreover, the Senate Finance Committee introduced a provision that would have prohibited the Office of Economic Opportunity Legal Services from financing lawsuits that would challenge federal policy on welfare. Long suggested that a broader range of factors would be considered to determine whether a man acted as a substitute father, including whether he was the father of a half sibling or visited the house frequently. Nonetheless, Long's assurance that the Senate did not intend to "go back to a situation where the family was pushed off welfare if the mother 'from time to time was "friendly" with' a male consort" was disingenuous.[149] As seen in the case of Sylvester Smith, such provisions left wide latitude for kicking families off the welfare rolls. This proposal only failed once liberals in Congress threatened to hold up an increase in Social Security payments if the substitute father provisions, along with several others, were not dropped.[150]

After this failed attempt to restore substitute father laws, FAP was unsuccessfully reintroduced one last time in the Ninety-Second Congress. Critics from both sides continued to lambast the bill. The National Welfare Rights Organization referred to FAP as an "Illfare Plan" and denounced the federal liens, $1,000 fine, and potential jail time all as excessive punishments.[151] NWRO activists also objected to the impossibly low guaranteed income and punitive work requirements.[152] Moynihan referred to all the attempts to pass FAP in the Ninety-Second Congress as a "farce."[153]

Finally, FAP was officially defeated in October 1972. All the restrictions put on FAP could not convince conservatives that enshrining welfare as a right rather than a privilege was in any way desirable.[154] FAP's failure was a double-edged sword. FAP could have enshrined a minimum income as a fundamental human right in the United States, which would have provided some level of protection for many women and children. No other minimum income plan achieved this level of success. In other ways, however, its failure was a victory. The prescribed minimum income was humiliatingly low, and with it, the federal government could have imposed broader and more powerful restrictions against poor men.[155]

But legislators' efforts against poor fathers and their partners remained aggressive, especially in comparison to the federal government's relative neglect of other men who failed to provide support until the mid-1980s. Welfare rights activists noted and objected to Congress's protection of deserting fathers whose children were not on welfare. As the NWRO had pointed out during debate on FAP, federal law would punish fathers for failing to pay child support *only* if their children were on welfare. The NWRO demanded that the federal government "attempt to secure support from absent parents and spouses by referring such cases for action under state law which *apply equally to all persons*."[156] Instead the policies targeted the poor fathers who were the least likely to be able to provide support for their children.

The new measures innovated by the federal and state governments affected poor men of all races. Unlike substitute father laws, these federal measures did not depend on social workers to carry them out. They operated more universally on the basis of participation in the welfare system. Alabama, Connecticut, Pennsylvania, and Illinois, among other states, forced mothers to release the names and addresses of fathers when applying for welfare and to cooperate with the state in trying to attain support under the 1950 Notification of Law Enforcement Officials Amendment to the Social Security Act.[157] Once again, women faced pressure to ally with the state against their former partners. In addition, three federal policies targeted only fathers whose children were on welfare: these fathers could be tracked via their Social Security numbers, they could be charged with a federal crime, and a lien could be taken on their federal benefits. For instance, in 1965, Congress implemented a rule that allowed courts to find the address of a deserting parent using Social Security or the Internal Revenue Service (IRS) in certain circumstances. In the details of the law, those circumstances applied exclusively to the fathers of children on welfare or who had applied for welfare benefits. In fact, Social Security was only allowed to give this information to "a welfare agency or court on condition that information be transmitted through a welfare agency, that an actual public assistance case be involved and a court order for support [had] been issued."[158] Such provisions of course excluded fathers whose children were not receiving assistance. Over the course of the next ten years, Congress rejected bills that gave mothers who were not on welfare access to the IRS or Social Security Locating Service, citing fathers' privacy rights as their rationale for restricting these locator services. Similarly, Congress opted not to make defaults on child support payments a federal crime or take liens on federal benefits for non-welfare fathers.[159]

A 1975 Social Security Act amendment remedied some of these differences but still disproportionately targeted the fathers of children on welfare. This new legislation ordered each state to establish its own child support enforcement agency, increased the federal presence in procuring child support, and ostensibly aimed to include all fathers who neglected to provide support. Most importantly, this law finally allowed non-welfare mothers to make use of the federal government's Parent Locator Service, despite continued concern about non-welfare fathers' privacy.[160] A committee report on the bill declared that its aim was to increase the collection of support for families "not on welfare as well as those on welfare."[161] Nonetheless the text that followed this inclusive statement focused almost entirely on the problem of AFDC children.[162] In the brief paragraph that addressed families not on welfare, the report stated that the bill would deal with the problem of AFDC fathers' neglect and reluctantly conceded that "the problem of nonsupport is broader than the AFDC rolls."[163]

Legislators clearly intended these rules to benefit taxpayers rather than mothers or children. Mothers and children received a shamefully modest "pay-through" of a father's payment until the welfare benefit had been fully repaid.

In the first year of the new policy, mothers and children got only 40 percent of the first fifty dollars collected from the father.[164] The percentage of pay-through remained low thereafter. Instead a biological father's child support would go directly to the state to offset the costs of AFDC payments.[165] In 1981, the chief of the Illinois Bureau of Child Support hired researchers to determine how to improve Illinois's performance in regard to the collection of child support compared to other states. In the resulting report, the researchers noted, "this requirement, like the AFDC centered directives of earlier years emphasizes the revenue generating approach rather than the concept of parental responsibility."[166] By 1985, the system had collected $6.8 billion from fathers of children on AFDC.[167] By 1999, $82.8 million was collected from fathers of children on Temporary Assistance for Needy Families (TANF), the successor to AFDC, in Illinois, but only $6.7 million of this "passed through" to families.[168]

Finally in 1984, the Congressional Caucus on Women's Issues championed an imperfect law where all fathers finally faced the same penalties in law—just as the NWRO had called for over a decade before—even though fathers of children on welfare continued to face disproportionate punishment in practice. When this law was enacted in 1985, states had to garnish wages and to put liens on the property of all fathers.[169] But instances of imprisonment, for example, disproportionately affected less privileged fathers. By this point, imprisonment for failure to pay support was rare, but prosecution remained at the discretion of local officials. Only fathers who refused to pay support were supposed to face jail sentences, but in many cases, courts imprisoned fathers who were not able to pay. In particular, courts' failure to determine a father's real income, judges' assumption that a father could earn at least a minimum wage and that he would work full time year round, state legislatures' mandated minimum awards, and the lack of counsel for indigent fathers all led poor fathers to be imprisoned more frequently than more privileged fathers.[170] Moreover some evidence suggests that counties with more poor fathers sometimes pursued jail sentences disproportionately. In Michigan in the 1970s, the county with the relatively well-off cities of Ann Arbor and Ypsilanti jailed very few men who failed to pay child support even though the county overall had a 44 percent default rate. In contrast, the county that contained working-class Flint jailed significantly more men despite a much lower default rate of only 26 percent.[171]

*   *   *

In the postwar period and beyond, state and federal policy makers attempted to capitalize on male sexuality as an easier and more socially acceptable means of stemming the dependence of women and children. The most pernicious element of this system, however, was the way in which it set men and women against one another. Laws regulating men operated in tandem with punitive measures against women to limit mothers' access to welfare rights or to make their claim on those rights more costly or dangerous. Lawmakers and bureaucrats particularly made use of cruel and stringent regulations of fathers to control poor women of color. Then innovations conceived of to punish black men were used against all poor men. These twinned regulations of male and female sexuality accomplished the double work lawmakers intended. They both punished working-class sexuality and eliminated the government's responsibility to care for women and children. In effect, the regulations tried to enforce the thick breadwinner-homemaker model of family on the poor, which was otherwise being broken down through no-fault divorce and state ERAs for families not on welfare.

CHAPTER 5

Sham Marriages, Real Love, and Immigration Reform

In *United States v. Windsor*, the 2013 case that famously overturned the Defense of Marriage Act, Justice Anthony Kennedy ruminated on the ways in which the federal government may legitimately refuse to recognize a marriage. He concluded that while the federal government could not constitutionally deny a same-sex marriage granted by one of the fifty states, it *could* deny a couple who married fraudulently in order to "procur[e] an alien's admission [to the United States] as an immigrant."[1] Legally Kennedy made the exclusion of a scamming immigrant more legitimate than excluding a gay partner. With this case, Kennedy sought to establish his liberal bona fides and his legal expertise even as he orchestrated a sea change in the meaning of marriage otherwise.

While marriage fraud became a possible means of procuring citizenship in the nineteenth century, it did not become the frightening specter that Justice Kennedy evoked until after the Hart-Celler Act, officially known as the Immigration and Nationality Act, had established family relationships and employment as the two dominant possible means of entry in 1965.[2] The INS and then Congress defined a "fraudulent" marriage much more loosely after the law's passage than they had prior to 1965; in effect, government agencies designated an increasing number of marriages as fraudulent. Culminating with the 1986 Immigration Marriage Fraud Amendments, the federal government used the specter of marriage fraud to limit how many immigrant spouses gained permanent residence in the United States.

What caused the government to fear immigrant marriage soon after Hart-Celler? Following changes to both welfare and state marriage laws, government agencies worried that immigrant spouses would become dependent on federal welfare benefits. The reduction of husbands' thick breadwinning obligations recounted in Chapter 2 could leave divorced immigrant wives impoverished, but some welfare policies allowed immigrant spouses to claim federal benefits. In order to prevent indigent immigrant wives from getting welfare, the government began to use the specter of marriage fraud to deport some of these immigrant spouses instead. Marriage fraud was sold as a gender-neutral policy but nonetheless focused on women as the recipients of the most controversial welfare benefits. In essence, immigrant wives' expanding need for and access to welfare caused the government to see fraud where they previously had not.

In the 1970s, state governments seemed happy to set men free from the obligation to be breadwinners—so long as their wives and children would not become dependent on the government. Government officials believed that middle-class wives would support themselves, but welfare offered a reason to retain some men's breadwinning obligations. Congress and the Supreme Court eliminated the suitable home and substitute father rules that had previously barred many black women's access to welfare, but other government agents still tried to hold the partners of welfare recipients responsible for these women and children. Immigrant spouses—also imagined as not white—seemed similarly likely to go on welfare. The INS and then Congress turned to deportation to stem the threat that immigrant women would join the welfare rolls. Race and dependence therefore remained central concerns in the regulation of marriage.

At the same time, however, political economy and race were not the only sources of anxiety about immigrant marriages. In the call for immigrants to marry only for love—and for their marriages to be better than citizens' marriages—was a bitterness or wistfulness for the fault divorce era that had just passed by. Marriages between immigrants and citizens became some of the only marriages on which the government could impose "thick expectations," in the words of legal scholar Mary Anne Case.[3] Similar to couples in domestic partnerships, a citizen and an immigrant who chose to marry had to prove the legitimacy of their relationship by cohabiting, commingling finances, and consummating the marriage. In contrast, for citizen couples, a marriage certificate alone bestowed all of the benefits of marriage even if the couple lived apart, kept separate bank accounts, did not reveal their marriage to friends and family, and did not remain sexually exclusive. After the changes to divorce law in the 1970s, including the introduction of no-fault divorce and the systematic breakdown of breadwinning and homemaking, all citizen marriages were bona fide. Nearly at the same moment that white middle-class couples gained the privilege of these thin expectations for marriage, the government increasingly mandated thick expectations for marriages between a citizen and an immigrant spouse. Unlike citizen spouses, marriages between a citizen and an immigrant had to be "good" marriages.[4]

Regulating Immigration and Marriage

In 1855, Congress established that a free white woman of any nationality became a U.S. citizen upon marrying an American man if she met naturalization requirements.[5] But people of color and immigrant husbands did not have the same access to naturalization via marriage. Husbands could not give citizenship to African women until 1870, Asian women were excluded, and American wives could not offer their husbands the gift of naturalization.[6] In these early years, women immigrants posed fewer political problems than male immigrants. Only male immigrants engendered fears about employment competition. Most restrictions on females immigrating were based on morality—particularly prostitution—or race. Prostitutes threatened to undermine the nation's ethical values; women of other races threatened to produce nonwhite children. Often these two categories converged in legislation. Congress effectually defined all Chinese women as prostitutes and excluded them as dangers to the nation in the 1875 Page Act. Congress dealt with other prostitutes with the 1891 provision that allowed immigration restriction on the basis of moral turpitude.[7] American wives could not bestow citizenship on even white immigrant husbands until passage of the Cable Act in 1922.[8]

Nonetheless, with this 1855 congressional act, the United States added an incentive to marry beyond those that already existed—that sexual intercourse was illegal outside of marriage; that the children produced outside of marriage became bastards; and that men and women alike depended on a household exchange of labor. Not long thereafter, government officials began noting incidents of marriage fraud. White prostitutes could marry to evade moral restrictions and seemingly did. In 1909, the INS found the attorney general lackadaisical about the problem of marriage fraud: "the bureau pressed so hard on the attorney general of the United States to agree that he conceded that a marriage joined 'merely for the purpose of evading the immigration laws' might be invalid."[9] Though it was lax, enforcement had begun. Immigration law did allow Chinese American men to bring in immigrant wives. Because it was difficult to travel to China to meet and marry a Chinese woman, many Chinese American men relied on matchmaking from afar. But Congress feared that marriage fraud would allow Chinese prostitutes to come into the United State en masse. In 1924, Congress outlawed proxy marriages and made no exceptions to racial quotas for spouses.[10] For several years thereafter, Congress assumed that racial exclusion largely solved the problem of immigration fraud.

During the Great Depression Congress proposed a new bill, later referred to as the Gigolo Act of 1937, that would protect women from predatory men who married them only to gain citizenship. This was of course an era of cracking down on immigrants generally, as they were considered an unnecessary drain on the nation's scant resources.[11] But the bill's sponsors suggested that such a "gigolo" could drain an individual woman's scant resources as well. In fact, the chairman of the congressional committee declared that his concern was first for the women involved. He noted, "gigolos . . . practically rob the poor box of the girls who have been saving their money for years and each one believes that she has secured a husband who not only deserts her but takes her money."[12] The chairman was also angry that these men retained their citizenship status. Even when these women had their marriages annulled, he explained, there was nothing that could be done to withdraw citizenship from their husbands. The new act took a much different tack than past immigration policies, which had identified fraud as largely visible in a person's race.

The increase in soldier marriages to foreign nationals during World War II further loosened explicit racial restrictions on immigration, which introduced even further fears about marriage fraud. The War Brides Act of 1945 and the Soldiers' Bride Act of 1947 enabled soldiers to bring wives home without qualifying under the immigration quota.[13] Then the 1952 McCarren Walter Act eased up on Asian exclusions from immigration and also allowed all spouses to come into the country without regard to quotas.[14] While racial discrimination nonetheless persisted, the new system privileged the rights of spouses.

Nonetheless, the U.S. Department of State worried about the practice of "de facto" marriage in Hong Kong. In China, de facto marriages were the equivalent of a common-law marriage, since registering marriages was a relatively new practice. If an American spouse hoped to extend his or her American citizenship to his or her wife, the couple often procured a brand-new marriage license in Hong Kong despite a long-established marriage. Or so they said. The State Department had its doubts since, in its opinion, Hong Kong did not verify the identity of these potential spouses sufficiently. An alleged spouse could turn out to be a concubine or even a blood relative who could not qualify under the overtaxed quota for siblings and parents. The consulate general reported to the State Department that it had uncovered a de facto marriage that turned out to involve a brother and his sister.[15] In 1961, in the INS's internal publication, the supervisory investigator of the central office described the use of marriage to circumvent the national origins quotas in other countries as well. In particular he identified Greek, Portuguese, and Spanish nationals as the common perpetuators of marriage fraud due to these countries' small quotas.[16]

Some government officials also feared that marriage fraud would be carried out in the name of Cold War politics. In his opus, *Masters of Deceit*, J. Edgar Hoover concentrated one of his case studies on a "promising young Communist" who married a Hungarian woman who also seemed "promising Party material." By arrangement the two divorced three years later. The same promising young man then married another foreign Communist in Elkton, Maryland. Finally, when the loyal party member met a woman he truly wished to marry, a Communist lawyer procured an annulment for him on the basis that his second wife had violated a prenuptial agreement to join his church.[17]

These guilty spouses met a rigorous definition of fraud established by immigration officials that contrasted sharply with the definition of a genuine marriage. Marriage was understood to be when "the two parties have undertaken to establish a life together and assume certain duties and obligations."[18] More literally, this meant that a couple intended the marriage to be genuine, consummated the marriage, lived together, and presented themselves as married. Immigrant and citizen spouses had thick obligations, but they were no thicker than those of any other husband or wife. By contrast, court cases illustrated this rigorous definition of fraud. In the 1953 case *Lutwak v. United States*, multiple couples were convicted of fraud after they married and fulfilled none of the thick obligations of marriage. Three veterans had been paid to go to Paris and marry three Poles living there. They agreed to wed solely for the Poles to gain admission to the country and planned to dissolve the marriages immediately. When the couples returned to the United States, they went their separate ways. The court found that none of the couples had consummated the marriage; none lived together; one spouse particularly presented himself as single in society; and all proceeded to try to dissolve the marital ties.

Even a more ambiguous case did not raise the ire of the courts in ways we might expect. In 1962, Adria Gonzalez and Jose Diogo were accused of arranging marriages for Jose Diogo, Domingo Das Canas Costa, and Manuel Vilanova Gonzalez who allegedly married for citizenship rights. For instance, Adria Gonzalez contacted a woman named Emma Mercado and offered her a trip to Portugal. While she was there, Mercado would meet Costa whom she would marry. In Mercado's words, the arrangement ensured that "the future will be more rosy for me, that I wouldn't have to work anymore.'" Mercado and Costa married in Portugal, sexually consummated the marriage, and traveled back to the United States. Other than the trip, no money exchanged hands. Almost two years later, however, Costa won a divorce in New York (where the only grounds for divorce was adultery). At the same time, Adria Gonzalez arranged more conventionally fraudulent marriages for Jose Diogo and Manuel Vilanova Gonzalez. Their wives received a $250 payment; they did not consummate their marriages; they did not live with their spouses. They almost immediately pursued divorce proceedings.

Mercado was considered blameless in this account (though she would not be today), but the court considered whether Costa and the other husbands had made false statements by declaring themselves married. The U.S. government pursued criminal charges for false statements, false statements in an application for a visa, and conspiracy to defraud the United States. At stake was not deportation, but up to five years in jail. Nonetheless, in his ruling, Judge Waterman rejected the government's charges. He declared that in fact Costa had not lied by declaring himself married since it was difficult to say whether the marriage was a sham or not. But the judge said that even Diogo and Manuel Vilanova Gonzalez, who had not in fact consummated their marriages and whose wives had been paid, had not lied when they declared themselves married. Because of course, legally, the accused were married. If each husband had answered to the contrary that he was not married, this too would have constituted a lie. In a dissent to Waterman's ruling, Judge Clark declared that his colleagues imagined "knowingly making a false claim against the government" was impossible. But even Clark thought Costa could not be determined to be lying given that he had consummated the marriage.[19] Judge Weinfeld, of the Southern District of New York, ruled on a related case in 1962. He too determined the government had not proven its case of false statements. The assistant U.S. attorney general disputed the ruling, arguing that a California judge had already held that a sham marriage was not a marriage. Weinfeld responded that the California ruling was not binding upon him.[20] Thus, even in the early 1960s, judges were slow to identify a marriage as fraudulent.

In 1965, Congress would largely dismantle the previous race-based immigration system and thus disorder the uneasy accord the INS had with immigration fraud heretofore. The Hart-Celler legislation ended the system of national origins quotas that had for four decades enshrined a racial hierarchy of immigrants, with the lowest on the ladder not allowed in at all. In its place, Hart-Celler vaulted two new values to the apex of American life—skilled labor and family reunification. The decision by Congress to privilege those with sought-after skills was only mildly contested. Family reunification was even more widely embraced. While husbands had long been able to give their spouses and children citizenship—and even wives had sometimes been able to do so since 1922—Hart-Celler extended these patriarchal privileges to a person's parents and siblings. It also offered permanent residents non-quota naturalization for their spouses and children. Finally it allowed in family members—spouses and children—who had previously been excluded due to being deemed feebleminded, insane, or epileptic. In other words, the bill expanded who was in the household but retained the logic of the household.

The legislation's sponsors assumed that the citizens who brought immigrant family members to the United States would be breadwinners. As advocates of what Robert Self has called breadwinner liberalism, they argued that it was possible to expand the household because a breadwinner would take care of dependent immigrants.[21] New York representative Emanuel Celler, for example, suggested that the majority of the immigrants accepted under these new rules would be elderly parents, wives, and children rather than workers who would take jobs away from American men. Celler moreover cited the provision of immigration law that would continue even under Hart-Celler— that each candidate would have to satisfy the public charge test that had long been the centerpiece of immigration law.[22] Only those citizens capable of taking care of wives, parents, and children—breadwinners—could bring family members into the country. The then-assistant secretary for labor and Self's quintessential breadwinner liberal Daniel Patrick Moynihan echoed these defenses. He claimed that "half the immigrants to the United States these days are women or children or older persons who don't compete for jobs with anyone."[23] Since skilled workers could not get in without employment, the immigrants posing a threat of joining the welfare rolls were household members, and they posed no threat as the dependents of a breadwinner.[24]

In 1965, most ordinary citizens also seemed sanguine about admitting these household members. In a survey sent out for the Cleveland hearings on immigration reform, Congress asked Ohio constituents how the nation should prioritize alien applicants for admission according to five categories: relatives of United States citizens, skilled workers, relatives of aliens living in United States, semiskilled workers, and victims of communist persecution. Of the thirty-two surveys Congress received back, twenty-seven ranked relatives of U.S. citizens as either first or second. If the surveyed placed these relatives second, it was usually behind victims of communist prosecution.[25] Even a man who opposed immigration of any kind during periods of unemployment higher than 3.5 percent made an exception for families with a first-degree blood relationship.[26] Selma Samols of the Women's International League for Peace and Freedom described the legislation as the "most humane document" because it recognized the inviolability of the family.[27] As Michigan governor George Romney succinctly put it, "Firmly, I believe that our present quota system should be abolished and that people from other countries should be allowed entrance on the basis of ability, skills and character, with special emphasis on uniting families."[28] Protecting the household, even a household expanded past the nuclear family, seemingly fit into the scheme of American values. As before with the frustrated 1909 missive from the INS, the federal government did not worry much about the problem of marriage fraud.

But other nascent changes were brewing that would vastly alter the perception of the immigration reform after 1965. First of all the Great Society expanded the vast system of welfare benefits reserved for women and children alone. Foremost among these benefits was Aid to Dependent Children, which became Aid to Families with Dependent Children. Following the civil rights movement, almost all women had claim to, if not access to, these welfare benefits. Quickly thereafter, many of these women were imagined to be women of color even though white women continued to be the majority of welfare recipients. Second, marriage law reform on the state level left divorced husbands and wives without the alimony that they nominally could have counted on heretofore. Third, the economy had entered a period of decline when breadwinning was increasingly difficult for all husbands. These changes in the political economy registered among the few objectors to the Hart-Celler Act and predominated thereafter.

Though many dissenters wanted to preserve the racial order that Hart-Celler threatened to upend, opponents to Hart-Celler feared that immigrants would introduce new welfare costs. For example, a doctor who examined potential immigrants at the embassy in Manila recommended that a family only be allowed to give citizenship status to two children in order to prevent certain national groups from profiting from the lack of a restriction.[29] Other citizens who wrote into Congress disliked the prospect of a growing welfare roll in any form. Fred Bryant, a manufacturer's representative from Downey, California, argued that the country was already burdened with citizens on relief or welfare. He thought an influx of new potential welfare recipients was dangerous in an era of 5 to 6 percent unemployment and increasing automation.[30] Similarly, Helen I. Loken, from Eau Claire, Wisconsin, worried about the welfare and relief rolls.[31] Robert W. Wayman, from Muncie, Indiana, also wanted to limit all immigration because of "excessive unemployment and . . . mounting welfare costs."[32] Though only a few dissenters believed that family-based immigration introduced potential welfare recipients to the country, such anxieties found their way into official INS policy and congressional action thereafter.

The INS began conceptualizing ways to keep newly admitted family members from becoming the responsibility of the United States, and one means was to make the thick expectations of marriage even thicker. By the mid-1970s, the INS used much less evidence than courts had in the 1950s and 1960s to establish a case of fraud. Typical was the case of Sang Chul Bark and his wife, whose marriage differed greatly from the marriage in question in *Lutwak*. Bark and his wife had met and been "sweethearts" in Korea for several years until Bark's wife moved to the United States as a permanent alien. In 1968 Bark himself went to the United States as first a business visitor and then a student. Reunited, the Barks married in Hawaii in May of 1969. Bark's wife applied for a permanent resident visa for her husband.[33]

After their marriage, however, trouble began rather quickly. Bark was displeased that his "wife could and did leave as she pleased when they were together." The two quarreled and then separated. This brought Bark's petition under consideration for marriage fraud. The immigration judge looked at this case, which in many ways did not resemble the *Lutwak* case at all. The couple had known each other for many years, dated in their native Korea, and lived together as man and wife in the United States. Seemingly no money changed hands. In other words, they married "for love" rather than immigration purposes. But the immigration judge highlighted two basic qualities of the Bark's marriage: first, the couple had conflicting testimony about how much time they spent together, and second, the couple did not live together at the time of the trial. The immigration judge ruled that the marriage was a sham.

Bark sued to prevent his deportation. He and his wife claimed that what they had was a good marriage, but that even good marriages ended. And luckily for Bark, the United States Court of Appeals for the Ninth Circuit agreed. First, the ruling rejected the idea that the INS could consider how much time a couple spent together. Married couples separated for many reasons, they said, citing obligations or opportunities related to the military, education, employment, illness, poverty, and domestic difficulties. Establishing a quota of time that a couple would need to spend together would violate the right to privacy enshrined in the famous birth control case *Griswold v. Connecticut* in 1965. If citizens were thus protected from these requirements, then so must be residents and aliens: the ruling established that "aliens cannot be required to have more conventional or more successful marriages than citizens." Finally, the ruling argued that the immigration judge and Board of Immigration Appeals considered the wrong question—whether the couple still lived together did not matter; what their intentions were at the point of marriage was the only significant query. The reasoning for this case was echoed in the 1980 case *Matter of Boromand*.[34] Together the two cases established a burden of proof for fraud that deeply frustrated the INS and citizens who considered the government too lax on immigrant spouses.

The Immigration Marriage Fraud Amendments

If the Ninth Circuit had stymied the INS in *Bark v. INS*, Congress granted the INS much of its power back when it passed the Immigration Marriage Fraud Amendments in 1986. This legislation barred spouses from gaining citizenship or permanent residence if they had been married for less than two years. Congress was already in the midst of rethinking immigration policy in 1986. The 1986 Immigration Reform and Control Act (IRCA) both imposed sanctions against employers for hiring undocumented immigrants and offered amnesty to undocumented immigrants who had resided in the United States since at least 1982. The legislation actually did less than Congress represented it doing—historian Roger Daniels suggests that the word "knowingly" in the law allowed employers to continue to hire immigrants without danger to their freedom or livelihood. Moreover, the law itself prevented warrantless searches of outdoor working spaces, vastly limiting enforcement. In essence IRCA provided already-gutted sanctions.[35] In contrast, the Immigration Marriage Fraud Amendments did more than Congress represented it doing. Though ostensibly it would only target the perpetrators of sham marriages, in reality it targeted a much broader pool of spouses and built full enforcement into its design.

In 1986, Congress considered an amendment to the Immigration and Nationality Act that would reorder how men and women gave their spouses citizenship. In hearings in September of 1986, Congress expressed frustration that even though section 241(c) of the act assumed that any marriage that lasted less than two years was entered into fraudulently, courts like the Ninth Circuit had rejected the premise that a marriage must be viable for a spouse to qualify for citizenship or permanent status.[36] Foremost among the changes that the Marriage Fraud Amendments would offer was a mandatory two-year conditional status for the recently married. This meant essentially that the burden would be on the spouses to prove any marriage that lasted less than two years was not an instance of marriage fraud. If he or she could not prove this, the immigrant spouse would be deported. By holding that any marriage that lasted less than two years was not bona fide, the new law assumed thick expectations for marriage for immigrants, despite evidence to the contrary that native marriages ended just as quickly for other reasons. Accusations of marriage fraud allowed the INS to get rid of these spouses that might receive public aid.

The hearings in Congress on the Immigration Marriage Fraud Amendments dwelled on cases where much more deception was evident than in the *Bark* case. The language of the hearings was stark: there was marriage fraud, and there were "bona fide" marriages. Alan C. Nelson, the commissioner of the Immigration and Naturalization Service, alleged that elaborate conspiracies arranged by a set of marriage fraud professionals, often referred to as arrangers or brokers, were behind the majority of instances of marriage fraud. These brokers had professionalized much more than Adria Gonzalez, who had arranged a few marriages for friends and acquaintances. For instance, one lawyer in New York was disbarred because of his role in facilitating 260 quick divorces for sham marriages.[37] In Chicago, a "ring" of eight marriage fraud brokers specialized in marriage fraud between Pakistani men and women on welfare. In Newark, another marriage fraud broker had set up two hundred sham marriages using fake New York marriage licenses.[38] An operation in Belle Glade, Florida, was caught paying $10,000 to single mothers to marry immigrants in a funeral parlor.[39]

The hearings alleged that these schemes extended beyond the border. In the Caribbean, the embassy fretted that marriage fraud had reached "folkloric proportions."[40] In the Dominican Republic, "marriage arrangers" also served as travel agents. An American citizen would receive an all-expenses-paid trip to the Dominican Republic, stay in accommodations for the weekend, marry an aspiring citizen on Saturday, and receive an additional $300 to $400 fee.[41] Nelson and other experts spoke of fees ranging from $3,000 to $5,000. More troubling to Nelson though were those cases where the fee could reach as high as $20,300 for marriages that included services from attorneys and an accord that ensured that the citizen would not be responsible for any of his or her spouse's debts.[42] In general, government officials believed most brokers were sophisticated members of the organized crime world, earning up to $100,000 a year in marriage fraud alone.[43] Of course the line between a ring and an individual could be blurry. One organization, characterized as a "ring" in the press, actually ran a bit of a family business: one woman, her husband, and their two daughters entered into fourteen separate sham marriages.[44] This family resembled Adria Gonzalez more than many of the other brokers Congress identified.

The hearings also suggested that marriage fraud entrepreneurs carefully prepared spouses for interrogation from the INS. They helped to create the illusion of a thick marriage. Couples were given "crib sheets" of questions the INS commonly asked and then were coached by an attorney. The couple would exchange apartment keys and open a joint bank account. The new spouse would be introduced to landlords and neighbors to make the couple look bona fide.[45] In the Caribbean, brokers supplied enthusiastic witnesses and a paste wedding cake to appear in photographs.[46] Brokers would also supply basics like a fake address, a doctor to do the necessary blood work, a clergyman, and a notary public. Sometimes brokers employed a runner to accompany nervous citizens to their weddings and ensure they recognized their spouses.[47]

According to the hearings, brokers also found willing citizens to marry immigrants. Chicago officials had noted that women on welfare were popular candidates. An anonymous embassy indicated that potential citizen spouses usually had less education, worked for lower wages, and were much younger than their immigrant spouses. Sometimes they did not even share a language, though experts disagreed about how much shared language was necessary for proving a bona fide relationship.[48] The embassy identified military men and members of cults as particularly likely to accept an offer from a marriage fraud broker.[49] A Canadian post suggested that lonely women also were potential candidates, and that they hoped the sham marriage would become a "real" marriage thereafter.[50] Still other participants were phantoms, men and women who had agreed to marry an immigrant and then abandoned the task suddenly. In these cases, a broker would replace them with an imposter. In other cases, brokers would begin with an imposter. To get these fake identities, one runner stole the identities of U.S. citizens through her high school yearbook, and another was a notary public who took them from income tax records.[51]

The congressional hearings particularly dwelled on citizens who unknowingly married someone seeking only citizenship. These men and women were akin to the victims of the Depression-era gigolos. For example, Patricia Beshara married a man in New York City, only to discover later on that he wanted only citizenship. He bragged to her that the INS could not get him if he remained with her for two years. Beshara went to the INS to try to get her husband deported. She complained that he had had twenty affairs, that he had broken her jaw, and that he stole all her money. The INS's response was that any marriage could "be like that."[52] For Beshara and Congress, this was unacceptable—at least for marriages that were not bona fide. In its coverage of the proposed legislation, the U.S. press highlighted cases where the immigrant spouse readily admitted to duping or making payments to his or her citizen spouse. In fact, Beshara was a popular figure in press coverage of the legislation.[53]

Nonetheless the rules for detecting marriage fraud did not reflect the circumstances of these highly publicized cases, and instead the proposed legislation broadened the definition of fraud way beyond these instances where the distinction between bona fide and sham seemed at least discernable. The proposed solution—that any marriage that lasted less than two years was a sham—was a blunt instrument that did not match the specific examples of fraud that its sponsors brought to Congress. Nor was staying together two years or more sufficient to prove a marriage bona fide.

The spirit of the legislation echoed INS's logic in *Bark v. INS*: immigrants *were* required to have better marriages than citizens. Though the legislation had stated that cohabitation, ownership of property jointly, filing of joint tax returns, insurance beneficiary forms, a shared bank account, and the birth of a child (provided that the couple could prove paternity) should be sufficient to prove a bona fide marriage for the still-married, these couples nonetheless had to submit to a marriage fraud interview, which could be invasive. The sponsors of the bill were not shy about the same invasions of marital privacy that had concerned the Ninth Circuit in *Bark v. INS*. Vernon D. Penner Jr. of the Bureau of Consular Affairs indicated that protecting both privacy and "the integrity of our visa" were potentially—and acceptably—not possible.[54] The interview purported to prove that a marriage was bona fide, but in the case of a divorce, even meeting these thick expectations was not sufficient.

Proving that a marriage had ended for "legitimate" reasons was designed to be exceedingly difficult in the proposed legislation.[55] When Assistant Attorney General John Bolton advised Ronald Reagan on whether to sign the bill into law, the only weakness Bolton identified in the bill was the difficulty in determining what constituted a "good cause" for terminating the marriage.[56] A divorce was, for all intents and purposes, a conviction of marriage fraud. He advised Reagan to sign the bill anyway. Jules E. Coven, in his testimony against the new law, stated, "Quite candidly I must add that this presumption is regarded by the immigration bar as an extremely high hurdle and that no immigration lawyer I know would presume to attempt to overcome it unless thoroughly convinced of the validity of the marriage in question."[57]

There would be few means of convincing the INS, and even fulfilling thick obligations was not enough if the spouses only did so for a couple years. Obtaining a fault divorce was one way for the alien spouse to suggest that he or she at least was blameless in the divorce, but fault divorces were not even available in many states by 1986. These difficulties were so extensive that even victims of domestic violence could find themselves deported under the rubric of marriage fraud. Since spouses alone could file a petition with the INS, and they also had full power to withdraw a petition, citizen spouses would hold a great deal of power over immigrant spouses. A husband could keep his wife cowed by threatening to divorce her within two years, or withdrawing the petition. She could not leave an abusive situation if she wanted to remain in the United States.[58] In fact, reuniting was the only way that Congress laid out for a divorced couple to really restore the immigrant spouse's status. The legislation premised that as long as the initial intention for marriage was genuine, a couple could petition to have the deported spouse brought back on another conditional visa so long as the marriage resumed.[59] Moreover Congress insisted that no money needed to have changed hands in order to constitute fraud. Congress's report suggested that a marriage entered into as a favor was as dangerous, perhaps even more dangerous, than a marriage entered into for a small fee.[60] Even Nelson attributed much less pernicious motives to spouses than pure financial gain, including "feel[ing] sorry" for the person who would be deported, being pressured by friends or family, or objecting to the system of immigration.[61]

The committee on the amendment made it so difficult to prove a marriage bona fide that, in the end, its members conceded that the law was not really intended to root out fraud but instead to reduce the overall number of marriage visas. The failures of the system were built in by design. As the committee put it in the House hearing: "The Committee realizes that, in contemporary

American society, not all marriages last for two years. It is important to remember, however, that the reason an alien spouse or alien son or daughter receives special treatment is the emphasis our immigration laws place on family reunification."[62] Congressmen expressed regret but no real solutions about marriages that ended due to domestic violence or other "reputable" reasons.[63] In essence, the intended effect was grounded in immigration reform rather than the prevention of marriage fraud rings.

The practical goal of the Immigration Marriage Fraud Amendments was to reduce the number of immigrant spouses overall. Congress expected that fewer spouses would become citizens through marriage via this legislation. The INS had varied but specific ideas about how many "fraudulent" marriages they could expect to identify. Studies indicated that while the number of marriages had increased 60 percent between 1962 and 1984, the number of visa-creating marriages had jumped from 23,962 to 149,296. This 600 percent increase suggested a preponderance of fraud cases to the INS.[64] The committee that considered the amendment estimated 30 percent of immigrant marriages to citizens to involve fraud—this number was cited again to President Reagan as reason enough to sign the bill.[65] They based this on the contrast between the 600 percent increase in visa-creating marriages and the 60 percent increase in the overall marriage rate.[66] The Department of Justice further noted that 45 percent of fiancées never adjusted their status, but there was no evidence that those fiancées left the country. While there was also no indication that all these fiancées remained in the country either, the Justice Department did take note that other fiancées gained visas based on marriages to someone other than the original petitioner. All of this suggested to the Department of Justice that the 30 percent number could be even higher.[67] The Congressional Budget Office estimated that the cost of the amendment would be slim, and that in fact it might save the government money since they anticipated a 15 percent decrease in applications due to the deterrent effect alone.[68] The INS presented this as a statistical model to understand how many marriages were fraudulent, but alternatively we can see this as a quota for how many marriages that INS agents should identify as "fraudulent."

Four economic concerns motivated Congress to establish a quota for citizen-immigrant marriages. Like the citizen objectors to the Hart-Celler Act in 1965, the Ninety-Ninth Congress worried about the fiscal costs of immigrants. Most simply, it was easier and cheaper to expel those guilty of marriage fraud via an automatic mechanism than it was to individually investigate suspected cases. In its report to Congress, the Congressional Budget Office had cited a reduction in investigations as one reason to shift the burden of proof to immigrants.[69] The INS relied on tips from anonymous letters, family members, and angry spouses and investigated up to twenty-one thousand cases in order to find incidents of potential fraud.[70] These investigations involved much more extensive attention than the interviews conducted at the end of the second year of marriage.[71]

Second, Congress finally recognized that spouses could be workers. Women had the right to give citizenship to their husbands, always recognized as workers. Also wives had increasingly entered the workforce, which meant that more immigrant spouses would work rather than be dependents. Alan C. Nelson, the commissioner of the INS, complained that giving citizenship through marriage allowed "significant numbers of unskilled laborers to enter the market-place."[72] Similarly, Roger Conner, the executive director of the Federation for American Immigration Reform, reminded the congressmen that the right to work in the United States was an "incredibly valuable commodity" that should be protected from marriage fraud perpetrators.[73] In 1981, the INS had suggested that the growing requirement to offer proof of status to employers encouraged an immigrant to "either purchase counterfeit documents or become a permanent resident": "Since most illegal aliens cannot qualify for an immigrant visa or for adjustment of status, and many find the complexities of a labor certification fraud intimidating, a sham marriage scheme is particularly appealing."[74] Marriage was increasingly an easier route to employment rights than other forms of immigration fraud.

Third, Congress worried that some citizens who married immigrants nonetheless received welfare benefits. Roger Conner and David North, the director of the Center for Labor and Migration Studies, testified that all INS offices should follow New York City's example. New York City's vaunted policy was to check any female citizen with children who married to make sure she was not receiving AFDC. These experts worried that aliens would illegally get citizenship at the same time that women would illegally receive welfare.[75]

Finally, Congress objected that immigrant spouses made use of entitlements—especially AFDC—that were supposed to be granted only to citizens and permanent residents. This fear, as can be seen in the Hart-Celler debates, had been around for quite some time. But average citizens increasingly expressed their fears that immigrants would end up on the welfare rolls to their legislators. In 1974, a former welfare recipient wrote to her congresswoman to pinpoint immigrants as undeserving of welfare benefits. She characterized them as taking jobs, living spaces, and particularly money via welfare from citizens.

All of it was "unfair for hard-working people to have to support self-imposing, non-productive bums."[76] What distinguished this woman in her own mind from the other people who received welfare was perhaps her race, perhaps her citizenship.

Fears about immigrants sapping the welfare system were so extensive that some politicians expended significant effort trying to dispel these rumors. Patsy Mink, the congresswoman from Hawaii from 1965 to 1977 and again from 1990 to 2002, spent the bulk of her highly acclaimed career trying to counteract these concerns. For example, in 1973, Mink had to reassure the chairman of the State Commission on Manpower and Full Employment that Filipinos made up less than 1 percent of the welfare rolls. Mink explained that it was a deportable offense in 1973 to go on the welfare rolls and that "there are simply no hoards coming in off the planes and going on welfare."[77] It is notable that Filipinos were targeted as particularly likely to go on welfare, indicating again that race remained a motivating fear for some of those who opposed immigration. Decades later, Mink again assured a constituent that "in point of fact, illegal aliens are already barred from receiving any and all federal assistance programs" including AFDC.[78] Officially this was still true even though the practice of welfare distribution was highly complicated by this point. But other legislators encouraged constituent fears. Illinois senator Charles Percy suggested to his colleagues that one third of all immigrants who entered the country between 1972 and 1975 had begun receiving welfare benefits by 1976, which was a number well above official estimates.[79] In the end, fearful legislators began to outnumber legislators who saw scant justification for draconian reform.

The perceived threat of immigrants receiving welfare carried new relevance by 1986 with the invention of the welfare queen trope and heightened attention to immigration policy.[80] The mythical welfare queen, like her immigrant counterpart, used fraud to live the high life on the average taxpayer's dime. Also like her immigrant counterpart, she was a woman of color who continued to have children with the entitlement that the government gave to her. The fear of immigrants making use of government entitlements was an important component in the formulation of the Immigration Marriage Fraud Amendments. Richard E. Norton, the deputy assistant commissioner for investigations at the INS, explained in congressional hearings that the spouses of U.S. citizens were entitled to a wide range of benefits, including on-base billeting, health benefits, Social Security, Supplemental Security Income (SSI), and unemployment compensation. Alan Nelson, the INS commissioner, sup-

Figure 7. Patsy Mink, the congresswoman from Hawaii, appeared at Honolulu International Airport with President Lyndon B. Johnson the year after Johnson signed the Hart-Celler Act in 1965. Mink tried to fight fears that immigrants would use up welfare resources the whole of her career. Courtesy of the LBJ Presidential Library.

plemented Norton's testimony with his own catalogue of benefits: "obviously you have got the Social Security, the supplemental security income, SSI, unemployment compensation, HUD-subsidized housing, the AFDC Program, food stamps, numerous Department of Education–funded programs including student loans and opportunity grants. You have got Small Business Administration loans. Mr. Norton has already hit the military, and there are probably others there, but there is quite a panoply of various social benefits that are available out there for people who have no right to obtain them."[81]

What's notable is how Nelson characterized these spouses. They were no longer the immediate family members who deserved to be with their citizen spouses. Instead they were people who did not have any right to social benefits.

Even though these men and women officially did not have any right to government entitlements, most provisions in place to prevent access were less effective in practice by 1986. The government had only deported about twenty-two thousand immigrants from 1908 to 1980 for becoming a public charge.[82] By the 1970s, the number of immigrants deported for becoming public charges had become miniscule. Of the nearly one hundred thousand immigrants deported between 1971 and 1975, only seventeen were deported as public charges.[83]

The small number of deportations for becoming a public charge was not because immigrant spouses received aid from a sponsoring citizen. Even though citizens were required to file a financial affidavit pledging to financially support immigrant parents, children, and spouses after 1931, these affidavits were not enforced after the 1958 case *Department of Mental Hygiene of the State of California v. Renel.*[84] In this case, Samuel Renel and his wife had sponsored two of her nephews so they could immigrate to the United States. One nephew was eventually committed to a California mental health facility at a cost of $4,721.61 to the state. California tried to recoup these costs from the Renels, but two appellate courts concluded that the affidavits imposed no contractual obligation. Instead affidavits were imposed to "lend an air of solemnity to a moral obligation."[85] In the next couple decades, the Michigan Supreme Court and the California Court of Appeals made similar rulings that affidavits imposed only a moral obligation.[86] Similarly the INS rarely used an option to require a citizen to post bonds up to $5,000 that he or she forfeited if the sponsored immigrant became a public charge.[87] Usually, if an immigration officer believed that the sponsor had the means and intention of supporting the immigrant, he or she did not demand a bond.[88] This sort of discretion, clearly, could be used unevenly.[89] For example, a study of 199 newly arrived immigrants receiving SSI showed that most had sponsors who had failed to support them. Of the 199, 113 had affidavits on file, 37 had been refugees who did not need affidavits, and another 25 could not be located.[90] Congress complained about this situation periodically.[91] By 1986 then, it was well-established that sponsoring citizens did not have to take care of the immigrant sponsored.

Without their sponsors' support, some immigrant wives were clearly in need, and many of these wives received welfare benefits even though they were not supposed to be eligible for them.[92] U.S. immigration law stated not only that the United States could exclude those likely to be a public charge but also that "any alien lawfully admitted shall be deported who 'has within five years after entry become a public charge from causes not affirmatively shown to have arisen after entry.' "[93] In practice, however, courts and bureaucracies protected immigrant wives' right to receive welfare. For instance, in the 1971 case *Graham v. Richardson*, the Supreme Court affirmed that alien residents who had become indigent based on circumstances that arose after entry were indeed eligible for aid. The court also reaffirmed a state's obligation to provide aid to a lawfully admitted immigrant. The ruling struck down an Arizona state law that imposed a residency requirement of fifteen years in the state of Arizona.[94]

Another loophole that allowed immigrant wives to receive welfare benefits was a rule that guaranteed privacy to welfare recipients. A U.S. Department of Health, Education, and Welfare stipulation barred any state from disclosing information about a welfare applicant or recipient without his or her consent. So while going on welfare after immigrating was grounds for deportation, the INS had nearly no means of determining this information.[95] In addition to the lack of information available to the INS on who had received welfare, public charges were only deportable if they failed to repay public assistance upon demand. This too allowed evasions that frustrated critics. The Supplemental Security Income program did not in fact demand repayment, which meant that those who had received assistance would not qualify for deportation.[96]

A 1977 case firmly established that even some undocumented immigrant wives could draw on the welfare system. Gayle McQuoid Holley, an undocumented Canadian immigrant, had moved to the United States as a girl on a student visa. Then in 1959 she married Norman McQuoid. In the next several years, the couple had six children and then separated in 1966. Holley applied for welfare benefits for herself and her minor children and received them until 1974. Then New York State passed a law barring the distribution of welfare benefits to undocumented immigrants residing in the state. The state cut off AFDC payments to Gayle Holley, while retaining them for her children. The Second Circuit considered whether New York's new law was in conflict with the law set out by HEW.[97]

The Second Circuit ruled both expansively and conservatively. First it established that lawful immigrants were in fact eligible for welfare benefits according to the text of the law. But then it went further and established that

Holley, "although unlawfully residing in the United States," was eligible as well. The ruling stated that Holley was entitled to receive benefits "under color of law" because she had fully disclosed her situation to the INS, received permission from the INS to stay "for humanitarian reasons," married, had children, and most significantly would live in the United States until the sixth child reached his majority. Essentially, the INS did not plan to deport Holley because doing so would "involve consequences, or inflict suffering, beyond what the authors of the law contemplated." In this case, deporting their mother would hoist the children into the foster care system, a cultural and financial effect that the court envisioned as more harmful than Holley's continued presence. And therefore, New York had to grant Holley welfare benefits.[98]

The Second Circuit believed itself to be dealing narrowly with this case—it saw Holley's condition as both permanent enough to get benefits but also temporary since she would be deported after her children were grown. It also saw her situation as exceptional. It counted her as part of a "minuscule subclass of aliens" whom the INS was not considering deporting at that time, presumably due to the six minor American citizens in her care. The court was also careful to distinguish between her and "the hordes who have unlawfully entered surreptitiously."[99] Perhaps Holley's Canadian origins protected her from relegation to membership in the alleged hordes. But as states and citizens alike became more opposed to immigrant household members receiving public aid, the federal government soon shared their skepticism.

Congress attempted its first substantial limit to welfare for immigrant wives in 1980. In H.R. 4904, the House had proposed that a recent immigrant was required to include her sponsor's income with hers when applying for aid. This method, referred to as deeming, in effect resembled the strategy California and other states took in implementing their substitute father laws. As the National Immigration Forum later noted in a 1994 issue brief on the costs and contributions of immigrants, this "deeming" of income would have disqualified many women from being eligible for AFDC benefits even though many women did "not have access to all of their sponsor's income."[100] The concept of deeming was based on the Social Security laws that counted the income and resources of an applicant's spouse or parents living in the same household. But an immigrant who applied for aid and her sponsor often did not live together if they were divorced. Without cohabitation, many sponsored immigrants would not actually be able to draw on his or her sponsor's income.[101] Certainly no law required sponsors to support immigrants since the 1958 *Renel* case.[102] Moreover, if a sponsor had refused to disclose his or her income to his or her sponsor, she would automatically become ineligible for AFDC. In essence, indigent immigrants would find themselves incredibly vulnerable to their sponsors' whims. Congress's failure to pass this bill (which it did pass in 1991) helped spur support for the Immigration Marriage Fraud Amendments.[103] Immigrant wives would be prevented from drawing too heavily on the social safety net by designating formerly bona fide marriages as frauds.

For all these reasons, reformers successfully implemented a two-year waiting period for all immigrant spouses via the 1986 Immigration Marriage Fraud Amendments. The perfunctory debate, which one sponsor characterized as "something of a love feast," only glanced over the surface of the issues at hand.[104] Supporters touched on marriage fraud rings, the growing number of immigrant spouses, and the fear of scam artists "trifl[ing]" with "a very sacred institution."[105] The amendment passed by voice vote in Congress in the fall of 1986, and Reagan signed the bill into law on November 10. After this, the attorney general had two years to determine that the marriage was not entered into in order to evade immigration laws, that no money had changed hands, and that the marriage was still intact.[106]

The 1986 Immigration Marriage Fraud Amendments particularly left victims of domestic violence inordinately vulnerable to abuse on one hand or deportation on the other. Notably, women were most likely to be these domestic violence victims. As the *Washington Post* indicated in 1990, "The 1986 Immigration Reform Act and the Immigration Marriage Fraud Amendment have combined to give the spouse applying for permanent residence a powerful tool to control his partner."[107] The *Post* particularly highlighted the case of an undocumented Latin American woman who fled to a domestic violence shelter after her husband broke two fingers and severely bruised her neck and chest. Her husband controlled her passport, her money, her children, and presumably any hope of ever gaining documented immigration status. After a few days in the shelter and with few legitimate choices, she returned to her husband.

Congress later passed reforms aimed to help abused immigrant spouses, but they had limited effects. Ostensibly, the 1990 Immigration Act and 1994 Violence Against Women Act (VAWA) allowed battered immigrant wives to petition the government to stay even if they otherwise qualified for deportation.[108] But exceptions remained. First, a terrorism bill made it so any immigrant who entered the country illegally could be deported without a hearing, including battered wives. Most significantly, additional legislation limited a wife's access to legal aid clinics that had the legal expertise to tap these protections for victims of domestic violence. This made it more difficult for a battered wife—who had been married less than two years or who had entered the country illegally—to petition a judge effectively. For example, a Cuban wife and her child fled her abusive husband. Her husband then charged her with parental kidnapping. Her employer procured legal aid for her, but because of her status as an undocumented immigrant, she could not accept this aid. The pro bono lawyer she found could not meet with her ahead of the day of the hearing. She and her son went to the courthouse to meet the lawyer, only to be greeted by and then shot in the face by her husband. Guards then shot her husband as well, also in front of their nine-year-old son.[109] The National Network on Behalf of Battered Immigrant Women called the protections given to immigrant spouses under the 1990 amendments and VAWA "merely illusory" without assistance from attorneys.

In the end, the INS had achieved through legislation what the courts had struck down in *Bark*. The new marriage fraud provisions had at their roots an exceedingly thick assumption—any marriage that did not last two years was automatically considered a fraud, much like the marriage of the Barks. The effects of these thick expectations fell most heavily on the most vulnerable—particularly immigrant women and their children abused by citizen spouses.

CHAPTER 6

Gay Marriage and "Homosexual Households"

In December of 1976 Wayne Schwandt, a graduate of the Wesley Theological Seminary, married John Fortunato, a former Carmelite brother. In its coverage of the church wedding, the *Washington Post* noted, "the devastating irony is . . . that these two homosexuals may be the only people who really believe in good old red-blooded American marriage anymore." While men and women had cast marriage as war, this gay couple still had faith in it. The paper's evident ruefulness was tinged with optimism, however. The *Post* and the couple both believed that perhaps this marriage could help "define what heterosexual marriage sex roles are—and are not—in an age when many male/female couples seem to spend a lot of time in the trenches, slugging out some dimly understood 5,000 year-old battle of the sexes."[1] Gay couples could show the irrelevance of gender to marriage—and thereby save it for everyone. Perhaps only a small minority of the American population at this time—gay or straight—believed that gay couples could fix the rapidly changing institution of marriage. But even the fact that this couple sought to marry in the Episcopal Church—and that some mainstream commentators saw a wisp of hope in this—indicated how much marriage had changed already. Both this journalist and this couple were observing the still-unfolding effects of eliminating legal gender roles from marriage.

The lengths to which some gay couples went to form families stood in striking contrast to the fracturing bonds between husbands and wives who owed each other little in marriage law. As we have seen, state legislatures throughout the country tried to grant individualist equality to husbands and wives within traditional marriage—largely via no-fault divorce, husbands were no longer financially responsible to their wives, and wives no longer owed their husbands their household and reproductive labor. Legally, if not in practice, spouses related to each other as individual men and women rather than as interdependent members of a household by the mid-1980s. If some husbands and wives found equality by discarding their obligations to support their families, some gay men and lesbians hoped to take the remaining mutual obligations on.[2]

Though state marriage law reform thinned spouses' mutual obligations to each other, federal-sponsored marriage benefits remained intact. Husbands and wives received tax breaks, Social Security, and other household benefits from the government, even if they owed one another very little. But although federal and state governments had made these remaining benefits gender-neutral, they nonetheless refused to extend them to gay couples. There were no legally recognized obligations between gay partners or from the government. Creating "homosexual households," as one judge would call them, seemingly would come only at an additional cost to taxpayers at a moment of fiscal retrenchment. Federal and state governments preserved household benefits only for heterosexual families.

Even fewer resources to support private households were available to single people, gay or straight, but government actors used the ones that existed to separate gay couples. As with "man in the house" laws and the Immigration Marriage Fraud Amendments, lawmakers and bureaucrats combined a legal strategy with a moral rationale. Over the course of the 1970s, gay liberation activists won very limited rights for individual gay men and lesbians. But even after some federal agencies and courts were mildly barred from discriminating explicitly against gay men and lesbians, they could easily target gay couples under the law. If sexuality was not a choice, the composition of one's household certainly was. Indeed, same-sex households represented an easier target for discriminatory legal treatment than did any gay man or woman living alone.

This was a moral strategy too, however, premised on a counterintuitive assumption by gay marriage opponents that the fight for gay family was a selfish impulse. Gay marriage opponents within state and federal governments consistently characterized gay couples as selfish or self-obsessed for wanting to marry rather than sacrificing for the needs of their children or society. Like ERA opponents, gay marriage opponents performed a monumental bait and switch to predict that gay marriage would destroy marital obligations even after both breadwinning and homemaking were already vastly reduced in practice and in law. Worst of all, they claimed, gay families would further encourage individual needs and desires rather than collective thick responsibility (ignoring that divorce law had already done so). The IRS, the Department of Housing and Urban Development (HUD), INS, judges determining child custody and visitation rights, and the Supreme Court all acted to break up gay couples and gay households out of fear of the selfishness that they claimed homosexual households embodied.

We know about some of this generation of discriminations from other historians of sexuality.[3] But when we examine them collectively, we can see that government institutions prohibited, for same-sex couples, the very right to form a household—to live together, to shelter children, to be dependent on one another. These markers of a household notably became the thick obligations that gay couples later had to perform to prove they were part of a domestic partnership, but in the 1970s, government agents used many tools at their disposal to break these households up. These policies provided government actors with an additional and particularly virulent "stick" to coerce gay men and lesbians to keep their private relationships closeted.[4]

The Campaign to Win Marriage

Many gay men and women joined radical feminists and members of the counterculture in rejecting the institution of marriage. But not all gay men and lesbians repudiated marriage, and both the gay community and the legal system found gay marriage supporters difficult to overlook. The *Advocate*'s journalist Rob Cole commented that the number of gay men and lesbians marrying, even in the absence of legal recognition, made "it plain that many Gays do want a formal union and do want to be considered morally bound to each other—at least in their own community if not in the straight world."[5] Later, Cole echoed his own sentiment from 1970: "the gay rush to the altar may continue to confound straights and fellow Gays alike, but there seems to be little doubt that there are going to be more and more such marriages, and a good bet that eventually the legal barriers will fall."[6] Those who clamored for gay marriage, even if their expectations for success were low, forced the gay community as a whole to pay attention to the legal barriers to marriage.

Activists cited a range of reasons for embracing same-sex marriage. Early on, especially during the era of the baby boom and the homophile movement, some activists endorsed marriage as a potential means of earning the acceptance of heterosexuals. Some gay men and women, like *ONE* contributor Randy Lloyd, perceived a "promiscuous" lifestyle as innately morally inferior.[7]

Others used a moral distinction between promiscuous and non-promiscuous gay men and women to argue that gay marriage would bring acceptance of the homosexual lifestyle from heterosexuals. For example, one contributor to the gay periodical *ONE* identified fears parents had that gay men and lesbians molested children and purportedly were unable to sustain a long-term relationship as the two main obstacles to heterosexual acceptance of gay rights.[8] These postwar assumptions about respectability persisted into the post-Stonewall era for some gay marriage advocates. In a 1972 interview, one gay activist—a member of the Metropolitan Community Church, which was founded by Troy Perry and quickly caught on among gay men and lesbians in major American cities—declared, "Right now, we have to show society that we can last, and that there is real love in a gay relationship, that can keep two people together for a long time regardless of what happens."[9] Similarly in 1972, the Washington Metropolitan Community Church also promoted marriage as a means of refuting the reputation homosexual relationships had for being instable and transient.[10]

As the homophile era waned and gay liberation rose, a new generation of gay marriage supporters declared that depriving same-sex couples of the right to marry was a violation of their civil rights. Michael Boucai suggests that most of the couples who sought legal battles for gay marriage intended these as "a political exercise."[11] Richard Baker and James McConnell, a Minnesota couple that initiated a media firestorm over their repeated attempts to marry beginning in the early 1970s, argued, "homosexuals should enjoy the same rights that heterosexuals do. We're guaranteed this by the Constitution."[12] Baker elaborated later that year that the ability to deprive gay men and lesbians of certain rights made them second-class citizens.[13] Another man suing for marriage rights explained that he did not support the institution of marriage for homosexuals or heterosexuals, but he would attempt to win that right until marriage itself was abolished.[14] Gay men and lesbians of color specifically linked their struggle as gay men and women to the civil rights movement. Conrad Balfour, the Minnesota commissioner of human rights and an early gay rights supporter, "publicly equated racial discrimination with that imposed on gay people" when he defended the right of two gay men to marry.[15] The *Advocate* reported that a black lesbian couple from Milwaukee argued for marriage rights in terms of civil rights: " 'The law should protect us and help us the way it does any two straight people who love each other and want to live together,' Ms. Burkett explained. 'That's our civil rights. That's what this is all about.' "[16]

Finally, marriage became a more attractive institution to some gay and lesbian activists as legislatures and courts gradually fractured the gender imperatives of marriage. If military perks, child support, and other benefits had previously only been benefits husbands could give to wives, the shift to gender-neutral benefits made them seem within the grasp of gay couples. These entitlements had tremendous value, as activists noted. But marriage imposed obligations even as it gave benefits, most of which fell on the wealthier partner in the marriage even after divorce law reform. Nonetheless same-sex couples sought the privileges and the obligations alike. Baker and McConnell, the pioneering Minnesota couple, told an interviewer that they believed that "sexual preference is not a reason to deny a couple inheritance rights, property privileges, or tax benefits in this day and age."[17] Baker and McConnell also cited "redress under wrongful death statutes," "alienation of affections statutes," and "one form of joint property ownership which in Minnesota is available only to wedded couples, providing advantages against creditors."[18] In covering a lawsuit by two lesbians in Texas for the right to marry, a journalist cited military dependent benefits, workmen's compensation benefits, and community property for wives, in addition to the protection of the homestead from creditors as potential windfalls for the wives of lesbians. Such benefits "translated into dollars and cents, mean[t] quite a lot."[19] The intersection of the respectability, rights, and benefits of marriage led a diverse group of gay men and women to fight for their place in the institution.

In articulating gay men and lesbians' demands for the privileges and obligations accorded married heterosexual couples—privileges that it seemed unlikely any mainstream institution would soon afford them—activists at times explicitly used measures that had stripped gender out of marriage law. One particular link was no-fault divorce, which in and of itself troubled "traditional" marriage. In a 1974 debate about gay marriage broadcast on WGBH's show *The Advocates*, Florida American Civil Liberties Union lawyer Tobias Simon was troubled that he could not identify a head of family in a gay marriage and therefore "both parties to the homosexual marriage [would] always be equal."[20] In part, Simon's evidence for this claim was that the grounds for a fault divorce for a gay marriage could not be identified. The broader conundrum, of who would lead the family in a gay marriage, depended entirely on the continuation of gender difference in marriage and fault in divorce. One of Simon's opponents in this debate, Elaine Noble, an instructor at Emerson College and member of the lesbian rights group Daughters of Bilitis, countered simply that it was straight couples that were questioning the lack of equality in marriage.[21] Both sides of this televised debate saw deep links between gender equality between husbands and wives and gay marriage.

In Washington DC, a campaign by gay activists and their allies unequivocally tied gay marriage to the breakdown of breadwinner and homemaker roles via no-fault divorce legislation. In May of 1975, African American councilman Arrington Dixon (D-Ward 4) proposed a no-fault divorce law that closely resembled the Illinois divorce law discussed in Chapter 2. Like Illinois's law, it provided recognition for women's labor in the home in property settlements and child support awards. Like Illinois's law, it attempted to make alimony an infrequent and temporary provision. Property, custody, and child support would be distributed without recognition of fault.[22] One advocate noted that "at all points, it makes no distinctions as to gender."[23] None of this was coincidental; like Illinois's law, it was based on the Uniform Marriage and Divorce Act.[24]

The DC bill's most striking feature, distinguishing it from no-fault divorce laws in all other states, was its deliberate legalization of gay marriage. By 1975, state legislatures were actively involved in the same-sex marriage question. Several states, including nearby Maryland, had in the early 1970s rewritten nineteenth-century laws that did not explicitly define marriage as the union between a man and a woman so as to prohibit same-sex marriage more clearly.[25] The DC law was unique in that it not only defined marriage as an institution between two persons rather than a man and a woman but also barred discrimination against gay parents when it came to child custody.[26] The bill also did not carry a residency requirement, which meant that a DC marriage license was available to anyone and additionally could even lead to national recognition of same-sex marriage under the Constitution's full faith and credit clause.[27] Dixon, a fixture in local DC politics in the 1970s, called attention to the inclusion of same-sex couples as one of the significant changes to marriage law the bill introduced. He had invited the Washington president of the gay rights organization the Mattachine Society, Dr. Franklin Kameny, and the president of the Gay Activist Alliance, Cade Ware, to testify before the city council.[28]

Like black politicians in Chicago and elsewhere, Dixon represented the inclusion of rights for gay men and lesbians as an opportunity to fight for social justice for everyone.[29] He noted to the press, it would be a "dichotomy if we go around oppressing other minorities."[30] Of course, black gay and lesbian couples also wanted to marry, which Dixon did not note in his advocacy of the bill, but may have been obvious to him if he read the black press carefully at this time.[31] To make the spirit of social justice for all even more visible in the bill, Dixon also deleted the requirement that a person's race be noted on all marriage licenses and legitimized any children born of interracial unions prior to 1866.[32] Dixon saw himself as presenting a marriage law that treated everyone, no matter one's race, gender, or sexual identity, equally.[33]

For a time, it seemed plausible that this remarkable piece of legislation—linking black, gender, and gay equality, shepherded through by an African American council member—might become law. In July of 1975, Kameny wrote a letter to the *Sexual Law Reporter* assuring readers that "the bill has VERY high probability of enactment into law, probably in the next 3 to 4 months." Indeed he even referred to it as "the bill (or more properly, the law-to-be)."[34] Kameny's confidence had been stoked in part by the public hearings held on July 7 and 8, when almost no one raised significant opposition to the bill's inclusion of same-sex marriage.[35] Others shared Kameny's hope. A same-sex couple who had been barred from marrying in nearby Maryland planned to remarry in DC on the assumption that the bill would pass quickly.[36] That said, gay activists were not naïve, and even Kameny noted that the unexpected could occur. And occur it did.

The tide changed quickly, and by early August Kameny was pleading with Dixon not to strip the gay marriage language from the no-fault bill. Kameny and the Gay Activists Alliance also urged the gay community to demonstrate public support for the bill more strongly.[37] Blaming a theocracy of reactionary black Baptist clergymen for the trouble, Kameny implored "the gay community and others who believe in personal freedom" to remind the thirteen council members (including Marion Barry) that there were "more of us than there are of those clergymen."[38] Kameny's increasing bitterness toward the Baptist clergymen produced little change in support for the marriage bill.

Activists' efforts to pass the gay marriage bill failed. Though Arrington Dixon continued to voice his concern for the civil rights of all minority groups, he bowed to pressure and dropped the section of the law that granted marriage to gay men and lesbians on Christmas Eve of 1975.[39] To Dixon's mind, the gender progress of the no-fault bill was imperiled by redefining marriage as an institution between two persons. Jettisoning the gay marriage clause did not save the no-fault provisions of the bill in 1976.[40] The hope for gay marriage legislation had ended. In 1977, the divorce reform law passed as a mere shadow of its former self, stripped both of gay marriage and of no-fault divorce provisions.[41]

Though Dixon's pairing of gender and gay equality in statutory reform failed, gay activists also tried to sue on the basis that same-sex couples ought to be treated equally as marriage lost its gendered properties. The most familiar gay marriage suit from the era was *Baker v. Nelson*.[42] In 1971, Richard John Baker and James Michael McConnell sued the Hennepin County District Court clerk in Minnesota to issue them a marriage license. Baker and McConnell argued that their marriage bid would "force the legislature to take a fresh look at a lot of statutes on the books," including the property rights embedded in marriage and the "laws that treat[ed] wives and husband unequally."[43]

Baker and McConnell brought their case against marriage inequality too early—divorce and gender discrimination laws only stripped sex roles from Minnesota marriage law a few years after their suit. County attorney George Scott, who countered their claims to marriage, based his case on the still-operational legal distinction between gender roles in marriage. He argued, "granting the license would produce legal chaos because all of the law is written in terms of husband and wife, for whom different duties and rights are specified."[44] The supreme courts of Minnesota and of the United States both rejected Baker and McConnell's claims, and in doing so invoked the still salient stability of gender distinctions in marriage.[45] The Minnesota Supreme Court ruling was based on gender distinctions still present in the law. The U.S. Supreme Court simply refused to hear the case, thus confirming the Minnesota Supreme Court ruling. Minnesota's reasoning therefore continued to influence a myriad of courts even after laws on gender and marriage began to change shortly thereafter. This account of *Baker v. Nelson* is familiar, but as Mary Anne Case has shown, Baker and McConnell also used gender-based subterfuge to "pass" as a heterosexual couple.

Finally some gay and lesbian couples tried to sue with valid marriage licenses in hand that they had gained through subterfuge. During this time, the easiest way for a same-sex couple to get a marriage license was to trick the marriage license bureau into thinking the same-sex couple was an opposite-sex couple. The ruse of passing as a heterosexual couple through literal or effective drag exploited stereotypical gender norms.[46] The use of subterfuge was contradictory.[47] The most successful passers never made it into the press or to the attention of government officials, but also had no effect on either the law itself or public awareness of gay couples' exclusion from marriage benefits. The least successful passers exposed themselves to the press to make the point that gay couples were excluded from marriage rights and benefits. Most of the couples I cite below saw themselves as activists. While other gay rights activists identified employment discrimination, the prospect of sodomy arrests, or violence as more pressing concerns, these gay couples wished to make the public aware of their desire to take on the very obligations of marriage that other spouses were trying to abandon.

Again, Baker and McConnell led the way in advertising their desire to take on gendered obligations by passing as a straight couple. While they waited for their ruling to come down from a state district court, McConnell adopted Baker in order to ensure Baker's right to inherit, to sue in case of wrongful death, and to pay in-state tuition at the University of Minnesota Law School.[48] McConnell was essentially using adoption to legally take on the benefits and obligations of a breadwinner. The couple also used the name change component of adoption to attempt to pass as an opposite-sex couple. As part of the adoption, Judge Lindsay G. Arthur approved Baker's name change to Pat Lyn McConnell. The new legal name was conspicuously and deliberately androgynous to allow Baker to pass as a woman on paper. The couple then took a short trip to Mankato, Minnesota, to establish residence there.[49] On August 9, 1971, Mike McConnell went to the courthouse alone and applied for a marriage license for himself and Pat Lyn McConnell, whose presence was not mandated by law. On paper, Pat Lyn McConnell successfully passed as a bride-to-be. It was only at this point that a university publicist originally from Mankato happened to recognize the McConnell name and address in the list of marriage licenses in her hometown newspaper. The publicist notified the press, after which "the county attorney at Mankato, John Corbey, suddenly declared the license 'defective' and unusable."[50] Baker and McConnell litigated the validity of this license separately, and a few years later it was officially struck down.

Other gay and lesbian couples also deployed the passing strategy to try to gain access to the broad range of marriage rights and responsibilities. As in Mankato, the Rockville, Maryland, marriage law required only one party to be present. Michele Bush and Paulette Hill successfully applied for a marriage license there.[51] In this case, a name change wasn't even necessary; the two women seemingly took advantage of the similarity between Michele and Michael, and the clerk claimed he issued the license "unwittingly."[52] The Maryland assistant attorney general argued that even though Maryland law barred gay marriage, the license would remain valid because "the clerk has no authority to alter such records at a later point in time, either on his own initiative or at the request of the parties."[53] Nonetheless the couple had planned to be remarried in Washington, DC, if Dixon had succeeded with his no-fault law. They saw this as a safeguard because even a valid license meant little given that "Maryland law [held] their marriage to be illegal."[54]

In California, gay couples attempted to make use of a law that allowed churches to legitimize common law marriages.[55] In these "contract marriages," the state had no part in determining who could and could not legally marry; only a church official held the authority for a contract marriage. In July of 1970, Neva Joy Heckman and Judith Ann Belew gained notoriety when Rev. Troy D. Perry, the founder and pastor of the Metropolitan Community Church, married them under the contract law provision. This prompted Assemblyman Alister McAlister (D-San Jose) to introduce a law that would require contract marriage couples to file a confidential certificate with the county clerk.[56] The new law did not immediately stop same-sex marriages, but it also showed the modesty of gay couples' successes in marrying. When the law took effect in March of 1972, the county clerk's office in Los Angeles recorded twenty-seven marriages conducted without a license, including marriages of "uncounted homosexual couples."[57] Because these unlicensed marriages were confidential, a spokesman for the county clerk explained, "the clerk has no choice but to record certificates of unlicensed marriage which are tendered with the $5 fee, even if the 'groom' is designed 'Howard William Armstrong' and the 'bride' as 'Edward Douglas Barnes.' "[58] But like the legitimate yet illegal licenses from Minnesota and Maryland, these certificates did not yield same-sex couples concrete recognition from the California or federal governments. By 1976, the majority of couples using contract marriages were Mexican émigrés rushing to marry before the preferential status for Mexican immigration was eliminated.[59]

Gay couples' most publicized means of securing a marriage license was to have one spouse dress in drag while applying for a license. In October of 1972, Antonio Molina and William "Billie" Ert applied for a license just outside of Houston. Ert, who worked as a female impersonator at a nightclub, wore a wig and a mini-skirt to apply for the license. Deputy Clerk Sandra Kalinowki issued the license because "she was 'most definitely' under the impression that Billie was a female. He wore a wig and 'held his throat like something was the matter with it and said something about having laryngitis.' "[60] Moreover both presented valid voter registrations, driver's licenses, and Social Security cards.[61] It was only after the two married using the license—and presented themselves to the press—that the county clerk refused to accept the completed document for filing.[62] Although the couple sued, the judge in the 130th judicial district ruled with the county clerk.[63] Similarly, in Las Vegas in 1977, two women obtained a marriage license in what the *Advocate* called "one of the first tries at a legal gay marriage in two years." Christina Asumendi and her spouse, L. T. "Cal" Callahan, obtained a license because the clerk thought "Callahan—who dresse[d] in men's clothing—was male." The response from the state was more immediate and less confused by 1977: the "newlyweds barely had time to finish a honeymoon before the local district attorney declared their marriage illegal—because both spouses were women.'"[64] These marriages raised awareness but did not yield rights.

The publicity for passing marriages prompted California officials to introduce new laws to prevent same-sex couples dressed in drag from marrying. In 1970, Los Angeles county clerk William G. Sharp wanted the premarital health certificate to indicate the sex of the applicant. He explained: the county had already "had some applicants whom we felt to be of the same sex . . . and there's no way we can determine this."[65] Even though Sharp indicated that the clerks had rejected couples they thought might be dressed as a member of the opposite sex, he thought "it was possible under the present system that there had already been marriages in the state between persons of the same sex through what would amount to legal deceit."[66] Sharp feared that the state would never know of such deceit unless one spouse filed for an annulment.[67] San Francisco's county clerk, Martin Mongan, similarly told the *San Francisco Chronicle* that "gay couples may already have been issued marriage licenses" through subterfuge.[68] This is certainly possible. For example, a black lesbian couple in Chicago, Edna Knowles and Peaches Stevens, reported to *Jet* that they had procured a marriage license without specifying how.[69] Nonetheless lawmakers and bureaucrats did a thorough job of excluding the vast majority of gay and lesbian couples from the vast majority of the marital rights and obligations that they sought.

Barring (Benefits to) "Homosexual Households"

If these gay and lesbian couples were exceptional in publicly seeking marriage rights, many gay men and lesbians nonetheless wanted families.[70] Legal marriage was a controversial topic, but family was widely embraced as politically if not personally desirable. For some, this meant simply children. Some gay men and lesbians, of course, had biological children in marriages that later failed. Journalist Chris McNaughton explained that child custody was seen as a particular priority in the fight for equal rights in part because "gay parents are as likely as any to want custody. Like all parents, they are attached to their children and believe that their having custody will be in the best interest of the kids."[71] Lesbians also began experimenting with alternative insemination.[72] One woman explained that "what's happening now is that women who came out in their early 20's and are now 30 are saying, 'Wait a minute—why do I have to choose not to be involved in a family just because I'm a lesbian?' "[73] Other gay men and lesbians arranged to be licensed as foster parents.

Some gay men and lesbians, however, wanted committed relationships with partners and envisioned families that included paramours alongside their children. This desire to construct a household with a partner and/or children became a political battle over the acceptability of "homosexual households" in a myriad of court cases and bureaucratic policies fought out over the course of the 1970s. Mark Strasser, Amelie-Marie George, and Daniel Rivers, in particular, have analyzed the way courts barred custody and visitation for parents who planned to cohabit with a homosexual partner.[74] In essence, growing up in—or at least visiting—the household of an actively gay parent was considered possibly in the best interest of the child, but growing up in a "homosexual household" rarely was. Douglas NeJaime has suggested that even LGBTQ men and women who eschewed marriage in favor of alternatives such as domestic partnerships "appeal[ed] to marital forms to gain nonmarital support" in the 1980s and 1990s.[75] This was certainly true in the 1970s as well; couples highlighted how closely they resembled married couples. But while LGBTQ activists had limited successes in the 1980s and 1990s, examining the 1970s also shows us that courts and bureaucrats fiercely rejected couples' attempts even to resemble married couples.

Lawmakers, judges, and bureaucrats thwarted gay couples' attempts to form stable households on the legal premise that being part of a homosexual household was a choice and the moral assumption that making such a choice was selfish, self-interested, or hedonistic. These officials alleged that the desire for a household showed that a parent cared more about his or her own sexual pleasure than his or her child's sexual health and identity. This critique of selfishness was the same that ERA opponents had made of homemaker entitlements. If states had comfortably reduced mutual obligations in the family via divorce law, custody, and visitation, courts seemed deeply uncomfortable with the bargain and hypocritically accused only gay families of such selfishness. That blame had real-world effects ranging from losing custody to losing the right to cohabit with a partner. Courts intervened to break up same-sex partnerships, using child custody and visitation rights as their legal apparatus for doing so.[76]

Nonetheless gay men and lesbians fiercely fought for custody and visitation rights for children born from previous marriages and at first perceived some success beginning in the late 1960s. It seemed that, through concerted activism, they might be successful in defending their rights as parents.[77] In 1967, a California appeals court ruled that a parent's homosexuality did not automatically render him or her unfit.[78] By the mid-1970s, courts reluctantly but nearly universally nodded to parents' constitutional rights: "the court is not required to find that a homosexual mother, by virtue of that fact is an unfit parent."[79] Committing sodomy did not infringe on a homosexual's right as a parent, courts reasoned, even when sodomy was a crime. For example, in the New Jersey case *In the Matter of J.S. & C.*, the court observed that other criminals, such as bank robbers, were allowed full visitation rights.[80] While comparing homosexuality to bank robbing was hardly an expression of acceptance, the definitive articulation of parents' legal rights as parents, even if they were gay or lesbian, was still a landmark decision. Another opinion stated, "although she is an admitted *practicing* homosexual, the trial court found that homosexuality, per se, did not render her unfit as a parent. The court made no effort to restrict her preferred sexual activity, although deviate sexual intercourse remains a crime in this State."[81] Practicing homosexuality—having casual sex with someone of the same gender—could not legally justify depriving a parent of his or her rights.

Nonetheless, courts' acknowledgment of gay parents' parental rights was in many ways only a posture, and courts could use "the best interest of the child" to deprive gay parents of custody and visitation rights. Judges in fact could use multiple different reasons to conclude that gay parents were not the best custodians for their children, including, famously, cases where parents were politically active in gay rights efforts.[82] Nonetheless, having a gay partner was a particularly prevalent rationale among judges. A single gay parent was legally fine, courts sometimes ruled; a cohabiting gay parent was not. A lower court in New York in *Di Stefano v. Di Stefano* concluded that a mother's inability to separate her sexuality and her role as a mother would injure her children.[83] The New Jersey court that noted that bank robbers were allowed full visitation rights nonetheless asserted that a bank robber who exposed his children to bank robbing would lose his rights.[84]

Throughout the 1970s and early 1980s cohabiting parents knew their chances for custody were slim. Carl Zuckerman, lawyer for the Community Service Society in New York, explained this system concisely in 1969. He believed that "most judges would not place a child in a home shared by Lesbians."[85] Similarly, a 1978 "Gay Parents' Legal Guide to Child Custody" explicitly warned parents that judges might force a parent to choose his or her children over his or her lover.[86] The guide was supposed to represent the collected wisdom of lawyers and gay parents across the country. Thus this concentrated account of experiences and legal rulings made clear that casual sex with someone of the same gender was within the rights of a gay or lesbian parent, but maintaining a committed relationship with a long-term partner, by contrast, would not be. Even the *Advocate* reported, "lesbian mothers have been denied custody of their children or given custody only on the condition that they live apart from their lover or otherwise deny their sexuality. The same is true of gay men, who in current precedent are lucky if they even get to visit their kids."[87]

Courts believed a parent's partner posed a much greater threat not in or of himself but because it indicated that the parent was making selfish decisions. In each case opponents alleged a gay parent who cohabited cared more for his or her lifestyle than for his or her child's development. The selfishness of a homosexual household produced homosexual children—either through sexual abuse, gender confusion, or a more accepting approach to homosexuality from two gay role models. For instance, in one famous Texas case discussed further below, a mother and her partner were considered poor role models in part because they allowed their son to wear a YWCA t-shirt. Wearing a t-shirt for the women's branch of the Christian group was considered potentially confusing for the child's gender identity. The child's father also accused the mother and her partner of hosting sexually explicit parties at the house that the child was witness to, which the mother denied.[88] The shirt and the parties indicated to the court that the mother was too self-absorbed to show the proper concern for her son's heterosexual development. Though the scientific inquiry into whether gay parents produced gay children had mixed results in the courtroom, this particular court saw clear danger to this child from a lesbian household.[89]

In multiple appellate cases across different states, courts used their legal ability to deprive custody from cohabiting gay or lesbian parents on the basis of their selfishness. In a 1975 California case, *Chaffin v. Frye*, a self-identified lesbian, Lynda Mae Chaffin, fought to regain custody from a married couple who had cared for her daughters for several years. The ruling explicitly established that the court would not deny custody solely on the basis of the mother's homosexuality. Instead the court denied the mother custody because she "has lived with her female companion since 1968 and will continue to live with her in the same apartment that the children would live in."[90] Her children reported that they were aware their mother was homosexual and had never seen her engaged in any homosexual activity; moreover, Chaffin stated that she and her partner had not engaged in sexual activity in two years. The court characterized these statements as "self-serving" and ruled "in exercising a choice between homosexual and heterosexual households for purposes of child custody a trial court could conclude that permanent residence in a *homosexual household* would be detrimental to the children and contrary to their best interests."[91] Sex and sexual identity did not necessarily appear nearly as dangerous to judges as did two women and children constituting a household.

Similarly, in the North Dakota case *Jacobson v. Jacobson*, the court ruled that the mother's intention to live with her partner and children, rather than her sexuality, was the problem. The ruling stated, "Sandra's homosexuality may, indeed, be something which is beyond her control. However, living with another person of the same sex in a sexual relationship is not something beyond her control."[92] Sandra Jacobson, in this case, lost her bid for custody because of her announced intention to live with her partner. The court made the explicit point that a parent's sexual identity might be protected legally, but his or her household choices were not. Moreover, after the court acknowledged that asking Sandra to give up her partner may be "too much to ask," the ruling nonetheless noted that "concerned parents in many, many instances have made sacrifices to varying degrees for their children."[93] This court, like many others, characterized Sandra's desire to create a family as an act of selfishness rather than the act of a woman seeking to take on the broader obligations of family.

Other rulings also claimed that parents' commitment to their partners destabilized the household for their children. In the New York case *In the Matter of Jane B., an Infant*, the court determined homosexuality alone was not sufficient legal ground to deny custody but "that living with her mother while Lucie Q. lives there in a lesbian relationship with the mother is not for the best interests and welfare of the child."[94] In another case, the probate court ruled, "the environment in which [Brenda] proposes to raise the children, namely, a Lesbian household, creates an element of instability that would adversely affect the welfare of the children." What made the household "Lesbian" was Brenda's insistence on "living in an active practicing homosexual relationship with a young teacher."[95] In *Kallas v. Kallas*, the Utah plaintiff "specifically object[ed] to the overnight visitation in the presence of defendant's lesbian lover."[96] Some children were even sent to foster care rather than be allowed to remain with a lesbian mother and her partner.[97]

Though courts' accusation that cohabiting gay parents were selfish rarely reached the awareness of anyone beyond these parents' friends and families, a few cases became so public that they shaped the perceptions—and fears—of many gays and lesbians across the country. The most widely publicized of these was the battle by a Texas nurse, Mary Jo Risher, who fought her husband, Douglas Risher, over custody of her younger son, Richard. NOW helped fund the legal costs for the case, and it got extensive coverage in media ranging from the *Los Angeles Times* to the *Lesbian Tide*. Risher then tried to turn the publicity to her advantage and published a book about her experiences titled *By Her Own Admission* in 1977. She promoted her cause all over the country, appearing on seventy-five TV programs and one hundred radio interviews.[98] A year later, her story was lightly fictionalized for a TV movie, *A Question of Love*, starring Gena Rowlands and Ned Beatty. None of this publicity helped Risher get custody of her son, however.

Risher's defeat as a partnered lesbian was as typical as the story of her divorce. Mary Jo and Douglas Risher divorced in 1971, and Mary Jo won custody of her two sons. Soon thereafter Mary Jo began easing herself into the small lesbian community in Dallas, and in 1973 Mary Jo met another mother named Ann Foreman. Mary Jo gave Ann a diamond ring, and later on the two decided together that they were married "the same as if they had a legal right to marry and make a life for themselves and their kids."[99] The couple began living together with Mary Jo Risher's sons and Ann Foreman's daughter. After Mary Joe's eldest son, Jimmy, told his father Douglas that Mary Jo and Ann Foreman's relationship was sexual in nature, Douglas tried to coerce Mary Jo into giving up custody. When she refused, he told her that she would find out what it would be like to pay child support and to have her own children testify against her.[100] He then sued for custody on the basis that Mary Jo was "living in a homosexual relationship as man and wife" and that "children should be removed from immoral and undesirable environment[s]."[101]

Douglas's lawyer asked questions of Mary Jo and Ann Foreman that again raised the issue of whether Mary Jo was a selfish or self-sacrificing mother. During the trial, Douglas Risher's lawyer challenged Ann Foreman about the nature of her household, querying whether they acted like a family.[102] Foreman established they were a family, both in how the children felt about each other and in that they had bought property together. The lawyer then asked Mary Jo whether she loved Ann or her sons more. Mary Jo balked at the question, explaining that the question made no sense—that it "would be like asking me at the time I was married to Mr. Risher if I loved him more than I loved

Jimmy."[103] Nonetheless the lawyer persisted: "if . . . it came to the choice of the son you've got left and being a homosexual, which would you choose ma'am?" Mary Jo said that she would not lose her son, but that response came too late. Even though Douglas was revealed to have been arrested for drunk driving, had broken his wife's nose, and had coerced the eighteen-year-old daughter of a coworker to have an abortion to hide their affair, the jury saw his "heterosexual household" as a better situation for Richard than Mary Jo's "homosexual household." In 1977, the Texas Fifth District Court dismissed Mary Jo Risher's appeal.[104] What Douglas Risher's lawyer asked of Mary Jo Risher—would she choose her child or her partner—was the question silently asked of all partnered gay parents. Like Kallas and Jacobson before her, having already chosen to form a homosexual household made Mary Jo Risher selfish and unsuited for raising her son even if being a lesbian had not.

Though citing the presence of a partner was only one of multiple rationales at hand for judges to deprive parents of custody, some judges did in fact grant custody or visitation in cases where parents agreed to live apart from a partner. These judges used custody rulings to force couples apart, illustrating again the power courts had to enforce the family form they desired. One New Jersey judge granted a mother known only as M.P. custody because she had not violated an order that she "not share Joyce's company at any time when the children were present" after she had first lived with her partner Joyce.[105] The judge also cited the fact that "she never displayed any sexual behavior in the presence of her children, and that she refrains from any demonstration of affection toward other women when the girls [were] present."[106] M.P.'s willingness to forgo a relationship while her children were minors met the court's strict interpretation of acting in the best interests of her children. In another case, a lower court preserved visitation rights for a father on the condition that he was "restricted from having any male overnight guests other than members of his lawful family when the younger two children stayed overnight."[107] Similarly, in the 1972 California case *Mitchell v. Mitchell*, the court ruled that the mother could retain custody only on the condition that she not live with or see her lesbian partner while the children were home.[108] Just a year later, in the Oregon case *A. v. A.*, the judge granted custody to the father of two boys only because the mother had had no contact with them—including birthday cards—for the past ten years. Nonetheless, the judge prohibited the "defendant's [business] partner or any other man from living in the family home." The defendant's business partner had lived with the family for the past two years, moving out only immediately prior to the trial. Though we can only speculate on the status of the two men's personal relationship, it is clear that the business partner had been part of the household prior to the trial.[109] These "selfless" parents who sacrificed their own relationships were able to retain custody.

The financial costs of this policy were aptly demonstrated in a consolidated Washington case that proved to be the striking exception to the rule that barred parents from living with same-sex partners. The early legal rounds of *Schuster v. Schuster* and *Isaacson v. Isaacson* illustrated the deep distaste the courts had for gay families. Two women separated from their husbands and began living together with all six of their children. Their husbands subsequently filed for divorce and custody of the children. As in the other cases described above, the court ruled that the women could retain custody on the condition that they live separately. After this, the story took a different turn. The two women followed the letter of the ruling and established separate apartments in the same building, but they also cultivated an eight-person household where "the Isaacson and Schuster children would refer to one another as brother or sister" and "there was a 'cross-over' of the parent roles between Ms. Isaacson and Ms. Schuster for the nurturing and assistance of the children."[110] The husbands took their former wives back to court, asking for custody in light of their wives' alleged violation of the court order.

Instead of ruling that the couple must separate to properly demonstrate their selfless parenting, the court surprisingly allowed the new family to stay together. The court in modification proceedings ruled that the women could retain custody *and* that "the living arrangement did not prove to be against the best interests of the children, except it added a financial burden."[111] The Supreme Court of Washington concurred, allowing the women to retain custody and to continue to form a blended family. This case, however, was still exceptional in the 1970s and even beyond, and the judge's reasoning clearly showed the stakes of these rulings.[112] Most gay couples had few satisfying options: they could separate, they could give up custody, or they could spend significantly more money living up to the letter, if not the spirit, of the law. Gay and lesbian households that contained children, then, had nearly no protection in the law.

Some judges extended the assumption that cohabiting gay and lesbian parents were selfish to unmarried heterosexual couples. In the case *DeVita v. DeVita*, tried in the Superior Court of New Jersey in 1976, a father contested a trial court order that he not have a female spend the night in his home while his children were present for visitation. The father argued that the ruling violated his privacy and cited several cases where courts ruled that a mother's sexual misconduct with various men did no harm to her children and therefore the mother could not be deprived of custody. The court, however, found that these cases dealt with the much more traumatic issue of custody, rather than visitation rights. Instead, they found the greatest parallel case in two gay household cases, *In the Matter of Jane B.* and *In the Matter of J.S. & C.* Though the New Jersey Superior Court showed its distaste for gay sex, it nonetheless identified both straight and same-sex cohabitation as a choice, rather than an immutable component of the parents' identities. Like in the two gay parent visitation cases, the court put conditions on DeVita's rights, DeVita argued that these restrictions were a violation of his constitutional right of privacy, and the court found instead that "there is no great inconvenience to the father in precluding his female friend from staying overnight on every other weekend when the children are present in the house. If he wants the children on those weekends he can give up his wish to have his friend stay there."[113]

Judge J. A. D. Antell's dissent highlighted the coercive nature of cohabitation rulings for gay and straight couples alike. Though Antell argued that homosexuality posed a threat that straight cohabitation did not, his analysis illuminated the shared constraints straight and same-sex cohabiting households faced. Antell emphasized that the father in *DeVita v. DeVita* was involved in a long-term committed relationship with a woman with children of her own. The father considered his family and his partner's to form a household, much like those of the lesbian mothers and gay fathers cited above. Though the couple was considering marriage, they "regard[ed] themselves as having formed a nonceremonialized family unit consisting of themselves and their respective children." The goals of the majority ruling, in Antell's opinion, were to try to "make the father toe the line" in regards to sexual propriety. And finally, Antell believed, "the only certain consequence of these unreasonable ground rules is that defendant will now have to choose between his friend and his children, and in place of natural, spontaneous feelings these relationships will be increasingly governed by the process of cold and deliberate analysis. However he chooses he must now pay a price, and this may eventually strain his relationship with the children." What the courts were largely silent about in rulings about homosexual households—the ways in which they were forcing parents to choose between their children and their partners—Antell was explicit about in regards to a straight relationship. The goal of these cohabitation rulings was to break up relationships, and courts continued to do so for many years or even decades, depending on the state.[114]

But the option that DeVita had to keep his living situation in place—the choice to marry his partner—was simply not available to a partnered gay parent who wanted to retain custody. That this option was out of gay and lesbian couples' grasp had been clear since another famous gay marriage case from 1971, *Jones v. Hallahan*. Marjorie Jones's suit claimed that Kentucky denied her the right to marry, the right of association, and the right to free exercise of religion. Scholars have suggested that Jones's desire to marry was more political than genuine, but it is difficult to judge her devotion to her partner Tracy Knight in 1971 based on how they felt about each other years after their break-up. At the time Jones and Knight committed considerable resources and took significant risks to make their marriage possible.[115]

In practical terms, in fact, Jones seemingly sued in order to be able to cohabit with Knight and also retain custody of her fifteen-year-old son. Instead of living together, the couple told the *Advocate*, "the son lives at her home under the supervision of a housekeeper, while Miss Knight lives at Mrs. Jones' massage parlor and reducing salon." This precaution was necessary in part because Jefferson County, Kentucky, county attorney J. Bruce Miller threatened to have "state agencies look into taking action against the mother for 'contributing to the delinquency of a minor.' "[116] Jones even made it clear, "until we get this straightened out to where we can live together under one roof, I do not have Tracy at the house other than occasionally for dinner or if I have a few friends in."[117] The arrangement also reinforced, however, the fact that Jones acted as the breadwinner in the household, taking responsibility for both Knight and her son, despite expensive legal hurdles. Jones presumably could not afford the expense of two rents, which forced Knight to live full-time in Jones's commercial establishment. In addition to attorney costs, the couple also had to pay a housekeeper to stay with Jones's teenage son. A marriage license could allow all three—mother, son, and partner—to reside together. Jones and Knight planned to create a household once the marriage was officially consecrated—and protected—by the state.

Jefferson County's attorney did not seem to see Jones as a breadwinner caring for both her partner and her child, and instead he accused Jones of acting selfishly. He argued that the Jones and Knight did not have "the requisites of a happy home, the love and affection desired by society, with the proper concern for the children involved."[118] He continued by noting that he saw "simply the pure pursuit of hedonistic and sexual pleasure on the part of the parties hereto."[119] The county attorney saw selfish sexual desire in Jones and Knight's suit and obscured Jones's sacrifices for and devotion to her family. No matter the contradictions imbedded in this accusation, it was one that couples repeatedly faced. The Kentucky court silently deferred to Miller in many ways, by stating simply that what Jones and Knight proposed was not in fact a marriage, and their bid for a marriage license, like so many other attempts in the 1970s, failed. Importantly, when Jones and Knight lost, they also lost the opportunity to live together with Jones's son.

Similarly, the IRS, HUD, the INS, and the Supreme Court also granted limited benefits to gay and lesbian individuals but would not grant marriage benefits to same-sex couples for fear that the "selfish" desire for marital obligations threatened society or family itself. Custody was only the most effective way of breaking up homosexual households. This fear about custody formed a larger framework for barring homosexual households in the 1970s. Government agencies inflicted solitude upon the members of gay and lesbian couples by working to break up gay and lesbian households.

Baker and McConnell were not only pioneers in attempting to procure a marriage license; they were also pioneers in using a license to try to gain tax benefits reserved for married couples. They first tried to use their Mankato license to establish a household in the eyes of the IRS. In their case, this meant that their tax rate would actually increase. In this Baker and McConnell perhaps hoped to illustrate that they would take on the gender-neutral thick obligations of marriage; not merely the thin version enacted on the state level.[120] Perhaps due to the presumably unusual willingness to pay extra taxes, or simply due to inattention, the U.S. Internal Revenue Service initially seemed to condone the Mankato marriage. In 1972, "the IRS collected the extra tax without comment, and for 1973 it sent the Form 1040 with both men's names on the mailing label."[121] Baker and McConnell's initial optimism proved short-lived, however. The IRS ruled against Baker and McConnell in 1975, disallowing their right to file as a married couple.[122] Baker also tried to claim veterans' benefits for McConnell as his dependent spouse, in particular education benefits. The Eighth Circuit court rejected this claim in 1976.[123] They affirmed the Veterans Administration (VA) ruling that McConnell simply was not Baker's spouse.[124]

Again, many other couples followed Baker and McConnell's example and tried to win benefits from a host of government agencies only to discover that other agencies recognized gay and lesbian households only on the rare occasion that it was in the government's financial interest to do so. Kenneth Bland and Ronald Malvin applied for a marriage license because Bland found himself ineligible for food stamps on the basis of his partner's income. Bland told the *Advocate*, "the government says Ron and I can't file a joint income tax return unless we are legally married, . . . but when I went to inquire about eligibility for food stamps, the welfare department told me that since we have a joint checking account, they would combine the income of our family unit together as though we were married—making me ineligible for the stamp program."[125] Bland, of course, was not rejected on the basis of his sexuality. First, after 1973, straight cohabiting couples were also barred from receiving food stamps.[126] Second, gay men and lesbians received food stamp benefits even if their sexuality was widely known.[127] For example, a Louisiana man named George Parker received food stamps after his conviction for sodomy.[128] It was Bland's homosexual household that barred him from food stamp benefits. On his own, he would be eligible. As it was, Bland could give up food stamps or give up Malvin. This choice was not an accident. Increasingly government workers, particularly judges determining custody and visitation rights, posed this choice to the poor and to gay parents, two groups vulnerable to government coercion.

The Department of Housing and Urban Development was among the most visible of the federal agencies to try to forcibly break up homosexual households, albeit after a brief loosening of HUD policy.[129] The saga began in 1976 when the Housing Authorization Act of 1976 charged HUD with opening up public housing to single people.[130] Priscilla Banks, the HUD housing program specialist, took an expansive approach to Congress's orders. Among the other new regulations, she introduced a provision that unmarried couples—heterosexual and homosexual alike—could live in public housing as long as they met the income limitations and demonstrated a "stable family relationship." Though Banks intended to help straight unmarried couples as well, she included gay and lesbian couples deliberately. Given that local authorities would interpret the meaning of stable families, Banks hoped that they would include gay couples on the local level. In essence, HUD's new provision would welcome homosexual households into one of the main benefits of marriage to low-income families. Banks then "held [her] breath," hoping the provision would come into effect on May 9 without disruption.[131]

As with the inclusive DC no-fault bill, the inclusive HUD provision quickly gained and then lost support. Banks had worried she would encounter a backlash when the new regulations were first released, but instead she received only six letters that mentioned the new definition of family at all.[132] Opposition and praise for the new regulations were equally matched. One HUD supporter in Charlotte, North Carolina, explained, "these people need roofs over their heads, too."[133] One opponent who managed public housing in Florida thought that the legal disputes over what constituted a stable family relationship would create a nightmare. Only Joseph Alden, the executive director of the Albany Housing Authority, argued that HUD should specifically exclude same-sex couples.[134] But then in June, the provision came to the attention of Representative Edward Boland (D-MA), who proposed an amendment to a HUD appropriation bill that would cut the new provision.[135] In the House debate, Boland argued that the unmarried couples who could provide a good situation for children should not be denied access to public housing, but he did not approve of extending housing rights to gay couples. He recast the provision as an unintended addition: "unfortunately, since promulgation, these regulations have given rise to other interpretations of 'stable family relationships,' namely homosexual couples. This development was not contemplated by the Department and poses an issue which it is unprepared to deal with at this time."[136] Speaking for HUD, Boland stated that "the issue of homosexual rights is too emotional and sensitive in thrust for local authorities to have to deal with."[137] Lesbians and gay men were welcome in public housing, but their partners certainly were not.

Other congressmen joined Boland in blocking public housing for gay families. Speaking for the minority, Representative Coughlin argued that "the way to change a dictionary definition of family is not through a regulation of HUD." Representative Hagedorn expressed support for a "live and let live" principle but feared that HUD's provision would also create an important precedent. Hagedorn further argued that the means of eliminating such discrimination should reside within Congress itself, rather than with bureaucrats within HUD. The House conceded quickly to Boland, casting a voice vote after only five minutes of debate.[138] In the end, Banks's attempt to extend the benefits of households to gay and unmarried couples failed. A gay man or lesbian could only live in HUD housing as a single gay man or lesbian. For those in need of affordable housing, this choice was immensely coercive.[139]

If these were all effective means of breaking up homosexual households, deportation was the most effective way. The definitive example was Richard Adams, who unsuccessfully tried to gain permanent residency for his immigrant partner, Anthony Sullivan. Sullivan, an Australian citizen, met Adams on a vacation in 1971. Enamored after a short time, Sullivan checked with the Australian consulate in Los Angeles to see if Adams could be granted a visa to Australia. The consulate worker told Sullivan that Adams would not be given a visa due to his Filipino racial heritage.[140] Sullivan left the country without

Adams, but the two kept in touch after the visit and fell in love via "a prolific correspondence."[141] Sullivan eventually came to the United States to be with Adams. For a while he bounced across the border to maintain his visa until Sullivan, "like thousands of gay aliens each year who love American citizens of the same sex," married a woman in a bid to gain citizenship.[142] But a few months later, Sullivan and his wife learned that they would have to consummate the marriage to qualify Sullivan for citizenship. A trial cohabitation ended poorly, and Sullivan annulled the sham marriage.[143] After a period of limbo, Adams and Sullivan managed to marry in Boulder, Colorado, during a week in 1975 when a clerk granted several same-sex couples marriage licenses. At the end of the week, the state attorney general stopped the clerk from issuing any further marriage licenses.

Adams then petitioned the INS to grant Sullivan a permanent resident visa on the basis of this marriage, but the federal government rejected the claim. Initially the INS responded, "You have failed to establish that a bona fide marital relationship can exist between two faggots."[144] Although the INS was quickly reprimanded for its choice of words, marital benefits for Sullivan were less forthcoming. The INS issued a new rejection. It cited *Baker* and *Jones* and argued that Congress had not intended gay marriage as a means of visa petition since neither partner could perform the wife's "duties and obligations."[145] Adams and his allies attempted to counter these claims by emphasizing repeatedly the sacrifices the couple made to be a couple, including their careers, inheritance, and more.[146] Nonetheless, even Sullivan's mother characterized his suit as selfish.[147]

Adams sued to try to establish his ability to perform marital obligations in a world without prescribed gender roles in marriage. He evoked gender equality as his legal rationale: "the argument that one party to a marriage must assume 'female duties and obligations' falls of its own weight."[148] But again, Sullivan's supposed inability to contribute as a homemaker to the household was a key point in the ruling. The presiding judge in the 1979 appeal suggested that the benefits of marriage should not accrue to gay couples in part because there was as yet no "mutual obligation to support" in place.[149] In 1980, a United States district court in California ruled against Adams and Sullivan.[150] The couple fled to Europe to avoid separation. They returned a short while later, and Sullivan lived as an undocumented immigrant.[151] Thus immigration policy was another means that government actors had to split up gay couples that were less resourceful or less willing to sacrifice than Sullivan and Adams.

For some time, the problem of the homosexual household in immigration

"SORRY ABOUT THE WORDING, BUT REALLY, A BONAFIDE MARRIAGE _DOES_ PRODUCE CHILDREN, DOESN'T IT?"

Figure 8. This political cartoon represented Richard Adams and Anthony Sullivan's attempt to win a visa on the basis of the couple's marriage license from Colorado. Sullivan holds "the Infamous 'Faggot' Letter" in his hand (United States Department of Justice Immigration and Naturalization Service, "Decision: Richard Frank Adams," November 24, 1975, box 1, folder 1: Case Records, 1974–1976, Sullivan v. INS Records, ONE Archives, University of Southern California Libraries). Courtesy of the ONE Archives, University of Southern California Libraries.

was different from what custody judges, the IRS, HUD, and other government agencies enacted since the INS had more discretion to discriminate against single gay men and lesbians until 1980. Most famously, the INS and then the Supreme Court determined that Canadian Clive Michael Boutilier was ineligible for naturalization due to his homosexual activity both before and after his immigration to the United States.[152] On this basis, Boutilier was deemed a psychopathic personality and deported. The United States was not always consistent about its discrimination, however. In *Fleuti v. Rosenberg*, *Matter of Belle*, and *In re. Labady*, courts ruled that immigrants with homosexual identities were not necessarily ineligible for citizenship.[153] But from the mid-1960s until 1980, the INS blocked most gay or lesbian immigrants. In 1980, the INS at last relaxed its policy on gay and lesbian immigrants—so long as those immigrants did not confess to homosexual activity. The enactment of this policy was imperfect. Border agents seemingly still pried into private documents and made arbitrary decisions on immigrants. Nonetheless, the *Boutilier* era had passed in important ways.

Being part of a homosexual household became a certain block from immigration. By the time that Adams and Sullivan lost their case in 1982, Sullivan could have successfully naturalized in the United States if he had entered on the basis of being a skilled worker. But the partners of gay and lesbian citizens were still ineligible for citizenship until the Defense of Marriage Act was overturned in 2013, long after the 1980 change in INS policy.[154]

Feminists' efforts to strip gender out of marriage did not help gay couples. Instead government workers barred the possibility of gay marriage—and proceeded to break up homosexual households when they had leverage to do so. What husbands had asked for in no-fault divorce statutes—independence from their wives—government agencies had inflicted upon gay couples, stemming from moral and monetary concerns. There were no legally recognized obligations between gay partners, and there were no legally recognized obligations to gay partners from the government.

The End of Marriage as We Know It

The backlash to the marriage revolution came into full bloom in 1996 even if its foundations were in place as early as the 1970s. Few states enforced a breadwinner-homemaker household, and few families lived it in practice. Nonetheless lawmakers continued to apply the principle selectively. First, Clinton-era welfare reform in the 1990s innovated new methods to target poor men to ensure they paid for dependents. Second, the INS began enforcing citizens' financial responsibility for their former spouses, which effectively barred the poor from marrying noncitizens without a cosponsor. Third, Congress maintained the fiction that gay marriage represented the selfish acts of individuals rather than a shared commitment to a united household economy. It passed the Defense of Marriage Act to prevent alleged self-interested same-sex couples from taking advantage of federal household benefits. By 1996, lawmakers had fully implemented the central contradiction of marriage policy: marriage for the poor imposed obligations, and marriage for the privileged valued individual property rights above all.

Welfare

In the late postwar period, states and then Congress tried to hold black men responsible for black women and their children—regardless of marriage, biological ties, or even their ability to provide. Black men became the excuse to deprive black women of welfare, and states selectively punished those men who failed to support women and children. Three court cases from 1968 until 1971 stalled this process to some degree—*King v. Smith*, *Lewis v. Martin*, and *Wyman v. James*. Nonetheless, Congress and state legislatures continued to focus on fathers whose children were on welfare, often to the exclusion of other fathers, for decades thereafter. For example, near the end of his second term, Reagan's Office of Policy Development still complained that *King v. Smith* "drastically reduced the legal presumptions favoring marriage and the family."[1]

Devaluing the homemaking labor of women on welfare became a central tenet of welfare reform in the 1990s. This was made easier by the rapid drop in full-time homemakers overall in the American population.[2] Democratic president Bill Clinton fulfilled his vow to "remake welfare as we know it." Above all, Clinton made welfare's benefits temporary, which was reflected in welfare's new name—Temporary Assistance for Needy Families. The shift from AFDC to TANF echoed the shift from alimony to maintenance. With both alimony and welfare, the temporary payments were designed simply to set women back on their feet—to make them independent as quickly as possible.[3] But mothers receiving TANF faced pressures that divorced wives did not, and moreover the treatment of TANF fathers differed a great deal from the treatment of divorced husbands.[4]

Strategies that thickened the breadwinning obligations of fathers whose children were on welfare were also central to welfare reform. In June of 1996, President Clinton announced new rules requiring mothers to provide "detailed" information on the father of their children in order to be eligible for welfare.[5] In proposing these new rules to the American Nurses Association, Clinton argued, "Our system should say to mothers: If you want our help, help us to identify and locate the fathers [*sic*] so he can be held accountable." He followed this with a more aggressive admonition to fathers: "And it should say to fathers: We're not going to just let you walk away from your children and stick the taxpayers with the tab. The government did not bring the child into the world, you did."[6] Once again, the federal government passionately pursued certain fathers—men whose children were on welfare, again often imagined to be black by the politicians who sought welfare reform in the first place.[7]

Congress similarly endorsed a system that sought payment from fathers through any means at hand—by restricting access to drivers' licenses and passports, garnishing federal tax returns, and tracking fathers' movements.[8] Senator Byron Dorgan of North Dakota announced in congressional debate "Deadbeat dads, avoiding your responsibility is over."[9] But pursuing fathers was once again a strategy to cut AFDC costs, rather than help children or their mothers. When the IRS tax intercept system seized a father's federal tax refund for failing to pay child support, the money went first to the state if the father's child had ever received welfare payments—even if the child was no longer on TANF. The states themselves were not alone in enjoying these payments, however, since the law mandated that the states pass on 50 to 75 percent of those funds on to the federal government. Even when the fathers owed mothers years of back pay on child support—as many did—the garnished return went first to the federal and state governments. Under Clinton welfare reform, enforcing fathers' obligations was designed to benefit the government first. This was also evident in the incentive structure built to get women on AFDC to comply. Most mothers and children saw only a $50 pay-through each month, and this scant amount was clearly a means only to incentivize mothers to disclose information on fathers' whereabouts. Even some members of the House of Representatives acknowledged how paltry $50 was at the end of the twentieth century. A House bill unsuccessfully recommended that women should get as much as $400 pay-through.[10]

As before, many women did not wish to turn over information on their children's father for a range of reasons. This was especially true when women on welfare feared retributive violence from their children's fathers. An early proposal for welfare reform during the Clinton administration proposed an exemption for disclosing a father's whereabouts in the case of rape, incest, or domestic violence.[11] The Personal Responsibility and Work Opportunity Reconciliation Act (PRWORA) also contained a Family Violence Option. This option was supposed to give applicants twenty days to show good cause for why a father should not be contacted for child support. But states had to opt in to these protections. Illinois, for example, only implemented this option in 2002 with grave ramifications in the interim. For instance one Illinois resident named Jessie Diaz testified to the Illinois House of Representatives that delaying implementation of the policy had put her in danger. She left her partner due to domestic violence in April of 2001 in order to protect her two daughters and unborn son. When she sought cash assistance to move out of the domestic violence shelter she lived in, her caseworker told her she must apply for child support to qualify. Diaz withdrew her application and borrowed money from a family member instead. But with her information in hand, the Department of Human Services sent her former partner notice anyway. Once he knew Diaz's whereabouts, he immediately went to her new apartment and kicked her in her postpartum stomach until she bled. The danger of domestic violence was real, and women experienced it due to policies that privileged fiscal concerns over the well-being of the poor.[12]

A more contemporary tragedy illustrates that a woman on TANF also might not want to disclose her children's father's identity or whereabouts in order to protect him. In April of 2015, Walter L. Scott ran from the police when he was pulled over for a broken taillight in North Charleston, South Carolina. The police then fatally shot Scott in the back. As his relatives later revealed, Scott may have run in part because he owed over $18,000 in child support. Scott had already served time for failing to pay child support, which had cost Scott his job and ballooned the child support he owed even further. Though the police obviously do not kill every man who owes child support, any encounter with the police can be dangerous for poor men. Scott's experiences with imprisonment were even more representative. As the *New York Times* noted in its follow-up coverage, "many critics assert that punitive policies are trapping poor men in a cycle of debt, unemployment and imprisonment."[13] In particular, the *Times* cited a 2007 Urban Institute Study that revealed that men who earned less than $10,000 represented over 70 percent of the child support debt owed in nine states, including Illinois. These men were also expected to pay 83 percent of their income in child support, a far cry from the maximum of 50 percent owed by men with over six children who went through divorce proceedings in Illinois. The protections in place for divorced men apparently did not accommodate men with low or no income.

In addition to this, states like New York and California revived home searches for live-in boyfriends. In 1995, New York City mayor Rudy Giuliani's administration instituted new policies that screened AFDC applicants via fingerprinting, an extended interview, a survey of utility bills, a credit check, and a computer search. Applicants who passed these provisional checks then had to submit to a home visit, the details of which resembled ones that Sylvester Smith endured. According to the *New York Times*, a field investigator on a home visit checked the mailbox for the names "of other people who might live with the applicant and possibly contribute to household income."[14] The field investigator also interviewed landlords, building supervisors, and neighbors; the investigator perhaps excluded grocers only because supermarkets had wiped out the intimate grocery transaction that Smith had experienced in the postwar South.

After the implementation of PRWORA, such policies withstood court challenges. For example, lawmakers in San Diego County implemented a new policy called Project 100% that echoed Giuliani's policy. Applicants submitted to home visits where investigators searched closets, drawers, medicine cabinets, refrigerators, purses, and mail.[15] Applicants who refused the search were automatically denied benefits on the presumption that they were hiding boyfriends. After losing benefits for refusing a search, several applicants sued the county for violating the Fourth Amendment, just as Barbara James had in *Wyman v. James* (1971). The case reached the United States Court of Appeals for the Ninth Circuit in 2007, which denied the request for rehearing *en banc* because the justices determined that unannounced home visits to welfare programs did not constitute a search. This ruling allowed the snooping and unannounced searches that *Wyman* had disallowed. A dissenting judge called the policy "nothing less than an attack on the poor."[16]

During the George W. Bush administration, the federal government also adopted policies that incentivized marriage for welfare recipients.[17] These initiatives echoed the film *Claudine*. After Claudine's caseworker, Miss Kabak, discovered Claudine's secret boyfriend, played by James Earl Jones's character, in the closet, she continually pressured him to marry Claudine in order to take the family off AFDC. (He did.) Similarly states rerouted huge sums of TANF money to private entities that encouraged women on welfare to marry. Even the comic strip *Boondocks* critiqued the "healthy marriage initiatives" for assuming marriage rather than education or healthcare would better alleviate poverty.[18] We should consider this old-school method in the context of a marriage law that had dispensed with the responsibility of breadwinning for the majority of American men.

Into the present day, then, the welfare system still pits poor men and women against one another. Laws regulating men operate in tandem with punitive measures against women to limit mothers' access to welfare rights or to make their claim on those rights more costly or dangerous. In effect, welfare policy continues to try to impose the breadwinner-homemaker model of family on the poor, even though this legal model broke down long ago through no-fault divorce and state ERAs for families that were not on welfare.

Immigration

Like the backlash against the fathers of children on welfare, the backlash against immigrant spouses only grew in the 1990s. Amid the general anti-welfare sentiment, immigrant spouses lost even more rights, and Congress began to target their citizen spouses as well by thickening their breadwinning obligations considerably. This trend actually led to almost half of the savings introduced by Clinton-era welfare reform.[19]

Even after the Immigration Marriage Fraud Amendments, the increasing number of immigrant spouses and dissatisfaction with amnesty fueled the immigrant marriage backlash. In some ways, the 1986 legislation seemed to be effectively reducing incidents of marriage fraud. In 1994, over 5,000 spouses out of a total of 95,000 had their conditional status terminated on the basis of fraud. The majority of these spouses came from Asia and North America (mostly Mexico and the Caribbean).[20] On the other hand, the 1986 legislation did not effectively decrease the number of overall immigrants admitted as immediate relatives. By 1993, the number of immigrants who gained citizenship by marriage was around 150,000 a year.[21] This was a significant increase over the 1970s numbers, when the number was close to 50,000 immigrant spouses, and even over the 1986 number of approximately 140,000.[22] In 1994, most of these immigrant spouses were from Mexico, the Dominican Republic, the Philippines, the United Kingdom, Canada, and Germany.[23] Many Americans still found immigrant spouses threatening. For example, the *Houston Post* published an op-ed by immigration expert Jim Hastings stating that family reunification had become too widespread. Hastings argued that the balance of visas should be shifted away from family members, who garnered 95 percent of visas, to skilled laborers.[24]

By 1990 it was possible for Congress to consider again significantly narrowing the family reunification principle. Though some aspects of the 1990 immigration legislation were promising—for example, victims of domestic violence were no longer automatically denied a visa if they divorced within two years—overall, the proposed bills indicated the increasing skepticism about family reunification. The S. 358 Immigration Act proposed including immediate relatives of U.S. citizens under the yearly quota of immigrants. Prior to this, immediate family members had always been exempt from overall limits to immigrants.[25] The annual limit for all family members would be 480,000 per year. Similarly the Smith Amendment to H.R. 4300 proposed a cap on the immediate family members of permanent residents and U.S. citizens based on the premise that immigrants exacerbated unemployment, decreased wages, and increased welfare benefits.[26] Representative Bryant offered an amendment that only marginally scaled back this impulse. It provided for a five-year hiatus when spouses and children of permanent residents would not be subject to immigration limits.[27] In the end, Congress did not place a quota on citizens' spouses and children but did limit the immediate family members of permanent residents as part of the amnesty deal. Within ten years, the backlog of spouses and children of permanent residents numbered 1.1 million.[28]

Nor were immigration opponents satisfied that the benefits of immigration outweighed the costs despite evidence to the contrary. Immigration advocates argued that immigrants contributed far more than they received in taxes.[29] One study concluded that immigrants paid $70.3 billion in taxes and received only $42.9 billion in benefits back. It further noted that undocumented workers fared the worst, paying into unemployment insurance and Social Security, but never receiving these benefits. This helped keep Social Security solvent, an unintended but also protected boon to the federal government.[30] But immigration opponents nonetheless insisted that immigrants overburdened the welfare system. Representative Lamar Smith of Texas claimed, "IMMIGRANTS DO NOT PAY MORE IN TAXES THAN THEY RECEIVE IN WELFARE BENEFITS!!" which he based on the work of George Borjas at Harvard University. He also argued that 20 percent of immigrants were on welfare, immigrants became increasingly likely to go on welfare the longer they stayed in the country, and they cost the American government $25 billion a year.[31]

As the 1980s wore into the 1990s, the public's focus shifted to undocumented immigrants and their access to welfare and other aid. This concern existed despite much more careful provisions against undocumented immigrants receiving federal benefits such as welfare, particularly AFDC.[32] Nonetheless, undocumented immigrants could receive AFDC on behalf of their citizen children.[33] The director of Income Security for the United States General Accounting Office estimated the national, state, and local costs of these benefits to the citizen children of noncitizen women at $479 million in 1992, or 2 percent of the annual cost of AFDC.[34] Whether opponents were aware of these distinctions or not, they certainly saw an enormous burden in undocumented men and women. For example, the *New York Times* focused in particular on an unmarried mother who had swum across the Rio Grande and then acquired access to the Special Supplemental Nutrition Program for Women, Infants, and Children (WIC). She had also delivered a son "at public expense" at Ben Taub General Hospital in Houston, Texas.[35] *Reader's Digest* published an extensive piece titled "Welfare for Illegal Aliens?" that alleged incorrectly that a quarter of all AFDC clients were illegal immigrants.[36]

Press coverage that exaggerated the use of welfare by immigrants prompted a flood of constituent responses into Representative Patsy Mink's office. For instance, one constituent wrote to Mink about his fears that the Fourteenth Amendment had created an entire population of "illegal" immigrants who could receive welfare benefits via children born in the United States.[37] Another also objected to the illegal immigrants "pour[ing] over our southern borders" due to the increased welfare and prison costs.[38] A third constituent asked Mink to support a policy that, among other things, insisted illegal immigrants should not receive welfare, nor should any of their children born on U.S. soil gain U.S. citizenship.[39] Yet another constituent deplored the "millions upon millions" given to illegal citizens for welfare, medical care, and more.[40]

In essence, many Americans believed that documented and undocumented immigration alike still threatened to increase welfare costs, a problem that Congress dealt with in a multistep process in the 1990s, culminating with PRWORA.[41] Every form of welfare reform that circulated during this time proposed one restriction or another for immigrants. One Republican proposal included an outright ban on over sixty federal programs for all documented immigrants.[42] Other Republican proposals just excluded refugees from all these programs. A third proposal mandated that federal programs report any immigrant who received benefits for more than a year in order to initiate deportation on the basis of being a public charge.[43]

Though Clinton's legislation was comparatively less punitive—a point his administration quickly pointed out to critics when given the opportunity—his proposal also sought to end the distribution of benefits to immigrants.[44] Clinton made use of "deeming" to exclude legal residents from receiving benefits. Deeming counted a sponsor's income as part of an immigrant's income whether or not he or she had access to any of it—much like the alleged partners of substitute fathers. His plan made the window under which a sponsor's income was deemed five years. During this time, a sponsor's income would have to be below $40,000 for immigrants to be eligible for welfare. In effect, many immigrants would be excluded from welfare benefits, no matter whether their sponsor helped them or not.[45] As one congressional study explained while comparing Senate and House versions of welfare reform, there was not necessarily an enormous difference between the various schemes: "the House bill bars legal immigrant access to AFDC, Food Stamps, non-emergency Medicaid, and Title XX block grants. In contrast, the Senate bill merely restricts access to these programs (and most needs-based programs) via deeming."[46] The National Council of State Legislatures objected that deeming would shift the burden of supporting poor immigrants exclusively to the states.[47] Congresswoman Patsy Mink, who had battled against the poor treatment of immigrants when she had last served in Congress, declared the provisions "punitive to Non US Citizens" and vowed to "fight against harsh anti-immigrant measures."[48] Despite her efforts, the various provisions including deeming made most immigrants ineligible for welfare.

In the end, welfare reform severely limited immigrants' access to all federal, state, and local means-tested benefits. Legislation that passed both houses in the summer of 1996 eliminated all legal residents from eligibility for five years, including for AFDC.[49] It also extended deeming—counting a sponsor's income with an immigrant's to determine eligibility for welfare programs—to AFDC, food stamps, and Social Security until an immigrant attained citizenship.[50] New immigrants would have to work at least forty quarters to qualify for benefits.[51] States could decide to continue to support legal residents only on their own dime.

Finally, of course, even AFDC ceased to exist when PRWORA replaced it with TANF. TANF incorporated or increased many of the restrictions for immigrants. First, under TANF, states could determine for themselves whether to continue TANF benefits for legal residents already receiving benefits.[52] Second, there was a five-year ban on TANF for new documented immigrants, as there was on most federal means-tested benefits. After the federal five-year ban ended, states could decide to maintain an immigrant spouse as ineligible for TANF. Moreover, after the five-year federal ban was over, immigrant spouses were subject to deeming for TANF and other federal benefits until they became citizens or worked for forty quarters.[53] Exemptions for one year were allowed for "some battered spouses and children, and those at risk of going hungry or becoming homeless."[54] There was also a blanket exception for immigrants who entered before August of 1996, but individual states could opt to exclude these immigrants as well.[55] In the end, PRWORA established a broad ban on aid for most immigrant spouses. This ban also ensured that welfare reform saved the federal government money. According to some estimates, the restrictions on TANF for immigrants of all sorts accounted for 44 percent of the total savings yielded by PRWORA.[56]

In 1996, Congress passed independent immigration reform that also prevented immigrant spouses from becoming dependent on government benefits by strictly enforcing sponsors' obligations.[57] This law, which was intended to cut immigration by 40 percent, drew its inspiration from earlier bills. Lamar Smith, the sponsor of H.R. 2202 and of a proposed reduction in immigration overall in H.R. 1915, had pioneered legislative proposals that made a sponsor's obligation legally binding.[58] Senator Alan Simpson (R-Wyoming) sponsored a similar bill in the Senate.[59] In 1993, Senator Reid of Nevada sponsored the

Immigration Stabilization Act of 1993, which sought to provide financial stability by enforcing financial affidavits. Reid aimed to hold all immigrants to the "same degree of financial accountability that current law requires for the sponsors of Amerasian immigrants."[60] In the version that became law, "sponsors who fail to support sponsored aliens are legally liable to the sponsored aliens and to any government agency that provides sponsored aliens needs-based assistance."[61] Sponsors remained liable until the immigrant spouses became citizens or worked for forty quarters.[62]

The new enforcement of a sponsor's thick financial obligations was an incredibly popular component of the bill. For instance, the board of supervisors for the County of Los Angeles wrote to every congressperson to endorse the provision in H.R. 2202 that required all immigrant sponsors to be legally and financially responsible for the health and welfare of every immigrant they sponsored.[63] The chairman of the Los Angeles County board insisted that this would prevent "aliens *legally* [in] the United States from *abusing the system*."[64]

Congress also restricted who could sponsor an immigrant in the first place. Immigration H.R. 2202 proposed that anyone sponsoring an immigrant had to have an income of at least 200 percent of the poverty level.[65] Sponsors had to submit documentation such as a recent tax return and a form indicating that he or she understood that his or her assets and income could be drawn from if the immigrant became a public charge.[66] The only loophole in the bill for spouses who earned less than 200 percent of the poverty line was to find a cosponsor willing to accept "joint and several liability with the petitioner."[67] As the Urban Institute noted, this posed a serious barrier to all potential sponsors, even spouses. Approximately 46 percent of all Americans earned below double the poverty level of 1994, and thus were too poor to sponsor an immigrant.[68] One congressional study noted that the 200 percent above the poverty line requirement would even prevent many service members in the U.S. military, a group particularly prone to both low wages and marrying foreign spouses abroad, from "bringing their foreign spouses home to live with them in the United States."[69] Marrying a foreigner would become an option *only* for the affluent, the report rightly complained.[70] The Senate bill moderated this provision only slightly. A spouse had to earn at least 125 percent of the poverty line.[71]

The bill again proposed a ceiling on how many immigrants could be admitted in a year, ending the policy that allowed citizens' spouses and children in without any limits. This meant that a U.S. citizen with a spouse or children would have joined a queue if too many immigrants were admitted in any given year.[72] Sponsors, even if they were citizens who earned above 200 percent of the poverty line, still would not necessarily get to bring in their spouses and children. Objectors found this provision the most irresponsible. The Chrysler/Berman/Brownback amendment eliminated this provision via a vote of 238 to 183.[73] Though the 200 percent provision was in place for most spouses, this was lowered for military members.[74] Another provision denied the right of noncitizen parents to claim benefits on behalf of their citizen children.[75] H.R. 2202 passed by a vote of 333 for and 87 against on March 21, 1996.

And finally if all else failed, the government left accepted immigrants on their own. Even qualified immigrants could not naturalize if their sponsor had any outstanding debts to the government.[76] This was a means of enforcing the affidavits, but again immigrants were forced to depend on sponsors, even " 'dead beat' sponsors."[77] This left new immigrants as permanent residents indefinitely and deprived them of many of the benefits of citizenship.[78] Other critics maintained that even five years of deeming kept battered women particularly vulnerable, perhaps forcing them to stay with their abusers just to keep body and soul together.[79] And like the proposals in welfare reform, using benefits for a year within the first few years of an immigrant's arrival was a deportable offense. Once again, a victim of domestic abuse could be deported at the whim of her citizen abuser.[80]

By 1996 there was a dual system for dealing with immigrant spouses in need of aid. Immigrant spouses who had resided in the United States less than two years were deported. Immigrant spouses who gained legal residency became legally dependent on their citizen spouses regardless of whether the spouse provided for him or her. Citizen spouses, regardless of gender, who divorced after less than two years had no support obligation at all; his or her spouse was often deported as a perpetrator of a sham marriage. But those who divorced after two years faced a situation much like the partners of women on welfare. They faced a thick support obligation that most spouses no longer bore. Even these provisions have not proved satisfying to immigration critics, and President Donald Trump has endorsed an immigration policy that would sharply limit family reunification visas.[81]

Gay Marriage

Though today we see a much different trajectory for gay marriage than for immigration or welfare, 1996 looked similarly dismal for gay marriage activists following a brief run of successes in the early 1990s. In 1993, the Hawaii Supreme Court ruled in *Baehr v. Lewin* (later *Baehr v. Miike*) that Hawaii could not deny licenses to gay and lesbian couples without a "compelling state interest."[82] Though local civil rights attorney Dan Foley had sought equal protection for gays and lesbians, instead the Hawaiian Supreme Court found in favor of the couples by applying strict scrutiny to gender discrimination. In other words, predictions that anti-feminists had made during the ERA battle at last seemed to be coming true. Later that year, the *New Yorker* profiled Tom Stoddard in the immediate aftermath of the Hawaii Supreme Court's decision regarding his upcoming marriage to Walter Rieman. Stoddard was both professionally and personally involved in the decision. He had been the executive director of Lambda Legal Defense and Education Fund since 1986. When he was appointed to the position, he had stated, "In fact, [being gay] often involves being part of a family in every possible sense: as spouse, as parent, as child. Society needs to foster greater stability in gay relationships."[83]

The issue of gay marriage was more personal to Stoddard in 1993 than it had been when he took the reins at Lambda Legal in part because Rieman had been diagnosed with AIDS in the interim. Though Stoddard and Rieman both expressed concern about participating in the traditional institution, in the spirit of gay marriage dissenters, the couple nonetheless married in light of Stoddard's battle with AIDS. Emotionally, marriage would provide what Stoddard described as closure in light of his illness. But marriage would also enable Stoddard to share Rieman's health insurance. In the 1990s, winning the benefits of marriage remained a major goal in part because the need for health-care benefits had grown. Like Rieman, many men and women sought health insurance or access to the 1993 Family and Medical Leave Act for their partners.[84] Finally, the passage of time also revealed how crucial divorce and other benefits were for unhappy couples—especially after former couples sought and failed to win recourse in cases of domestic violence, adultery, and custody battles.[85]

The *New Yorker* article nonetheless reminded its readers that Hawaii's decision had not yet led to gay marriage for Stoddard and Rieman or for anyone else. Lamba Legal put out a call to research the full faith and credit clause and the statutes of each state in order to determine a course of action if couples were denied the right to file a joint tax return, to give each other health insurance through their workplace, or to purchase a family membership.[86] The letter stated that "if you're married, you're married; this is one country; and it's a fundamental right." But it also quickly acknowledged, "we also know that, as always, lesbians and gay men will have to fight against the tendency of some in politics and the judiciary to create a 'gay exception' to even the clearest principle of constitutional law or fairness."[87]

Lambda Legal's anticipation of a fight was prescient. The same questions that seemed so promising to Lambda—that the full faith and credit clause could introduce same-sex marriage nationwide—prompted Hawaii and Congress to act. In reaction to *Baehr*, the Hawaii legislature passed a statute that defined marriage as between a man and a woman, allegedly in order to protect children.[88] Gay couples eventually received only domestic partnerships, with all the thick obligations that marriage had largely dispensed with.[89] In Congress, Wisconsin representative James Sensenbrenner Jr. submitted this very letter from Lamdba into the official record as evidence that the Defense of Marriage Act (DOMA) was necessary. Representative Robert Barr again evoked committed gay couples' selfishness. Without DOMA, he claimed, "the flames of hedonism, the flames of narcissism, the flames of self-centered morality are licking at the very foundation of our society: the family unit."[90]

Lawmakers also protested the expense of gay marriage. Sensenbrenner numbered the mentions of spouse in federal law at three thousand, declaring that when Congress passed Social Security survivor, Medicare, veteran, pension, and health insurance benefits—"some of them decades ago"—it had "assumed that the benefits would be to the survivors or to the spouses of traditional heterosexual marriages."[91] Sensenbrenner perhaps drew on constituent letters like one that Hawaii representative Patsy Mink received the month before he made his own statement: "Social security benefits are intended for widows and widowers, and their young children. I do not want my tax dollars used to provide benefits to homosexual 'partners.'"[92] DOMA explicitly proposed to prevent the extension of these benefits, and it proved mostly uncontroversial in Congress. The Defense of Marriage Act passed Congress and became law on September 21, 1996.

Since that time, however, activists for marriage equality have achieved much more than welfare or immigration rights activists. Just a few years later, in 1999, the Vermont Supreme Court ruled in *Baker v. State of Vermont* that gay couples must have access to the same rights as straight married couples. Vermont granted these rights in the form of civil unions.[93] Then in 2003, the Massachusetts Supreme Judicial Court ruled in *Goodridge v. Department of Public Health* that gay couples had the right to marry in Massachusetts.[94]

Even amid this initial round of success, however, marriage equality campaigners walked a difficult road. For instance, many gay parents still could not consider their custody rights secure given that the law varied from state to state. In 2000, the U.S. Supreme Court rejected nonparents' rights to seek visitation if the biological parent did not wish the nonbiological parent to have them in *Troxel v. Granville*.[95] This posed difficult questions for gay parents who were barred in some states from adopting their partners' biological children or from engaging in joint adoption (whereby gay or lesbian parents adopt a child when neither is the biological parent). Often then one partner legally retained sole custody. When couples remained together, this posed few practical problems. But following a breakup, the nonadoptive parent could lose all rights to custody or to visit a child he or she had been raising with his or her partner.

These men and women may have acted as parents but were strangers according to the law. For instance, in the 2006 Massachusetts case *A.H. v. M.P.*, A.H. petitioned for joint custody of her ex-partner's biological child. The couple had decided to have children together. M.P. birthed the child and became "Mommy." A.H. became "Mama." Two years later but prior to *Goodridge*, the couple decided to end their relationship. A.H. hoped to continue her relationship with the child, but M.P. fought her. The case made it to the Massachusetts Supreme Judicial Court, which denied A.H. joint custody because she had not yet completed her adoption of the child nor provided care that the court deemed equivalent to M.P.'s stay-at-home care. In other words, unless couples took advantage of legal means of establishing parenthood, Massachusetts did not grant "de facto" parental rights.[96] A crucial mistake in paperwork cost A.H. the child she had helped raise, but other states disallowed second-parent adoption entirely. This meant gay nonbiological parents had no custody rights in some states. For instance, the Virginia Supreme Court ruled in *Davenport v. Little-Bowser* that the second parent's name could only be entered on a child's birth certificate when a court in another state ordered this.[97] In many cases like this, parents lost their children according to their address. The denial of marriage rights continued to significantly impair gay men and lesbians' household rights. But this denial too began to give way.

Despite many states' attempts to halt what they termed "judicial activism," a tumble of decisions culminating with *United States v. Windsor* overturned DOMA. In *Windsor*, the question of gender had fallen away.[98] Officially, Justice Kennedy's decision rested on the fact that states retained the right to determine marriage—including being allowed to offer marriage to same-sex couples. But Kennedy's ruling also highlighted his belief that marriage bans denied gay couples dignity under the law, which prompted many lower courts to interpret *Windsor* broadly and enact marriage equality in thirty-seven states by 2015. *Windsor* forecast *Obergefell v. Hodges*, which finally granted marriage rights to gay and lesbian couples. The decision also brought careful attention to the significant civil rights that marriage bestows to this day in the United States.[99]

A question remains, however, about what it means that we have achieved success in terms of marriage equality in light of the defeats so obvious in welfare and immigration policy. It is possible of course that *Obergefell* forecasts progress for immigrant spouses, black fathers, and the poor, all of whom still suffer rather than benefit from marriage laws. But upon observing the political activism and money that went into the marriage equality fight, this seems unlikely.[100] Instead, it's also possible that the gay couples that have received the right to marry may have simply joined the other advantaged couples that benefit from marriage. Elite gay couples have been granted access to the privileges of the elite and left behind less privileged queer men and women.[101] Rather than speaking to changes in marriage, marriage rights for gay couples may speak more to the changing status of gay couples in modern America. Marriage itself has increasingly become an institution for the privileged and for the powerful within the family itself.

A third possibility is that gay and lesbian couples have gained access to marriage only in the institution's death throes. Certainly we know that fewer people marry today even in the United States, where there are certainly material advantages to marrying. Fewer couples can afford to marry in the first place—they lack the capital for a wedding, to marry someone who is not a citizen, to provide for one another, to divorce, to cohabit. But overall, the innovations in marriage from the 1970s—granting women property rights to their household labor and ending men's support obligations—suggests an enduring neoliberal individualist turn in regard to family life. As Arlie Hochschild noted in 1989, "the growing instability of marriage creates an anonymous, individualist 'modern' form of oppression [of women]."[102] But like so many other changes in the 1970s, many critics attributed the individualization of family members solely to feminism without acknowledging the role of activist ex-husbands. Law professor William A. Stanmeyer stated in hearings on the ERA extension that he feared the "pure contract notion of marriage." He warned that "the atomization of the family unit" must be avoided.[103] Similarly, Pastor Charles Stanley, representing the Southern Baptists Convention, repudiated the ERA for its promise that "husbands and wives will no longer be considered one, but two separate, independent individuals with their legal rights living together."[104] Cultural critics like Christopher Lasch joined the chorus.[105] Chicano activist and state chairman of the Partido de La Raza Unida de Nuevo Mexico Juan José Peña blamed multiple parties for the "rugged individualism" of the Anglo family, including capitalism, but highlighted feminists and homosexuals particularly.[106]

But atomization preceded feminism and has persisted alongside it. We can see the atomization of the family as originating as early as the American Revolution. At this point, fathers lost their patriarchal power over their sons, who became their equals in law and politics in theory if not in practice.[107] By the time of Tocqueville's visit to the United States in 1831, he identified the spirit of "individualism" as having profound effects on the family, including that marriage was more egalitarian, the family had become more child-centered, and family life had been privatized.[108] The married women's property acts, if not designed to do so originally, nonetheless began the process of making wives self-owning liberal individuals.[109]

Despite the deep roots behind this trend, the family *is* increasingly atomized beginning with the rise of no-fault divorce and continuing today. After the Cold War ended in the early 1990s, even the military reduced the services and benefits it provided to soldiers' wives in the all-volunteer army. Instead it promoted a program of "self-reliance."[110] The Family Medical Leave Act was a half measure, and Bill Clinton could not convince Congress to provide paid leave for family medical emergencies. According to Daniel H. Pink, a former aide to the secretary of labor and the chief speech writer for Al Gore, this was because blanket government solutions did not accommodate individual needs.[111] Government skepticism toward family obligations has spread to the private sector. For instance, large corporations like UPS and corporate-state hybrids like the University of Virginia are getting out of the marriage business—they have ceased providing health care for spouses as an employee benefit if the spouse has his or her own health care.[112] These entities are not alone. A survey by an actuarial firm noted a sudden drop in spousal coverage in a survey of employers in 2015.[113]

The trend away from providing benefits to a household illustrates a major break with the twentieth-century bargain whereby corporations offered benefits to prevent the imposition of a larger social welfare state.[114] Though the Affordable Care Act for now fills in many of these gaps in most states, it was designed to perpetuate a system where most Americans receive their health care from private employers. The overall effect of reducing spousal access to health-care benefits is to push more Americans onto the open marketplace for benefits.

I would suggest that atomization is not inherently destructive—in Europe, for example, individuals receive safety-net entitlements as a right of citizenship. But in the United States, we face the worst of both worlds. We lack individual rights as citizens to health care, pensions, unemployment insurance, and more, and now the household model that we have relied on imperfectly instead is being broken down. This reflects a larger trend throughout society since the 1970s, as neoliberalism has begun to touch the economy, the workplace, politics, leisure spaces, and much more.[115] We perhaps face the rise of the neoliberal individual via the end of marriage just as we have with the end of the union, the political party, and the bowling league.

Critiquing the atomization of the family, as Stanmeyer put it, is one of the few areas that the left and the right agree on. The raising of children and the care of the sick and elderly have become increasingly individualized endeavors—and most often women are solely responsible for this labor. While both sides decry this development, they have deeply divided solutions.[116] The right wants to reinforce old gender norms and marriage. The left hopes to expand family rights to every form of family—or better yet to grant the social welfare benefits we give through marriage to all men and women on the basis of their residency in the United States. Both see hope for these solutions in future activism and policy reform. But historians have repeatedly hazarded predictions that do not come true, and perhaps the only certain answer is that the relationship between gender, sexuality, family, and economics will be rewritten again in our future.

NOTES

Introduction

1. Kristin Celello, *Making Marriage Work: A History of Marriage and Divorce in the Twentieth-Century United States* (Chapel Hill: University of North Carolina Press, 2009).

2. Judy Syfers, "Why I Want a Wife," *Ms. Magazine* insert in *New York Magazine*, December 20, 1971, 56. Emphasis in original.

3. Charles V. Metz, *Divorce and Custody for Men: A Guide and Primer Designed Exclusively to Help Men Win Just Settlements* (Garden City, NY: Doubleday & Company, Inc., 1968).

4. Hendrik Hartog, *Man and Wife in America: A History* (Cambridge, MA: Harvard University Press, 2000); Amy Dru Stanley, *From Bondage to Contract: Wage Labor, Marriage, and the Market in the Age of Slave Emancipation* (Cambridge: Cambridge University Press, 1998).

5. Under the fault divorce regime, only an innocent spouse could win a divorce from his or her spouse on the basis of a number of different grounds. These grounds varied by state, but in all states, judges could deny a divorce to a spouse who could not convincingly establish a ground for divorce or who was equally guilty of violating the marriage contract. The potential of being denied a divorce shaped how many spouses sought divorces—or convinced them not to pursue one in the first place.

6. Hartog, *Man and Wife in America*.

7. Linda Gordon, *Pitied but Not Entitled: Single Mothers and the History of Welfare 1890–1935* (Cambridge, MA: Harvard University Press, 1998); Suzanne Mettler, *Dividing Citizens: Gender and Federalism in New Deal Public Policy* (Ithaca, NY: Cornell University Press, 1998); Alice Kessler-Harris, *In Pursuit of Equity: Women, Men, and the Quest for Economic Citizenship in 20th-Century America* (New York: Oxford University Press, 2001); Nancy Cott, *Public Vows: A History of Marriage and the Nation* (Cambridge, MA: Harvard University Press, 2000); Michael Willrich, *City of Courts: Socializing Justice in Progressive Era Chicago* (Cambridge: Cambridge University Press, 2003); Nancy MacLean, "Postwar Women's History: The 'Second Wave' or the End of the Family Wage?," in *A Companion to Post-1945 America*, ed. Jean-Christophe Agnew and Roy Rosenzweig (Malden, MA: Blackwell Publishing, 2006), 235–59; Margot Canaday, "Heterosexuality as a Legal Regime," in *The Cambridge History of Law in America*, ed. Michael Grossberg and Christopher Tomlins (New York: Cambridge University Press, 2008), 442–71; Eileen Boris, "Labor's Welfare State: Defining Workers, Constructing Citizens," in Grossberg and Tomlins, *Cambridge History of Law in America*.

8. Ruth Rosen, *The World Split Open: How the Modern Women's Movement Changed America* (New York: Penguin Books, 2006); Sara Evans, *Tidal Wave: How Women Changed America at*

Century's End (New York: Free Press, 2010); Christine Stansell, *The Feminist Promise: 1792 to the Present* (New York: Modern Library, 2010).

9. For earlier feminist attacks on marriage, see Carole Pateman, *The Sexual Contract* (Stanford, CA: Stanford University Press, 1988); Elaine Tyler May, *Homeward Bound: American Families in the Cold War Era* (New York: Basic Books, 1988); Jeanne Boydston, *Home and Work: Housework, Wages, and the Ideology of Labor in the Early Republic* (New York: Oxford University Press, 1990); Reva Siegel, "Home as Work: The First Women's Rights Claims Concerning Wives' Household Labor, 1850–1880," 103 *Yale Law Journal* (1994): 1073–218; Gordon, *Pitied but Not Entitled*; Stanley, *From Bondage to Contract*; Cott, *Public Vows*; Hartog, *Man and Wife in America*; Mary Anne Case, "Marriage Licenses," *Minnesota Law Review* 89 (2005): 1758–97; Christina Simmons, *Making Marriage Modern: Women's Sexuality from the Progressive Era to World War II* (Oxford: Oxford University Press, 2009). For scholarship that traces how the private sphere transformed during second-wave feminism, see Robert Self, *All in the Family: The Realignment of American Democracy Since the 1960s* (New York: Hill and Wang, 2012); Serena Mayeri, *Reasoning from Race: Feminism, Law, and the Civil Rights Revolution* (Cambridge, MA: Harvard University Press, 2014); George Chauncey, *Why Marriage: The History Shaping Today's Debate over Gay Equality* (New York: Basic Books, 2004); Cott, *Public Vows*; Celello, *Making Marriage Work*; Jill Elaine Hasday, "Contest and Consent: A Legal History of Marital Rape," *California Law Review* 88 (October 2000): 1373–506; Canaday, "Heterosexuality as a Legal Regime"; Kessler-Harris, *In Pursuit of Equity*.

10. For an outstanding history of men's cultural revolt, see Barbara Ehrenreich, *The Hearts of Men: American Dreams and the Flight from Commitment* (Garden City, NY: Anchor Press/Doubleday, 1983).

11. Self, *All in the Family*; Natasha Zaretsky, *No Direction Home: The American Family and the Fear of National Decline, 1968–1980* (Chapel Hill: University of North Carolina Press, 2007); MacLean, "Postwar Women's History"; Marisa Chappell, *The War on Welfare: Family, Poverty, and Politics in Modern America* (Philadelphia: University of Pennsylvania Press, 2009).

12. Mary Anne Case, "What Feminists Have to Lose in Same-Sex Marriage Litigation," *University of California Los Angeles Law Review* 57 (2009–10): 1199–233. See also Susan Frelich Appleton, "Leaving Home? Domicile, Family, and Gender," *UC Davis Law Review* 47 (June 2014): 1453–519.

13. Karen M. Tani, *States of Dependency: Welfare, Rights, and American Governance, 1935–1972* (New York: Cambridge University Press, 2016).

14. Martha Fineman, *The Illusion of Equality: The Rhetoric and Reality of Divorce Reform* (Chicago: University of Chicago Press, 1991).

15. Self, *All in the Family*; Rebecca E. Klatch, *Women of the New Right* (Philadelphia: Temple University Press, 1987); Donald G. Mathews and Jane Sherron De Hart, *Sex, Gender, and the Politics of ERA: A State and the Nation* (New York: Oxford University Press, 1990); Pamela Abbott, *The Family and the New Right* (London: Pluto Press, 1992); Dallas A. Blanchard, *The Anti-Abortion Movement and the Rise of the Religious Right: From Polite to Fiery Protest* (New York: Twayne Publishers, 1994); Donald T. Critchlow, *Phyllis Schlafly and Grassroots Conservatism* (Princeton, NJ: Princeton University Press, 2005); Matthew D. Lassiter, "Inventing Family Values," and Marjorie J. Spruill, "Gender and America's Right Turn," in *Rightward Bound: Making America Conservative in the 1970s*, ed. Bruce J. Schulman and Julian E. Zelizer (Cambridge, MA: Harvard University Press, 2008), 13–28 and 71–89; J. Brooks Flippen, *Jimmy Carter, the Politics of Family, and the Rise of the Religious Right* (Athens: University of Georgia Press, 2011); Stacie

Taranto, *Kitchen Table Politics: Conservative Women and Family Values in the Seventies* (Philadelphia: University of Pennsylvania Press, 2017).

16. For more on feminism's "dangerous liaison with neoliberalism," see Nancy Fraser, *Fortunes of Feminism: From State-Managed Capitalism to Neoliberal Crisis* (London: Verso, 2013), 83–110.

Chapter 1

1. Isaiah Berlin, "Two Concepts of Liberty," in *Four Essays on Liberty* (Oxford: Oxford University Press, 1957).

2. For the use of "thick" and "thin" expectations, see Mary Anne Case, "What Feminists Have to Lose in Same-Sex Marriage Litigation," *University of California Los Angeles Law Review* 57 (2009–10): 1199–233.

3. Norma Basch, *Framing American Divorce: From the Revolutionary Generation to the Victorians* (Berkeley: University of California Press, 1999), 21.

4. Blanche Glassman Hersh, *The Slavery of Sex: Feminist-Abolitionists in America* (Urbana: University of Illinois Press, 1978); Norma Basch, *In the Eyes of the Law: Women, Marriage, and Property in Nineteenth-Century New York* (Ithaca, NY: Cornell University Press, 1982); Amy Dru Stanley, *From Bondage to Contract: Wage Labor, Marriage, and the Market in the Age of Slave Emancipation* (Cambridge: Cambridge University Press, 1998).

5. Stanley, *From Bondage to Contract*, 180.

6. Nancy F. Cott, *Public Vows: A History of Marriage and the Nation* (Cambridge, MA: Harvard University Press, 2000), 52–55.

7. Lawrence Foster, *Religion and Sexuality: The Shakers, the Mormons, and the Oneida Community* (Chicago: University of Illinois Press, 1984).

8. See also Cott, *Public Vows*; Ellen DuBois, *Women's Suffrage and Women's Rights* (New York: New York University, 1998); Linda K. Kerber, *No Constitutional Right to Be Ladies: Women and the Obligations of Citizenship* (New York: Hill and Wang, 1998).

9. Nancy F. Cott, *The Grounding of Modern Feminism* (New Haven, CT: Yale University Press, 1987), 157. See also Elaine Tyler May, *Great Expectations: Marriage and Divorce in Post-Victorian America* (Chicago: University of Chicago Press, 1980); Kristin Celello, *Making Marriage Work: A History of Marriage and Divorce in the Twentieth-Century United States* (Chapel Hill: University of North Carolina Press, 2009); Rebecca L. Davis, *More Perfect Unions: The American Search for Marital Bliss* (Cambridge, MA: Harvard University Press, 2010); and Christina Simmons, *Making Marriage Modern: Women's Sexuality from the Progressive Era to World War II* (Oxford: Oxford University Press, 2009).

10. Cott, *Public Vows*, 157. See also Margot Canaday, "Heterosexuality as a Legal Regime," in *The Cambridge History of Law in America*, ed. Michael Grossberg and Christopher Tomlins (New York: Cambridge University Press, 2008): 442–71.

11. U.S. Bureau of the Census, *Historical Statistics of the United States: Colonial Times to 1970, Bicentennial Edition*, part 1 (Washington, DC: Government Printing Office, 1975), 49.

12. "Marriage and Divorce Statistics," *NCHStats: A Blog of the National Center for Health Statistics*, http://nchspressroom.wordpress.com/2007/07/06/marriage-and-divorce-statistics/; U.S. Department of Health, Education, and Welfare, *Vital Statistics of the United States, 1960*, vol. 3, *Marriage and Divorce* (Washington, DC: Public Health Service, 1964); United States Department of Commerce, U.S. Census Bureau, and United States Economics and Statistics Administration, *Statistical Abstract of the United States: 2012* (Washington, DC: U.S. Census Bureau, 2012), 384.

13. Elizabeth Waldman, "Labor Force Statistics from a Family Perspective," *Monthly Labor Review* (December 1983): 17.

14. Waldman, "Labor Force Statistics from a Family Perspective," 17.

15. Elizabeth H. Pleck, *Not Just Roommates: Cohabitation After the Sexual Revolution* (Chicago: University of Chicago Press, 2012); and Beth Bailey, *Sex in the Heartland* (Cambridge, MA: Harvard University Press, 2002). See also Rickie Solinger, *Wake Up Little Susie: Single Pregnancy and Race Before Roe v. Wade* (New York: Routledge, 1992).

16. Waldman, "Labor Force Statistics from a Family Perspective," 18.

17. U.S. Bureau of the Census, *Historical Statistics of the United States: Colonial Times to 1970*, 1:139–40.

18. Linda J. Waite, *U.S. Women at Work* (Santa Monica, CA: Rand, 1981), 1.

19. U.S. Department of Health and Human Services, *Vital Statistics of the United States, 1980*, vol. 3 *Marriage and Divorce* (Hyattsville, MD: National Center for Health Statistics, 1985).

20. Waite, *U.S. Women at Work*, 11.

21. Nancy F. Cott, *Bonds of Womanhood: "Woman's Sphere" in New England, 1780–1835* (New Haven, CT: Yale University Press, 1997); Kerber, *No Constitutional Right to Be Ladies*; Stanley, *From Bondage to Contract*.

22. Alice Kessler-Harris, *Out to Work: A History of Wage-Earning Women in the United States* (New York: Oxford University Press, 2003); Annelise Orleck, *Common Sense and a Little Fire: Women and Working-Class Politics in the United States, 1900–1965* (Chapel Hill: University of North Carolina Press, 1995); Jacqueline Jones, *Labor of Love, Labor of Sorrow: Black Women, Work, and the Family, from Slavery to the Present* (New York: Basic Books, 1985).

23. William Chafe, *The American Woman: Her Changing Social, Economic, and Political Roles, 1920–1970* (New York: Oxford University Press, 1972); Karen Anderson, *Wartime Women: Sex Roles, Family Relations, and the Status of Women During World War II* (Westport, CT: Greenwood Press, 1981); Susan Hartmann, *The Home Front and Beyond: American Women in the 1940s* (Boston: Twayne, 1982).

24. Lizabeth Cohen, *A Consumer's Republic: The Politics of Mass Consumption in Postwar America* (New York: Vintage Books, 2003); Nelson Lichtenstein, *State of the Union: A Century of American Labor* (Princeton, NJ: Princeton University Press, 2013); Kathleen Frydl, *The G.I. Bill* (New York: Cambridge University Press, 2011).

25. Robert O. Self, *All in the Family: The Realignment of American Democracy Since the 1960s* (New York: Hill and Wang, 2013); Jefferson Cowie, *Stayin' Alive: The 1970s and the Last Days of the Working Class* (New York: New Press, 2012); Natasha Zaretsky, *No Direction Home: The American Family and the Fear of National Decline, 1968–1980* (Chapel Hill: University of North Carolina Press, 2007); Nancy MacLean, "Postwar Women's History: The 'Second Wave' or the End of the Family Wage?," in *A Companion to Post-1945 America*, ed. Jean-Christophe Agnew and Roy Rosenzweig (Malden, MA: Blackwell Publishing, 2006), 235–59.

26. Waite, *U.S. Women at Work*, 8.

27. Susan Strasser, *Never Done: A History of American Housework* (New York: Pantheon Books, 1982); Ruth Schwartz Cowan, *More Work for Mother: The Ironies of Household Technology from the Open Hearth to the Microwave* (New York: Basic Books, 1983); Annegret S. Ogden, *The Great American Housewife: From Helpmate to Wage Earner, 1776–1986* (Westport, CT: Greenwood Press, 1986); and Glenna Matthews, *"Just a Housewife": The Rise and Fall of Domesticity in America* (New York: Oxford University Press, 1987).

28. "The Social Role of the Suburban Wife Questionnaire 1050101," n.d., box 21, folder 7,

Helena Znaniecka Lopata Papers, Women and Leadership Archives, Loyola University Chicago.

29. Ibid.

30. Arlie Hochschild, *The Second Shift: Working Families and the Revolution at Home* (New York: Penguin Books, 2012).

31. Waldman, "Labor Force Statistics from a Family Perspective," 18.

32. U.S. Department of Health and Human Services, *Vital Statistics of the United States, 1980*, vol. 3.

33. Cowan, *More Work for Mother*, 9.

34. Margaret Mead and Frances Balgley Kaplan, eds., *American Women: The Report of the President's Commission on the Status of Women and Other Publications of the Commission* (New York: Scribner, 1965), 9; Carolyn Johnston, *Sexual Power: Feminism and the Family in America* (Tuscaloosa: University of Alabama Press, 1992), 247–49; Christine Stansell, *The Feminist Promise: 1792 to the Present* (New York: Modern Library, 2010).

35. Mead and Kaplan, *American Women*, 9.

36. Ibid., 70.

37. Ibid., 69.

38. Ibid., 204, 281.

39. Ibid., 342.

40. Ibid., 375.

41. Stansell, *Feminist Promise*; Sara M. Evans, *Personal Politics: The Roots of Women's Liberation in the Civil Rights Movement and the New Left* (New York: Knopf, 1979); Ruth Rosen, *The World Split Open: How the Modern Women's Movement Changed America* (New York: Viking, 2000); Estelle B. Freedman, *No Turning Back: The History of Feminism and the Future of Women* (New York: Ballantine Books, 2002); Sara M. Evans, *Tidal Wave: How Women Changed America at Century's End* (New York: Free Press, 2003).

42. Dorothy Sue Cobble, *The Other Women's Movement: Workplace Justice and Social Rights in Modern America* (Princeton, NJ: Princeton University Press, 2004), 185.

43. For more on feminist critiques of marriage, see Celello, *Making Marriage Work*, 103–32 and Johnston, *Sexual Power*, 246–50.

44. Brenda D. Eichelberger to Edwina Moore, CBS-TV, November 7, 1974, box 2, folder L-M-N 1974, Brenda Eichelberger Papers, Chicago History Museum; Benita Roth, *Separate Roads to Feminism: Black, Chicana, and White Feminist Movements in America's Second Wave* (Cambridge: Cambridge University Press, 2004); Volchita Nachescu, "Race Matters?" (paper presented March 19, 2010 at Newberry Library, Chicago); Wini Breines, *The Trouble Between Us: An Uneasy History of White and Black Women in the Feminist Movement* (New York: Oxford University Press, 2006); Kimberly Springer, *Living for the Revolution: Black Feminist Organizations, 1968–1980* (Durham, NC: Duke University Press, 2005).

45. Peggy Pascoe, *What Comes Naturally: Miscegenation Law and the Making of Race in America* (Oxford: Oxford University Press, 2009).

46. Carol Kleiman, "When Black Women Rap, the Talk Sure Is Different," *Chicago Tribune*, June 1, 1975, 13, box 2, folder 14, Eichelberger Papers; Ouida Lindsey, "Black Feminists vs. Racism, Sexism," *Sunday Sun-Times*, June 20, 1976, box 2, folder 14, Eichelberger Papers.

47. Mead and Kaplan, *American Women*, 221–22.

48. Jacquelyn Grant, "Theological/Biblical Basis for ERA: 'Black Theology and the Black Woman,'" in *ERA and Ethnic Minority Women: Report from Consultation on Ethnic Minority*

Involvement in the Equal Rights Amendment, pamphlet, n.d., 21, box 2, folder 8, series 1, Records of the National Alliance of Black Feminists (hereafter cited as NABF Records), National Archives for Black Women's History, Mary McLeod Bethune Council House, Washington, DC (hereafter cited as NABWH).

49. Peter Wallenstein, *Tell the Court I Love My Wife: Race, Marriage, and Law* (New York: St. Martin's Press, 2014), 202; Randall Kennedy, *Interracial Intimacies: Sex, Marriage, Identity, and Adoption* (New York: Pantheon Books, 2003), 25.

50. Laura F. Edwards, "The Marriage Covenant Is at the Foundation of All Our Rights: The Politics of Slave Marriages in North Carolina After Emancipation," *Law & History Review* 14, no. 1 (1996): 91–107.

51. Pauli Murray in U.S. Congress, Senate, Committee on the Judiciary, *Equal Rights 1970: Hearings Before the Committee on the Judiciary of the United States Senate on S.J. Res. 61 and S.J. Res. 231, Proposing an Amendment to the Constitution of the United States Relative to Equal Rights for Men and Women*, 91st Cong., 2nd sess., 1970, 429.

52. Brenda Daniels-Eichelberger, "Blacks and the Equal Rights Amendment," submitted to *WIN Magazine*, August 12, 1980, 3–4, box 6, folder 16, series 6, NABF Records, NABWH.

53. Serena Mayeri, "Historicizing the 'End of Men': The Politics of Reaction(s)," *Boston University Law Review* 93 (2013): 729–44.

54. These numbers obscured the differences between divorced and never-married women. "Women, Black Families," *Chicago Defender*, March 4, 1971, 18.

55. See also Alexis Herman, "Keynote Address: ERA and Ethnic Minority Women," in *ERA and Ethnic Minority Women: Report from Consultation on Ethnic Minority Involvement in the Equal Rights Amendment*, pamphlet, n.d., 39, box 2, folder 8, series 1, NABF Records; and Frankie Muse Freeman, "The Equal Rights Amendment: What's in It For Black Women?," pamphlet, 1975, box 2, folder 8, series 1, NABF Records.

56. Brenda Eichelberger, "Black Feminist Attacks Myths," *Chicago Defender*, March 27, 1978, box 6, folder 14, series 6, NABF Records.

57. "More About NABF!" flier printed by the Black Feminist Press, 1976, box 4, folder 3, series 3, NABF Records; Freeman, "Equal Rights Amendment"; National Alliance of Black Feminists Membership letter, July/August 1979, box 2, folder 19, series 1, NABF Records; Case study, Operation Cope, Instructor Mary Oyewole, October 25, 1974, box 3, folder 12, series 22, National Council of Negro Women, Inc. Records, NABWH.

58. Janet Boles, *The Politics of the Equal Rights Amendment: Conflict and the Decision Process* (New York: Longman, 1979); Susan D. Becker, *The Origins of the Equal Rights Amendment: American Feminism Between the Wars* (Westport, CT: Greenwood Press, 1981); Gilbert Steiner, *Constitutional Inequality: The Political Fortunes of the Equal Rights Amendment* (Washington, DC: Brookings Institution,1985); Jane Mansbridge, *Why We Lost the ERA* (Chicago: University of Chicago Press, 1986); Mary Francis Berry, *Why ERA Failed: Politics, Women's Rights, and the Amending Process of the Constitution* (Bloomington: Indiana University Press, 1986); Joan Hoff, *Rights of Passage: The Past and Future of the ERA* (Bloomington: Indiana University Press, 1986); and Donald Matthews and Jane Sherron De Hart, *Sex, Gender, and the Politics of ERA: A State and the Nation* (New York: Oxford University Press, 1990).

59. Cott, *Grounding of Modern Feminism* and Becker, *Origins of the Equal Rights Amendment*.

60. By the time Congress began holding hearings, labor had dropped their objections to the

ERA in recognition of the state and federal government's concerted disassembly of protective legislation. Cobble, *Other Women's Movement*.

61. U.S. Congress, Senate, Committee, *Equal Rights 1970*, 1.

62. Karl E. Campbell, *Senator Sam Ervin, Last of the Founding Fathers* (Chapel Hill: University of North Carolina Press, 2009), 13.

63. Barbara Brown, Thomas I. Emerson, Gail Falk, and Ann E. Freedman, "The Equal Rights Amendment: A Constitutional Basis for Equal Rights for Women," *Yale Law Journal* 80 (April 1971): 875–985.

64. *Equal Rights for Men and Women*, H.J.R. 208, 92nd Cong., 1st sess., *Congressional Record* 117 (October 12, 1971): H 35,789.

65. Dr. Bernice Sandler, at U.S. Congress, House, Committee on the Judiciary, *Equal Rights for Men and Women 1971, Hearings Before Subcommittee No. 4 of the Committee on the Judiciary, House of Representatives Ninety-Second Congress, First Session on H.J. Res. 35, 208, and Related Bills Proposing an Amendment to the Constitution of the United States Relative to Equal Rights for Men and Women and H.R. 916 and Related Bills Concerning the Recommendations of the Presidential Task Force on Women's Rights and Responsibilities*, 92nd Cong., 1st sess., 1971, 267.

66. Murray in U.S. Congress, Senate, Committee, *Equal Rights 1970*, 433.

67. U.S. Congress, Senate, Committee of the Judiciary, *The "Equal Rights" Amendment: Hearings Before the Subcommittee on Constitutional Amendments of the Committee of the Judiciary on S.J. Res. 61 to Amend the Constitution So As to Provide Equal Rights for Men and Women*, 91st Cong., 2nd sess., 1970, 126.

68. U.S. Congress, Senate, Committee, *Equal Rights 1970*, 1.

69. Statement of Paul A. Freund, at ibid., 78.

70. *Equal Rights for Men and Women*, H.J.R. 208, H 35,784. On conservatives accepting equality in the public sphere, Donald T. Critchlow, *Phyllis Schlafly and Grassroots Conservatism: A Woman's Crusade* (Princeton, NJ: Princeton University Press, 2005); *Equal Rights for Men and Women*, H.J.R. 1068, 92nd Cong., 2nd sess., *Congressional Record* 118 (March 22, 1972): S 9517; "Eagle Forum: The Alternative to Women's Lib," pamphlet, box 115, folder Eagle Forum, ERAmerica Records, Library of Congress.

71. *Equal Rights for Men and Women*, H.J.R. 208, H 35,784.

72. *Equal Rights for Men and Women*, H.J.R. 1068, S 9517. See also ibid., S 9520.

73. Ibid., S 9522.

74. As of January 1965, just a few years before California passed no-fault divorce, twenty-eight states included nonsupport by husbands as grounds for absolute divorce. Mead and Kaplan, *American Women*; Superior Court of Cook County, Case No. 46s 3701, *Dorothy M. Weber v. Harold T. Weber*, March 27, 1946, Cook County divorce record, Archives Department, Records and Archives, Clerk of the Circuit Court of Cook County, Illinois, Chicago, IL (hereafter cited as CCA); *Eileen C. Steggall v. Joseph E. Steggall*, January 16, 1975, Judgment for Divorce, 74 D 12626, CCA. Cook County divorce records did not make note of race until the 1980s when a new form included a check box for race. Cook County officials erratically filled this check box in. I therefore have very little evidence for determining what race any of these divorcing men and women were.

75. Robert J. Levy, *Uniform Marriage and Divorce Legislation: A Preliminary Analysis* ([Chicago?]: National Conference of Commissioners on Uniform State Laws, 1968), 135. *Bennet v. Bennet* 27 Ill. App. 2nd 24 (1960). "The ERA—Opposing View, Mrs. Frances Fortier Council of

Catholic Women," n.d. box 11, folder 21, Chicago Catholic Women Records, Women and Leadership Archives, Loyola University Chicago.

76. See Fred E. Schoenlaub, "Use of Contempt Powers in the Enforcement of Alimony and Support Decrees," *Journal of the Missouri Bar* 23 (September 1967): 396–415. Jail time was permitted because "alimony allowed by a decree of court is not founded on contract, and hence imprisonment for nonpayment is not imprisonment for debt." Lomax Pittman, "Contempt," in *The American and English Encyclopaedia of Law*, ed. S. Garland et al., 2nd ed., vol. 7 (1898), 41. See also "Transfer of the Separate Property of One Spouse to Another in Lieu of or in Addition to Permanent Alimony 1," A Survey Prepared for the New York County Lawyers Association, Special Committee on Matrimonial Law (mimeo., 1966) quoted in Levy, *Uniform Marriage and Divorce Legislation*, 135.

77. "Alimony Row," *Ebony*, March 1951, 41.

78. Elaine Markoutsas, " 'Good Old Days' of Alimony Row Fade," *Chicago Tribune*, June 6, 1976, 28; "Alimony Row," 39. For similar practices in Kentucky, see John W. Murphy Jr., "Enforcement of Alimony Decrees in Kentucky," *Kentucky Law Journal* 41 (March 1953): 335–36.

79. Theodore S. White, "Enforcement of Alimony Provisions of Matrimonial Decrees in New York," *Syracuse Law Review* 136 (Fall 1951): 143; Testimony by Hazen E. Kunz, May 26–27, 1950 published in "Issue 19," *Ohio State Bar Association Reports* 23 (1950): 407. See also William B. Elmer, "Pay-as-You-Go Alimony," *Michigan State Bar Journal* 29 (March 1950): 18–21. Lisa Levenstein, *A Movement Without Marches: African American Women and the Politics of Poverty in Postwar Philadelphia* (Chapel Hill: University of North Carolina Press, 2009): 72.

80. Jail was considered the last resort. Diane Serafin Blank, "Enforcement of Interspousal Obligations: A Proposal," *Women's Rights Law Reporter* 2 (June 1975): 13–25. For examples of the press's coverage of Alimony Row, see the annual Christmas coverage including " 'Alimony Row' Doors Opened for Christmas," *Chicago Tribune*, December 25, 1963, D5 and also "Free Husband So Wife Can Sleep Again," *Chicago Tribune*, January 14, 1960, C8.

81. Jones, *Labor of Love, Labor of Sorrow*; Julie Saville, *The Work of Reconstruction: From Slave to Wage Labor in South Carolina 1860–1870* (Cambridge: Cambridge University Press, 1996); Stanley, *From Bondage to Contract*.

82. Paul Jacobsen, *American Marriage and Divorce* (New York: Rhinehart, 1959), 127. See also J. Thomas Oldham, "Changes in Economic Consequences of Divorce, 1958–2008," *Family Law Quarterly* 42 (2008): 429. The U.S. Bureau of the Census did not keep track of the number of women receiving alimony from 1906 until 1978. Jacobsen's work is one of the few available sources for determining this rate.

83. Lenore Weitzman and Lyudmila Workman, "Alimony Demographics," *Journal of Contemporary Legal Issues* 20 (2011–12): 108–10.

84. Twila L. Perry, "Alimony: Race, Privilege, and Dependency in the Search of Theory," *Georgetown Law Journal* 82 (September 1994): 2481–520.

85. For the history of middle-class reformers' desire to keep household labor out of the purview of Congress, see Vanessa May, *Unprotected Labor: Household Workers, Politics, and Middle-Class Reform in New York, 1870–1940* (Chapel Hill: University of North Carolina Press, 2011). For a history of dependency, see Nancy Fraser and Linda Gordon, *Fortunes of Feminism: From State-Managed Capitalism to Neoliberal Crisis* (London: Verso, 2013), 83–110.

86. Kessler-Harris, *Out to Work*, 184. After initial opposition, Ruth Bader Ginsburg concluded in 2008 that time had proved that the "opening wedge" strategy worked. Ruth Bader Ginsburg, "*Muller v. Oregon*: One Hundred Years Later," *Willamette Law Review* 45 (2009): 372.

For Ginsburg's original thinking, see Nancy Wolloch, *A Class by Herself: Protective Laws for Women Workers, 1890s–1990s* (Princeton, NJ: Princeton University Press, 2015), 83.

87. Berlin, "Two Concepts of Liberty."

88. See Self, *All in the Family.*

89. U.S. Congress, Senate, Committee, *The "Equal Rights" Amendment*, 16.

90. Ibid., 676.

91. Edith M. "Peggy" Parkey at U.S. Congress, House, Committee, *Equal Rights for Men and Women 1971*, 538.

92. *Equal Rights for Men and Women*, H.J.R. 1068, 92nd Cong., 2nd sess., *Congressional Record* 118 (March 22, 1972): S 9523

93. *Henderson v. Henderson*, 224 Pa. Super. 185; 303 A.2d 843 (1973).

94. *Wiegand v. Wiegand*, 226 Pa. Super. 278; 310 A.2d 426 (1973).

95. Linda W. Knight, "Comments: Male Alimony in Light of the Sex Discrimination Decisions of the Supreme Court," *Cumberland Law Review* 6 (1975–76): 594. For Florida, see "Case Summaries: Divorce," *Women's Rights Law Reporter* 1 (1971–74): 33.

96. *Pfohl v. Pfohl*, 345 So. 2d 376 (1977).

97. Knight, "Comments," 592; Agnes Pek Dover, "Financial Equality in Marriage and Parenthood: Sharing the Burdens as Well as the Benefits," *Catholic Law Review* 29 (1979–80): 733–50.

98. Serena Mayeri, *Reasoning from Race: Feminism, Law, and the Civil Rights Revolution* (Cambridge: Harvard University Press, 2011). See also Stansell, *Feminist Promise*, 201, 306.

99. *Trammel v. U.S.*, 445 U.S. 40 (1980).

100. See in particular Mayeri, *Reasoning from Race*; Amy Leigh Campbell, *Raising the Bar: Ruth Bader Ginsburg and the ACLU Women's Rights Project* (Princeton, NJ: Xlibris Corporation, 2003); and Cary Franklin, "The Anti-Stereotyping Principle in Constitutional Sex Discrimination Law," *New York University Law Review* 85 (April 2010): 83–173.

101. Campbell, *Raising the Bar*, 31–62.

102. Mayeri, *Reasoning from Race*, 69–75.

103. *Frontiero v. Richardson*, 411 U.S. 677 (1973).

104. Ibid.

105. Ibid., 5. Seemingly only 52 percent of military wives would have counted as dependent under the standard applied to husbands.

106. *Frontiero v. Richardson.*

107. *Weinberger v. Wiesenfeld*, 420 U.S. 636 (1975).

108. Ruth Polatschek to Mr. Frank C. Genovese, October 10, 1978, box 1, folder The Community Approach to Disability and Employment' etc (2), Babson-Bernays Competition Records, Schlesinger Library on the History of Women in America, Radcliffe Institute, Harvard University, Cambridge, MA.

109. *Weinberger v. Wiesenfeld*, 643. In *Kahn v. Shevin*, the Supreme Court retreated from its approach in *Frontiero* to approve of the use of gender distinctions for the sake of benevolent purposes. *Kahn v. Shevin*, 416 U.S. 351 (1974).

110. *Califano v. Goldfarb*, 430 U.S. 199 (1977).

111. Lower courts had awarded alimony to dependent men prior to this of course. Constitutional Amendments, H.J.R. 18, 79th General Assembly, *State of Illinois Floor Debate Transcriptions* (May 1, 1975): H 27; "Wins Alimony from Wife," *Chicago Tribune*, November 25, 1965, 26; Henry Wood, "Wife Leaves So Cabbie Sues for Alimony," *Chicago Tribune*, September 4, 1970,

A3; John Oswald, "Wife Will Pay Spouse Prior to a Divorce," *Chicago Tribune*, February 1, 1969, B12; and "Jobless Man Wins Alimony," *Chicago Tribune*, November 17, 1979, 3.

112. *Orr v. Orr*, 440 U.S. 268 (1979).

113. Ibid.

114. Ibid., 281.

115. *Kirchberg v. Feenstra*, 450 U.S. 455 (1981).

116. In the early history of the United States, love was seen as a source of comfort or as a revolutionary means of enacting an egalitarian society. Marriage became a more emotive relationship rather than a purely material exchange. Jan Lewis, *The Pursuit of Happiness: Family and Values in Jefferson's Virginia* (Cambridge: Cambridge University Press, 1983); Andrew Cayton, *Love in the Time of Revolution: Transatlantic Literary Radicalism & Historical Change, 1793–1818* (Chapel Hill: University of North Carolina Press, 2013); May, *Great Expectations*; Davis, *More Perfect Unions*; Simmons, *Making Marriage Modern*; and William Leach, *True Love and Perfect Union: The Feminist Reform of Sex and Society* (New York: Basic Books, 1980).

117. For more on radical feminists on marriage, see Evans, *Personal Politics*; Alice Echols, *Daring to Be Bad: Radical Feminism in America, 1967–1975* (Minneapolis: University of Minnesota Press, 1989); Celello, *Making Marriage Work*, 108–9; Johnston, *Sexual Power*, 250–63; John D'Emilio and Estelle B. Freedman, *Intimate Matters: A History of Sexuality in America* (New York: Harper & Row, 1988); and Jane F. Gerhard, *Desiring Revolution: Second-Wave Feminism and the Rewriting of American Sexual Thought, 1920 to 1982* (New York: Columbia University Press, 2001).

118. Shulamith Firestone, *The Dialectic of Sex; the Case for Feminist Revolution* (New York: Morrow, 1970), 126.

119. Ann Oakley, *Woman's Work: The Housewife, Past and Present* (New York: Pantheon Books, 1974), 3.

120. Firestone, *Dialectic of Sex*, 139.

121. Kate Millett, "Sexual Politics" and CWLU, "Position Paper of the Revolutionary Union on Homosexuality and Gay Liberation," box 15, folder CWLU—Projects—Liberation School Course Material—1972 "Political History of CWLU," Chicago Women's Liberation Union Papers, Chicago History Museum, Chicago, IL (hereafter cited as CWLU Papers).

122. Sheila Cronan, "Marriage," in *Radical Feminism*, ed. Anne Koedt, Ellen Levine, and Anita Rapone (New York: Quadrangle Books, 1973), 216.

123. Betsy Warrior, "Housework: Slavery or Labor of Love," in *Radical Feminism: A Documentary Reader*, ed. Barbara A. Crow (New York: New York University Press, 2000), 209.

124. Pat Mainardi, "The Politics of Housework," in *The Politics of Housework*, ed. Ellen Malos (Cheltenham, UK: New Clarion Press, 1995), 85.

125. Rae André, *Homemakers, the Forgotten Workers* (Chicago: University of Chicago Press, 1981), 59; Marlene Dixon, "Why Women's Liberation," box 28, folder Women's Liberation movement—articles by Marlene Dixon, CWLU Papers; "Position Paper of the Revolutionary Union on Homosexuality and Gay Liberation"; Firestone, *Dialectic of Sex*, 207; Warrior, "Housework," 212; Oakley, *Woman's Work*, 61.

126. Power of Women Collective, "Deciding for Our Selves," in *All Work and No Pay: Women, Housework, and the Wages Due*, ed. Wendy Edmond and Suzie Fleming (London: Power of Women Collective, 1975), 120.

127. Dixon, "Why Women's Liberation."

128. Mariarosa Dalla Costa and Selma James, *The Power of Women and the Subversion of the Community* (Bristol, UK: Falling Wall Press, 1975), 33–4.

129. Barbara Ehrenreich, "Socialist/Feminism and Revolution," July 4, 1975, box 15, folder CWLU—Projects—Liberation School Course Material—1972 "Political History of CWLU," CWLU Papers.

130. Conference Summary, "the first national women's liberation conference," Thanksgiving, 1968, Camp Hastings, Lake Villa, IL, box 1, folder "Marya—Women's Movement" (6), Marya Randall Levenson Papers, Schlesinger Library.

131. Dixon, "Why Women's Liberation." Notably Rae André cited John Kenneth Galbraith's 1973 work, *Economics and Public Purpose*. Quoted in André, *Homemakers*, 59.

132. Karen Sacks, "Social Bases for Sexual Equality: A Comparative View," *Sisterhood Is Powerful: An Anthology of Writings from the Women's Liberation Movement*, ed. Robin Morgan (New York: Vintage Books, 1970), 462; André, *Homemakers*, 60; CWLU, "Position Paper of the Revolutionary Union on Homosexuality and Gay Liberation."

133. Juliet Mitchell, "Women: The Longest Revolution," *New Left Review*, November-December 1966, 19.

134. Firestone, *Dialectic of Sex*, 207.

135. Los Angeles Wages for Housework Committee, "Sisters Why March?," in Edmond and Fleming, *All Work and No Pay*, 123.

136. Cronan, "Marriage," 219–20.

137. André, *Homemakers*, 60; Los Angeles Wages for Housework Committee, "Sisters Why March?," 123.

138. Mitchell, "Longest Revolution," 35.

139. Mariarosa Dalla Costa, "A General Strike," in Edmonds and Fleming, *All Work and No Pay*, 126. See also Power of Women Collective, "The Home in the Hospital," in ibid., 87.

140. "Come Testify: How Government and Business Pimp Off *Your* Work. A Street Trial: Women vs. Business and Government," box 11, folder 541, Coyote (Organization) Records, 1962–1989, Schlesinger Library.

141. "The American Family: Future Uncertain," *Time*, December 28, 1970, 38–46.

142. Oakley, *Woman's Work*, 226–27. See also Firestone, *Dialectic of Sex*, 206, 208.

143. *Born in Flames*, directed by Lizzie Borden (1983).

144. "College Sponsors Essay Contest," *NRTA News Bulletin*, February 1978, box 3, folder 345 Received Crt 2/78 (4), Babson-Bernays Records.

145. Kay D. Ress to NOW, July 16, 1981, L335, box 185, folder 10, National Organization for Women, General, MC496, Schlesinger Library.

146. Lois Allen, "A Practical Program to Achieve Economic Justice for Homemakers," October 2, 1978, #549, box 1, folder Editorial for NRA Journal Sept-Oct 1952 Issue, Babson-Bernays Records.

147. Gwen Cramer, "A Practical Program to Achieve Economic Justice for Homemakers," September 21, 1978, #76, p. 1, box 1, folder Editorial for NRA Journal Sept-Oct 1952 Issue, Babson-Bernays Records. See also Virgnia E. Delebar to Frank C. Genovese, October 14, 1978, box 1, folder The Community Approach to Disability and Employment' etc (2), Babson-Bernays Records; Bonnie L. and James M. Fleck, "A Practical Program to Achieve Economic Justice for Homemakers," September 30, 1978, #314, p. 7, box 1, folder Rehabilitation—A Public Trust Journal of Rehabilitation Nov-Dec 1952 (3), Babson-Bernays Records.

148. Ida Mae Fedoruk, "A Practical Program to Achieve Economic Justice for Homemakers," October 1, 1978, #687, p. 3, box 1, folder Editorial for NRA Journal Sept-Oct 1952 Issue, Babson-Bernays Records. See also Elizabeth Marrocoo, "A Practical Program to Achieve Economic

Justice for Homemakers," September 29, 1978, #546, box 1, folder Rape Booklet 26 (8), Babson-Bernays Records; Lyn W. Kurpiewski, "A Practical Program to Achieve Economic Justice for Homemakers," October 2, 1978, #45, box 1, folder Editorial for NRA Journal Sept-Oct 1952 Issue, Babson-Bernays Records.

149. Ruth Polatschek to Frank C. Genovese, October 10, 1978.

150. Luigi J. Santucci to Sirs, September 29, 1978, #1002, box 2, folder 3, Babson-Bernays Records. This model, however, compensated "fairly" only when someone other than husbands compensated housewives, since husbands of course were ultimately limited by their own incomes. Carol T. Reed, "How Should Housewives be Paid?," 3, box 1, folder The Community Approach to Disability and Employment' etc (2), Babson-Bernays Records.

151. Russell Bryan to Mr. Frank C. Genovese, June 20, 1978, #1201, box 2, folder 19, Babson-Bernays Records.

152. Ruth Polatschek to Mr. Frank C. Genovese, October 10, 1978.

153. Alberta M. Sevigny, "A Practical Program to Achieve Economic Justice for Homemakers," October 1, 1978, #103, p. 2, box 1, folder Politics 12/72 23 (11), Babson-Bernays Records; Phillip J. Weber, "A Practical Program to Achieve Economic Justice for Homemakers," September 8, 1978, #137, box 1, folder Politics 12/72 23 (11), Babson-Bernays Records; Frances Peterson, "A Practical Program to Achieve Economic Justice for Homemakers," September 26, 1978, #402E, box 1, folder #25 Politics TFRE Agenda Items (16), Babson-Bernays Records.

154. Some contestants argued that compensation should be the sole privilege of women married to wealthy men. Ruth Polatschek to Mr. Frank C. Genovese, October 10, 1978.

155. Don Kovar and Kitty Kovar, "A Practical Program to Achieve Economic Justice for Homemakers," October 2, 1978, #548, box 1, folder Article for the International News Service, Dec 31, 1952 (9), Babson-Bernays Records.

156. For a wonderful study of cohabitation, see Pleck, Not Just Roommates.

157. See also Paul O'Neil, "The Only Rebellion Around," Life Magazine, November 30, 1959, 114–30.

158. Marvin M. Mitchelson, Living Together (New York: Simon and Schuster, 1980), 18.

159. Dan J. Peterman, Carl A. Ridley, and Scott M. Anderson, "A Comparison of Cohabiting and NonCohabiting College Students," Journal of Marriage and the Family 36 (May 1974): 344. See also Carl Danziger, Unmarried Heterosexual Cohabitation (San Francisco: R&E Research Associates, 1978), 32.

160. Danziger, Unmarried Heterosexual Cohabitation, 36.

161. Judy Klemesrud, "An Arrangement: Living Together for Convenience, Security, Sex," New York Times, March 4, 1968, 40. See also Arno Karlen, "The Unmarried Marrieds on Campus," New York Times, January 26, 1969, 80.

162. "American Family," 37.

163. Mitchelson, Living Together, 138.

164. Miriam E. Berger, "Trial Marriage: Harnessing the Trend Constructively," Family Coordinator 20 (January 1971): 40. See also Karlen, "Unmarried Marrieds on Campus."

165. Bailey, Sex in the Heartland, 208.

166. Ibid., 204. Barnard publicly punished LeClair anyway. Pleck, Not Just Roommates, 71–92.

167. Eleanor D. Macklin, "Heterosexual Cohabitation Among Unmarried College Students," Family Coordinator 21 (October 1972): 467–68; Danziger, Unmarried Heterosexual Cohabitation, 32. For more on Macklin, see Pleck, Not Just Roommates, 119–46.

168. Karlen, "Unmarried Marrieds on Campus," SM31.

169. Danziger, *Unmarried Heterosexual Cohabitation*, 70.

170. Roy Ald, *Sex off Campus* (New York: Grosset & Dunlap, 1969), 76–77.

171. Benjamin David Zablocki, *Alienation and Charisma: A Study of Contemporary American Communes* (New York: Free Press, 1980), 120.

172. Noreen Cornfield, "The Success of Urban Communes," *Journal of Marriage and the Family* 45 (February 1983): 115–26.

173. Kerry L. Conlon, "Countercultural Communes: Rejection or Reflection of Conventional Mainstream Gender Norms?" (MA thesis, Rutgers University–Newark, 2014), 61.

174. Judson Jerome, *Families of Eden: Communes and the New Anarchism* (New York: The Seabury Press, 1974).

175. Mitchelson, *Living Together*, 63.

176. Macklin, "Heterosexual Cohabitation Among Unmarried College Students," 465.

177. Nick Stinnett, *The Family and Alternate Life Styles* (Chicago: Nelson-Hall, 1978), 97.

178. Ibid., 97.

179. Ald, *Sex off Campus*, 24.

180. Conlon, "Countercultural Communes"; Ron E. Roberts, *The New Communes: Coming Together in America* (Englewood Cliffs, NJ: Prentice-Hall, Inc., 1971), 42–43; and William Smith, *Families and Communes: An Examination of Nontraditional Lifestyles* (Thousand Oaks, CA: Sage, 1999), 95–104.

181. Danziger, *Unmarried Heterosexual Cohabitation*, 56. A sociology professor at Ohio State who conducted her own study of one hundred students concluded that women were frustrated that their partners did not share household tasks. Pleck, *Not Just Roommates*, 136.

182. Klemesrud, "An Arrangement: Living Together for Convenience, Security, Sex," 40.

183. Ald, *Sex Off Campus*, 31.

184. Ibid., 108.

185. Danziger, *Unmarried Heterosexual Cohabitation*, 54–55, 70. See also Macklin, "Heterosexual Cohabitation Among Unmarried College Students," 465.

186. Ald, *Sex off Campus*, 119.

187. Danziger, *Unmarried Heterosexual Cohabitation*, 65.

188. Conlon, "Countercultural Communes."

189. Michael Boucai, "Glorious Precedents: When Gay Marriage Was Radical," *Yale Journal of Law & the Humanities* 27 (2015): 1–82.

190. Paul Britton, "Should a Homosexual Be Advised to Marry?," *ONE*, September 1962, 18.

191. See also Didgeon, "Reflexions on Love and Marriage," *ONE*, July 1966, 10.

192. Hermann Stoessel, "The Decline and Fall of Marriage," *ONE*, April 1959, 7.

193. Ibid.

194. E. B. Saunders, "Reformer's Choice: Marriage License or Just License?," *ONE*, August 1953, 11.

195. Jim Kepner, "Not for Us All, the Wedding Ring," *Advocate*, October 14, 1970, 2, 7.

196. "Lesbian Marries for Money," *Body Politic*, October 1978, 16.

197. Herbert Gant, "The 3rd Choice," *ONE*, October 1966, 6.

198. Ibid., 9.

199. Scott Anderson, "Working Relationships: A New Study Looks at Alternate Ways of Making Relationships Wash," *Advocate*, February 7, 1980, 18.

200. Liza Cowan, "Nesting," *DYKE: A Quarterly* 3 (1976): 30–31.

201. Gant, "3rd Choice," 7.

202. Carl Wittman, "A Gay Manifesto," 1970, in *Out of the Closets: Voices of Gay Liberation*, ed. Karla Jay and Allen Young (New York: New York University Press, 1992).

203. Martha Shelley, "On Marriage," *Ladder*, October/November 1968, 46–47.

204. "Record Share of Americans Have Never Married," Pew Research Center Social & Demographic Trends, September 24, 2014, http://www.pewsocialtrends.org/2014/09/24/record -share-of-americans-have-never-married/.

Chapter 2

1. Walter D. Johnson, *Policy Implications of Divorce Reform: The Illinois Example* (Springfield: Illinois Legislative Studies Center, 1979), 197. See also Walter D. Johnson and S. Kay Zimka, *An Evaluation of the Illinois Child Support Enforcement Program* (Springfield, IL: Center for Policy Studies and Program Evaluation, 1981).

2. Dr. Walter D. Johnson to Honorable Herbert V. Huskey, State Representative, April 27, 1977, box 4, folder Displaced Homemakers, 1977, Susan Catania Papers, Abraham Lincoln Presidential Library and Museum, Springfield, IL (hereafter cited as ALPLM). In a study of child support default in Michigan, another scholar noted that default rates in his sample jumped 20 percent after 1969. David L. Chambers, *Making Fathers Pay: The Enforcement of Child Support* (Chicago: University of Chicago Press, 1979), 114 and appendix 7G.

3. State of Illinois, Family Study Commission, *Report and Recommendations to the Members of the 76th General Assembly* (Chicago: 1969), 32. See also Laura F. Edwards, "The Marriage Covenant Is at the Foundation of All Our Rights: The Politics of Slave Marriages in North Carolina After Emancipation," *Law & History Review* 14, no. 1 (1996): 91–107; Michael Willrich, "Home Slackers: Men, the State, and Welfare in Modern America," *Journal of American History* 87, no. 2 (2000): 460–89; Erica Ryan, *Red War on the Family: Sex, Gender, and Americanism in the First Red Scare* (Philadelphia: Temple University Press, 2014); and Alice Kessler-Harris, *In Pursuit of Equity: Women, Men, and the Quest for Economic Citizenship in 20th-Century America* (New York: Oxford University Press, 2001).

4. Lisa Levenstein, " 'Don't Agonize, Organize!': The Displaced Homemakers Campaign and the Contested Goals of Postwar Feminism," *Journal of American History* 100 (March 2014), 1114–38; Mary Ziegler, "An Incomplete Revolution: Feminists and the Legacy of Marital-Property Reform," *Michigan Journal of Gender & Law* 19 (2013): 259–92; Suzanne Kahn, "The Next Battle for Marriage Equality," *Dissent* (Winter 2016): 25–34.

5. Cynthia Lee Starnes, *The Marriage Buyout: The Troubled Trajectory of U.S. Alimony Law* (New York: New York University Press, 2014), 37; Jocelyn Elise Crowley, *Defiant Dads: Fathers' Rights Activists in America* (Ithaca, NY: Cornell University Press, 2008), 110–11; Lisa Levenstein, *Movement Without Marches: African American Women and the Politics of Poverty in Postwar Philadelphia* (Chapel Hill: University of North Carolina Press, 2009).

6. John Dorfman, "Divorce: The High Cost of Leaving . . . ," reprinted in ADAM pamphlet, box 15, folder Divorce, 1973–1978, Catania Papers, ALPLM.

7. Robert Self, *All in the Family: The Realignment of American Democracy Since the 1960s* (New York: Hill and Wang, 2013).

8. Barbara Ehrenreich, *The Hearts of Men: American Dreams and the Flight from Commitment* (Garden City, NY: Anchor Press/Doubleday, 1983). Legal scholars have shown that many men objected to paying alimony and even had an occasional ally in the legislature. Nonetheless the dominant narrative still treats the changes to marriage law as an unintended consequence of

good faith change and alimony dissenters as minor players. Mary E. O'Connell, "Alimony After No-Fault: A Practice in Search of a Theory," *New England Law Review* 437 (1988): 437–514; Starnes, *Marriage Buyout*; Allen M. Parkman, *Good Intentions Gone Awry: No-Fault Divorce and the American Family* (Oxford: Rowman and Littlefield, 2000); Deborah Dinner, "The Divorce Bargain: The Fathers' Rights Movement and Family Inequalities," *Virginia Law Review Association* 102 (2016): 79–152; Crowley, *Defiant Dads*; J. Herbie DiFonzo, *Beneath the Fault Line: The Popular and Legal Culture of Divorce in Twentieth-Century America* (Charlottesville: University Press of Virginia, 1997).

9. Bob Norman, "Miss Gold-Digger of 1953," *Playboy* (December 1953): 6–8. See also Charles Wilner, *Alimony: The American Tragedy* (New York: Vantage Press, Inc., 1952).

10. Ruth Schwartz Cowan, *More Work for Mother: The Ironies of Household Technology from the Open Hearth to the Microwave* (New York: Basic Books, 1983).

11. Ronald Reagan "Live Better Electronically" commercial, https://www.youtube.com/watch?v=u5Lz1C53RwI.

12. Sandra Pesmen, "Just a Housewife? Whoever Said That?," *Star*, September 8, 1971, box 53, folder 1, Eleanor F. Dolan Papers, Women and Leadership Archives (hereafter cited as WALA), Loyola University Chicago (hereafter cited as LUC).

13. "The Social Role of the Suburban Wife Questionnaire 1810102," n.d. box 21, folder 7, Helena Znaniecka Lopata Papers, WALA, LUC; "The Social Role of the Suburban Wife Questionnaire 1800076," box 22, folder 6, Lopata Papers; "The Social Role of the Suburban Wife Questionnaire 1810125," box 21, folder 9, Lopata Papers.

14. George T. Horback, "Alimony Laws," *Chicago Daily Tribune*, January 1, 1963, 16.

15. *Borowitz v. Borowitz*, 19 Ill. App. 3d 176; 311 N.E.2d 292 (1974).

16. Vera Glaser, "Easing the Pain (But Not the Cost) of Splitting Up," *Chicago Tribune*, September 25, 1973, B1.

17. Carol Kleiman, "Working Woman," *Chicago Tribune*, January 28, 1968, N3.

18. The women who did approve were disproportionately black, poor, and held only grade school educations. The Roper Organization, *The Virginia Slims American Women's Opinion Poll*, vol. 3, *A Survey of the Attitudes of Women on Marriage, Divorce, the Family and America's Changing Sexual Morality* ([New York?]: Roper Organization, Inc., 1974), 57.

19. Norman, "Miss Gold-Digger of 1953," 7–8; Glaser, "Easing the Pain (But Not the Cost) of Splitting Up," B1.

20. Dorfman, "Divorce."

21. Paul Jacobsen, *American Marriage and Divorce* (New York: Rhinehart, 1959), 127; J. Thomas Oldham, "Changes in Economic Consequences of Divorce, 1958–2008," *Family Law Quarterly* 42 (2009): 419, 429.

22. Twila L. Perry, "Alimony: Race, Privilege, and Dependency in the Search of Theory," 82 *Georgetown Law Journal* (September 1994): 2481–520.

23. Walter D. Johnson, "Divorce, Alimony, Support and Custody: A Survey of Judges Attitudes in One State," *Family Law Reporter* 3 (1976): 4003; *Rose Merz v. John H. Merz*, 55 S 18614, Report of Proceedings, April 9, 1956, box 4A-11-Y-07, Cook County divorce record, Archives Department, Records and Archives, Clerk of the Circuit Court of Cook County, Illinois, Chicago, IL (hereafter cited as CCA); *Commissioner of Internal Revenue v. Lester*, 366 U.S. 302 (1961) confirmed that wives counted alimony as their income for tax purposes, which meant men could subtract the alimony amount from their annual income. Because alimony acted as a tax deduction for ex-husbands, many couples arranged to pay part of a child custody award as alimony.

Draft of "A Guide to Survival for a Woman Facing Divorce in New York," box 7, folder 1, Betty Blaidell Berry Papers, Schlesinger Library on the History of Women in America, Radcliffe Institute, Harvard University, Cambridge, MA; Catherine East to Judy Goldsmith, President-Elect National Organization for Women, November 20, 1982, box 12, folder 21, Catherine Shipe East Papers, Schlesinger Library; Hon. Julia Ashbey, Hon. Anthony P. Tunney, and Lynn Hecht Schafran, Esq., "National Judicial Education Program Presentation, 'The Economic Consequences of Divorce; Child Support and the Feminization of Poverty,' " New Jersey Statewide Conference on Child Support Enforcement, May 9, 1982, box 30, folder 694, National Association of Women Judges (U.S.) Records, 1966–1997, Schlesinger Library.

24. Robert J. Levy, *Uniform Marriage and Divorce Legislation: A Preliminary Analysis* ([Chicago?]: National Conference of Commissioners on Uniform State Laws, 1968), B-6, and Leslie Joan Harris, "A 'Just and Proper Division': Property Distribution at Divorce in Oregon," *Oregon Law Review* 78 (1999): 742.

25. The community property model was unpopular, however, and the joint tax return was invented in part to avoid a swing toward community property in the 1940s. Lizabeth Cohen, *Consumer's Republic: The Politics of Mass Consumption in Postwar America* (New York: Alfred Knopf, 2003), 145.

26. Johnson, "Divorce, Alimony, Support and Custody," 4002.

27. *ERA Educational Study Pack*, ed. Thelma Stacy rev. ed. (San Diego, CA: San Diego County Chapter NOW, 1979), box 4, folder 2, Homemakers' Equal Rights Association Papers (hereafter cited as HERA Papers), WALA, LUC. Husbands usually paid their wives' lawyers after the divorce decree, but lawyers who accepted this faced delayed and uncertain payment.

28. *Anthony W. Silainis v. Anna Irene Silainis*, 45 C 10227, Report of Proceedings, April 2, 1946, box 3A-39-Z-22, CCA.

29. *Amelia Hightower v. Jefferson Hightower*, 55 S 18623, Complaint for Divorce, October 4, 1956, box 4A-11-Y-07, CCA.

30. In a 1986 study of lawyer-client interactions in forty divorce cases, lawyers said they usually tried to convey the contradictory and incoherent nature of the legal system instead of any sense of formal justice. Presumably some clients who opted for settlements identified them as their best option in an imperfect system. Austin Sarat and William L.F. Felstiner, "Law and Strategy in the Divorce Lawyer's Office," *Law & Society Review* 20 (1986): 93–134.

31. *Arvilla Caputo v. John Caputo*, 64 D 4423, Complaint for Divorce, August 17, 1965, Domestic Case Files Reel 64-94 Domestic Relations from 4414 to 4474, CCA.

32. *Truly Anthony v. Edward L. Anthony*, 64 D 8736, Complaint for Separate Maintenance, June 19, 1964, Domestic Case Files Reel 64-176 Division Domestic Relations from 8732 to 8771, CCA.

33. *Lucille V. Becker v. William C. Becker*, 64 D 8738, Complaint for Divorce, June 22, 1964, Domestic Case Files Reel 64-176 Division Domestic Relations from 8732 to 8771, CCA.

34. Roman L. H. Niel to NOW, July 30, 1981, L621, box 185, folder 16, National Organization for Women Records, General, MC496, Schlesinger Library on the History of Women in America, Radcliffe Institute, Harvard University, Cambridge, MA; *May Stamer v. Louis Stamer*, 45 C 10230, Report of Proceedings, February 21, 1946, box 3A-39-Z-22, CCA.

35. U.S. Department of Commerce, Bureau of the Census, *Child Support and Alimony: 1978* (Current Population Reports, Special Studies: Series P-23, No. 112), 2.

36. *Priscilla Hill v. Robert E. Hill*, 45 C 10229, Complaint for Separate Maintenance, May 13, 1946, box 3A-39-Z-22, CCA.

37. Johnson, "Divorce, Alimony, Support and Custody," 4004.

38. See for example, *Dorothy Thomas v. Howard Frank Thomas*, 45 S 20346, Report of Proceedings, March 20, 1945, box 3C-9-H-44, CCA. *Goldie Pavloff v. Paul Pavloff*, 55 C 11753, Report of Proceedings, February 9, 1956, box 4A-11-Y-07, CCA. *Helena Whitfield v. Sstor* Whitfield, 65 D 7021, Divorce decree, July 19, 1965, Superior Court Decrees Reel 65 D-32, Division Divorce, from 01 to 2015, CCA.

39. U.S. Department of Commerce, *Child Support and Alimony*, 2.

40. Johnson, *Policy Implications of Divorce Reform*, 197.

41. Johnson, "Divorce, Alimony, Support and Custody," 4003.

42. Judge Daniel A. Covelli, "Remarks and Comments by Members of the Judiciary of the Circuit Court of Cook County, IL Before the Members of the Committee on the Study of Divorce Laws of the Family Study Commission on Marriage, Divorce, Parental Responsibility of the State of Illinois," 74, May 24, 1968, box 1, folder Divorce Laws—Remarks, Bernard B. Wolfe Papers, Manuscripts Division, Abraham Lincoln Presidential Library, Springfield, IL.

43. "The Alimony Backlash," *Miami Herald*, November 10, 1974, 10G.

44. Martha Patton, "Money in Your Pocket: In Divorce Court, Equal Rights Are No Advantage," *Chicago Tribune*, August 17, 1975, A9.

45. Johnson, "Divorce, Alimony, Support and Custody," 4003.

46. *Zablocki v. Redhall*, 434 U.S.374 (1978).

47. Johnson, *Policy Implications of Divorce Reform*, 128. The two different surveys were based on the 1965 survey conducted by Una Rita Quenstedt and Carl F. Winkler in "What Are Our Domestic Relations Judges Thinking?," in *Monograph* (Chicago: American Bar Association, 1965), 5, and the 1975 schedule suggested by the Lake County Bar Association.

48. Johnson, *Policy Implications of Divorce Reform*, 199–200. In 1975, the equivalent of $12.50 in 1965 would have been $21.35, according to the Bureau of Labor Statistic's inflation calculator. This means that dropping the recommendation by $4.00 had the effect of over double that.

49. Quoted in Carol Kleiman, "Alimony: Debunking the Rich Divorce Myth," *Chicago Tribune*, August 1, 1972, B1. For members of the council, see "Advisory Council of Women Named: Nixon Chooses Panel of 20 to Check on Status," *New York Times*, August 17, 1969, 41.

50. Johnson, "Divorce, Alimony, Support, and Custody," 4004.

51. U.S. Department of Commerce, *Child Support and Alimony*, 1.

52. Though the press did not cover the decision-making behind this shift, prison administrators had wide discretion to operate the prison as they wished. Keramet Reiter, *23/7: Pelican Bay Prison and the Rise of Long-Term Solitary* (New Haven, CT: Yale University Press, 2016).

53. Elaine Markoutsas, " 'Good Old Days' of Alimony Row Fade," *Chicago Tribune*, June 6, 1976, 28.

54. The rates fluctuated widely by county. Seventeen men per 10,000 served jail times for default in one Michigan county versus 123 per 10,000 in another. David L. Chambers, *Making Fathers Pay: The Enforcement of Child Support* (Chicago: University of Chicago Press, 1979), 320; Richard Lempert, "Organization for Deterrence: Lessons from a Study of Child Support," *Law & Society Review* 16 (1981–82): 513–68; Elizabeth G. Patterson, "Civil Contempt and the Indigent Child Support Obligor: The Silent Return of the Debtor's Prison," *Cornell Journal of Law & Public Policy* 18 (2008–9): 117.

55. Crowley, *Defiant Dads*, 34–36; and Dinner, "Divorce Bargain."

56. "Early, undated proposal," ASDM letterhead, Section 2: "Archives of Coalition-building

Attempts within the Men's/Fathers' Movement," Men's Fathers' Movement Archive (hereafter cited as MFMA), http://www.mensdefense.org/Downloads/.

57. Michael S. Kimmel, *Manhood in America: A Cultural History* (New York: Free Press, 1996); Michael Schwalbe, *Unlocking the Iron Cage: The Men's Movement, Gender Politics, and American Culture* (New York: Oxford University Press, 1996); Rhys H. Williams, *Promise Keepers and the New Masculinity: Private Lives and Public Morality* (Lanham, MD: Lexington Books, 2001).

58. Terri Schultz, "Our Town: Champion of Divorced Males Turns Lions into Lambs," *Chicago Tribune*, November 1, 1970, NW3.

59. Dinner, "Divorce Bargain," 89.

60. Charles V. Metz, *Divorce and Custody for Men: A Guide and Primer Designed Exclusively to Help Men Win Just Settlements* (Garden City, NY: Doubleday & Company, Inc., 1968).

61. "Charles Metz Services Set for Tomorrow," *Chicago Tribune*, March 29, 1971, A14; Complaint, December 11, 1970, *Metz v. Ogilvie*, 70C 3099, box 143, D-40-1-1-5-4, United States District Court [hereafter USDC], Chicago, Civil Case Files, National Archives and Records Administration, Great Lakes (hereafter cited as NARA Great Lakes).

62. Schultz, "Our Town," NW3; "Opening Statement," Coalition of American Divorce Reform Elements (CADRE) founding meeting, February 13, 1971, 4, Section 1: Organizing Papers of CADRE/NCFP, Men International, and subsequent revival efforts, MFMA. By 1980, they did thirty thousand consultations, and the charge was seventy-five dollars. Susan K. Bass, "Divorce: The Male Perspective," *Chicago Tribune Magazine*, March 18, 1980, 34.

63. For an excellent account of men's divorce groups in California, see Dinner, "Divorce Bargain," 81–152; and Schultz, "Our Town," NW3. For another example, see also the Northern Virginia (NOVA) chapter of Fathers United for Equal Rights or Men's International. Marci DeWolf, "United by Divorce," *Chicago Tribune*, March 1, 1981, J1. NOVA, founded in 1976, served over two thousand men in half a decade. Fathers United in Virginia specifically advocated for "a law limiting the time required for alimony payments." The Society for the Emancipation of the American Male (SEAM), based out of Ann Arbor, Michigan, fought for "restoring the American patriarchy" and opposed "discriminatory divorce, alimony, and child custody laws.'" Carol Kleiman, "Working Woman: You Mean He's Not the Boss," *Chicago Tribune*, May 11, 1969, p F4. See also the National Council for Family Preservation, CADRE, and MEN International, which were all founded to try to bring local groups under one umbrella organization. Sheila Wolfe, "Men Assail Selves in Divorce Gouging," *Chicago Tribune*, May 8, 1971, 5. Richard F. Doyle to Gentlemen, undated, Section 2: Archives of Coalition-building Attempts within the Men's/Father's Movement, MFMA. CADRE sought to coordinate fifteen other organizations' efforts. Though initially ASDM provided office space, ASDM was not a member of this coalition due to a dispute. R. F. Doyle to CADRE, n.d., Section 1: Organizing Papers of CADRE/NCFP, Men International, and subsequent revival efforts, MFMA. MFMA and "Opening Statement," CADRE founding meeting, Feb. 13, 1971, Section 1: Organizing Papers of CADRE/NCFP, Men International, and subsequent revival efforts, MFMA.

64. Patricia Krizmis, "Divorces Costly, Unfair, Group Says," *Chicago Tribune*, September 7, 1969, 20.

65. Metz, *Divorce and Custody for Men*, 6–10, 69.

66. Ibid., 125. Other divorced men activists took this line up later. Lou J. Filczer to All Concerned Divorce Reformers Re. Cadre, Section 2: Correspondences and publicity relating to CADRE/NCFP, MFMA.

67. "ADAM Hits Genetic Test Legislation," *Chicago Defender*, August 21, 1973, 13.

68. Chuck Phillips, MD, "Unity," essay, undated, Part 4: Correspondences relating to subsequent revival efforts, MFMA.

69. "Elgin, IL," *Encyclopedia of Chicago*, http://www.encyclopedia.chicagohistory.org/pages /420.html.

70. Daniel Amneus, press release, "Men's Rights Coalition Formed," February 7, 1977, Section 3: Correspondences and Publicity relating to Men International, MFMA. Later MEN International drew on civil rights experience yet again to conjecture that the problems they were having organizing were due to FBI interference. Chairman Richard F. Doyle to Temporary members and supporters, MEN International, May 18, 1977, Section 3: Correspondence and Publicity relating to Men International, MFMA.

71. *Kohler v. Ogilvie*, 53 F.R.D. 98; (1971); "Group Seeks to Void Illinois Divorce Laws," *Chicago Tribune*, December 13, 1970, 2.

72. Complaint, December 11, 1970, 13, *Metz v. Ogilvie*, 70C 3099, box 143, D-40-1-1-5-4, USDC Chicago, Civil Case Files, NARA Great Lakes.

73. Ibid.

74. Ibid.

75. Ibid. In essence, Metz's lawyer was making a disparate impact argument before the revolutionary disparate impact case *Griggs v. Duke Power Company* was argued before the U.S. Supreme Court and before gender became a protected class in *Reed v. Reed*. Ibid., 13. See also Memorandum in Reply to Motion to Dismiss, January 27, 1971, ibid., 5.

76. Memorandum in Support of Motion to Dismiss. January 8, 1971, ibid., 4. See also Memorandum in Reply to Motion to Dismiss, ibid.

77. Opinion, *Kohler v. Ogilvie*, 70C 3099, box 143, D-40-1-1-5-4, USDC Chicago, Civil Case Files, NARA Great Lakes.

78. Other divorced men's organizations also pursued legislative change as the most effective tactic. See David Christopherson to Nat Denman, April 4, 1971, Section 2: Correspondences and publicity relating to CADRE/NCFP, MFMA.

79. See "Elrod Bills Ask Rights for Men!," *Lerner Booster Newspapers*, May 5, 1969, William B. Kelley Papers in possession of Chen K. Ooi, Chicago.

80. Charles L. VanDuzee, Secretary Treasurer, National Council for Family Preservation, to Richard F. Doyle, May 4, 1971, Section 2: Correspondences and publicity relating to CADRE/NCFP, MFMA.

81. Representative Marvin R. Dee, Chairman, *1974 Report of the Divorce Lawyers Practices Committee* (Springfield, IL: Divorce Lawyers Practices Committee, 1974).

82. Metz, *Divorce and Custody for Men*, 3–5, 92.

83. Ibid., 140.

84. Dee, *1974 Report of the Divorce Lawyers Practices Committee*.

85. Richard Templeton to Mr. Wilcox, n.d., Ephemeral Materials, [1988–,?] folder American Society of Divorced Men, Wilcox Collection of Contemporary Political Movements, University of Kansas Libraries, Lawrence, KS.

86. Kleiman, "Alimony," B1.

87. Terri Schultz, "Bra-Burner Tactics Out as Lawsuits Gain Ground," *Chicago Tribune*, June 28, 1971, 1.

88. "Divorce's Flip Side: The Ripped-Off Male," *Potpourri*, May 1973, box 7, folder Marriage and Divorce, Goudyloch (Giddy) Dyer Papers, ALPLM; Judy Vanslyke, "Men Want Divorce from

Laws That Bind Them to Ex-Wives," *Chicago Tribune*, October 28, 1971, N1; "News Brief," *Chicago Tribune*, November 23, 1971, 3.

89. Lou Filczer, "Men for E.R.A.," *Chicago Tribune*, March 22, 1973, 16.

90. ADAM membership pamphlet, received September 1990, Ephemeral Materials, [1988–?], folder, American Divorce Association for Men, Wilcox Collection of Contemporary Political Movements.

91. "Divorce's Flip Side," 2.

92. Vanslyke, "Men Want Divorce," N1, and Bob Cromie, "A.D.A.M. Wants More than Apples," Chicago Tribune, March 21, 1973, 10.

93. Louis J. Filsczer, American Divorce Association for Men to Representative Catania, "Subject: The Fault with No-Fault," memo, n.d., and Rebuttal WGN Editorial #75-R20, Monday, May 5, 1975, box 15, folder Divorce, 1973–1978, Catania Papers.

94. Mandatory counseling was a failed early element of no-fault. Herbert Jacob, *Silent Revolution: The Transformation of Divorce Law in the United States* (Chicago: University of Chicago Press, 1988).

95. Parkman, *Good Intentions Gone Awry*.

96. "Economic Protection of Dependent Spouses and Children in Divorce Law and Practice," series VI–X, MC477, box 11, folder 16, East Papers.

97. See Herma Hill Kay, "Equality and Difference: A Perspective on No-Fault Divorce and Its Aftermath," *University of Cincinnati Law Review* 56 (1987): 62. See also Starnes, *Marriage Buyout*, 44.

98. SB 252 Family Law Act, box GO72, folder Legislation—Divorce Reform 1969 (2/4), Legal Affairs Unit, Ronald Reagan Governor's Office Collection, Ronald Reagan Presidential Library, Simi Valley, CA (hereafter cited at RRPL). See also, James A. Hayes, "California Divorce Reform: Parting Is Sweeter Sorrow," *American Bar Association Journal*, July 1970, 663, box GO72, folder Legislation—Divorce Reform 1969 (1/4), Legal Affairs Unit, Ronald Reagan Governor's Office Collection.

99. Statement of Harvey L. Zuckman in Support of Bill No. I-89 before the Council of the District of Columbia, July 7, 1975, 4, box 113, folder 5, Frank Kameny Papers, Library of Congress.

100. Parkman, *Good Intentions Gone Awry*, 73.

101. SB 252 Family Law Act, box GO72, folder Legislation—Divorce Reform 1969 (2/4), Legal Affairs Unit, Ronald Reagan Governor's Office Collection.

102. Senator Donald L. Grunsky and Assemblyman James A. Hayes, *Family Law Act SB 252 and AB 530 Making Supplemental Changes Effect January 1, 1970* (Sacramento, CA: Joint Rules Committee, 1969), 29, box GO72, folder Legislation—Divorce Reform, 1969 (3/4), Legal Affairs Unit, Ronald Reagan Governor's Office Collection. This law was changed in California in 1973. *Report of the California Advisory Commission on the Status of Women: California Women* (Sacramento, CA: The Commission, 1973), box GO 209, folder Research File—Women, Status of [Advisory Commission Report], Research Files, Ronald Reagan's Governor Papers Collection.

103. Kay, "Equality and Difference," 44. See also Herma Hill Kay, "An Appraisal of California's No-Fault Divorce Law," *California Law Review* 75 (1987): 291–319.

104. Kay, "Equality and Difference," 59; Ellen Shulte, "The Peaceful Revolution," *Los Angeles Times*, December 15, 1968, and "Senate-Assembly Conferees Agree on Divorce Reform Bill," *Los Angeles Times*, July 24, 1969, Marriage and Divorce [Pre-Marriage Equality], ONE Subject File, ONE National Gay & Lesbian Archives, University of Southern California Libraries, Los Angeles,

CA; Seymour Korman, "Californians Await Easier Divorce Law," *Chicago Tribune*, December 29, 1969, A10; "Reagan Signs Bill Liberalizing Laws on Divorce in California," *Chicago Tribune*, September 6, 1969, N6; Seymour Korman, "Assembly OK's Divorce Bill in California," *Chicago Tribune*, June 23, 1969, A8; Parkman, *Good Intentions Gone Awry*, 79–81.

105. Noble C. Overom to George Partis, March 17, 1971, Section 2: Archives of Coalition-building Attempts within the Men's/Father's Movement. MFMA.

106. Joseph Epstein, "Divorce: Part Two," *Chicago Tribune*, November 12, 1972, 51.

107. Table Comparing Existing Law to SB 252, as Amended June 13, 1969, Prepared by James A. Hayes, Assemblyman, 39th District, box GO72, folder Legislation—Divorce Reform, 1969 (2/4), Legal Affairs Unit, Ronald Reagan Governor's Office Collection. See also Parkman, *Good Intentions Gone Awry*, 75–77.

108. "NOW Task Force on Marriage and Divorce Elizabeth Coxe Spalding, National Coordinator," box 1, folder 4, Elizabeth Coxe Spalding Papers, Papers of NOW officers, 1970–1977, Schlesinger Library. See also Ziegler, "Incomplete Revolution," 259–92.

109. Sheila Cronan, "Marriage," in *Radical Feminism*, ed. Anne Koedt, Ellen Levine, and Anita Rapone (New York: Quadrangle Books, 1973), 218.

110. Stacy, *ERA Educational Study Pack*.

111. Jo Ann Budde, Housewives for ERA, to House Judiciary Committee Hearing on the Equal Rights Amendment, n.d., box 13, folder 6, ERA Central Records, Chicago History Museum.

112. *Debrey v. Debrey*, 132 Ill. App. 2d 1072 (1971), 3. Emphasis added.

113. Ill. Rev. Stat. ch. 68, IP 8 (1975) as quoted in Illinois, *Smith-Hurd Illinois Annotated Statutes*, permanent ed. (St. Paul, MN: West Publishing Co, 1934), 457; *Everett v. Everett*, 25 Ill. 2d 342; 185 N.E.2d 201 (1962), 4.

114. Amy Stanley, "Conjugal Bonds and Wage Labor: Rights of Contract in the Age of Emancipation," *Journal of American History* 75 (September 1988): 471–500; Reva Siegel, "Home as Work: The First Women's Rights Claims Concerning Wives' Household Labor, 1850–1880," *Yale Law Journal* 103 (1994): 1073–217.

115. *Stotlar v. Stotlar*, 50 Ill. App. 3d 790; 365 N.E.2d 1097; (1977); *Harding v. Harding*, 18 Ill. App. 3d 550; 310 N.E.2d 19; (1974); *Katz v. Katz*, 10 Ill. App. 3d 39; 293 N.E.2d 904; (1973); *Demos v. Demos*, 8 Ill. App. 3d 906; 290 N.E.2d 304; (1972). Sheila Cronan highlighted a similar assumption in New York case law in Cronan, "Marriage." See, for instance *Garlock v. Garlock*, 279 NY 337; 18 N.E.2d 521; (1939).

116. Critiques of marital rape had been part of the first-wave feminist agenda. Jill Elaine Hasday, "Contest and Consent: A Legal History of Marital Rape," *California Law Review* 88 (October 2000): 1413–41.

117. *People v. Alexander*, 116 Ill. App. 3d 855, 452 N.E.2d 591 (1983).

118. J. C. Barden, "Confronting the Moral and Legal Issue of Marital Rape," clipping, box 31, folder 4, Dolan Papers.

119. Sheribel Rothenberg and Marian Barnes, *The Legal Status of Homemakers in Illinois* (Washington, DC: U.S. Government Printing Office, 1977), 9.

120. HERA-Ohio newsletter, vol. 1, no. 2., January 1982, box 1, folder 13, HERA Papers, WALA, LUC.

121. Rothenberg and Barnes, *Legal Status of Homemakers in Illinois*, 9.

122. "Displaced Homemaker Forum," *Network News: The Newsletter of the Displaced Homemakers Network*, vol. 4, no. 1, February 1982, 4, box 115, folder Displaced Homemakers Network, ERAmerica Records, Library of Congress.

123. Budde to House Judiciary Committee Hearing on the Equal Rights Amendment.

124. Levenstein, "'Don't Agonize, Organize!,'" 144–68 and Kahn, "Next Battle for Marriage Equality." As Amy Stanley and Reva Siegel have shown, women in the years immediately before and after the Civil War also made "the claim that wives were entitled to property rights in their household labor." Stanley, "Conjugal Bonds and Wage Labor," 486; Siegel, "Home as Work," 1075. At the turn of the century, a group of middle-class women fought to make housework more like waged work or share it communally or with husbands. Susan Strasser, *Never Done: A History of American Housework* (New York: Pantheon Books, 1982), 185; Eileen Boris, *Home to Work: Motherhood and the Politics of Industrial Homework in the United States* (Cambridge: Cambridge University Press, 1994); Christina Simmons, *Making Marriage Modern: Women's Sexuality from the Progressive Era to World War II* (Oxford: Oxford University Press, 2009).

125. Sylvia Porter, "Social Security Reflects Old Bias Toward Women," April 1980, clipping, box 10, folder 121, ERA Illinois Records, Special Collections and University Archives, University of Illinois at Chicago.

126. Rothenberg and Barnes, *Legal Status of Homemakers in Illinois*.

127. Margaret Mead and Frances Balgley Kaplan, eds., *American Women: The Report of the President's Commission on the Status of Women and Other Publications of the Commission* (New York: Scribner, 1965), 69.

128. Ibid.

129. In her epilogue to *American Women,* cultural anthropologist Margaret Mead envisioned an even bolder solution where every adult was guaranteed an adequate income. Only elite workers, including engineers, teachers, scientists, and homemakers, would earn anything more. *American Women*, 191–92.

130. Quoted in Metz, *Divorce and Custody for Men*, 71.

131. National Conference of Commissioners on Uniform State Laws, *Uniform Marriage and Divorce Act* (Chicago: 1970), 3–6. For more on an earlier era of uniform marriage law advocacy, see Nicholas L. Syrett, *American Child Bride: A History of Minors and Marriage in the United States* (Chapel Hill: University of North Carolina Press, 2016), 165–201.

132. Parkman, *Good Intentions Gone Awry*, 71.

133. See Kay, "Equality and Difference," 46; National Conference of Commissioners on Uniform State Laws, *Uniform Marriage and Divorce Act*, 29–30.

134. National Conference of Commissioners on Uniform State Laws, *Uniform Marriage and Divorce Act*, 5.

135. National Conference of Commissioners on Uniform State Laws, *Uniform Marriage and Divorce Act*. See also Mary Ann Glendon, "Matrimonial Property: A Comparative Study of Law and Social Change," *Tulane Law Review* 49 (November 1974): 21–83.

136. Barbara Brown, Thomas I. Emerson, Gail Falk, and Ann E. Freedman, "Equal Rights Amendment: A Constitutional Basis for Equal Rights for Women," *Yale Law Journal* 80 (April 1971): 946.

137. Homemakers' Equal Rights Association pamphlet, box 1, folder 2, HERA Papers.

138. "An Open Letter to All Housewives for ERA," *News for and from Housewives for ERA*, vol. IV, no. 1, May-June 1975, box 115, folder Housewives for ERA, ERAmerica Records; HERA Fourth Annual Convention August 7–9, 1981, Clarke College, Dubuque, Iowa program, box 1, folder 1, HERA Papers.

139. HERA Fourth Annual Convention August 7–9, 1981 Clarke College, Dubuque, Iowa

program; Housewives for ERA Second Annual Convention. Saturday, June 2, 1979, Broadview Hotel and Convention Center. 400 West Douglas Wichita, Kansas. box 1, folder 1, HERA Papers.

140. Anne Bowen Follis to HERA Board Member, November 10, 1981, box 1, folder 6, HERA Papers.

141. HERA Homemakers' Equal Rights Association pamphlet, n.d., box 1, folder 2, HERA Papers; *News for and from Housewives for ERA*, vol. III, no. 1, February 22, 1975, box 13, folder 6, ERA Central Records.

142. Statement by Jo Ann Budde, Housewives for ERA House Human Resources Committee Hearing on the Equal Rights Amendment, June 12, 1974, box 22, folder 6, ERA Central Records.

143. Terri Wedoff, "President's Perspective" in HERA Newsletter, June/July/August 1981, box 19, folder 204, ERA Illinois Records.

144. Resolution on Financial Compensation for Homemakers, box 1, folder 25, HERA Papers. HERA rejected wages for housework in Proposals for Consideration, June 1, 1978, box 3, folder 2, HERA Papers.

145. Homemakers' Equal Rights Association, "A Right Is a Right Is a Right," pamphlet, n.d., box 1, folder 2, HERA Papers.

146. Ziegler, "An Incomplete Revolution," 259–92.

147. Housewives for ERA pamphlet, n.d., box 1, folder 2, HERA Papers.

148. Statement by Jo Ann Budde, Housewives for ERA House Human Resources Committee Hearing on the Equal Rights Amendment.

149. "Dear Coordinators and Leaders," *HERA Coordinator News*, n.d., box 2, folder 1, HERA Papers; "'Roses' for Roses Day," *News for and from . . . Homemaker's Equal Rights Association of Illinois*, Fall 1979, 4, box 3, folder 4, HERA Papers.

150. HERA Illinois—State Board Meeting, May 31, 1983, Home of Kerri C. Tedrowe, box 3, folder 2, HERA Papers; "Dear Coordinators and Leaders," *HERA Coordinator News*. See the letters in box 2, folder 2, HERA Papers: Betty Lou Reed to Shirley, n.d.; Adeline J. Geo-Karis to Ms. Jamie Gentzkow, February 26, 1980; Ronald E. Griesheimer to Sharon Clay Rose, March 28, 1980.

151. Minutes, HERA State Board, June 8, 1981, 22 Pine Circle, Cary, IL 60013, box 3, folder 2, HERA Papers; Press Release, HERA of Illinois, April 28, 1982, box 1, folder 22, HERA Papers.

152. Beth Brinkman Cianci to Friend, October 22, 1980, box 1, folder 1, Beth Brinkmann Cianci Papers, WALA, LUC; Karri Clay Tedrowe, President Illinois HERA, to HERA Member, n.d., box 2, folder 1, HERA Papers.

153. Judith I. Avner, "Using Connecticut Equal Rights Amendment at Divorce to Protect Homemakers' Acquisition of Marital Property," *University of Bridgeport Law Review* 4 (1982–83): 265–81.

154. *Henderson v. Henderson, Holmes v. Holmes, Rand v. Rand, Silvia v Silvia*, and *Conway v. Dana* from Avner, "Using Connecticut Equal Rights," 277.

155. Greta A. Mikus, Legal Assistant, Commonwealth of PA Office of the Governor, to Nina Gaspich, Joliet, IL, August 25, 1975, box 9, folder 103, ERA Illinois Records.

156. Series of myths featured in *New Directions for Women*, vol. 10, no. 5, September/October 1981, box 1, folder 1, ERA Illinois Records; *Friedman v. Friedman*, 521 S.W.2d 111 (1975).

157. *DiFlorido v. DiFlorido*, 459 Pa. 650; 331 A.2d 179 (1975).

158. Kim E. Green, "State ERAs Are Working," *New Directions for Women*, vol. 10, no. 5 September/October 1981, 1, box 1, folder 1, ERA Illinois Records.

159. Norman, "Miss Gold-Digger of 1953," 8.

160. A Bill for an Act in Relation to Domestic Relations, HB 3910, 79th General Assembly, *State of Illinois Floor Debate Transcriptions* (June 8, 1976): H 26; Beverly A. Susler and Eloise Johnstone, "Looking to the Future to Correct Evils of the Past," *DePaul Law Review* 23 (1973–1974): 349–50.

161. Bill for an Act in Relation to Domestic Relations, HB 3910 (June 8, 1976), H 64; Bill for an Act in Relation to Domestic Relations, HB 3910 (June 16, 1976), H 45.

162. Bill for an Act in Relation to Domestic Relations, HB 3910 (June 8, 1976), H 65.

163. Ibid., H 48.

164. "Toward a New Divorce Law," *Chicago Tribune*, June 28, 1977, B2.

165. Ray Mosley, "Divorces Go on While Court Rules," *Chicago Tribune*, January 3, 1978, 3; A Bill for an Act in Relation to Marriage and Divorce, SB 801, 80th General Assembly, *State of Illinois Floor Debate Transcriptions* (June 23, 1977): H 144–50.

166. The phrase "of the marital and non-marital property" ensured that the new act covered cases similar to *Debrey v. Debrey*. The house in question in *Debrey* was considered nonmarital property—the husband had inherited it—but its preservation due to the wife's housework would have rendered it in part her property. *In re. Gustke* (1979) and *In re. Glidden* (1979), as well as the Missouri cases *Stark v. Stark* (1976) and *Cain v. Cain* (1976). See Illinois, *Smith-Hurd Illinois Annotated Statutes*, 454.

167. Illinois, *Smith-Hurd Illinois Annotated Statutes*, , chap. 40, "Domestic Relations," 523.

168. Ibid., 472.

169. Ibid., H 61. See ibid., 52. Alan J. Dixon, ed., *Illinois Blue Book, 1977–1978* (Springfield, IL: Office of the Secretary of State, 1978): 111.

170. Bill for an Act in Relation to Domestic Relations, HB 3910 (June 8, 1976), H 50.

171. Bill for an Act in Relation to Marriage and Divorce, H 103-4.

172. Louis J. Filczer, president, American Divorce Association for Men, to the editor, n.d., clipping, box 7, folder Divorce—1977 SB 801, Goudyloch (Giddy) Dyer Papers.

173. Bill for an Act in Relation to Marriage and Divorce, H 98.

174. Ibid.

175. Ibid., H 142. Community property was proposed in Illinois. Laura S. Rasmussen, JD, "An Act Relative to the Establishment of Valid Contracts Between Husband and Wife Concerning the Rights and Obligations of the Spouses," model bill, box 8, folder Interspousal Contract, 1977–1978, Catania Papers, ALPLM.

176. Bill for an Act in Relation to Domestic Relations, HB 3910 (June 8, 1976), H 52.

177. Ibid. Herma Hill Kay suggests that in California this moderation of the homemakers' contribution was accidental due to changes between the 1970 and 1973 versions of the Uniform Marriage and Divorce Act. Judges then took advantage of this change. Kay, "Equality and Difference," 50–51. Robert J. Levy also argued that gender inequality was a problem of how the laws were applied. In Minnesota, the legislature even changed its statute to make the value of the homemakers' contribution more clear. Robert J. Levy, "A Reminiscence About the Uniform Marriage and Divorce Act—and Some Reflections About Its Critics and Its Policies," *Brigham Young University Law Review* 1991 (1991): 43–77. But in Illinois, this distinction seemed much more accepted ahead of time.

178. Illinois, *Smith-Hurd Illinois Annotated Statutes*, 524.

179. Bill for an Act in Relation to Marriage and Divorce, H 146.

180. The legislators who consistently opposed the ERA and abortion funding but who favored no-fault were Keats, Schlickman, Williams, Walsh, Boucek, Mahar, Laurino, Wolf, Conti, DiPrima, Doyle, Terzich, Simms, Rigney, VonBeckman, Tuerk, Schisler, R. Walsh, Steele, Flinn, Winchester, Giglio, Jacobs, Bluthardt, and Birchler. State of Illinois, *Journal of the House of Representatives*, vol. no. 17, May 4, 1977, 1699 for HB 333. In addition, eight additional senators vacillated on the ERA, including voting against it in this session, but voted for the Marriage and Dissolution of Marriage Act. These eight were Laurino, Nardulli, Domico, Huff, Vitek, Taylor, Dawson, and Mulcahey. Legislators Action on ERA--How They Voted, box 96, folder Illinois State ERA, ERAmerica Records; John W. Lewis, ed., *Illinois Blue Book, 1971–72* (Springfield, IL: Office of the Secretary of State, 1972); Michael J. Howlett, ed., *Illinois Blue Book, 1973–74* (Springfield, IL: Office of the Secretary of State, 1974); Michael J. Howlett, ed., *Illinois Blue Book, 1975–76* (Springfield, IL: Office of the Secretary of State, 1976); Dixon, *Illinois Blue Book, 1977–1978*; State of Illinois General Assembly, *Journal of the House of Representatives*, June 23, 1977, 36; 4773.

181. "Dispute over Illinois Divorce Law Dramatizes Need for ERA," *The Times of the 27th*, vol. 2, no. 7, May 1978, box 96, folder Illinois State ERA, ERAmerica Records.

182. Metz, *Divorce and Custody for Men*, 81, and Filczer to the editor. Joseph won in a lower court with this argument. Ray Mosley, "Divorces Go on While Court Rules," *Chicago Tribune*, January 3, 1978, 3; Stan Twardy, "Marriage and Property," *Chicago Tribune*, January 5, 1978, B2.

183. *Kujawinski v. Kujawinski*, 71 Ill. 2d 576; 376 N.E.2d 1382 (1978).

184. See Table 1 for if and when women in other states received homemaker entitlements.

185. Fern Schumer, "Fairness New Byword," *Chicago Tribune*, March 24, 1981, C1.

186. Gordon H. Lester, "Child Support and Alimony: 1989," *Current Population Reports*, ser. P-60, no. 173 (Washington, DC: U.S. Department of Commerce, 1991), 14.

187. Ziegler, "Incomplete Revolution," 259–92.

188. Starnes, *Marriage Buyout*, 39.

189. Arlie Hochschild, *The Second Shift: Working Families and the Revolution at Home* (New York: Penguin Books, 2012). For statistics on women's extra household labor today, see "Balancing Paid Work, Unpaid Work and Leisure," Organization for Economic Co-operation and Development (OECD), http://www.oecd.org/gender/data/balancingpaidworkunpaidworkandleisure.htm.

190. Moreover, a woman had to be a wife to profit from her household labor in Illinois. Though Wisconsin in *Watts v. Watts* and California in *Marvin v. Marvin* both allowed cohabiting partners to share marital property, the Illinois Supreme Court ruled against this in 1978 in *Hewitt v. Hewitt*. *Marvin v. Marvin*, 18 Cal. 3d 600 (1976); *Watts v. Watts*, 137 Wis.2d 506 (1987); and Elizabeth Pleck, *Not Just Roommates: Cohabitation After the Sexual Revolution* (Chicago: University of Chicago Press, 2012), 149, 160.

191. More unusually, this settlement did include a cost-of-living increase. *Marie T. Scharpenter and Theodore Paul Scharpenter*, 85 D 12499, judgment for dissolution of marriage, July 3, 1985, reel 85D84, CCA. See also *Rogelio Rivas v. Paula Rivas*, 85 D 11528, judgment for dissolution of marriage, July 3, 1985, reel 85D84, CCA.

192. *Nancy E. Mertz and Alan D. Mertz*, 85 D 5358, judgment of dissolution of marriage, May 1, 1985, reel 85D54, CCA; *Mary Beth Simon and Richard Simon*, 84 D 10823, judgment for dissolution of marriage, July 3, 1985, reel 85D84, CCA.

193. *John Golliday and Louvenia Golliday*, 84 D 485, judgment for dissolution of marriage, May 1, 1985, reel 85D54, CCA.

194. *In re. Marriage of Tatham*, 173 Ill. App. 3d 1072; 527 N.E.2d 1351; 1988. See also *In re. Marriage of Banach*, 140 Ill. App. 3d 327; 489 N.E.2d 363; 1986; Leslie Joan Harris, "A 'Just and Proper Division': Property Distribution at Divorce in Oregon," *Oregon Law Review* 78 (1999): 735–65; and Katherine Silbaugh, "Turning Labor into Love: Housework and the Law," *Northwestern University Law Review* 91 (1996–97): 1–86.

195. *Pfohl v. Pfohl*.

196. Hochschild, *Second Shift*.

197. "Illinois Gets Divorce Reform; Judge Says Legislators Duped," *Chicago Tribune*, September 24, 1977, B5. See also Michael Hirsley and Charles Mount, "Foes Charge State's Divorce Reform Is Just the Opposite," *Chicago Tribune*, October 9, 1977, 40.

198. Elaine Markoutsas, "Alimony by Any Other Name Still Costs," *Chicago Tribune*, November 8, 1981, K5.

199. Markoutsas, "Alimony by Any Other Name Still Costs," K5.

200. Schumer, "Fairness New Byword," C1.

201. *Report of the California Advisory Commission on the Status of Women: California Women*. See Table 1.

202. Sharon Johnson, "No-fault Divorce Survives Decade Despite Its Faults," *Chicago Tribune*, April 29, 1979, J1.

203. Jane Bryant Quinn, "Laws Put Divorced Housewives in Financial Jeopardy," *Chicago Tribune*, July 27, 1982, C1.

204. Mike Wheeler, New England School of Law, to Ms. East, December 7, 1973, ser. VI–X, MC477, box 11, folder 15, East Papers.

205. Elaine Markoutsas, "Divorce Soars as Alimony Ups," *Chicago Tribune*, April 11, 1976, 22. Other scholars estimated that alimony awards were reduced from one out of ten cases to one out of twenty. Lenore Weitzman quoted in Glaser, "Easing the Pain (But Not the Cost) of Splitting Up," B1.

206. U.S. Bureau of the Census, Current Population Reports, Series P-60, No. 173, *Child Support and Alimony: 1989* (Washington, DC: U.S. Government Printing Office, 1991). Catherine East to Judy Goldsmith, President-Elect National Organization for Women, November 20, 1982.

207. Schumer, "Fairness New Byword," C1.

208. Homemakers' Equal Rights Association of Kansas, newsletter, vol. 1, no. 4, March/April 1982, box 1, folder 10, HERA Papers.

209. For work on how fathers began to demand visitation rights in exchange for these child support payments, see Deborah Dinner, "The Divorce Bargain: The Fathers' Rights Movement and the Dual System of Family Law" (American Society for Legal History Conference, 2014).

210. Johnson, "No-fault Divorce Survives Decade Despite Its Faults," J1. However, Weitzman and Herbert Jacob both argue that no-fault did not affect child support payments. Lenore J. Weitzman, *The Divorce Revolution: The Unexpected Social and Economic Consequences for Women and Children in America* (New York: Free Press, 1985): 265; and Herbert Jacob, "Another Look at No-Fault Divorce and Postdivorce Finances of Women," *Law and Society Review* 23(1989): 95–115.

211. Johnson and Zimka, *Evaluation of the Illinois Child Support Enforcement Program*, 22.

212. See To Amend Title 18, United States Code, to Make a Misdemeanor the Flight, in Interstate or Foreign Commerce, By Any Person Who Is the Parent of a Minor Child or Who Is a Married Man, If Such Person So Flees with the Intent of Evading His Legal Responsibilities with

Respect to the Support or Maintenance of His Minor Child or of His Wife, S. 2160, 90th Cong. (1967); To Make It a Crime to Move or Travel in Interstate or Foreign Commerce to Avoid Compliance With Certain Support Orders, and For Other Purposes, H.R. 7972, 91st Cong. (1969); To Amend Title 18, United States Code, to Make a Misdemeanor the Flight, in Interstate or Foreign Commerce, By Any Person Who Is the Parent of a Minor Child or Who Is a Married Man, If Such Person So Flees with the Intent of Evading His Legal Responsibilities with Respect to the Support or Maintenance of His Minor Child or of His Wife, S. 2701, 92nd Cong. (1971) ; To Amend Chapter 73 of Title 10, United States Code, to establish a Survivor Benefit Plan, and For Other Purposes, H.R. 10670, 92nd Cong. (1971). For the concession on locating absent fathers, see PL 93-647. See also "Law on Runaways Sought," *New York Times*, February 9, 1967, 26; Marjorie Hunter, "Senate Panel Votes a U.S. Role in Tracing Deserting Fathers," *New York Times*, May 19, 1972, 47; "Major Provisions of Senate Bill on Social Security and Welfare," *New York Times*, June 14, 1972, 32; "To Collect a Debt to Children," *New York Times*, August 9, 1983, A22.

213. Levy, *Uniform Marriage and Divorce Act Legislation*, compiled appendices. Arizona, Indiana, Michigan, Mississippi, Nebraska, New Mexico, North Carolina, Oregon, South Carolina, Utah, Washington, West Virginia, Wisconsin, and Wyoming allowed liens and Alaska, Connecticut, Delaware, Florida, Kansas, Louisiana, Missouri, New York, North Carolina, Oklahoma, Washington, West Virginia, Wisconsin, and Wyoming allowed garnishment.

214. Anna Marie Smith, *Welfare Reform and Sexual Regulation* (Cambridge: Cambridge University Press, 2007), 98; Russell B. Long, *Social Services Amendments of 1974: Report of the Committee on Finance, United States Senate to Accompany H.R. 17045 to Amend the Social Security Act to Establish a Consolidated Program of Federal Financial Assistance to Encourage Provision of Services by the States (Together with Separate Views), December 14, 1974*, (Washington DC: U.S. Government Printing Office, 1974), 2.

215. White House Staffing, Survey of Administration Accomplishments on Behalf of Women, July 25, 1984, box 15F, folder Women (3 of 3), Faith Ryan Whittlesey Papers, RRPL.

216. "To Collect a Debt to Children," A22.

217. For a contemporary reflection on this new law, see Joseph L. Lieberman, "Time to Get Tough on Child-Support Payments," *New York Times*, October 12, 1985, 27. For the full bill, see A Bill to Amend Part D of Title IV of the Social Security Act to Assure, Through Mandatory Income Withholding, Incentive Payments to States, and Other Improvements in the Child Support Enforcement Program, That All Children in the United States Who Are in Need of Assistance in Securing Financial Support from Their Parents Will Receive Such Assistance Regardless of Their Circumstances, and For Other Purposes, H.R. 4325, 98th Cong. (1984). Crowley, *Defiant Dads*.

218. Smith, *Welfare Reform and Sexual Regulation*, 112.

219. This law also officially introduced no-fault grounds, in addition to no-fault custody and property distribution.

220. A Bill for an Act in Relation to Support and Maintenance, HB 3068, 83rd Congress, *State of Illinois Floor Debate Transcriptions* (May 17, 1984): H 193-209; 94th General Assembly, Regular Session, May 21, 1985, 7; State of Illinois, 83rd General Assembly, House of Representatives, Transcription Debate, May 17, 1984, 193–209; Jim Edgar, ed., *Illinois Blue Book, 1983–1984*, (Springfield, IL: Office of the Secretary of State, 1978): 110.

221. A Bill for an Act to Amend an Act in Relationship to Support and Maintenance, HB 2431, 84th Congress, *State of Illinois Floor Debate Transcriptions*, (May 20, 1985): H 34-45; Illinois General Assembly, Legislative Information System, "Status of All Legislation by Sponsor,"

January 22, 1985, 6; State of Illinois, 94th General Assembly, Regular Session, May 21, 1985, 7; State of Illinois, 94th General Assembly, Regular Session, May 24, 1985, 228; Illinois General Assembly, Legislative Information System, "Status of All Legislation by Sponsor," December 27, 1985, 5.

222. Bill for an Act to Amend an Act in Relationship to Support and Maintenance, H38, 43.

223. Johnson, *Policy Implications of Divorce Reform*, 128. The two different surveys were based on the 1965 survey conducted by Una Rita Quenstedt and Carl F. Winkler in "What Are Our Domestic Relations Judges Thinking?," in *Monograph* (Chicago: American Bar Association, 1965), 5 and the 1975 schedule suggested by the Lake County Bar Association.

224. Weitzman, *The Divorce Revolution*; Jay Matthews, "Divorce Study Shows Men Get Richer," *Washington Post*, May 31, 1982, box OA9999, folder EXPOSE [Ex-Partners of Servicemen for Equality], Dee Jepsen Papers, RRPL.

225. Starnes, *Marriage Buyout*, 37; Crowley, *Defiant Dads*, 110–11.

226. Hochschild, *Second Shift*, 251.

227. Linda Bailiff Marshall, "Rehabilitative Alimony: An Old Wolf in New Clothes," *NYU Law Review and Social Change* 667 (1984–85): 667–93.

228. Martha Fineman, *The Illusion of Equality: The Rhetoric and Reality of Divorce Reform* (Chicago: University of Chicago Press, 1991); and Weitzman, *Divorce Revolution*.

229. "Entered House Illegally: Judge Drops Rape Charge, Fines Husband $65," *Chicago Tribune*, March 8, 1979, B1.

230. SB 16, 81st General Assembly, *State of Illinois Floor Debate Transcriptions* (February 7, 1979): S 17.

231. Ibid., S 18.

232. SB 519, 81st General Assembly, *State of Illinois Floor Debate Transcriptions* (May 25, 1979): S 10; SB 123, 82nd General Assembly, *State of Illinois Floor Debate Transcriptions* (May 19, 1981): S 130; Marianne Taylor, "Bill Would Allow Wife to Charge Spouse with Rape," *Chicago Tribune*, March 13, 1983, 1; "Group to Help Victims of Rape," *Chicago Tribune*, November 4, 1982, NWC4; "State to Explain New Sex Assault Law," *Chicago Tribune*, March 2, 1984, DuPage edition, B3; Polly Poskin, "History of the Anti-Rape Movement in Illinois," http://vawnet.org/sites/default/files/assets/files/2016-10/IL-ICASA_historyantirapemvt.pdf. Other organizations including the Illinois National Organization for Women, the District of Columbia Rape Task Force, the New York University Law School Clinical Program in Women's Legal Rights, the New York Radical Feminists, and many more worked against marital rape. Joseph R. Tybor, "New Rape Law Knocks Down Barriers to Prosecution," *Chicago Tribune*, October 9, 1983, C1.

233. SB 123, 82nd General Assembly, *State of Illinois Floor Debate Transcriptions* (May 19, 1981): S 130.

234. SB 519, 81st General Assembly, *State of Illinois Floor Debate Transcriptions* (May 25, 1979): S 10.

235. A Bill for an Act to Create the Offense of Sex, H.B. 606, 83rd General Assembly, *State of Illinois Floor Debate Transcriptions* (May 10, 1983): H 168–69.

236. Ibid., H 169.

237. Ibid., H 170.

238. Ibid., H 170–71.

239. H.B. 606, 83rd General Assembly, *State of Illinois Floor Debate Transcriptions* (July 1, 1983): S 94.

240. Ibid., S 99–100.

241. Colin O'Donnell, "Senate Panel Passes Reform in Rape Law," *Chicago Tribune*, June 8, 1983, B1.

242. Fifty had been found guilty. Andy Knott and Thomas Powers, "Sex-Crime Law Has Some Doubters," *Chicago Tribune*, July 1, 1984, B4. Just a few months later, the legislature changed the law to eliminate a thirty-day report clause on all rape but marital rape, leaving in a condition of marital rape in Illinois that persists into the twenty-first century. A Bill for an Act in Relation to Certain Criminal Offenses and the Prosecution of Such Offenses, SB 1424, 83rd General Assembly, *State of Illinois Floor Debate Transcriptions* (June 14, 1984): H 61.

243. *Planned Parenthood of Southeastern Pennsylvania v. Casey*, 505 U.S. 833 (1992).

Chapter 3

1. Serena Mayeri, *Reasoning from Race: Feminism, Law, and the Civil Rights Revolution* (Cambridge, MA: Harvard University Press, 2011), 81–84.

2. Donald T. Critchlow, *Phyllis Schlafly and Grassroots Conservatism: A Woman's Crusade* (Princeton, NJ: Princeton University Press, 2005); Donald G. Mathews and Jane Sherron DeHart, *Sex, Gender, and the Politics of ERA: A State and the Nation* (New York: Oxford University Press, 1990), 59.

3. Critchlow, *Phyllis Schlafly and Grassroots Conservatism*, 221.

4. Ilene Rose Feinman, *Feminist Soldiers and Feminist Antimilitarists* (New York: New York University Press, 2000); Neil J. Young, *We Gather Together: The Religious Right and the Problem of Interfaith Politics* (New York: Oxford University Press, 2105), 158.

5. Illinois had an opportunity to pass the ERA with a simple majority, but allegedly did not due to Richard J. Daley's order to punish a rival. Shortly thereafter, Illinois enacted its new state constitution with a provision that required three-fifths of the Illinois legislature to pass the ERA, rather than the simple majority required in most states. The ERA did not have enough support to pass with a three-fifths majority. Attorney General William J. Scott issued an opinion that the extraordinary vote should not be required, but a special three-judge federal panel, including Judge John Paul Stevens a few months before he joined the Supreme Court, ruled that a state legislature had the power to determine its own voting margins. Jim Edgar, interview by Mark DePue, May 21, 2009, 156–61, Jim Edgar Oral History Project, Abraham Lincoln Presidential Library and Museum, Springfield, IL; "4 Sue to Upset Defeat of Equal Rights," *Chicago Tribune*, May 9, 1973, B10; "State Can Set Own ERA Vote Margin," *Chicago Tribune*, February 21, 1975, A1. For examples of other states, see Janet K. Boles, *The Politics of the Equal Rights Amendment: Conflict and the Decision Process* (New York: Longman, 1979); Mary Frances Berry, *Why ERA Failed: Politics, Women's Rights, and the Amending Process of the Constitution* (Bloomington: Indiana University Press, 1986); Jane J. Mansbridge, *Why We Lost the ERA* (Chicago: University of Chicago Press, 1986); Matthews and DeHart, *Sex, Gender, and the Politics of ERA*.

6. The Equal Employment Opportunity Act of 1972, passed just days after the ERA, finally gave teeth to the Equal Pay Act of 1963 and the Civil Rights Act of 1964. Similarly Title IX, the Higher Education Act passed on June 23, 1972, eradicated the most obvious abuses in education. Congress dealt with women's access to credit with the Equal Credit Opportunity Act of 1974. *Reed v. Reed* began applying equal protection and substantive due process to the category of gender. *Reed v. Reed*, 404 U.S. 71 (1971).

7. See for example, Robert Cross, "Dialog: Phyllis Schlafly," *Chicago Tribune Magazine*, November 9, 1975, 26, clipping, box 1, folder 1, ERA Illinois Records, Special Collections and University Archives, University of Illinois at Chicago; *Phyllis Schlafly Report*, vol. 8, no. 10, ser.

2, March 1975, box 12, folder 1, ERA Central Records, Chicago History Museum; "Warning! Equal Rights Amendment Is Dangerous to Women!!!," flier from League of Housewives, box 1, folder 12, ERA Central Records; Robert Smith, clipping from *Minneapolis Tribune*, September 5, 1976, sent out by STOP ERA from Chatham, IL, box 1, folder 1, ERA Illinois Records; STOP ERA, "You Can't Fool Mother Nature" pamphlet, box 1, folder 1, ERA Illinois Records; Rosemary Thompson, "What's Behind the Equal Rights Amendment," *Moody Monthly*, February 1974, 48, 51, box 1, folder 1, ERA Illinois Records; A Reply to Editorial CBS 2, March 21, 1974, from Ira Latimer, Executive Vice President of Illinois Small Business Men's Association, box 1, folder 12, ERA Central Records.

8. Barbara Ehrenreich, *The Hearts of Men: American Dreams and the Flight from Commitment* (Garden City, NY: Anchor Press/Doubleday, 1983); Rebecca E. Klatch, *Women of the New Right* (Philadelphia: Temple University Press, 1987); Mathews and DeHart, *Sex, Gender, and the Politics of ERA*; J. Brooks Flippen, *Jimmy Carter, the Politics of Family, and the Rise of the Religious Right* (Athens: University of Georgia Press, 2011); Robert O. Self, *All in the Family: The Realignment of American Democracy Since the 1960s* (New York: Hill and Wang, 2013); Neil J. Young, " 'The ERA Is a Moral Issue:' The Mormon Church, LDS Women, and the Defeat of the Equal Rights Amendment," *American Quarterly* 59 (September 2007): 623–44.

9. See for example, William E. Dunham, *The Baby Killers* (Belmont, MA: Review of the News, 1972); William E. Dunham, *O.S.H.A. Builds Fear* (Belmont, MA: Review of the News, 1973); and William E. Dunham, *Stop Socialized Medicine!* (Belmont, MA: Review of the News, 1970).

10. William E. Dunham, "Attack on Women," July 19, 1972, Review of the News, Belmont, MA, box 1, folder 1, ERA Illinois Records.

11. STOP ERA, "You Can't Fool Mother Nature."

12. "Do You Know . . . WHAT It Means?," pamphlet from ERA Opposed, Lake Forest, IL, box 1, folder 1, ERA Illinois Records. See also "Operation Wake-Up: A Coalition of Organization Opposed to the Equal Rights Amendment," box 124, folder anti misc articles, ERAmerica Records, Library of Congress.

13. *The Church and the Proposed Equal Right Amendment: A Moral Issue,* booklet put out by the Mormon Church, Church Magazines, Salt Lake City, UT, box 1, folder 1, ERA Illinois Records.

14. "We Believe," Association of Women Who Want to Be Women newsletter, volume 4, no. 8, October 1977, box 124, folder anti misc articles, ERAmerica Records.

15. "In Defense of Women's Rights—Why the Equal Rights Amendment Must NOT Be Ratified," STOP ERA Committee, box 26, folder Equal Rights Amendment [1/3], Elizabeth Dole Files, Ronald Reagan Presidential Library, Simi Valley, CA (hereafter cited as RRPL).

16. "How ERA Would Change Federal Laws," *Phyllis Schlafly Report*, November 1981, 2.

17. STOP ERA, "Hot Air Balloon," pamphlet, box 4, folder Equal Rights Amendment [1/3], Wendy Borcherdt Files, RRPL.

18. See, for example, a letter where a woman recounted both her mother's and her friend's surprise when left with less than half of the household wealth after a divorce. Kay D. Ress, Indianapolis, IN, to NOW, July 16, 1981, L335, box 185, folder 10, National Organization for Women Records (hereafter cited as NOW Records), Schlesinger Library on the History of Women in America, Radcliffe Institute, Harvard University, Cambridge, MA. See also unknown, Citrus Heights, CA, to NOW, undated, L554, box 185, folder 15, NOW Records.

19. John F. McManus, "The Birch Log: More about the ERA," column, March 13, 1975, box

124, folder anti misc articles, ERAmerica Records; Dorothy Sue Cobble, *The Other Women's Movement: Workplace Justice and Social Rights in Modern America* (Princeton, NJ: Princeton University Press, 2004).

20. Linda Gordon, *Pitied but Not Entitled: Single Mothers and the History of Welfare, 1890–1935* (New York: Free Press, 1994); Alice Kessler-Harris, *In Pursuit of Equity: Women, Men, and the Quest for Economic Citizenship in 20th-Century America* (New York: Oxford University Press, 2001).

21. Sylvia Porter, "Social Security Reflects Old Bias Toward Women," April 1980, clipping, box 10, folder 121, ERA Illinois Records.

22. Lisa Levenstein, " 'Don't Agonize, Organize!': The Displaced Homemakers Campaign and the Contested Goals of Postwar Feminism," *Journal of American History* 100 (May 2014): 1127. See also Suzanne Kahn, "The Next Battle for Marriage Equality," *Dissent* (Winter 2016): 25–34.

23. Elaine Donnelly, former member, Reagan/Bush Women's Policy Advisory, to Elizabeth Dole, Diana Lozono, Wendy Borcherdt, and Judy Peachee, memo, October 16, 1981, box 12, folder Task Force on Legal Equity for Women [II](2), Wendy Borcherdt Papers.

24. Eagle Forum, "The Blank Check Called 'ERA,'" pamphlet, box 1, folder 1, ERA Illinois Records.

25. "The Tremendous Powers of ERA," *Phyllis Schlafly Report*, December 1981, section 2, box 1, folder 2, ERA Illinois Records.

26. Mormon Church, *Church and the Proposed Equal Right Amendment*.

27. Nancy J. Rider, "What the ERA Would Do to American Women . . . ," *Review of the News*, December 8, 1976, box 1, folder 1, ERA Illinois Records.

28. Robert Cross, "Dialog: Phyllis Schlafly."

29. Mormon Church, *Church and the Proposed Equal Right Amendment*.

30. Victoria Moruzzi, "A Practical Program to Achieve Economic Justice for Homemakers," September 9, 1978, box 1, folder The Community Approach to Disability and Employment' etc (2), Babson-Bernays Competition Records, Schlesinger Library on the History of Women in America, Radcliffe Institute, Harvard University, Cambridge, MA.

31. STOP ERA, "You Can't Fool Mother Nature."

32. Keith Kathan, "Meet: Happiness of Womanhood INC (HOW)," newsletter, December 11, 1972, box 1, folder 10, ERA Central Records.

33. Eagle Forum, "Blank Check Called 'ERA.'"

34. Jennifer Baker to Frank C. Genovese, October 1, 1978, #1498, box 2, folder 15, Babson-Bernays Records.

35. Ibid.

36. C.F. Berry to unknown, June 11, 1978, box 3, folder Foreign Exchange (12), Babson-Bernays Records.

37. "Proposed 27th Amendment to U.S. Constitution/The Truth about the Equal Rights Amendment," box 1, folder 12, ERA Central Records.

38. STOP ERA, "You Can't Fool Mother Nature."

39. "Legal Developments Arising from Cases Brought Under State ERAs," undated pamphlet, box 9, folder 103, ERA Illinois Records.

40. Essay by Marilyn P. Desaulniers sent to Ervin, March 8, 1972, box 273, folder 11302, Sam J. Ervin Papers, Subgroup A: Senate Records #3847A (hereafter cited as Ervin Senate Papers), Southern Historical Collection, Wilson Library, University of North Carolina at Chapel Hill, Chapel Hill, North Carolina (hereafter cited at SHC-UNC).

41. "Quotations About the ERA, Women's Lib," *About the ERA*, an insert in the *Richmond News Leader*, box 1, folder 1, ERA Illinois Records.

42. Congressman John G. Schmitz, "Look Out! They're Planning to Draft Your Daughter," box 1, folder 10, ERA Central Records. Susan Huck ghostwrote this document. Susan Huck to Mrs. Holiday, undated, box 273, folder 11314, Ervin Senate Papers.

43. Rockford Illinois chapter of STOP ERA, *ERA—Let the Authorities Speak*, booklet, box 1, folder 2, ERA Illinois Records; "The Dan Smoot Report: Reject or Rescind the ERA," *Review of the News*, vol. 10 no. 11, March 13, 1974, box 1, folder 12, ERA Central Records.

44. Jenkin Lloyd Jones, "Women are Having Second Thoughts About Equal Rights Amendment," clipping, box 33, folder Willis Whichard Papers for use on specific campaigns/ideol anti, Senator Willis P. Whichard Papers, 1965–1998, collection number 4426, SHC-UNC.

45. Patricia Sanlin, Jacksonville, NC, to "sir," March 28, 1972, box 273, folder 11302, Ervin Senate Papers.

46. "How ERA Will Hurt Divorced Women," *Phyllis Schlafly Report*, vol. 7, no. 10, May 1974, section 2, box 1, folder 12, ERA Central Records.

47. Ibid.

48. Thompson, "What's Behind the Equal Rights Amendment?."

49. Operation Wake-Up: A Coalition of Organizations Opposed to the Equal Rights Amendment, "Resolutions," box 124, folder anti misc articles, ERAmerica Records.

50. For more on this, see Ehrenreich, *Hearts of Men*. Klatch attributes this lack of responsibility and selfishness to men and women. In this case, however, it was men's irresponsibility and women's conscientiousness that was the problem. Klatch, *Women of the New Right*, 119–94.

51. "The Precious Rights ERA Will Take Away from Wives," *Phyllis Schlafly Report*, vol 7, no. 1, section 2, August 1973, box 1, folder 11, ERA Central Records.

52. Robert Cross, "Dialog: Phyllis Schlafly".

53. Paul Freund, "Why the ERA Proposal 'Leaves the Mind So Unsatisfied,'" *About the ERA*, an insert in the *Richmond News Leader*, box 1, folder 1, ERA Illinois Records; "What's Wrong with 'Equal Rights' for Women?," *Phyllis Schlafly Report*, vol. 5, no. 7, February 1972, box 124, folder Phyllis Schlafly Report, ERAmerica Records.

54. "Quotations About the ERA, Women's Lib."

55. "How ERA Will Hurt Divorced Women."

56. Mormon Church, *Church and the Proposed Equal Right Amendment*.

57. Clipping from *Homefront: Institute for American Democracy*, vol. 7, no. 2, February 1973, box 1, folder 10, ERA Central Records.

58. "Will ERA Make Child-Care the State's Job?," *Phyllis Schlafly* Report, vol. 9, no. 5, November 1975, box 124, folder Phyllis Schlafly Report, ERAmerica Records.

59. Natasha Zaretsky, *No Direction Home: The American Family and the Fear of National Decline, 1968–1980* (Chapel Hill: University of North Carolina Press, 2007), 119; Self, *All in the Family*, 322–24.

60. Zaretsky, *No Direction Home*, 119.

61. Matthew D. Lassiter, *The Silent Majority: Suburban Politics in the Sunbelt South* (Princeton, NJ: Princeton University Press, 2007).

62. Allen J. Matusow, *Nixon's Economy: Booms, Busts, Dollars, and Votes* (Lawrence: University Press of Kansas, 1998).

63. Nancy MacLean, "Postwar Women's History: The 'Second Wave' or the End of the Family

Wage?," in *A Companion to Post-1945 America*, ed. Jean-Christophe Agnew and Roy Rosenzweig (Malden, MA: Blackwell Pub, 2006), 235–59; Zaretsky, *No Direction Home*; and Thomas J. Sugrue, *The Origins of the Urban Crisis: Race and Inequality in Postwar Detroit* (Princeton, NJ: Princeton University Press, 1996).

64. STOP ERA, "You Can't Fool Mother Nature."

65. Barbara H. K. Spink to Ellie Smeal, July 23, 1981, L286, box 185, folder 9, NOW Records.

66. Statement Anonymous, box 33, folder Willis Whichard Papers for use on specific campaigns/ideol anti, Whichard Papers.

67. Remarks made by Dr. Margaret Mead at the conference "Women at Work" sponsored by the Los Angeles County Federation of Labor, AFL-CIO, March 13, 1971, box 350, folder 13655, Ervin Senate Papers.

68. Schmitz, "Look Out! They're Planning to Draft Your Daughter."

69. "The Power of Suggestion: How Easily Are You Fooled?," box 1, folder 12, ERA Central Records.

70. Association of Women Who Want to Be Women, "Ladies! Have You Heard?," flier, box 1, folder 12, ERA Central Records.

71. Schmitz, "Look Out! They're Planning to Draft Your Daughter."

72. STOP ERA workshop, Springfield, IL, St. Nicholas Hotel, Friday, July 25, 1975, observed and reported back to ERA Central, box 1, folder 12, ERA Central Records.

73. See, for example, Mary Jane Downing-Yriart, "Proposed Plan of Compensation for Family Manager and Mother," box 3, folder 345 Received Crt 2/78 (4), Babson-Bernays Records; Wilma Wallace to Babson College, June 21, 1978, box 3, folder Foreign Exchange (12); Mrs. Myrtle Chell Hurley to Mr. Genovese from, June 15, 1978, #1429, box 2, folder 1; and Robin Larrabee to Professor Genevese, October 2, 1978, box 2, folder 15, all Babson-Bernays Records. See, for example, Sonya Michel, *Children's Interests/Mothers' Rights: The Shaping of America's Child Care Policy* (New Haven, CT: Yale University Press, 1999) and Elizabeth R. Rose, *A Mother's Job: The History of Day Care, 1890–1960* (New York: Oxford University Press, 1999).

74. Self, *All in the Family*.

75. Thompson, "What's Behind the Equal Rights Amendment?"

76. William E. Dunham, "The E.R.A. Mickey Mouse," December 18, 1974, box 1, folder 1, ERA Illinois Records.

77. Lee Rainwater and William L. Yancey, *The Moynihan Report and the Politics of Controversy: A Trans-Action Social Science and Public Policy Report* (Cambridge, MA: MIT Press, 1967), 30. The prospect of white families becoming like black families was a pervasive fear. As Natasha Zaretsky has argued about the 1970s, "Changes in the family were not only moving up the class ladder from the poor to the affluent, observers argued, but also traversing racial boundaries from black to white." Zaretsky, *No Direction Home*, 13. See also James T. Patterson, *Freedom Is Not Enough: The Moynihan Report and America's Struggle over Black Family Life—from LBJ to Obama* (New York: Basic Books, 2010).

78. Don Duncan, "Male-Liberation Movement Theorist Presents His Case," *Biotheology*, n.d., reprinted by Colorado Chapter, League of Housewives, folder D45I Equal Rights Amendment, sub-series 38, Daniel Walker Papers, RG 101, Illinois State Archives, Springfield, IL.

79. Matthews and DeHart, *Sex, Gender, and the Politics of ERA*.

80. "Voting Rights Act of 1965," *Duke Law Journal* 1966 (1966): 463–83.

81. "The Tremendous Powers of ERA's Section 2," *Phyllis Schlafly Report*, vol. 15, no. 5, December 1981, box 1, folder 2, ERA Illinois Records.

82. In fact, cases like *Relf v. Weinberger* indicated how unsettlingly successful the state could be in limiting the number of children black women could have. *Relf v. Weinberger*, 565 F.2d 722, 184 U.S. App. D.C. 147 (1977). More recent press suggests that this pattern of abuse continued well into the twenty-first century. Hunter Schwarz, "Following Reports of Forced Sterilization of Female Prison Inmates, California Passes Ban," *Washington Post*, September 26, 2014.

83. Lassiter, *Silent Majority*.

84. Schmitz, "Look Out! They're Planning to Draft Your Daughter."

85. Quoted in Glenn Schwendiman and Helen Schwendiman, "The Proposed Equal Rights Amendment to the United States Constitution (So Called Equal Rights Amendment)," February 6, 1975, folder D46I, sub-series 38, Daniel Walker Papers.

86. Mrs. Charles Dolivier to Senator Sam Ervin, December 23, 1971, box 273, folder 11303, Ervin Senate Papers.

87. Ibid.

88. Mrs. Cecil M. Long to Willis P. Whichard, state representative, February 28, 1973, box 34, folder ERA-No-Elsewhere 1973, Whichard Papers.

89. Schwendiman and Schwendiman, "Proposed Equal Rights Amendment." Others saw elite women's voices as overrepresented because they were the only women with the time, power, and money to effect changes in the law. Poem and comments by L.E. Cox, box 305, folder 12482, Ervin Senate Records.

90. Elizabeth Waldman, "Labor Force Statistics from a Family Perspective," *Monthly Labor Review*, December 1983, 19.

91. Arlene Skolnick, *Embattled Paradise: The American Family in an Age of Uncertainty* (New York: Basic Books, 1991), 108.

92. "Working Wives Increase Family Income and Status," *Family News and Features*, August 26, 1971, box 53, folder 1, Eleanor F. Dolan Papers, Women and Leadership Archive, Loyola University Chicago.

93. Ibid.

94. *Phyllis Schlafly Report*, vol. 8, no. 11, June 1975, box 1, folder 12, ERA Central Records; A Reply to Editorial CBS 2, March 21, 1974, from Ira Latimer.

95. STOP ERA, "If You Are Pregnant, Ill, Poor, Minority, or Disadvantaged . . . Beware of the Hook in ERA," pamphlet, box 1, folder 1, ERA Illinois Records; "Q and A: The Schlafly View of ERA, Liberation," *Washington Star*, January 18, 1976, A1, box 124, folder anti misc articles, ERAmerica Records.

96. Bette Jean (J. J.) Jarboe to Sam Ervin, "Statement of Intent," The International Anti-"Women's Liberation" League, June 19, 1973, box 350, folder 13,659, Ervin Senate Papers.

97. George Chauncey, *Why Marriage? The History Shaping Today's Debate Over Gay Equality* (Cambridge, MA: Basic Books, 2004); Peggy Pascoe, "Sex, Gender, and Same-Sex Marriage," *Is Academic Feminism Dead? Theory in Practice*, ed. The Social Justice Group at the Center for Advanced Feminist Studies (New York: New York University Press, 2000), 86–129.

98. *Baker v. Nelson*, 291 Minn. 310, 191 N.W.2d 185 (1971).

99. *Adams v. Howerton*, 673 F.2d 1036 (1982).

100. *Equal Rights for Men and Women*, H.J.R. 208, 92nd Cong., 2nd sess., *Congressional Record* 118 (March 21, 1972): S 9314.

101. This was the logic eventually cited by the Hawaiian Supreme Court in *Baehr v. Lewin*, 74 Haw. 645, 852 P.2d 44 (1993). See also Pascoe, "Sex, Gender, and Same-Sex Marriage."

102. Illinois Eagle Forum, "The ERA: (Equal Rights Amendment) Myths vs. Facts," pamphlet, box 1, folder 1, ERA Illinois Records.

103. Mormon Church, *Church and the Proposed Equal Right Amendment*.

104. State Representative William G. Batchelder on the Floor of the Ohio House—March 29, 1973, box 305, folder 12473, Ervin Senate Papers.

105. "Testimony of Prof. Ruth Bader Ginsburg, Professor of Law, Columbia Law School," *Equal Rights Amendment Extension: Hearings Before the Subcommittee on Civil and Constitutional Rights of the Committee on the Judiciary, House of Representatives, Ninety-Fifth Congress on H.J.Res. 638*, 95th Cong., 1st and 2nd sess., 1977–1978, 359, 134.

106. "Warning! Equal Rights Amendment is Dangerous to Women!!!"

107. "Quotations About the ERA, Women's Lib."

108. State Representative Betty J. Hoxsey, "Springfield Report: ERA Returns," *Moral Majority Report of Illinois*, vol. 1, no. 1, June–July (no year), box 117, folder Moral Majority, ERAmerica Records.

109. "Eagle Forum: The Alternative to Women's Lib," pamphlet, box 115, folder Eagle Forum, ERAmerica Records.

110. "Association of the W's: Newsletter," vol. 4, no. 8, October 1977, box 124, folder anti misc articles, ERAmerica Records.

111. Ervin was actually quoting Michigan Law Professor James White's congressional testimony. His selection of this particular quote, however, is significant. *Equal Rights for Men and Women*, S 9317.

112. Later courts would reject the extension of spousal privileges to gay partners. For instance, Richard Baker initiated the first gay marriage case with James McConnell in Minnesota in 1971. Baker then tried to claim veterans' benefits for McConnell as his dependent spouse, in particular education benefits. The Eighth Circuit court rejected this claim in 1976. Mary Anne Case, "Marriage Licenses," *Minnesota Law Review* 89 (2005): 1763; *McConnell v. Nooner*, 547 F.2d 54 (1976).

113. Illinois Eagle Forum, "ERA: (Equal Rights Amendment) Myths vs. Facts."

114. *Phyllis Schlafly Report*, vol. 8, no. 12, July 1975, box 124, folder Phyllis Schlafly Report, ERAmerica Records.

115. STOP ERA, "You Can't Fool Mother Nature."

116. "Should Marriage Between Homosexuals Be Permitted?," WGBH Boston, sponsored by *The Advocates*, May 2, 1974, available at http://openvault.wgbh.org/catalog/f4ae6e-should-marriage-between-homosexuals-be-permitted.

117. "Should Marriage Between Homosexuals Be Permitted?"

118. "Viewpoint with Ronald Reagan" (Reprint of a Radio Program entitled "Equal Rights Amendment—Con)," August 13, 1975, Louisiana, KHOM-AM, box 124, folder Ronald Reagan Radio Programs, ERAmerica Records.

119. Testimony by David Abrams, ERAmerica before Young Republicans, Washington, DC, May 19, 1976, box 144, folder Republican Platform Comm Hearing, ERAmerica Records.

120. Maureen Reagan, Testimony Before the Republican Platform Committee Hearing, June 14, 1976, box 144, folder Republican Platform Comm Hearing, ERAmerica Records.

121. Ibid.

122. "Viewpoint with Ronald Reagan."

123. Ibid.

124. Sam J. Ervin Jr., "Statement to House Judiciary Committee," reprinted in "E.R.A. Time Extension Bill Is Illegal," *Phyllis Schlafly Report*, July 1978.

125. "Testimony of Prof. William A. Stanmeyer, Indiana University School of Law," *Equal Rights Amendment Extension: Hearings Before the Subcommittee*, 359.

126. Ibid., 369–70.

127. Rudd, August 15, 1978, 95th Cong., 2nd sess. *Congressional Record*, 124, pt. 19:26200 (August 15, 1978).

128. Kindness, Ibid., 26216.

129. Treen, Ibid., 26238.

130. Bill Summary and Status, 95th Cong., H.J. Res. 638, Major Congressional Actions, https://www.congress.gov/bill/95th-congress/house-joint-resolution/638?q=%7B%22search%22%3A%5B%22%5C%22equal+rights+amendment%5C%22%22%5D%7D&r=30.

131. Abzug, notably, lost to Moynihan in the primary for a Senate race. Moynihan's Democratic credentials were clear, but so was his affiliation with the welfare reform movement. Bayh, on the other hand, spent all his political capital getting the ERA ratified by the rather conservative state of Indiana in 1977. Church groups in particular rallied against Bayh in favor of Danforth Quayle due to Bayh's positions on homosexuality, abortion, and the Equal Rights Amendment. Reginald Stuart, "Bayh Loses Indiana Senate Race; G.O.P. Novice Defeats Brademas," *New York Times*, November 5, 1980, A23. Elizabeth Holtzman, who cofounded the Congresswoman's Caucus, left her House seat to run without success for a seat in the Senate in 1980. Leslie Bennets, "Women in Office: How Have They Affected Women's Issues?," *New York Times*, November 4, 1980, B8.; "D'Amato Led Rivals in Raising of Funds," *New York Times*, December 14, 1980, 69; Phyllis Schlafly, "Election Dooms ERA and Women's Lib," *Eagle Forum*, November 1980, box 115, folder Eagle Forum, ERAmerica Records.

132. Schlafly, "Election Dooms ERA and Women's Lib."

133. https://www.govtrack.us/congress/votes/95-1978/h1324.

134. Schlafly, "Election Dooms ERA and Women's Lib."

135. Ibid. On the role of economics over family issues, see also Barbara Honegger to Elizabeth Dole, memo re: Decision to Implement Task Force on Legal Equity for Women, October 19, 1981, box 12, folder Task Force on Legal Equity for Women [II](2), Wendy Borcherdt Files.

136. Ervin became a friendly correspondent with Phyllis Schlafly. Sam J. Ervin Jr. to Mrs. Phyllis Schlafly, September 22, 1975, box 73, folder 883, Sam J. Ervin Papers, Subgroup B: Private Papers #3847B (hereafter cited as Ervin Private Papers), SHC-UNC; Donald T. Critchlow, *Phyllis Schlafly and Grassroots Conservatism: A Woman's Crusade* (Princeton, NJ: Princeton University Press, 2005), 185–210.

137. Buckley cited the *Yale Law Journal* in her letter, including pages numbers, but not the date or volume. It is difficult to say what she was reading for sure, but it is possible it was the Emerson article.

138. Mrs. Shay Buckley to Senator Ervin, May 21, 1975, box 73, folder 883, Ervin Private Papers.

139. Ibid.

140. *Rostker v. Goldberg*, 453 U.S. 57 (1981).

141. *McCarty v. McCarty*, 453 U.S. 210 (1981).

142. Agnes Boone to Ellie Smeal, August 12, 1981, L1054, box 185, folder 25, NOW Records.

143. Action for Former Military Wives, "The Supreme Court Cuts Lifeline to Thousands of Women and Children: These Statistics Were Compiled by a Professional Statistician, Fay Zeman," box OA9999, folder ACTION for Former Military Wives, Dee Jepsen Files, RRPL.

144. "Donahue Transcript #01042 Appearances: Phil Donahue Phyllis Schlafly (President of Eagle Forum) Eleanor Smeal (President of the National Organization for Women)," 11, box 185, folder 1, MC496, General, NOW Records. Schlafly's own organization, the Eagle Forum, did oppose the *McCarty* decision but still maintained that the ERA would not solve this problem. Susan Burton, Eagle Forum attorney, "McCarty Is Not an ERA Issue," box 4, folder Equal Rights Amendment [2/3], Wendy Borcherdt Files.

145. Uniformed Services Former Spouses' Protection Act, Public Law 97-252. USFSPA peeled back some of *McCarty* but still did not grant full equity to wives who lived in states that did not honors homemakers' entitlements, who divorced before 1982, or who were married less than twenty years. Beverly Stephen, ""New Military Benefits Are Good, However . . . ," *New York Daily News*, October 10, 1982, box OA 9999, folder EXPOSE [Ex-Partners of Servicemen for Equality], and Elizabeth H. Dole to Friend, October 19, 1982, box OA9999, folder Ex-Spouses Military Pension, both Dee Jepsen Files.

146. Ronald Reagan to Mrs. Ann King Petroni from Ronald, July 31, 1980, reprinted in *Reagan: A Life in Letters*, ed. Kiron K. Skinner, Annelise Anderson, and Martin Anderson (New York: Free Press, 2003).

147. "Remarks of the President at Signing Ceremony for Executive Order 12336 Establishing Task Force on Legal Equity for Women," press release, December 21, 1981, box 4, folder Equal Rights Amendment 1/3, Wendy Borcherdt Files.

148. Elaine Donnelly to Elizabeth Dole, Diana Lozono, Wendy Borcherdt, and Judy Peachee, memo, October 16, 1981.

149. Congressman Don Edwards and Marie McGlone, "Can Reagan Co-Opt the ERA?," *Ms. Magazine*, June 1982, 106, box 26, folder Equal Rights Amendment [3/3], Elizabeth Dole Files.

Chapter 4

1. Mimi Abramovitz, *Regulating the Lives of Women: Social Welfare Policy from Colonial Times to the Present* (Boston: South End Press, 1988).

2. Jennifer Mittelstadt, *From Welfare to Workfare: The Unintended Consequences of Liberal Reform, 1945–1965* (Chapel Hill: University of North Carolina Press, 2005), 86–91; Karen Tani, *States of Dependency: Welfare, Rights, and American Governance, 1935–1972* (Cambridge: Cambridge University Press, 2016).

3. For more on welfare rights, see, for example, Kenneth J. Neubeck, *Welfare Racism: Playing the Race Card Against America's Poor* (New York: Routledge, 2001); Ellen Reese, *Backlash Against Welfare Mothers: Past and Present* (Berkeley: University of California Press, 2005); Premilla Nadasen, *Welfare Warriors: The Welfare Rights Movement in the United States* (New York: Routledge, 2005); Annelise Orleck, *Storming Caesar's Palace: How Black Mothers Fought Their Own War on Poverty* (Boston: Beacon Press, 2005); Felicia Ann Kornbluh, *The Battle for Welfare Rights: Politics and Poverty in Modern America* (Philadelphia: University of Pennsylvania Press, 2007); and Nancy Fraser and Linda Gordon, *Fortunes of Feminism: From State-Managed Capitalism to Neoliberal Crisis* (London: Verso, 2013), 83–110.

4. Michael Willrich, "Home Slackers: Men, the State, and Welfare in Modern America," *Journal of American History* 87 (September 2000): 462.

5. Martin Gilens, "How the Poor Became Black: The Racialization of American Poverty in

the Mass Media," in *Race and the Politics of Welfare Reform*, ed. Sanford Schram, Joe Soss, and Richard C. Fording (Ann Arbor: University of Michigan Press, 2003), 105.

6. Frances Fox Piven and Richard A. Cloward, *Regulating the Poor: The Functions of Public Welfare* (New York: Pantheon Books, 1971).

7. Walter Goodman, "The Case of Mrs. Sylvester Smith," *New York Times*, August 25, 1968, SM62.

8. Eugene Genovese, *Roll, Jordan, Roll: The World the Slaves Made* (New York: Vintage Books, 1976); Amy Stanley, *From Bondage to Contract: Wage Labor, Marriage, and the Market in the Age of Slave Emancipation* (Cambridge: Cambridge University Press, 1988); Kathleen Brown, *Good Wives, Nasty Wenches, and Anxious Patriarchs: Gender, Race, and Power in Colonial Virginia* (Chapel Hill: University of North Carolina Press, 1996); Ira Berlin, *Many Thousands Gone: The First Two Centuries of Slavery in North America* (New York: Harvard University Press, 2000).

9. See, for example, Glenda Gilmore, *Gender and Jim Crow: Women and the Politics of White Supremacy in North Carolina, 1896–1920* (Chapel Hill: University of North Carolina Press, 1996); Gail Bederman, *Manliness and Civilization: A Cultural History of Gender and Race in the United States, 1880–1917* (Chicago: University of Chicago Press, 1995); Alex Lubin, *Romance and Rights: The Politics of Interracial Intimacy, 1945–1954* (Jackson: University Press of Mississippi, 2005); Peggy Pascoe, *What Comes Naturally: Miscegenation Law and the Making of Race in America* (Oxford: Oxford University Press, 2009); Peter Wallenstein, *Tell the Court I Love My Wife: Race, Marriage, and Law—An American History* (New York: St. Martin's Griffin, 2004).

10. Dorothy Roberts, *Killing the Black Body: Race, Reproduction, and the Meaning of Liberty* (New York: Vintage, 1997); Lisa Levenstein, *A Movement Without Marches: African American Women and the Politics of Poverty in Postwar Philadelphia* (Chapel Hill: University of North Carolina Press, 2009); Abramovitz, *Regulating the Lives of Women*; Rickie Solinger, *Wake Up Little Susie: Single Pregnancy and Race Before Roe v. Wade* (New York: Routledge, 1992); Martha F. Davis, *Brutal Need: Lawyers and the Welfare Rights Movement, 1960–1973* (New Haven, CT: Yale University Press, 1993); Linda Gordon, *Pitied but Not Entitled: Single Mothers and the History of Welfare, 1890–1935* (New York: Free Press, 1994); Gwendolyn Mink, *The Wages of Motherhood: Inequality in the Welfare State* (Ithaca, NY: Cornell University Press, 1995); Andrea Julie Sachs, "The Politics of Poverty: Race, Class, Motherhood, and the National Welfare Rights Organization, 1965–1975" (PhD diss., University of Minnesota, 2001); Nadasen, *Welfare Warriors*; Orleck, *Storming Caesar's Palace*; Marisa Chappell, *The War on Welfare: Family, Poverty, and Politics in Modern America* (Philadelphia: University of Pennsylvania Press, 2009) have all noted welfare rights activists' important critiques of heteronormative family policy.

11. See, for example, Laura F. Edwards, "The Marriage Covenant Is at the Foundation of All Our Rights: The Politics of Slave Marriages in North Carolina After Emancipation," *Law & History Review* 14, no. 1 (1996): 91–107; Katherine M. Franke, "Becoming a Citizen: Reconstruction Era Regulation of African American Marriages," *Yale Journal of Law & Humanities* 11, no. 2 (1999): 251–310; Susan O'Donovan, *Becoming Free in the Cotton South* (Cambridge, MA: Harvard University Press, 2007).

12. Jacqueline Jones, *Labor of Love, Labor of Sorrow: Black Women, Work, and the Family, from Slavery to the Present* (New York: Basic Books, 2009); Julie Saville, *The Work of Reconstruction: From Slave to Wage Labor in South Carolina, 1860–1870* (Cambridge: Cambridge University Press, 1996); Laura Edwards, *Gendered Strife and Confusion: The Political Culture of Reconstruction* (Urbana: University of Illinois Press, 1997).

13. Jill Quadagno, *The Color of Welfare: How Racism Undermined the War on Poverty* (New

York: Oxford University Press, 1994); Thomas J. Sugrue, *The Origins of the Urban Crisis: Race and Inequality in Postwar Detroit* (Princeton, NJ: Princeton University Press, 1996); Robert Self, *American Babylon: Race and the Struggle for Postwar Oakland* (Princeton, NJ: Princeton University Press, 2005); Elizabeth Hinton, *From the War on Poverty to the War on Crime* (Cambridge, MA: Harvard University Press, 2016).

14. Abramowitz, *Regulating the Lives of Women*, 318–19. See also Winifred Bell, *Aid to Dependent Children* (New York: Columbia University Press, 1965), 29–32 and Tani, *States of Dependency*, 204.

15. Some of these increasing numbers came from newly enfranchised black women claiming their rights to welfare as citizens. Linda Gordon, "Who Deserves Help? Who Must Provide?," *Lost Ground: Welfare Reform, Poverty, and Beyond*, ed. Randy Albelda and Ann Withorn (Cambridge, MA: Harvard University Press, 2002), 19.

16. Taryn Lindhorst and Leslie Leighninger, " 'Ending Welfare as We Know It' in 1960: Louisiana's Suitable Home Law," *Social Service Review* 77, no. 4 (2003): 564–84 and Gordon, *Pitied but Not Entitled*.

17. Sachs, "Politics of Poverty," 39–90.

18. Oral history interview with Arthur S. Flemming, Washington, DC, June 19, 1989, by Niel M. Johnson, http://www.trumanlibrary.org/oralhist/flemming.htm.

19. Appendix A, *Smith v. King*, Civil Action, No. 2495-N, in the United States District Court for the Middle District of Alabama, Northern Division, in MacDonald Gallion, Mrs. Mary Lee Stapp, and Mrs. Carol F. Miller, "Jurisdicitional Statement," *King v. Smith* 392 U.S. 309 (1968), 20.

20. U.S. Congress, Senate, Committee on Finance, "Major Differences in the Present Law and H.R. 4884 as Reported by the Committee on Finance," April 19, 1961, 87th Cong., 1st sess., 1961, S. Doc. ; Robert C. Lieberman, *Shifting the Color Line: Race and the American Welfare State* (Boston: Harvard University Press, 2001), 118–76.

21. "U.S. Judges Spoil Wallace's Image," *Chicago Defender*, August 5, 1975, 1.

22. *King v. Smith*, Jurisdictional statement, Appendix A, 24–25; Martin Garbus, *Ready for the Defense* (New York: Farrar, Straus, and Giroux, 1971), 148.

23. *King v. Smith*, Jurisdictional statement, Appendix A, 23.

24. *King v. Smith*, 392 U.S. 309 (1968) (No. 949); Garbus, *Ready for the Defense*, 194. Arkansas, Arizona, Connecticut, Indiana, Louisiana, Maine, Michigan, Mississippi, Missouri, New Hampshire, New Mexico, North Carolina, Oklahoma, South Carolina, Texas, Tennessee, Vermont, Virginia, and Washington, DC, had "substitute father" laws. Fred P. Graham, "Alabama Warns of Welfare Cut," *New York Times*, November 22, 1967, 54. Also, Garbus explained that he worried after the ruling that Alabama would not appeal but instead pass a law making other signifiers establish "substitute fatherhood," like eating a meal with the children. Goodman, "Case of Mrs. Sylvester Smith," SM67.

25. Gallion, et al., "Jurisdictional statement," 7. For more on *King v. Smith*, see Davis, *Brutal Need*; Piven and Cloward, *Regulating the Poor*; Mimi Abramovitz, *Under Attack, Fighting Back: Women and Welfare in the United States* (New York: Monthly Review Press, 1995); Anna Marie Smith, *Welfare Reform and Sexual Regulation* (Cambridge: Cambridge University Press, 2007); Lieberman, *Shifting the Color Line*, 118–76; Sachs, "Politics of Poverty"; Rickie Solinger, "The First Welfare Case: Money, Sex, Marriage, and White Supremacy in Selma, 1966, A Reproductive Justice Analysis," *Journal of Women's History* 22(Fall 2010): 13–38; and Elizabeth Pleck, *Not Just Roommates: Cohabitation After the Sexual Revolution* (Chicago: University of Chicago Press, 2012).

26. *King v. Smith*, 314.

27. Ibid.

28. "Curb on Welfare in Alabama Upset," *New York Times*, November 10, 1967, 10; Garbus, *Ready for the Defense*, 158.

29. Goodman, "Case of Mrs. Sylvester Smith," SM62.

30. *King v. Smith*, Jurisdictional statement, Appendix A, 23.

31. See in particular Solinger, "First Welfare Case" and Pleck, *Not Just Roommates* for an examination of *King v. Smith* and its effects on women.

32. Davis, *Brutal Need*, 64. Such rates were seemingly not representative of the population receiving welfare. For example, in one county, ten times as many African Americans received aid as whites, but "the cut-off ratio was forty to one." Garbus, *Ready for the Defense*, 160.

33. Goodman, "Case of Mrs. Sylvester Smith," SM62.

34. *King v. Smith*, 314.

35. *King v. Smith*, Jurisdictional statement, Appendix A, 30.

36. Goodman, "Case of Mrs. Sylvester Smith," SM62.

37. Ibid., SM28.

38. *King v. Smith*, Jurisdictional statement, submitted by MacDonald Gallion, 7.

39. Graham, "Alabama Warns of Welfare Cut," 54.

40. Goodman, "Case of Mrs. Sylvester Smith," SM67.

41. Garbus, *Ready for the Defense*, 159.

42. Wendy Edmond and Suzie Fleming, *All Work and No Pay* (London: Power of Women Collective, 1975), 96.

43. Garbus, *Ready for the Defense*, 187–88.

44. Ibid., 190.

45. Ibid., 157–58.

46. For an account of a similar system in the United Kingdom, see Pamela Abbot and Claire Wallace, *The Family and the New Right* (London: Pluto Press, 1992), 25.

47. Garbus, *Ready for the Defense*, 144.

48. Goodman, "Case of Mrs. Sylvester Smith," SM62.

49. Ibid., SM62.

50. Garbus, *Ready for the Defense*, 145–46.

51. Ibid., 145.

52. "Typical AFDC Family Smaller than 10 Years Ago: Average Number of Children Fell from 3 to 2," *Family Planning Perspectives* 15 (Jan-Feb 1983): 31–32.

53. Goodman, "Case of Mrs. Sylvester Smith," SM67.

54. Garbus, *Ready for the Defense*, 146.

55. Ibid., 146. See also Davis, *Brutal Need*, 60–68.

56. Martin Garbus, "Brief for Appellees," *King v. Smith*, 392 U.S. 309 (1968), 26–27. See also Davis, *Brutal Need*, 64.

57. Garbus, "Brief for Appellees," 23-4.

58. Garbus, *Ready for the Defense*, 148. Garbus also considered Arkansas and Georgia, but opted for Alabama.

59. Ibid., 155. The case went to Judge Frank J. Johnson who had famously desegregated the Alabama public school system.

60. Davis, *Brutal Need*, 65.

61. Davis, *Brutal Need*, 66; Tani, *States of Dependency*.

62. Abramovitz, *Under Attack, Fighting Back.*

63. *King v. Smith,* 309.

64. Edward V. Sparer, Paul Dodyk, Brian Glick, James Greenberg, James M. Nabrit, III, Leroy D. Clark, and Charles Stephen Ralson, "Brief for the NAACP Legal Defense and Education Fund, Inc., the National Office for the Rights of the Indigent, and the Center on Social Welfare Policy and Law," *King v. Smith* 392 U.S. 309 (1968), 2 and 5.

65. Ibid., 3.

66. *King v. Smith,* 333.

67. "Welfare: Trying to End the Nightmare," clipping, box 100, folder 1194, Hull House Association Records (hereafter cited at HHA Records), Special Collections and University Archives, University of Illinois at Chicago, Chicago, IL.

68. Goodman, "Case of Mrs. Sylvester Smith," SM67.

69. "Welfare: Trying to End the Nightmare."

70. Davis, *Brutal Need,* 136.

71. Robert Moffitt, *Telephone Survey of State AFDC Rules Regarding Cohabitation and Marriage* (Madison, WI: Institute for Research on Poverty, 1995).

72. Bill of Welfare Rights pamphlet put out by National Welfare Rights Organization, September 1, 1970, box 101, folder 1208, HHA Records.

73. *Goldberg v. Kelly,* 397 U.S. 254 (1970).

74. *Lewis et al. v. Martin,* No. 829, 397 U.S. 559; 90 S. Ct. 1285; 25 L. Ed. 2d 567 (1970).

75. Similarly, in 1971, the New Jersey Welfare Rights Organization successfully challenged a law that limited welfare benefits to children born to a married couple or adopted. *New Jersey Welfare Rights Organization v. Cahill,* 448 F.2d 1247 (1971). For more on other cases necessary to grant access for cohabiting families or single parents, see Pleck, *Not Just Roommates,* 59–65.

76. For example, in 1972, the Madison County Welfare Rights Organization still warned members, "If you have a boyfriend, the welfare department cannot force him to contribute to your support." "Welfare Rights Handbook: Your Rights Under the Illinois Welfare Rules," prepared by The Madison County Welfare Rights Organization, a chapter of National Welfare Rights Organization, September 1972, box 100, folder 1203, HHA Records.

77. Pleck, *Not Just Roommates,* 59–65.

78. For more on legal experts' conception of privacy, see Gwendolyn Mink, Samantha Ann Majic, and Leandra Zarnow, "Poverty Law and Income Support: From the Progressive Era to the War on Welfare," *The Cambridge History of Law in America,* vol. 3, ed. Michael Grossberg and Christopher Tomlins (New York: Cambridge University Press, 2011).

79. *Wyman v. James,* 400 U.S. 309 (1971).

80. Nadasen, *Welfare Warriors.*

81. For an academic take on this critique, see Mink, et al., "Poverty Law and Income Support."

82. Alice, "A Description of Chicago's Family Relations Court and How Women Fare in Its Proceedings," *Womankind,* April 1972, *CWLU Herstory Project,* https://www.cwluherstory.org /family/family-relations-court.

83. Andre Leo, "ADC: Marriage to the State," in *Radical Feminism,* ed. Anne Koedt, Ellen Levine, and Anita Rapone (New York: Quadrangle Books, 1973), 223.

84. Quoted in Guida West, *The National Welfare Rights Movement: The Social Protest of Poor Women* (New York: Praeger Special Studies, 1981), 89.

85. "Women, Black Families," *Chicago Defender,* March 4, 1971, 18.

86. Ibid.

87. Mary Lou to WRO, February 7, 1973, box 98, folder 1179, HHA Records.

88. Carol B Stack, *All Our Kin: Strategies for Survival in a Black Community* (New York: Harper & Row, 1974), 115.

89. Ibid., 114.

90. Ibid., 117–18.

91. Celestine Ware, "Black Feminism," in Koedt, *Radical Feminism*, 83.

92. Johnnie Tillmon and Nancy Steffen, "Welfare Is a Women's Issue," *Liberation News Service*, February 26, 1972, 15.

93. "Our $1 billion Heartache: 'ADC Father' Wants Work—Not Welfare," clipping, box 101, folder 1220, HHA Records.

94. Copy of the letter sent to Governor Ogilvie, n.d., box 100, folder 1198, HHA Records.

95. Leo, "ADC," 226.

96. Operation Cope, case study, instructor Mrs. Laverne Butler, series 22, box 3, folder 15, National Council of Negro Women, Inc., Records (hereafter cited as NCNW Records), National Archives for Black Women's History, Mary McLeod Bethune Council House (hereafter cited as NABWH).

97. Betsy Warrior, "Females and Welfare," in *Voices from Women's Liberation*, ed. Leslie B. Tanner (New York: Signet New American Library, 1970), 277.

98. Operation Cope, case study, instructor Miss Lillie Wharton, series 22, box 2, folder 18, NCNW Records.

99. Stacks, *All Our Kin*, 51, 58–59.

100. Serena Mayeri, "Historicizing the 'End of Men': The Politics of Reaction(s)," *Boston University Law Review* 93 (2013): 729–44; Marisa Chappell, "Demanding a New Family Wage: Feminist Consensus in the 1970s Full Employment Campaign," in *Feminist Coalitions: Historical Perspectives on Second-Wave Feminism in the United States*, ed. Stephanie Gilmore (Urbana, IL: University of Illinois Press, 2008), 252–84; Chappell, *War on Welfare*.

101. "DEMAND YOUR WINTER CLOTHES," flier, box 98, folder 1179, HHA Records.

102. Mrs. Jessie Muril Williams to Senator James Allen, August 21, 1973, series 1, box 1, folder 5, series 1, National Committee on Household Employment Records, NABWH.

103. Task Force on Public Aid, Church Federation of Greater Chicago, "The Illinois Welfare Scandal and YOU," pamphlet, April 1969, box 100, folder 1194, HHA Records; "To Welfare Rights Organization Member, Staff, and Friends," flier, March 10, 1972, box 101, folder 1208, HHA Records.

104. Operation COPE, case history, instructor Lillie Wharton, series 22, box 4, folder 16, NCNW Records.

105. Jean Chmurra to friends, March 11, 1970, box 99, folder 1183, HHA Records.

106. See, for example, Jones, *Labor of Love, Labor of Sorrow*; Saville, *Work of Reconstruction*; Stanley, *From Bondage to Contract*.

107. Leo, "ADC," 223.

108. Ibid., 225.

109. West, *National Welfare Rights Movement*, 89.

110. Campaign for Adequate Welfare Reform Now, "Twelve Reasons for Opposing the Welfare Reform Bill (Title IV of H.R. 1)," flier, June 16, 1971, box 540, folder 3, Patsy Mink Papers, Library of Congress.

111. Alexis Herman, "Keynote Address: ERA and Ethnic Minority Women" (ERA and

Ethnic Minority Women, report from Consultation on Ethnic Minority Involvement in the Equal Rights Amendment), 41–42, pamphlet, series 1, box 2, folder 8, series 1, Records of the National Alliance of Black Feminists, NABWH. The 1977 bill H.R. 10272, for example, did not include women on welfare in the provision, but the 1978 bill H.R. 28 did. U.S Congress, House of Representatives, H.R. 28, 95th Cong., 1st sess., January 4, 1977, box 1, folder Displaced Homemakers, Mariwyn Somers Papers, Schlesinger Library on the History of Women in America, Radcliffe Institute, Harvard University, Cambridge, MA.

112. Tillmon and Steffen, "Welfare Is a Women's Issue," 16.

113. Ginger Mack, Chicago Welfare Rights Organization, to Jane Addams Center, n.d., box 99, folder 1187, HHA Records.

114. Daniel Patrick Moynihan, "The Moynihan Report, The Negro Family: The Case for National Action," in *The Moynihan Report and the Politics of Controversy; a Trans-Action Social Science and Public Policy Report*, ed. Lee Rainwater and William L. Yancey (Cambridge, MA: MIT Press, 1967), 75.

115. Moynihan, "Negro Family," 93.

116. Ibid.

117. Peniel E. Joseph, ed., *Black Power Movement: Re-thinking the Civil Rights-Black Power Era* (New York: Routledge, 2006); and Jennifer Nelson, *Women of Color and the Reproductive Rights Movement* (New York: New York University Press, 2003).

118. Daniel Patrick Moynihan, *The Politics of a Guaranteed Income: The Nixon Administration and the Family Assistance Plan* (New York: Random House, 1973), 3.

119. "Fact Sheet: NWRO's Guaranteed Adequate Income Plan?," box 100, folder 1205, HHA Records. NWRO later asked for $6,500. The AFL demanded $3,500. H.R. 16311, 91st Cong., 2nd sess., *Congressional Record* 116 (April 16, 1970): H 12,041.

120. Advocates believed an unemployed father benefit and training would not only restore the black family, but also prevent rioting and other urban unrest. Quadagno, *Color of Welfare*, 117–34.

121. H.R. 16311, *Congressional Record*, 91st Cong., 2nd sess. 116 (April 15, 1970): H 11,878. Sachs reconciles Nixon's odd liberal stance by showing FAP's conservative roots in a Milton Friedman proposal for cash payments to the poor and Nixon's belief they could dismantle the New Deal state. Sachs, "Politics of Poverty," 211–12.

122. H.R. 16311 (April 15, 1970): H 11,887.

123. Ibid., H 11,898.

124. Moynihan, *Politics of a Guaranteed Income*, 30.

125. Statement of Roger A. Freeman, Senior Fellow, the Hoover Institution on War, Revolution and Peace, Stanford University, Stanford, CA, in U.S. Congress, Senate, Committee on Finance, *Hearings on H.R. 1 (Social Security Amendments of 1972) Titles III and IV (Public Assistance)*, 92nd Cong., 2nd sess. (January 27, 1972), 40–41. When the "welfare queen" scandal rocked several states in 1974, an investigatory committee reported that the fraud included husbands who "bring in several wives giving birth to children during the same month all paid by public aid." Progress Report by Investigative Unit, November 14 and 19, 1974, subseries 003, RG 616, Illinois State Archives, Springfield, IL.

126. Freeman statement, *Hearings on H.R. 1*, 48–49.

127. 92nd U.S. Congress, Committee on Finance, *Welfare Reform—Or Is It?: Address of Hon. Russell B. Long, Chairman, Committee on Finance and Supporting Material*, 92nd Cong., 1st sess., 1971, Committee Print 65-892, 5.

128. John Peter O'Brien, the supervisor of Milwaukee's Department of Public Welfare, in U.S. Congress, Senate, Committee on Finance, *Family Assistance Act of 1970, Hearings Before the Committee on Finance, United States Senate Ninety-First Congress, Second Session on HR 16311 An Act to Authorize A Family Assistance Plan Providing Basic Benefits to Low-Income Families with Children, to Provide Incentives for Employment and Training to Improve the Capacity for Employment of Members of Such Families, To Achieve Greater Uniformity of Treatment of Recipients Under the Federal-State Public Assistance Programs and to Otherwise Improve Such Programs, and for Other Purposes,* 91st Cong., 2nd sess., August 24–27, 31, and September 1, 9, and 10, 1970, pt. 3:1639.

129. Freeman statement, *Hearings on H.R. 1,* 41.

130. Moynihan, *Politics of a Guaranteed Income,* 31.

131. Ibid., 469.

132. Ibid., 467.

133. *Social Security Amendments of 1972,* H.R. 1, 92nd Cong., 2nd sess., *Congressional Record* 118 (October 4, 1972): S 33,628.

134. U.S. Congress, Senate, Committee on Finance, *Family Assistance Act of 1970: Hearings Before the Committee on Finance, United States Senate Ninety-First Congress, Second Session on HR 16311 (An Act to Authorize a Family Assistance Plan Providing Basic Benefits to Low-Income Families with Children, to Provide Incentives for Employment and Training to Improve the Capacity for Employment of Members of Such Families, To Achieve Greater Uniformity of Treatment of Recipients Under the Federal-State Public Assistance Programs and to Otherwise Improve Such Programs, and for Other Purposes),* 91st Cong., 2nd sess., July 21, 22, 23, 28, 29, and 30 and August 4, 6, 13, and 18, 1970, Administration Witnesses, pt. 2:467–68. See also Long, "Welfare Reform—Or Is It?," 8.

135. *Family Assistance Act of 1970,* pt. 2:468.

136. H.R. 16311 (April 15, 1970): H 11,880.

137. *Family Assistance Act of 1970,* pt. 2:689.

138. "Some Reasons Why NWRO Is Opposed to HR 1—Nixon's Family Assistance Plan (FAP)," box 101, folder 1208, HHA Records.

139. Elizabeth Wickenden, professor of Urban Studies, City University of New York, "HR1: Welfare Policy as an Instrument of Control," 3, box 101, folder 1208, HHA Records.

140. Elaine McLean & Friends, "Where Welfare Reform Is Now—June 1972 Olympia, Washington," box 101, folder 1208, HHA Records.

141. Sheila Tobias, president of ALERT to Senator Joseph J. Dinielli (CT), February 28, 1975, box 6, folder 1, Elizabeth Coxe Spalding Papers, Schlesinger Library. The Senate Finance Committee's gesture at dealing with women frightened of their former partners was "a requirement that mothers who are afraid to seek child support payments from the fathers of their children assign their rights to institute action in such cases to Federal, state or local lawyers or law enforcement officials." Marjorie Hunter, "Senate Panel Acts to Curb Welfare Costs and Suits against U.S.," *New York Times,* April 20, 1972, 14.

142. Warren Weaver Jr., "President's Welfare Plan Passes House, 243 to 155," *New York Times,* April 17, 1970, 1.

143. *Family Assistance Act of 1970,* pt. 2:523.

144. Moynihan, *Politics of a Guaranteed Income,* 494.

145. *Family Assistance Act of 1970,* pt. 2:1083.

146. Moynihan, *Politics of a Guaranteed Income,* 535.

147. Eve Edstrom, "Panel Move on Welfare Jolts Liberals," *Washington Post*, November 25, 1970, A1.

148. Robert Mann, *Legacy to Power* (New York: Paragon House, 1992).

149. Spencer Rich, "Welfare Measure Stiffened," *Washington Post*, December 30, 1970, A1.

150. Ibid.

151. Wickenden, "HR1," 3; NWRO, "Nobody Gets Hurt," packet, June 11, 1971, box 540, folder 3, Patsy Mink Papers.

152. "Fact Sheet: NWRO's Guaranteed Adequate Income Plan?"; "Some Reasons Why NWRO Is Opposed to HR 1."

153. Moynihan, *Politics of a Guaranteed Income*, 557.

154. Sachs, "Politics of Poverty," 201–40; *Social Security Amendments of 1972*, S 33,642– 33,657. See also Vincent J. Burke and Vee Burke, *Nixon's Good Deed: Welfare Reform* (New York: Columbia University Press, 1974), 180.

155. Brian Steensland, *The Failed Welfare Revolution: America's Struggle over Guaranteed Income Policy* (Princeton, NJ: Princeton University Press, 2008).

156. NWRO, "Nobody Gets Hurt." Emphasis added.

157. Levenstein, *Movement Without Marches*, 83–85; *King v. Smith*, Jurisdictional statement, Appendix D, 31; *Family Assistance Act of 1970*, pt. 2:969; and Confidential Memos to Senator Moore folder, speech to President Risely, President-elect Forney, and members of the association, subseries 003, RG 616, Illinois State Archives.

158. U.S. Congress, House of Representatives, Committee on the House of Ways and Means, *Summary of Major Provisions of H.R. 6675 The Social Security Amendments of 1965 as Reflected by the Agreement Reached between The House and Senate Conferees Together with Actuarial Data*, 89th Cong., 1st sess., July 24, 1965, 17; Mary Fisher Bernet, "The Child Support Provisions: Comments on the New Federal Law," *Family Law Quarterly* 9 (Fall 1975): 491–526.

159. See To Amend Title 18, United States Code, to Make a Misdemeanor the Flight, in Interstate or Foreign Commerce, By Any Person Who Is the Parent of a Minor Child or Who Is a Married Man, If Such Person So Flees with the Intent of Evading His Legal Responsibilities with Respect to the Support or Maintenance of His Minor Child or of His Wife, S. 2160, 90th Cong. (1967); To Make It a Crime to Move or Travel in Interstate or Foreign Commerce to Avoid Compliance With Certain Support Orders, and For Other Purposes, H.R. 7972, 91st Cong. (1969); To Amend Title 18, United States Code, to Make a Misdemeanor the Flight, in Interstate or Foreign Commerce, By Any Person Who Is the Parent of a Minor Child or Who Is a Married Man, If Such Person So Flees with the Intent of Evading His Legal Responsibilities with Respect to the Support or Maintenance of His Minor Child or of His Wife, S. 2701, 92nd Cong. (1971); To Amend Chapter 73 of Title 10, United States Code, to establish a Survivor Benefit Plan, and For Other Purposes, H.R. 10670, 92nd Cong. (1971). For the concession on locating absent fathers, see Public Law 93-647, *U.S. Statutes at Large*, 88 (1975): 2337–61. See also "Law on Runaways Sought," *New York Times*, February 9, 1967, 26; Marjorie Hunter, "Senate Panel Votes a U.S. Role in Tracing Deserting Fathers," *New York Times*, May 19, 1972, 47; "Major Provisions of Senate Bill on Social Security and Welfare," *New York Times*, June 14, 1972, 32; "To Collect a Debt to Children," *New York Times*, August 9, 1983, A22.

160. Bernet, "Child Support Provisions," 519–21.

161. U.S. Committee on Finance, *Social Services Amendments of 1974: Report of the Committee on Finance, United States Senate to Accompany H.R. 17045 to Amend the Social Security Act to Establish a Consolidated Program of Federal Financial Assistance to Encourage Provision of*

Services by the States (Together with Separate Views), by Russell B. Long. 93rd Cong., 2nd sess., 1974, S. Rpt. 93-1356, 2.

162. Ibid., 42–55.

163. Ibid., 55. With the Social Security Disability Amendments of 1980, Congress allowed the Social Security Administration to share wage information in 1980. Public Law 96–265, *U.S. Statutes at Large*, 94(1980): 441–81. In 1981, the IRS was allowed to withhold tax refunds for delinquent child support. Public Law 97-35, *U.S. Statutes at Large*, 95 (1981): 860–65. But still Congress repeatedly failed to make a unilaterally strong child support enforcement via the Economic Equity Act. For example, see A Bill to Ensure Economic Equity for American Women and Their Families by Promoting Fairness in the Workplace; Creating New Economic Opportunities for Women Workers and Women Business Owners; Helping Workers Better Meet the Competing Demands of Work and Family; and Enhancing Economic Self-Sufficiency Through Public and Private Pension Reform and Child Support Enforcement, S 2514, 103rd Cong., 2nd sess. (1994) and A Bill Entitled the "Economic Equity Act," S 888, 99th Cong., 1st sess. (1985). See also Kathryn Cullen-DuPont, *Encyclopedia of Women's History in America* (New York: Infobase Publishing, 2009), 52.

164. Long, *Social Services Amendments of 1974*, 54.

165. Ibid.; Walter D. Johnson and S. Kay Zimka, *An Evaluation of the Illinois Child Support Enforcement Program* (Springfield, IL: Center for Policy Studies and Program Evaluation, 1981), 20.

166. Johnson and Zimka, *Evaluation of the Illinois Child Support Enforcement Program*, 127–28.

167. Daniel Patrick Moynihan, "Securing the Future for American Families," *NCSEA News* 11 (August 1987), box II2380, folder 4, Daniel Patrick Moynihan Papers, Library of Congress. In 1986, AFDC granted benefits to seven million children. Moynihan, "Securing the Future for American Families."

168. Ann Patla, director, Illinois Department of Public Aid, to Sister Marcelline Koch, director, Project IRENE, June 8, 2000, box 11, folder 6, Project IRENE Records, 1996–2004, Women and Leadership Archives, Loyola University Chicago.

169. For press on this new law, see Joseph L. Lieberman, "Time to Get Tough on Child-Support Payments," *New York Times*, October 12, 1985, 27; Jocelyn Elise Crowley, *Defiant Dads: Fathers' Rights Activists in America* (Ithaca, NY: Cornell University Press, 2008).

170. Elizabeth G. Patterson, "Civil Contempt and the Indigent Child Support Obligor: The Silent Return of the Debtor's Prison," *Cornell Journal of Law & Public Policy* 18 (2008–9): 95–142.

171. David L. Chambers, *Making Fathers Pay: The Enforcement of Child Support* (Chicago: University of Chicago Press, 1979), 117.

Chapter 5

1. *United States v. Windsor*, 133 S. Ct. 2690 (2013).

2. Kerry Abrams insightfully argues that no fault divorce made immigrant marriages easier to leave and therefore immigrant marriage became a more palatable strategy for anyone truly seeking to perpetrate marriage fraud. Kerry Abrams, "Marriage Fraud," *California Law Review* 1 (February 2012): 144. Fraudulent marriages may have become more common, but this alone was not enough to account for the government's increasing concern about fraud. I argue that the growing concern about fraud resides in some of Abrams's other work, where she shows that the

state is concerned that citizen spouses not becoming a public charge. Kerry Abrams, "Immigration Law and the Regulation of Marriage," *Minnesota Law Review* 91 (2006–7): 1625. This chapter will argue that this fear of the public charge created this fear of fraud.

3. Mary Anne Case, "What Feminists Have to Lose in Same-Sex Marriage Litigation," 57 *University of California Los Angeles Law Review* 57 (2009–10): 1199–233.

4. Abrams, "Immigration Law and the Regulation of Marriage," 1625; Lee Ann Wang, "Of the Law, But Not Its Spirit: Immigration Fraud as a Legal Fiction and Violence Against Asian Immigrant Women," *UC Irvine Law Review* 3 (December 2013): 1221–50.

5. Nancy Cott, *Public Vows: A History of Marriage and the Nation* (Cambridge, MA: Harvard University Press, 2000), 133.

6. Nancy Cott, "Marriage and Women's Citizenship in the United States, 1830–1934," *American Historical Review* 103 (December 1998): 1440–74. For current-day manifestations of this differential system, see Kristin Collins, "When Fathers' Rights Are Mothers' Duties: The Failure of Equal Protection in *Miller v. Albright*," *Yale Law Journal* 109 (1999–2000): 1669–708.

7. Margot Canaday, *The Straight State: Sexuality and Citizenship in Twentieth-Century America* (Princeton, NJ: Princeton University Press, 2009), 218.

8. Cott, *Public Vows*, 165.

9. Ibid., 148.

10. Ibid., 154.

11. George J. Sanchez, *Becoming Mexican American: Ethnicity, Culture, and Identity in Chicano Los Angeles, 1900–1945* (New York: Oxford University Press, 1995).

12. U.S. Congress, House of Representatives, Committee on Immigration and Naturalization, bill "To Deport Certain Aliens Who Secured Preference-Quota or Non-Quota Visas Through Fraud By Contracting Marriage Solely to Expedite Entry to the United States, and for Other Purposes," *Hearing Before the Committee on Immigration and Naturalization, House of Representatives*, 74th Cong., 2nd sess., February 12, 1936, 2.

13. *United States v. Jose Diogo, Dimingo Das Canas Costa, and Manuel Vilanova Gonzalez*, 282 CA2 (1962), in CO1011.1 C (page 509 of NRC2013085093 FOIA Response document).

14. Canaday, *Straight State*, 218–20.

15. Operations Memorandum to Department of State from American Consul, Hong Kong, November 30, 1954, Unclassified U.S. Department of State Case No. F-2013-20069, Doc. No. CO5545240, (page 27 of FOIA envelope doc). For more on the larger crisis regarding immigration and Hong Kong, see also Mae Ngai, *Impossible Subjects: Illegal Aliens and the Making of Modern America* (Princeton, NJ: Princeton University Press, 2004), 202–24.

16. Ralph P. Harris, "Marriage Frauds to Circumvent Quota Limitations," *I and N Reporter* 9, no. 3 (January 1961): 29–31.

17. J. Edgar Hoover, *Masters of Deceit* (New York: Holt, 1958), 143–44.

18. *Lutwak v. United States*, 344 U.S. 611 (1953).

19. *United States vs. Jose Diogo, Dimingo Das Canas Costa, and Manuel Vilanova Gonzalez*.

20. O. I. Kramer, Associate Deputy Regional, to Deputy Associate Commissioner, United States Government memorandum, December 14, 1962, CO 1109.134 (NRC2013085093 FOIA Response page 534).

21. Robert Self, *All in the Family: The Realignment of American Democracy Since the 1960s* (New York: Hill and Wang, 2013).

22. "Many Misinformed on Pending Immigration Revision Proposal," in 89th Cong., 1st sess., *Congressional Record*, Proceeding and Debates, reprint, box 75, folder HR 2580 press

release, newspaper clippings 1 of 2, Records of the U.S. House of Representatives, 89th Congress, RG 233, National Archives, Washington, DC (hereafter cited as National Archives 1).

23. Address by Assistant Secretary of Labor Daniel Patrick Moynihan at Enchanted Forest Park, Chesterton, Indiana, September 27, 1964, box 152, folder 13, Daniel Patrick Moynihan Papers, Library of Congress.

24. Following the 1922 Cable Act and the 1934 Equal Nationality Act, women retained their citizenship following marriage and could extend their citizenship to husbands if their husbands were white, would not become a public charge, and did not leave the United States. See Cott, *Public Vows*; Cott, "Marriage and Women's Citizenship in the United States" 1440–74; and Candice Lewis Bredbenner, *A Nationality of Her Own: Women, Marriage, and the Law of Citizenship* (Berkeley: University of California Press, 1998), 151–94.

25. Questionnaire for Cleveland Hearings, box 77, folder HR 89th com on jud HR 2580 questionnaires returned 7 of 8, Committee on the Judiciary, Legislative Files: House Bills, Records of the U.S. House of Representatives, 89th Congress, RG 233.

26. Mrs. J. Boomis, Independence, KS, to Senate Judiciary Committee, May 27, 1965, box 3, folder RG 46 Sen89A.F12.1 Subcommittee on Immigration I & N Act-Proposed Revisions to, Committee on the Judiciary, Sen89A-E12, S.500 to S.500, HMFY 2005, Records of the U.S. Senate, RG 46, National Archives 1.

27. Mrs. Selma Samols, in U.S. Congress, House of Representatives, Committee on the Judiciary, *Hearings Before Subcommittee No. 1 of the Committee on the Judiciary House of Representatives on H.R. 2580 to Amend the Immigration and Naturalization Act, and for Other Purposes*, 89th Cong., 1st sess., March 3, 8, 10, 11, 18, 31; April 6; May 18, 20, 26, 27; June 1, 1965, 434.

28. George Romney to Honorable Michael Feighan, May 28, 1965, box 9, folder Sen89A-E12, S. 500, folder 1 of 11, Committee on the Judiciary, Records of the U.S. Senate, RG 46.

29. Dwight Dill, MD, to Honorable James Eastland, August 1, 1964, box 3, folder sen89a f12 1 subcommittee on immigration 9 and n act-proposed revisions to committee on the judiciary, Committee on the Judiciary, Records of the U.S. Senate, RG 46.

30. Fred Bryant to Michael Feighan, June 25, 1965, box 76, folder HR 89th com on the jud HR 2580 & 8662 I & N act acknowledged 6 of 8, Records of the U.S. House of Representatives, 89th Congress, RG 233.

31. Helen I. Loken to Michael Feighan, June 29, 1965, box 76, folder HR 89th com on the jud HR 2580 & 8662 I & N act acknowledged 6 of 8, Records of the U.S. House of Representatives, 89th Congress, RG 233.

32. Robert W. Wayman to Senators Vance Hartke and Birch Bayh and Congressman Ralph Harvey, June 30, 1965, box 76, folder HR 89th com on the jud HR 2580 & 8662 I & N act acknowledged 6 of 8, Records of the U.S. House of Representatives, 89th Congress, RG 233. See also Camilla A. Smith to Michael A. Feighan, July 6, 1965, ibid; H. V. Lind to Michael Feighan, July 3, 1965, ibid; Norman V. Boling to Michael Feighan, March 5, 1965, box 77, folder HR 89th com on the jud HR 2580 letters sent to mr feigham 8 of 8, Committee on the Judiciary, Legislative Files: House Bills, ibid.; Mrs. N. R. Nellie McCluskey (from Hamilton Montana) to Michael Feighan, February 10, 1965, box 75, folder 89th Com on the Jud., HR 2580, (Gen Covr.) 1 of 3, Committee on the Judiciary, Legislative Files: House Bills, HR 2580 (89 J .6) HM FY 98, ibid.; Statement by Kitty L. Reynolds, A Citizen, Arlington VA Before the Senate Judiciary Committee, Subcommittee on Immigration—June 25, 1965, box 2, folder RG 46 Sen89A.F12.1 Subcommittee on Immigration Hearing Misc (Ltrs re: Statements, extra, etc.), Committee on the Judiciary, Records of the U.S. Senate, RG 46.

33. *Bark v. INS*, 511 F.2d 1200 (1975).

34. *Matter of Boromand*, 17 N Dec. 450 (BIA 1980) in *United States v Qaisi*, 779 F. 2d 348 (1985).

35. Roger Daniels, *Guarding the Golden Door: American Immigration Policy and Immigrants Since 1882* (New York: Hill and Wang, 2004), 219–31. See also Jorge Bustamante, "Undocumented Migration from Mexico to the United States: Preliminary Findings of the Zapata Canyon Project," in *Undocumented Migration to the United States: IRCA and the Experience of the 1980s*, ed. Frank D. Edmonston, Barry Passel, and Jeffrey S. Bean (Santa Monica, CA: Rand Corp., 1990), 211–22.

36. *Amending the Immigration and Nationality Act to Deter Immigration-Related Marriage Fraud and Other Immigration Fraud: Mr. Thurmond, from the Committee on the Judiciary, submitted the following Report [To accompany S. 2270]*, 99th Cong., 2nd sess., September 26, 1986, S. Rep. 99-491., 2.

37. "Immigration Marriage Fraud," in *Hearing Before the Subcommittee on Immigration and Refugee Policy of the Committee on the Judiciary, United States Senate Ninety-Ninth Congress, First Session on Fraudulent Marriage and Fiance Arrangements to Obtain Permanent Resident Immigration Status 52-653*, July 26, 1985, 15.

38. Ibid., 16.

39. Ibid., 68.

40. Ibid., 29.

41. Robert Gilbert, "Document and Marriage Fraud in the Caribbean," *I and N Reporter* 23, no. 3 (Winter 1974–75): 37.

42. "Immigration Marriage Fraud," 13.

43. David Dec, "Marriage Fraud," *INS Reporter*, 30 (Winter 1981–82): 9.

44. David Tong, "Marrying Sham Lets Aliens Sneak In," *Star Advertiser*, undated clipping, box 306, folder 3, Patsy Mink Papers, Library of Congress.

45. "Immigration Marriage Fraud," 13.

46. Ibid., 29.

47. Dec, "Marriage Fraud," 8.

48. "Immigration Marriage Fraud," 33–34.

49. Ibid., 29.

50. Ibid., 30.

51. Dec, "Marriage Fraud," 8.

52. "Immigration Marriage Fraud," 47.

53. "'Thanks for the Ticket': Aliens Follow Bridal Path to Enter U.S., Senate Told," *Los Angeles Times*, July 26, 1985, 2.

54. "Immigration Marriage Fraud," 23–24.

55. Ibid., 71. Eventually divorcees could file a Waiver of the Joint Petition Form I-752 within ninety days of the two-year time limit to try to obtain permission to remain. Family-Based Immigration Summary, box 1344, folder 5, Patsy Mink Papers.

56. John R. Bolton, assistant attorney general, U.S. Department of Justice, to Honorable James C. Miller III, November 5, 1986, box 82, folder Nov. 10, 1986 [H.R. 3737], Executive Clerk, White House Office of the: Bill Reports Papers, Ronald Reagan Presidential Library, Simi Valley, CA.

57. "Immigration Marriage Fraud," 80–81.

58. National Immigration Forum, "Issue Brief: Immigrant Women," Fall 1994, box 1345, folder 2, Patsy Mink Papers.

59. *Amending the Immigration and Nationality Act to Deter Immigration-Related Marriage Fraud*, 7.

60. Ibid., 12.

61. "Immigration Marriage Fraud," 13.

62. *Amending the Immigration and Nationality Act to Deter Immigration-Related Marriage Fraud*, 8.

63. "Immigration Marriage Fraud," 33.

64. Ibid., 57.

65. James C. Miller III, director, Executive Office of the President, Office of Management and Budget, memorandum for the President, Subject: Enrolled Bill H.R. 3737—Immigration Marriage Fraud Amendments of 1986, November 5, 1986, box 82, folder Nov. 10, 1986 [H.R. 3737], Executive Clerk, White House Office of the: Bill Reports Papers.

66. *Amending the Immigration and Nationality Act to Deter Immigration-Related Marriage Fraud*, 6.

67. "Marriage Fraud, Pre-1986," box 287, Office of the Deputy Attorney General, Subject Files of Associate Deputy Attorney General Rex J. Ford, 1989–1993 (location: 230/61/19/7), Records of the Department of Justice, RG 60, National Archives 1.

68. *Amending the Immigration and Nationality Act to Deter Immigration-Related Marriage Fraud*, 15.

69. Ibid., 15.

70. Tong, "Marrying Sham Lets Aliens Sneak In."

71. Interviews to validate a "bona fide" marriage sometimes looked like interviews for paper wives and paper sons during the Chinese exclusion era. For more on immigration interviews of both types, see Guillermo Gleizer, "Regulating Administrative Discretion: Immigration and Marriage," *Yale Law & Policy Review* 4 (Spring/Summer 1986): 479–503; Ngai, *Impossible Subjects*; Erika Lee, *At America's Gates: Chinese Immigration During the Exclusion Era, 1882–1943* (Chapel Hill: University of North Carolina Press, 2003); Abrams, "Immigration Law and the Regulation of Marriage," 1625; Kerry Abrams, "Becoming a Citizen: Marriage, Immigration, and Assimilation," *Gender Equality* (2009): 39–59; Samantha L. Chetrit, "Surviving an Immigration Marriage Fraud Investigation: All You Need Is Love, Luck, and Tight Privacy," *Brooklyn Law Review* 77 (Winter 2012): 709–44.

72. "Immigration Marriage Fraud," 7.

73. Ibid., 64.

74. Dec, "Marriage Fraud," 8.

75. "Immigration Marriage Fraud," 58–59.

76. Ms. FC, Honolulu, to Patsy Mink May 14, 1974, box 305, folder 9, Patsy Mink Papers.

77. Patsy T. Mink to Mr. James J.M. Misajon, chairman, State Commission on Manpower and Full Employment, HI, October 4, 1973, box 305, folder 8, Patsy Mink Papers.

78. Patsy T. Mink to SP, December 7, 1995, box 1346, folder 5, Patsy Mink Papers.

79. Charles H. Percy to Colleague, draft, January 1979, box II1861, folder 6, Daniel Patrick Moynihan Papers.

80. Julilly Kohler-Hausmann, "'The Crime of Survival': Fraud Prosecutions, Community Surveillance, and the Original 'Welfare Queen,'" *Journal of Social History* 41 (Winter 2007): 329–54.

81. "Immigration Marriage Fraud," 37.

82. U.S. Department of Justice, *1994 Statistical Yearbook of the Immigration and Naturalization Service*, 166, box 1342, folder 1, Patsy Mink Papers.

83. "Report to the Congress by the Comptroller General of the United States, Number of Newly Arrived Aliens Who Receive Supplemental Security Income Needs to Be Reduced," 12, box II: 1861, folder 5, Daniel Patrick Moynihan Papers.

84. "Report to the Congress by the Comptroller General of the United States, Number of Newly Arrived Aliens Who Receive Supplemental Security Income Needs to Be Reduced," 10; Form V-3(a), revised November 16, 1959, American Embassy, Consular Section, Manila, Philippines, box 305, folder 7, Patsy Mink Papers.

85. *Department of Mental Hygiene of California v. Renel*, 10 Misc. 2d 405 (1958); *Department of Mental Hygiene of California v. Renel*, 8 Misc. 2d 615 (1957).

86. Michael J. Sheridan, "The New Affidavit of Support and Other 1996 Amendments to Immigration and Welfare Provisions Designed to Prevent Aliens from Becoming Public Charges," *Creighton Law Review* 31(1997–98): 741–66.

87. Form V-3(a), revised November 16, 1959; Patsy Mink to Ms. FC Honolulu, June 12, 1974, box 305, folder 9, Patsy Mink Papers.

88. Sheridan, "New Affidavit of Support and Other 1996 Amendments," 741–66.

89. *State v. Binder*, 356 Mich. 73 (1959); *County of San Diego v. Viloria*, 276 Cal. App. 2d 350 (1969).

90. "Report to the Congress by the Comptroller General of the United States, Number of Newly Arrived Aliens Who Receive Supplemental Security Income Needs to Be Reduced," 10.

91. Ibid., iii.

92. John A. Svahn, acting administrator of the Department of Health, Education, and Welfare, to the Honorable Patsy T. Mink, November 4, 1975, box 306, folder 3, Patsy Mink Papers.

93. *Graham v. Richardson*, 403 U.S. 365; 91 S. Ct. 1848, (1971).

94. Ibid.

95. The rule can be found in under sections 402(a)(9) and 1902(a)(7) of the Social Security Act. Svahn to Mink, November 4, 1975; "Rules on Welfare Shield Immigrants," July 23, 1975, box 306, folder 3, Patsy Mink Papers.

96. "Report to the Congress by the Comptroller General of the United States, Number of Newly Arrived Aliens Who Receive Supplemental Security Income Needs to Be Reduced," 5.

97. *Holley v. Lavine*, 553 F.2d 845 (1977). See also Sheridan, "New Affidavit of Support and Other 1996 Amendments," 741–66.

98. Ibid.

99. Ibid.

100. National Immigration Forum, "Issue Brief: Costs and Contributions of Immigrants," box 1342, folder 3, Patsy Mink Papers.

101. "Report to the Congress by the Comptroller General of the United States, Number of Newly Arrived Aliens Who Receive Supplemental Security Income Needs to Be Reduced," 19.

102. National Immigration Forum, "Issue Brief: Immigrants & Welfare," box 1342, folder 3, Patsy Mink Papers.

103. *Aziz v. Sullivan*, 800 F.Supp. 1374 (1992).

104. Mr. Frank, on H.R. 3737, 99th Cong., 2nd sess., *Congressional Record* 132 (September 29, 1986), pt. 19:27016.

105. Mr. McCollum, on H.R. 3737, ibid., pt. 19:27,015; Mazzoli on H.R. 3737, ibid., pt. 19:27,015; Mr. Frank, on H.R. 3737, ibid., pt. 19:27,016.

106. See https://www.congress.gov/bill/99th-congress/house-bill/3737?q=%7B%22search%22%3A%5B%22marriage+fraud+amendments%22%5D%7D&r=1.

107. Jorge Banales, "Abuse Among Immigrants: As Their Numbers Grow So Does the Need for Services," *Washington Post*, October 16, 1990, E5.

108. National Immigration Forum, "Issue Brief: Immigrant Women."

109. National Network on Behalf of Battered Immigrant Women to Senate Judiciary Committee Members, May 22, 1996, box 1345, folder 2, Patsy Mink Papers.

Chapter 6

1. Jeanette Smith, "'To Love, To Share, To Help': Taking the Vows, Making a Statement," *Washington Post*, December 12, 1976, K7.

2. For more on the desire to marry, see for example, Peggy Pascoe, "Sex, Gender, and Same-Sex Marriage," in *Is Academic Feminism Dead? Theory in Practice*, ed. The Social Justice Group at the Center for Advanced Feminist Studies, University of Minnesota (New York: New York University Press, 2000), 86–129; Mary Anne Case, "Marriage Licenses," *Minnesota Law Review* 89 (2005): 1758–97; George Chauncey, *Why Marriage? The History Shaping Today's Debate over Gay Equality* (Cambridge, MA: Basic Books, 2004); Dudley Clendinen and Adam Nagourney, *Out for Good: The Struggle to Build a Gay Rights Movement in America* (New York: Simon and Schuster, 1999); Joyce Murdoch and Deb Price, *Courting Justice: Gay Men and Lesbians v. the Supreme Court* (New York: Basic Books, 2001); Carlos A. Ball, *Same-Sex Marriage and Children: A Tale of History, Social Science, and Law* (Oxford: Oxford University Press, 2014).

3. Here I am particularly dependent on Elizabeth Pleck, *Not Just Roommates: Cohabitation After the Sexual Revolution* (Chicago: University of Chicago Press, 2012) and Clayton Howard, *The Closet and the Cul de Sac: Sex, Politics, and Suburbanization in Postwar California* (Philadelphia: University of Pennsylvania Press, forthcoming) on housing; on custody I am indebted to Daniel Rivers, *Radical Relations: Lesbian Mothers, Gay Fathers, and Their Children in the United States Since World War II* (Chapel Hill, NC: University of North Carolina Press, 2013); Marie-Amelie George, "The Custody Crucible: The Development of Scientific Authority About Gay and Lesbian Parents," *Law and History Review* 34 (May 2016): 487–529; and Nancy D. Polikoff, *Beyond Straight and Gay Marriage: Valuing All Families Under the Law* (Boston: Beacon Press, 2008).

4. Margot Canaday, "Heterosexuality as a Legal Regime," in *The Cambridge History of Law in America*, ed. Michael Grossberg and Christopher Tomlins (New York: Cambridge University Press, 2008), 442–71.

5. Rob Cole, "Gay Marriage 'Boom': Suddenly It's News," *Advocate*, August 5, 1970, 7.

6. Rob Cole, "Marriage Is an Evil that Most Men Welcome," *Advocate*, March 29, 1971, 1.

7. Randy Lloyd, "Let's Push Homophile Marriage," *ONE*, June 1963, 5.

8. Carol Bradford, "The Invisible Society," *ONE*, May 1962, 10.

9. "Troy Perry, Mate of 3 Years, Making It Formal," *Advocate*, June 21, 1972, 2.

10. The Mattachine Society of Washington, Inc. and The Metropolitan Community Church of Washington, news release, June 30, 1972, box 125, folder 12, Frank Kameny Papers, Library of Congress.

11. Michael Boucai, "Glorious Precedents: When Gay Marriage Was Radical," *Yale Journal of Law & the Humanities* 27 (2015): 54.

12. Rob Cole, "Two Men Ask Minnesota License for First Legal U.S. Gay Marriage," *Advocate*, June 10, 1970, 4.

13. Lors Bjornson, "Judge Nixes Marriage Bid," *Advocate*, December 9, 1970, 4.

14. "'Non-Believers' Seek License to Wed," *Advocate*, November 10, 1971, 12.

15. Bjornson, "Judge Nixes Marriage Bid," 1.

16. "Two Milwaukee Women Fight for Marriage License," *Advocate*, December 8, 1971, 5.

17. Cole, "Two Men Ask Minnesota License for First Legal U.S. Gay Marriage," 4.

18. Bjornson, "Judge Nixes Marriage Bid," 4.

19. Lex, "Male-Order Marriages?" *Advocate*, July 17, 1974, 30. On attempts by gay couples to win the right to divorce and earn community property, see "Spurned 'Wife' Sues to Become a Gay Divorcee," unidentified clipping; "David Files for Divorce from Robert," *Gazette Telegraph*, September 26, 1976; and "Gay Divorce May Precede Marriages," *Advocate*, February 14, 1973; all clippings, Marriage and Divorce [Pre-Marriage Equality], ONE Subject File, ONE National Gay & Lesbian Archives, University of Southern California Libraries, Los Angeles, CA (hereafter cited as ONE Archives). On a successful bid to win support, see "Lesbian to Pay Child Support," *San Francisco Chronicle*, June 7, 1978, ibid.

20. "Should Marriage Between Homosexuals Be Permitted?," WGBH Boston, sponsored by *The Advocates*, May 2,1974, available at http://openvault.wgbh.org/catalog/f4ae6e-should-marriage -between-homosexuals-be-permitted.

21. Ibid.

22. A Bill, No. 1-89 in the Council of the District of Columbia, May 6, 1975, with amendments proposed, July 7, 1975, box 113, folder 4, Kameny Papers.

23. Frank Kameny to the *Sexual Law Reporter*, July 12, 1975, box 113, folder 4, Kameny Papers.

24. Opening Statement of Councilmember Arrington Dixon, Public Hearings on Bill no. 1-89 "The District of Columbia Uniform Marriage and Dissolution Act," June 7–8, 1975, box 113, folder 5, Kameny Papers.

25. Pascoe, "Sex, Gender, and Same-Sex Marriage."

26. Bill, No. 1-89 in the Council of the District of Columbia, May 6, 1975.

27. Kameny to *Sexual Law Reporter*, July 12, 1975.

28. "Report on Meeting on Gay Marriage/Child Custody/No-Fault Divorce Called by Gay Activist Alliance," November 7, 1975, Gay Activist Alliance Records, Rainbow History Project, http://rainbowhistory.omeka.net/items/show/4938189.

29. Timothy Stewart-Winter, *Queer Clout: Chicago and the Rise of Gay Politics* (Philadelphia: University of Pennsylvania Press, 2016).

30. Lurma Rackley, "Legalized Homosexual Marriages Urged in D.C.," *Washington Star*, July 8, 1975, B1, box 113, folder 5, Kameny Papers.

31. "Two Females 'Married' in Chicago—To Each Other," *Jet*, October 15, 1970, 54; Frank Sharp, "Homosexual Clergyman Suspended from Methodist Ministry by Texas Conference," *Philadelphia Tribune*, June 29, 1971, 21; "Lesbians Still Plan Marriage," *Chicago Defender*, October 22, 1975, 25. See also "Two Milwaukee Women Fight for Marriage License," *Advocate*, December 8, 1971, 5.

32. Committee on the Judiciary and Criminal Law David A. Clarke, chairperson, to Members of the Council, June 24, 1976, Subject: Bill No. 1-89, the "District of Columbia Marriage & Divorce Act," box 113, folder 4, Kameny Papers.

33. Not everyone saw the fights as twinned. One constituent objected, "because we are members of a minority does not mean that we are obliged to support or agree with every philosophy and doctrine men can conceive." James S. Woods to the Honorable Arrington Dixon, July 15, 1975, box 113, folder 4, Kameny Papers.

34. Kameny to *Sexual Law Reporter*, July 12, 1975.

35. Ibid.

36. "License Will Stay on Books," *Advocate*, August 13, 1975, 6.

37. Frank Kameny to the Honorable Arrington Dixon, August 5, 1975, box 113, folder 4, Kameny Papers; "Report on Meeting on Gay Marriage/Child Custody/No-Fault Divorce Called by Gay Activist Alliance," November 7, 1975.

38. Franklin E. Kameny, "Gay Marriage Bill in Trouble: Gay Community Support Urgently Needed," box 113, folder 5, Kameny Papers; Frank Kameny to the Honorable Sterling Tucker, August 5, 1975, box 113, folder 4, ibid. For more on the power of black politicians in DC during this time, see Kwame Holmes, "What's the Tea," *Radical History Review* 122 (May 2015): 55–69.

39. "Dixon Alters Divorce Bill," December 25, 1976, unidentified clipping, box 113, folder 5, Kameny Papers.

40. LaBarbara Bowman, "Dixon Drops Bill for Homosexuals," *Washington Post*, December 24, 1975, D5.

41. *Dean vs. DC*, Superior Court of the District of Columbia Family Division, incomplete brief draft, box 125, folder 10, Kameny Papers.

42. For less famous cases, see the challenges by two California couples (one white gay and one black lesbian couple) in Rev. Murial Marushka, "Lesbian and Gay Male Couples Seek Marriage Licenses," press release, March 15, 1977, Coll 2012-0, Subject Files Gay Marriage, ONE Archives, and two Florida black lesbian couples in Kathy Scott, "4 Women Here Seek Licenses to Marry," *Tampa Tribune*, December 5, 1970, 17-A, in ibid.

43. Kay Tobin and Randy Wicker, *The Gay Crusaders* (New York: Catholic Book Agency, 1972), 153.

44. "Minnesota Gays to Challenge Refusal of Marriage License," *Advocate*, June 24, 1970, 1.

45. Pascoe, "Sex, Gender, and Same-Sex Marriage"; Case, "Marriage Licenses;" Chauncey, *Why Marriage?*; Clendinen and Nagourney, *Out for Good*; Murdoch and Price, *Courting Justice*.

46. Case, "Marriage Licenses."

47. Historians tracing racial passing have theorized the contradictions of passing very ably, and I am indebted to their insights for this. See in particular, Allyson Hobbs, *A Chosen Exile: A History of Racial Passing in American Life* (Cambridge, MA: Harvard University Press, 2014). It is of course important to note that these couples did not identify themselves as transgender or transsexual in their interactions with the press.

48. Lars Bjornsen, "Adoption Ploy Gets Mr. to Mr. License," *Advocate*, September 29, 1971, 1, 3. For another couple who used the adoption method, see Bayard Rustin and Walter Naegle in John D'Emilio, *Lost Prophet: The Life and Times of Bayard Rustin* (Chicago: University of Chicago Press, 2004).

49. Lars Bjornsen, "Marriage Case Goes to Top Court," *Advocate*, March 31, 1971, 19.

50. Bjornsen, "Adoption Ploy Gets Mr. to Mr. License," 1, 3.

51. "License Will Stay on Books," 6.

52. Lurma Rackley, "Legalized Homosexual Marriages Urged in D.C.," *Washington Star*, July 8, 1975, B1, box 113, folder 5, Kameny Papers.

53. "License Will Stay on Books," 6. Maryland was in fact one of the earliest of a rash of states to pass a law defining marriage as a union between one man and one woman. For more on these laws, inspired by the rise of gender equality, see Pascoe, "Sex, Gender, and Same-Sex Marriage."

54. "License Will Stay on Books," 6. It turns out that DC did not pass this ordinance for another thirty-five years.

55. "Two L.A. Girls Attempt First Legal Gay Marriage," *Advocate*, July 8, 1970, 5.

56. "No-License Marriage Law Tightened," *Advocate*, November 24, 1971, 22.

57. "Marriage Law Change Having Little Effect," *Advocate*, April 26, 1972, 18.

58. Ibid.

59. Myrna Oliver, "Marriages Without Blood Tests on Rise," *Los Angeles Times*, December 30, 1976, B3. For more on the intersection of immigration and marriage, see Chapter 5.

60. "Legal Gay Marriage in Texas?," *Advocate*, October 25, 1972, 3; Rob Shivers, "Texas Gay Marriage Apparently Within Law," *Advocate*, November 8, 1972, 7.

61. "Legal Gay Marriage in Texas?," 3; Shivers, "Texas Gay Marriage Apparently Within Law," 7.

62. Rob Shivers, "More Gays Seek Marriage Licenses: County Clerks Stop Joking, Start Fretting," *Advocate*, December 20, 1972, 16.

63. Shivers, "More Gays Seek Marriage Licenses," 16.

64. "Wedding Bell Blues: Courts Continuing Anti-Gay Marriage Trend," *Advocate*, February 9, 1977, 9.

65. "Clerk Wants Tighter Law Against Gay Marriages," *Advocate*, June 24, 1970, 2.

66. Ibid.

67. Ibid.; Michael Grieg, "Gay Married Life," *San Francisco Chronicle*, July 15, 1970, Gay Marriage, Coll 2012-0, ONE Subject Files, ONE Archives.

68. Cole, "Gay Marriage 'Boom,'" 6. In fact, passing marriages did remain an issue. See, for example, "Homosexuality and Annulment," *San Francisco Chronicle*, June 24, 1983, Marriage and Divorce [Pre-Marriage Equality], ONE Subject File, ONE Archives.

69. Stewart-Winter, *Queer Clout*, 141; "Two Females 'Married' in Chicago—To Each Other," 54.

70. For insightful work on queer domesticity during the postwar period, see Stephen Vider, " 'Oh Hell, May, Why Don't You People Have a Cookbook?': Camp Humor and Gay Domesticity," *American Quarterly* 65 (December 2013): 877–904.

71. Chris MacNaughton, "Who Gets the Kids?," *Body Politic*, June 1977, 12.

72. Rivers, *Radical Relations*, 171–80.

73. Sue Zemel, "Choosing to Parent," *Advocate*, April 30, 1981, 19.

74. Mark Strasser, "Fit to Be Tied: On Custody, Discretion, and Sexual Orientation," *American University Law Review* 46 (February 1997): 10–11; Rivers, *Radical Relations*; George, "Custody Crucible," 518–20. See also Nancy D. Polikoff, "The Child Does Have Two Mothers: Redefining Parenthood to Meet the Needs of Children in Lesbian-Mother and Other Nontraditional Families," *Georgetown Law Journal* 78 (February 1990): 459–576; Stephen B. Pershing, " 'Entreat Me Not to Leave Thee': *Bottoms v. Bottoms* and the Custody Rights of Gay and Lesbian Parents," *William & Mary Bill of Rights Journal* 3 (1994): 289–325; Amy D. Ronner, "*Bottoms v. Bottoms*: The Lesbian Mother and the Judicial Perpetuation of Damaging Stereotypes," *Yale Journal of Law & Feminism* 7 (1995): 341–73; Julie Shapiro, "Custody and Conduct: How the Law Fails Lesbian and Gay Parents and Their Children," *Indiana Law Journal* 71 (Summer 1996): 623–71; Rhonda R. Rivera, "Our Straight-Laced Judges: The Legal Position of Homosexual Persons in the United States," *Hastings Law Journal* 50 (April 1999): 1179–98; Pleck, *Not Just Roommates*, especially 159, 170.

75. Douglas NeJaime, "Before Marriage: The Unexplored History of Nonmarital Recognition and Its Relationship to Marriage," *California Law Review* 102 (2014): 91.

76. Other activity associated with a gay identity could also jeopardize a gay parent's rights, particularly being involved in gay liberation. See for example, Rivers, *Radical Relations*.

77. For accounts of the battle gay and lesbian groups took to gain custody, see especially Polikoff, "Child Does Have Two Mothers"; Rivers, *Radical Relations*; and George, "Custody Crucible," 487–529.

78. *Nadler v. Nadler*, 255 Cal. App. 2d 523; 63 Cal. Rptr. 352 (1967).

79. *In the Matter of Jane B.*, 85 Misc. 2d 525; 380 N.Y.S. 2d 858 (1976).

80. *In the Matter of J.S. & C.*, 129 N.J. Super. 486; 324 A.2d 90 (1974).

81. *Di Stefano v. Di Stefano*, 60 A.D.2d 976; 401 N.Y.S. 2d 637 (1978). Emphasis added.

82. See Rivers, *Radical Relations*, in particular.

83. *Di Stefano v. Di Stefano*.

84. *In the Matter of J.S. & C.*

85. Enid Nemy, "The Woman Homosexual: More Assertive, Less Willing to Hide," *New York Times*, November 17, 1969, 62.

86. Anti-Sexism Committee of the San Francisco-Bay Area Chapter of the National Lawyers Guild, "A Gay Parents' Legal Guide to Child Custody," 1978, box 30, folder 65, Betty Berzon Papers, 1928–2006, ONE Archives. See also the 1985 edition, Anti-Sexism Committee of the San Francisco-Bay Area Chapter of the National Lawyer's Guild, "A Lesbian & Gay Parents' Legal Guide to Child Custody," 1985, box 30, folder 65, Betty Berzon Papers, 1928–2006, ONE Archives.

87. Thom Willenbecher, "Gay Men Leave Straight Marriages," *Advocate*, February 22, 1979, 44.

88. Gifford Guy Gibson with Mary Jo Risher, *By Her Own Admission: A Lesbian's Fight to Keep Her Son* (Garden City, NY: Doubleday, 1977), 61.

89. George, "Custody Crucible."

90. *Chaffin v. Frye*, 45 Cal. App. 3d 43; 119 Cal. Rptr. 23 (1975).

91. Ibid. Emphasis added.

92. *Jacobson v. Jacobson*, 314 N.W.2d 81 (1981).

93. Ibid.

94. *In the Matter of Jane B.*, 85 Misc. 2d 527; 380 N.Y.S.2d 860 (1976).

95. Cited in *Bezio v. Patenaude*, 381 Mass. 569; 410 N.E.2d 1211 (1980). See also *Chaffin v. Frye*, 43 Cal. App. 3d at 43, 119 Cal. Rptr. at 23 and *In re Tammy* F. 1 Civ. No. 32648 Cal. App. (1973) cited in Rivera, "Our Straight-Laced Judges," 1114 and 1106.

96. *Kallas v. Kallas*, 614 P.2d 645 (1980).

97. Judy Y. Samelson, "Lapeer Court to Decide if Home Is Fit for Children," *Flint MI Journal*, September 27, 1973, box 15, folder Child Custody, Lesbian Legacy Collection, ONE Archives.

98. Beth Ann Krier, "A Lesbian's Battle for Son's Custody," *Los Angeles Times*, August 30, 1977, G1; "Books," *Body Politic*, September 1, 1977, 14; Terry Wolverton, "Custody's Last Stand," *Lesbian Tide*, September/October 1977, 30.

99. Gibson, *By Her Own Admission*, 61.

100. Ibid., 15.

101. Ibid., 85.

102. Ibid., 157.

103. Ibid., 142.

104. *Risher v. Risher*, 547 S.W.2d 292 (1977).

105. *M.P. v. S.P.*, 169 N.J. Super. 430; 404 A.2d 1259 (1979).

106. Ibid.

107. *In the Matter of J.S. & C.*, 129 N.J. Super. 488; 324 A.2d 92 (1974).

108. See the account in Rivera, "Our Straight-Laced Judges," 1111–12.

109. *A. v. A.*, 15 Ore. App. 356; 514 P.2d 359 (1973).

110. *Schuster v. Schuster, Isaacson v. Isaacson*, 90 Wn.2d 631; 585 P.2d 133 (1978).

111. Ibid. Another exceptional case prior to this, the 1973 Michigan case *People v. Brown*, held that "There was sufficient evidence to support the conclusion that the women were engaged in a lesbian relationship. However, there is very little to support the conclusion that this relationship rendered the home an unfit place for the children to reside." *People v. Brown*, 49 Mich. App. 365; 212 N.W.2d 59 (1973).

112. This rule was still in place as late as 2007 in Virginia. *A.O.V. v. J.R.V.* No. 0219-06-4, No. 0220-06-4, 2007 Va. App. LEXIS 64.

113. *DeVita v. DeVita*, 145 N.J. Super. 128; 366 A.2d 1355 (1976).

114. For cases in which state supreme courts continued to deprive cohabiting parents of their rights, see Rivers, *Radical Relations*, 76.

115. Boucai, "Glorious Precedents," 29, 51–53.

116. "Women Await Ruling on Wedding," *Advocate*, December 9, 1970, 4.

117. Ibid.

118. "Women to Fight for Kentucky License," *Advocate*, August 5, 1970, 6.

119. Ibid.

120. For a later articulation of this idea, see Roberta Achtenburg's attempt in 1985 to distinguish lesbian couples who hoped to provide mutual financial support to each other from unmarried heterosexual cohabiting couples. NeJaime, "Before Marriage," 123.

121. "Those Two Minnesota Boys Urge IRS to Tax Their Love," *Advocate*, July 17, 1974, 23.

122. Howard Erickson, "Joint Tax Return Denied for Minnesota Pair," *Advocate*, January 1, 1975, 6.

123. Case, "Marriage Licenses," 1763.

124. *McConnell v. Nooner*, 547 F.2d 54 (1976).

125. "Welfare Thinks They're a Couple, But License Bureau Won't Agree," *Advocate*, September 29, 1970, 4.

126. *United States Department of Agriculture v. Moreno*, 413 U.S. 528, 93 S. Ct. 2821, 37 L. Ed. 2d 782 (1973).

127. See for example, the case of Charles G. Harris, who retained his food stamps even as he faced extreme employment discrimination. Carey Winfrey, "Homosexual Sues to Limit Rights of Employer to Dismiss Workers," *New York Times*, May 1, 1978, B2.

128. *Parker v. State of Louisiana*, 261 So. 2d 364 (1972).

129. For more on how housing policy favored straight couples, see Margot Canaday, *The Straight State: Sexuality and Citizenship in Twentieth-Century America* (Princeton, NJ: Princeton University Press, 2009); Pleck, *Not Just Roommates*; and Clayton Howard, "Building a 'Family Friendly' Metropolis: Sexuality, the State, and Postwar Housing Policy," *Journal of Urban History* 39 (September 2013): 933–55.

130. *Stable Family Amendment*, HR 7554, 95th Cong. 1st sess., *Congressional Record* 123, pt. 16: 19076 (June 15, 1977); U.S. Congress, House of Representatives, Committee on Banking, Currency and Housing, *The Housing Authorization Act: Hearings before the Subcommittee on Housing and Community Development of the Committee on Banking, Currency and Housing, House of Representatives, Ninety-Fourth Congress, Second Session on H.R. 11769*, 94th Cong., 2nd sess., 1976, 312.

131. Judy Burke, "HUD to Allow Gays, Unmarried Couples in Public Housing," *Washington Post*, May 28, 1977, A2; "H.U.D. Will Accept Unmarried Couples for Public Housing," *New York Times*, May 29, 1977, 22.

132. Ibid.

133. "Public Housing for Gay Couples," *Advocate*, July 27, 1977, 14.

134. Burke, "HUD to Allow Gays, Unmarried Couples in Public Housing," A2; "H.U.D. Will Accept Unmarried Couples for Public Housing," 22.

135. "House Acts to Deny VA Benefits to 'Upgraded' Vietnam Veterans," *Los Angeles Times*, June 16, 1977, 9.

136. Representative Boland speaking on HR 7544, 95th Cong., 1st sess., *Congressional Record* 123, pt. 16: 19076–77 (June 15, 1977).

137. Mary Russell, "Taking 'Joy Rides' on the Floor," *Washington Post*, June 16, 1977, A1.

138. Representative Boland speaking on HR 7544, 95th Cong., 1st sess., *Congressional Record*, 19076–77.

139. See Pleck, *Not Just Roommates* for local concessions to gay and lesbian households in the 1980s.

140. A. Corbett Sullivan, "Adams/Sullivan Same Sex Marriage 1975," 2009, box 1, folder 4: Correspondence, 1975–1985, 2009, Anthony Corbett Sullivan v. Immigration and Naturalization Service Legal Records (hereafter cited as Sullivan v. INS Records), ONE Archives.

141. Press release, April 22, 1975, box 1, folder 1: Case Records: 1974–1976, Sullivan v. INS Records.

142. Press Release, December 3, 1975, Resumé of Events to this point, box 1, folder 1: Case Records, 1974–1976, Sullivan v. INS Records.

143. Press release, April 22, 1975, box 1, folder 1: Case Records: 1974–1976, Sullivan v. INS Records.

144. Bradley Altman, "Champagne in Limbo for Tony and Richard," *Advocate*, April 20, 1977, 45.

145. United States Department of Justice Immigration and Naturalization Service, file no. A 20 537 540 Diaty/Ditra, December 2, 1975, box 1, folder 1: Case Records, 1974–1976, Sullivan v. INS Records.

146. Anthony Sullivan & Richard Adams to Hon. Harry A. Waxman, February 1, 1985, box 1, folder 4: Correspondence, 1975–1985, 2009, Sullivan v. INS Records.

147. Mother to Tony, April 1, 1975, box 1, folder 4: Correspondence, 1975–1985, 2009, Sullivan v. INS Records.

148. Board of Immigration Appeals, In the Matter of Anthony Corbett Sullivan, No. A 20 537 540 Diaty/Ditra, page 4, box 1, folder 1: Case Records, 1974–1976, Sullivan v. INS Records.

149. Quoted in Statement of Anthony Corbett Sullivan, October 5, 1981, box 1, folder 2: Case Records, Sullivan v. INS Records.

150. *Adams v. Howerton*, 673 F.2d 1036 (1982).

151. Jeremy D. Gerber to Ronald Reagan, October 23, 1985, box 1, folder 1: Case Records, 1974–1976, Sullivan v. INS Records.

152. Canaday, *Straight State*, 214–54; Marc Stein, *Sexual Injustice: Supreme Court Decisions from Griswold to Roe* (Chapel Hill: University of North Carolina Press, 2013).

153. See in particular Canaday, *Straight State*, 214–54 and Stein, *Sexual Injustice*, 243–78. See also *Fleuti v. Rosenberg*, 302 F.2d 652 (1962); *In Re. Labady*, 326 F. Supp. 924 (1971).

154. *United States v. Windsor*. 133 S. Ct. 2675; 186 L. Ed. 2d 808 (2013).

Conclusion

1. The White House Office of Policy Development, "Report to the Domestic Policy Council on the Family," 21, box 1-F, folder Family Report to the Domestic Policy Council on the Final Draft, Kenneth T. Cribb Files, Ronald Reagan Presidential Papers, Ronald Reagan Presidential Library, Simi Valley, CA (hereafter cited as RRPL).

2. The percentage of women in the workforce overall grew from 29.6 percent in 1950 to 46.6 percent in 2000. Mitra Toossi, "A Century of Change: The U.S. Labor Force, 1950–2050," *Monthly Labor Review* 125 (May 2002): 16.

3. Rep. Christopher H. Smith of New Jersey speaking on Aid for America's Neediest Families, extension of remarks, 105th Cong., 2nd sess., *Congressional Record* 144 (June 16, 1998), pt 9: 12533.

4. Gwendolyn Mink, *Welfare's End* (Ithaca, NY: Cornell University Press, 2002).

5. See for example, Ruth Sidel, *Keeping Women and Children First* (New York: Penguin Books, 1996).

6. John F. Harris and Judith Havemann, "Clinton Vows Tougher Rules on Welfare Fathers," *Washington Post*, June 19, 1996, A02.

7. For the race politics of the Clinton-era reforms, see for example, Sidel, *Keeping Women and Children First*; Vee Burke, Joe Richardson, Carmen Solomon-Fears, Karen Spar, and Joyce Vialet, Education and Public Welfare Division, "New Welfare Law: The Personal Responsibility and Work Opportunity Reconciliation Act of 1996," box 1522, folder 6, Patsy Mink Papers, Library of Congress.

8. Senator Levin, speaking on *Personal Responsibility, Work Opportunity, and Medicaid Restructuring Act of 1996*, S 1956, 104th Cong., 2nd sess., *Congressional Record* 142 (July 18, 1996): S8101.

9. Byron Dorgan, ibid., S8094.

10. Sharon Parrott, "The TANF-Related Provisions in the President's Budget," Center on Budget and Policy Priorities, February 7, 2002, box 11, folder 8, Project IRENE Records, 1996–2004, Loyola University Chicago; H.R. 1471—Child Support Distribution Act of 2001, 107th Congress, https://www.congress.gov/bill/107th-congress/house-bill/1471?resultIndex=25.

11. Outline of Republican Welfare Reform Bill, November 1993, box 1255, folder 6, Patsy Mink Papers.

12. Diaz notably also could not afford to go to the hospital afterward. "Family Violence Option Now in Effect in Illinois," *Illinois Welfare News*, July 2002, 3, box 13, folder 5; Testimony of Jessie Diaz, Illinois House of Representatives, Human Services Committee, Subject Matter: "Access to IDHS Services," October 15, 2003, box 14, folder 1; Testimony Rose Karasti, Senior Policy Associate, Illinois House of Representatives, Human Services Committee, Subject Matter: "Access to IDHS Services," October 15, 2003, box 14, folder 1, all in Project IRENE Records.

13. Frances Robles and Shaila Dewan, "Skip Child Support. Go to Jail. Lose Job. Repeat," *New York Times*, April 29, 2015, A1.

14. David Firestone, "100,000 New Yorkers May Be Cut off Welfare in Crackdown," *New York Times*, August 8, 1995, B1.

15. Richelle S. Swan, Linda L. Shaw, Sharon Cullity, Mary Roche, Joni Halperin, Wendy M. Limpert, and Juliana Humphry, "The Untold Story of Welfare Fraud," *Journal of Sociology & Social Welfare* 35 (September 2008): 133–51.

16. *Sanchez v. County of San Diego*, 483 F.3d 969 (2007).

17. See for example, Anna Marie Smith, *Welfare Reform and Sexual Regulation* (Cambridge: Cambridge University Press, 2007); Sidel, *Keeping Women and Children First*; Martha Fineman and Terence Dougherty, ed., *Feminism Confronts Homo Economicus: Gender, Law, and Society* (Ithaca, NY: Cornell University Press, 2005); Linda C. McClain, *The Place of Families: Fostering Capacity, Equality, and Responsibility* (Cambridge, MA: Harvard University Press, 2006); Mink, *Welfare's End*; Kathryn Edin, "Few Good Men: Why Poor Mothers Don't Marry or Remarry," *American Prospect* 11 (January 2000): 26–31; and Angela Onwuachi-Willig, "The Return of the Ring: Welfare Reform's Marriage Cure as the Revival of Post-Bellum Control," *California Law Review* 93, no. 6 (2005): 1647–96.

18. Aaron McGruder, *Boondocks*, undated, Marriage and Divorce [Pre-Marriage Equality], ONE Subject Files, ONE National Gay & Lesbian Archives, University of Southern California Libraries, Los Angeles, CA ONE Archives (hereafter cited as ONE Archives).

19. Burke, Richardson, Solomon-Fears, Spar, and Vialet, "New Welfare Law."

20. U.S. Department of Justice, *1994 Statistical Yearbook of the Immigration and Naturalization Service*, 70–71, box 1342, folder 1, Patsy Mink Papers.

21. Joyce C. Vialet, "Immigration: Numerical Limits on Permanent Admissions," *CRS Report for Congress*, December 1, 1994, CRS-3, box 1218, folder 2, Patsy Mink Papers.

22. U.S. Department of Justice, *1994 Statistical Yearbook of the Immigration and Naturalization Service*, 17–18, box 1342, folder 1, Patsy Mink Papers.

23. U.S. Department of Justice, 1994 Statistical Yearbook of the Immigration and Naturalization Service, pp 17–18, box 1342, folder 1, Patsy Mink Papers.

24. Jim Hastings, "Immigration 'Reform' Bill Is a Sham and a Hasty Mistake," *Houston Post*, undated clipping, box 1070, folder 6, Patsy Mink Papers.

25. Democratic Study Group, U.S. House of Representatives, "Fact Sheet: Immigration Agreement," October 25, 1990, box 1070, folder 7, Patsy Mink Papers.

26. Democratic Study Group, U.S. House of Representatives, "Fact Sheet: Immigration Amendments," October 1, 1990, box 1070, folder 7, Patsy Mink Papers.

27. Ibid.

28. Joyce C. Vialet and Ruth Ellen Wasem, "Immigration: Analysis of Major Proposals to Revise Family and Employment Admissions," *CRS Report for Congress*, February 14, 1996, CRS-4, box 1344, folder 1, Patsy Mink Papers.

29. Julian Smith, "Immigration Exploitation Myths . . . or Reality?," *Washington Times*, March 11, 1996, A17, box 1342, folder 3, Patsy Mink Papers.

30. National Immigration Forum, "Issue Brief: Costs and Contributions of Immigrants," box 1342, folder 3, Patsy Mink Papers.

31. Lamar Smith to Colleague, March 20, 1996, box 1342, folder 3, Patsy Mink Papers.

32. Joyce Vialet, "Illegal Immigration: Facts and Issues," *CRS Report for Congress*, December 21, 1994, CRS-1-2, box 1346, folder 5, Patsy Mink Papers.

33. Joseph D. Delfico, "Benefits for Illegal Aliens: Some Program Costs Increasing, But Total Costs Unknown," September 29, 1993, box 1346, folder 8, Patsy Mink Papers.

34. Ibid.

35. Sam Howe Verhovek, "Stop Benefits for Aliens? It Wouldn't Be That Easy," *New York Times*, June 8, 1994, box 1346, folder 8, Patsy Mink Papers.

36. Randy Fitzgerald, "Welfare for Illegal Aliens?" *Reader's Digest*, June 1994, box 1218, folder 1, Patsy Mink Papers.

37. D. H. to Patsy Mink, March 22, 1994, box 1218, folder 2, Patsy Mink Papers.

38. C. R. to Patsy Mink, August [9?], 1994, box 1218, folder 2, Patsy Mink Papers.

39. P. P. to Patsy Mink, November 15, 1993, box 1218, folder 6, Patsy Mink Papers.

40. R. P. to Patsy Mink, November 16, 1994, box 1346, folder 6, Patsy Mink Papers.

41. On illegal immigrants as a threat to welfare, see for example, P. H. to Patsy Mink, October 8, 1991, and Congressman Elton Gallegly to Colleague, February 11, 1994, box 1070, folder 6, Patsy Mink papers.

42. Alice M. Rivlin, Executive Office of the President, Office of Management and Budget, to Patsy Mink, May 6, 1996, box 1345, folder 7, Patsy Mink Papers.

43. National Immigration Forum, "Issue Brief: Immigrants & Welfare," box 1342, folder 3; and Congressional Hispanic Caucus, "Issue Brief: Immigration Reform and Public Benefits (HR 2202, Title VI)," March 1, 1996, folder 2, both Patsy Mink Papers.

44. Alice M. Rivlin to Patsy Mink, May 6, 1996.

45. National Immigration Forum, "Issue Brief: Immigrants & Welfare"; Congressional Hispanic Caucus, "Issue Brief: Immigration Reform and Public Benefits (HR 2202, Title VI)."

46. "Five Major Immigrant Provisions at Issue in the House & Senate Welfare Reform Conference," undated flier, box 1346, folder 1, Patsy Mink Papers.

47. Chairman Ed Pastor and Ileana Ros-Lehtinen to Colleagues, March 19, 1996; James L. Lack, president NCSL, to Ed Pastor, March 4, 1996, box 1342, folder 3, Patsy Mink Papers; *Graham v. Richardson*, 403 U.S. 365 (1971).

48. Patsy Mink to Robert Ichikawa, August 15, 1996, box 1343, folder 4, Patsy Mink Papers.

49. Patsy Mink to Robert Ichikawa, American Immigration Lawyers Association, August 15, 1996, box 1343, folder 4, Patsy Mink Papers. See also Alert from U.S. Congresswoman Patsy T. Mink; Jon Jeter, "States Face Dilemma on Immigrants," August 13, 1996, clipping; and Joyce C. Vialet and Larry M. Eig, "Alien Eligibility for Benefits under H.R. 3734, Welfare Conference Agreement," all box 1343, folder 4, Patsy Minks Papers.

50. Congressman Xavier Becerra (D-CA), "Testimony Submitted to the Ways and Means Committee: Immigration and Welfare Benefits," 3, May 23, 1996, box 1344, folder 4, Patsy Mink Papers.

51. "Five Major Immigrant Provisions at Issue in the House & Senate Welfare Reform Conference."

52. Joyce C. Vialet, "Alien Eligibility for Public Assistance," *CRS Report for Congress*, December 18, 1997, CRS-3, box 1522, folder 1, Patsy Mink Papers.

53. Ibid.

54. National Immigration Forum, "What Public Benefits Can 'Qualified' Immigrants Receive?," January 1998, box 1346, folder 1, Patsy Mink Papers.

55. Ibid.

56. Burke, Richardson, Solomon-Fears, Spar, and Vialet, "New Welfare Law."

57. Vialet and Wasem, "Immigration: Analysis of Major Proposals to Revise Family and Employment Admissions," CRS-11. For more on this, see Kerry Abrams, "Becoming a Citizen: Marriage, Immigration, and Assimilation," *Gender Equality* (2009): 39–59 and Kerry Abrams, "Immigration Law and the Regulation of Marriage," *Minnesota Law Review* 91 (2006–7): 1625–1709.

58. Patsy Mink to AR, September 5, 1995, box 1343, folder 2; and Congressmen Howard L. Berman, Chris Smith, Dick Chrysler, and Sam Brownback to Colleague, "The Facts on Immigration #8: Is Your Child Part of Your Nuclear Family?" March 19, 1996, box 1344, folder 3, both Patsy Mink Papers.

59. Patsy Mink to AR, September 5, 1995.

60. The Federation for American Immigration Reform, "Title-By-Title Analysis of the Immigration Stabilization Act of 1993 Introduced by Senator Reid (D-Nev)," For Your Information, box II:592, folder 10, Daniel Patrick Moynihan Papers, Library of Congress.

61. Vialet, "Alien Eligibility for Public Assistance," CRS-5.

62. Ibid., CRS-6.

63. Michael D. Antonovich to Patsy Mink, March 19, 1996, box 1343, folder 5, Patsy Mink Papers.

64. Italics in original. Ibid.

65. Luis V. Gutierrez to Colleague, March 19, 1996, box 1342, folder 3, Patsy Mink Papers.

66. Family-Based Immigration Summary, box 1344, folder 5, Patsy Mink Papers.

67. Vialet and Wasem, "Immigration: Analysis of Major Proposals to Revise Family and Employment Admissions, CRS-4.

68. "Many American Families Will Remain Separated if an Immigrant's Sponsor Must Earn at Least 200% of the Poverty Level," flier, box 1342, folder 3, Patsy Mink Papers.

69. "Five Major Immigrant Provisions at Issue in the House & Senate Welfare Reform Conference."

70. Ibid.

71. Frances C. Berger, Association of the Bar of the City of New York, to Senator Daniel Patrick Moynihan, September 20, 1996, box II1859, folder 2, Daniel Patrick Moynihan Papers.

72. Vialet and Wasem, "Immigration: Analysis of Major Proposals to Revise Family and Employment Admissions."

73. The amendment also eliminated a provision that would have excluded undocumented children from school. Patsy Mink to Melba Bantay, April 8, 1996, box 1343, folder 3, Patsy Mink Papers.

74. Vialet, "Alien Eligibility for Public Assistance," CRS-3.

75. Patsy Mink to Robert Ichikawa, July 29, 1996, box 1343, folder 4, Patsy Mink Papers.

76. These debts were deemed enforceable in *Stump v. Stump*, 2005 U.S. Dist. LEXIS 26002 (2005).

77. Congressional Hispanic Caucus, "Issue Brief: Immigration Reform and Public Benefits (HR 2202, Title VI)."

78. It might have been worse. Another bill proposed deeming for a period of ten years after an immigrant's arrival. Deeming previously affected only AFDC, SSI, and food stamps; this legislation expanded it to more than fifty means-based programs. An immigrant spouse would only be eligible for AFDC, Medicaid, SSI, WIC, school lunch, and food stamps if his or her sponsor made so little that both the immigrant and citizen spouses together qualified. Memorandum for Senator Moynihan from Gray Maxwell, Ben Marsh, and Jon Secrest, "Subj: Final Vote on the Immigration Bill," May 2, 1996, box II1860, folder 2, Daniel Patrick Moynihan Papers.

79. AYUDA, Inc. and the Family Violence Prevention Fund, "Action Alert: 'Immigration in the National Interest Act' (H.R. 1915) Could Trap Battered and Abused Immigrant Women in Violent Situations," July 17, 1995, box 1345, folder 2, Patsy Mink Papers.

80. National Immigration Forum, "Fix '96: Restore America's Tradition as a Nation of Immigrants and a Nation of Just Laws," September 3, 1999, box 1629, folder 10, Patsy Mink Papers.

81. Peter Baker, "President Backs a Plan to Curtail Legal Migration," *New York Times*, August 3, 2017, A1.

82. "Marriage Project-Hawaii: Update June 1998," June 30, 1998, folder Marriage, Coll. 2012, ONE Subject Files Collection Bulk, ONE Archives.

83. "Talk of the Town: Tom and Walter Got Married," *New Yorker*, December 20, 1993, box 92, folder Gay Marriage and Commitment Ceremonies 1970, 1993, 1997–2006, n.d, (92.10), Barbara Gittings and Kay Tobin Lahusen Gay History Papers and Photographs MssCol 6397, New York Public Library.

84. Sue Fox, "Rule Nixes Gay Spouses from Family Leave Act," *Washington Blade*, January 10, 1997, 19, box 5, folder 21: Federal Employees, Charles W. Gossett Papers, ONE Archives.

85. On domestic violence, see "Attorney General Says Virginia Law Excludes Same-Sex Couples," *Washington Blade*, August 4, 1995, 6, box 5, folder Marriage Law/Family Law Conservative Legislation, Charles W. Gossett Papers. For the desire for access to divorce, see "Gay Divorce in Florida Becomes Quagmire," *Voice*, July 1, 1993, 4, box 5, folder Marriage Laws—Same sex, ibid. On custody, see "Lesbian Jailed for Defying Visitation Ruling" *Washington Blade*, August 11, 1995, 16, box 5, folder 19: Same Sex Marriage 2/3 1978–1995, ibid.

86. Evan Wolfson, Lambda Legal Defense and Education Fund, Jeffrey Gibson, ABA Section on Individual Rights and Responsibilities, chair Lesbian & Gay Committee, and Barbara Cox, California Western School of Law, to Attorneys, Academics, and Students, January 9, 1995, box 125, folder 12, Frank Kameny Papers, Library of Congress.

87. Ibid.

88. "House Gives Nod to Marriage Bill," *Garden Island*, February 4, 1994, folder Marriage, Collection 2012-0, ONE Subject Files Collection Bulk, ONE Archives.

89. Mary Anne Case, "Marriage Licenses," *Minnesota Law Review* 89 (2005): 1758–97

90. Rep. Robert Barr on *Defense of Marriage Act*, HR474, 104th Cong., 2nd sess., *Congressional Record* 142 (July 12, 1996), H 7482.

91. U.S. Congress, House of Representatives, Committee on the Judiciary, *Defense of Marriage Act, Hearing Before the Subcommittee on the Constitution of Committee on the Judiciary House of Representatives*, 104th Cong., 2nd sess., May 15, 1996, 32.

92. C. B. to Patsy Mink, April 9, 2002, box 1742, folder 7, Patsy Mink Papers.

93. *Baker v. Vermont*, 744 A.2D 864 (1999).

94. *Goodridge v. Department of Public Health*, 798 N.E.2d 941 (2003).

95. *Troxel v. Granville*, 530 U.S. 57 (2000).

96. *A.H. v. M.P.*, 447 Mass. 828 (2006).

97. *Davenport v. Little-Bowser*, 611 S.E.2d 366 (2005).

98. *United States v. Windsor*, 699 F. 3d 169 (2013).

99. *Obergefell v. Hodges*, 135 S. Ct. 2584; 192 L. Ed. 2d 609 (2015).

100. For example, marriage equality proponents spent $33.9 million on four state ballot initiatives in 2012. Juliet Eilperin, "Gay Marriage Fight Will Cost Tens of Millions" *Washington Post*, July 1, 2013, http://www.washingtonpost.com/blogs/the-fix/wp/2013/07/01/how-much-will-the-gay-marriage-fight-cost-over-the-next-three-years-tens-of-millions/.

101. This is a widespread critique, but see for example Nancy D. Polikoff, *Beyond Straight and Gay Marriage: Valuing All Families Under the Law* (Boston: Beacon Press, 2008) and Craig Willse and Dean Spade, "Freedom in a Regulatory State? Lawrence, Marriage and Biopolitics," *Widener Law Review* 11 (2005): 309–29.

102. Arlie Hochschild, *The Second Shift: Working Parents and the Revolution at Home* (New York: Viking, 1989), 250.

103. Testimony of Prof. William A. Stanmeyer, Indiana University School of Law, in U.S.

Congress, House of Representatives, Committee on the Judiciary, *Equal Rights Amendment Extension: Hearings Before the Subcommittee on Civil and Constitutional Rights of the Committee on the Judiciary, House of Representatives, Ninety-Fifth Congress on H.J.Res. 638*, 95th Cong., 2nd sess., May 19, 1978, 365. For a similar expression of fears of individualization in the family, see Republican senator Albert Lee Smith's remark that "one alarming trend in the assault on the family is the increasing imbalance in the courts between the view that family members are individuals with special needs for civil rights protection and the view that the family is a legal entity with certain rights and responsibilities." Deb re. Albert Lee Smith to E. H. D., New File: Family Protection Act, box 27, folder Family Protection Act-1982 (1), Elizabeth Dole Files, RRPL.

104. Charles Stanley, Southern Baptist Convention and Pastor, First Baptist Church, in U.S. Congress, Senate, Committee on the Judiciary, *Equal Rights Amendment Extension: Hearings Before the Subcommittee on the Constitution of the Committee on the Judiciary, United States Senate, Ninety-Fifth Congress on S.J. Res. 134*, 95th Cong., 2nd sess., date, 270.

105. Arlene Skolnick, *Embattled Paradise: The American Family in an Age of Uncertainty* (New York: Basic Books, 1991), especially 125–50.

106. Juan José Peña, "On the Question of the Chicano Family," *Partido de La Raza Unida de Nuevo Mexico: Discussion Bulletin Number 5*, 1979, New Mexico Highlands University—Donnelly Library, ArchiveGrid, https://beta.worldcat.org/archivegrid/collection/data/11277714.

107. Michael Grossberg, *Governing the Hearth: Law and Family in Nineteenth Century America* (Chapel Hill: University of North Carolina Press, 1985).

108. Steven Mintz and Susan Kellogg, *Domestic Revolutions: A Social History of American Family Life* (New York: Free Press, 1989), 43–45.

109. Amy Dru Stanley, *From Bondage to Contract: Wage Labor, Marriage, and the Market in the Age of Slave Emancipation* (Cambridge: Cambridge University Press, 1998); Barbara Welke, *Law and the Borders of Belonging in the Long Nineteenth Century United States* (New York: Cambridge University Press, 2010).

110. Jennifer Mittelstadt, *The Rise of the Military Welfare State* (Cambridge, MA: Harvard University Press, 2015).

111. Daniel H. Pink, *Free Agent Nation: The Future of Working for Yourself* (New York: Business Plus, 2001).

112. Jay Hancock, "UPS Won't Insure Spouses of Many Employees," *USA Today*, August 20, 2013, http://www.usatoday.com/story/money/business/2013/08/20/ups-spouses-health-insurance/2651713/; "University Employees Will See Significant Changes to Health Plan This Year," *UVA Today*, August 21, 2013, https://news.virginia.edu/content/university-employees-will-see-significant-changes-health-plan-year.

113. In 2015, 47 percent of respondents reported that they excluded or charged for spousal benefits, up from 20 percent in 2012. See Dan Cook, "Employers Dropping Spousal Coverage," May 15, 2015, BenefitsPro, http://www.benefitspro.com/2015/05/26/employers-dropping-spousal-coverage.

114. Elizabeth A. Fones-Wolf, *Selling Free Enterprise: The Business Assault on Labor and Liberalism, 1945–1960* (Urbana: University of Illinois Press, 1995).

115. David Harvey, *A Brief History of Neoliberalism* (Oxford: Oxford University Press, 2017); Daniel Rodgers, *Age of Fracture* (Cambridge, MA: Belknap Press, 2012), Jefferson Cowie. *Stayin' Alive: The 1970s and the Last Days of the Working Class* (New York: New Press, 2012); Robert D. Putnam, *Bowling Alone: The Collapse and Revival of American Community* (New York: Simon and Schuster, 2001). Notably, politicians otherwise associated with neoliberalism rejected the

idea that the family should be atomized. Margaret Thatcher declared there was no such thing as society, only individuals. But she maintained that there were families. Mary Abbott, *Family Affairs: A History of Family in 20th Century England* (London: Routledge, 2003). In their joint memoir, Milton Friedman and his wife, Rose Friedman, presented their family as a unit with a natural division of labor. Milton Friedman and Rose D. Friedman, *Two Lucky People: Memoirs* (Chicago: University of Chicago Press, 1998).

116. Scott Yenor, *Family Politics: The Idea of Marriage in Modern Political Thought* (Waco, TX: Baylor University Press, 2011) and Polikoff, *Beyond Straight and Gay Marriage*.

INDEX

ACKNOWLEDGMENTS

There are so many people to thank for their help. This project began at the University of Chicago, and many people there have continued to help me with it. I am very grateful for all the wisdom and support I've received from Amy Dru Stanley, George Chauncey, James Sparrow, and Christine Stansell. Amy has generously shared her brilliant insights (and many dinners), and her work is a constant inspiration as well. George's advice and encouragement has also been invaluable. Even from afar, he has asked me the hard questions that helped this work develop. Jim Sparrow has been a constant source of support and insightful feedback. Finally, Christine Stansell has been an irreplaceably enthusiastic and helpful critic.

The University of Chicago as a whole was also an amazing community. The Center for Sexuality and Gender Studies provided me with financial and intellectual support for several years running. I was honored to receive the James C. Hormel Fellowship in Lesbian and Gay Studies and the Center for Gender Studies Fellowship. Thanks to the University of Chicago History Department and the Freehling Grant Committee for financial support as well. Thanks to Mary Anne Case, Bill Sewell, Ramón Gutiérrez, David Goodwine, Craig Becker, Tom Stanley-Becker, Isaac Stanley-Becker, James Hormel, Debbie Nelson, Stuart Michaels, Gina Olson, Thom Bahde, Julia Brookins, Nancy Buenger, Mike Czaplicki, Joanna Grisinger, Allyson Hobbs, Roman Hoyos, Molly Hudgens, Kelly King-O'Brien, Monica Mercado, Carl Nash, Jess Neptune, Meredith Oda, Arissa Oh, Emily Remus, Hillary Reser, David Spatz, Tracy Steffes, Anthony Todd, Elizabeth Todd-Breland, Katie Turk, Kyle Volk, and Ellen Wu. Thomas Adams, Jon Levy, Sarah Potter, Gautham Rao, and Jennifer Vanore—all brilliant and all dear friends—particularly read things for me over and over again. Thank you!

I was lucky enough to spend two years in Oxford, Ohio, during a crucial period of writing. Allan Winkler, Drew Cayton, Mary Cayton, Charlotte

Goldy, Elena Albarrán, J. C. Albarrán, Nishani Frazier, Kelly Quinn, Damon Scott, Tatiana Seijas, Jose Amador, Kimberly Hamlin, Amanda McVety, Carla Pestana, and Rena Lauer were all wonderful companions and helpful interlocutors at Miami University.

Other kind souls have also helped me think about this project, including Will Baude, Eileen Boris, Kristin Cellelo, Nancy Cott, Deborah Dinner, Sarah Dubow, Gill Frank, Apryl Cox Jackson, Tom Foster, David Garrow, Dirk Hartog, Caley Horan, Lauren Kaminsky, Emily Twarog LaBarbera, Vanessa May, Elaine Tyler May, Sarah Milov, Ana Raquel Minian, Wendy Mink, Allison Perlman, Roderick Phillips, Elizabeth Pleck, Erica Ryan, Reuel Schiller, Nick Syrett, Stacie Taranto, Lauren Thompson, Lara Vapnik, and Jessica Weiss. Thanks especially to Linda Gordon and Christina Simmons, who were both so generous with their time and insights. A few venues have proved to be invaluable, including the Institute for Constitutional History, the Phil Zwickler Workshop, MADCAP at UVA, the NYC Women's History Reading and Writing Group, and the Seton Hall Contact Zones symposium. The J. Willard Hurst Summer Institute in Legal History fundamentally changed how I thought about this project, so thank you especially to Ari Bryen, Rohit De, Nate Holdren, Keramet Reiter, Chris Tomlins, Kim Welch, and above all Barbara Welke.

Thank you to the Schlesinger Library on the History of Women in America for providing financial support and Ellen Shea for research assistance. Similarly thank you to Loyola University Chicago's Women and Leadership Archive for the funds that allowed me to add some crucial evidence, and especially Nancy Freeman. I've also received assistance from many archivists, particularly those at the Abraham Lincoln Presidential Library, the National Archives for Black Women's History, the Library of Congress, and the ONE National Gay and Lesbian Archives at the University of Southern California. Thanks also to the Clerk of Cook County Archives, including Phil Costello and Lois Travis.

Thank you so much to the Center for Historical Research at Ohio State University. I would have never finished this book without the support and the feedback I received there. Thanks especially to Birgitte Soland, Dan Rivers, Susan Hartmann, Katherine Marino, Nick Abbot, and Clay Howard, all of whom generously and insightfully engaged in this project many times over.

My colleagues in the Federated History Department at the New Jersey Institute of Technology and Rutgers University–Newark are the best colleagues a person could ask for. Thank you to Dan Asen, Marybeth Boger,

Chuck Brooks, Karen Caplan, Susan Carruthers, Kornell Chang, Dar Desai, Gary Farney, Eva Giloi, Stuart Gold, Scott Kent, Mark Krasovic, Neil Maher, Lyra Monteiro, Maureen O'Rourke, Katia Passerini, Stephen Pemberton, Liz Petrick, Mary Rizzo, Karl Schweizer, Richard Sher, Christina Strasburger, Nukhet Varlik, Jess Witte-Dyer, and John Wolf. Thank you especially to Kyle Riismandel, Beryl Satter, Nancy Steffen-Fluhr, Whit Strub, and Caitlin Wylie for their insightful feedback on my work. And above all thank you to Tim Stewart-Winter who has read and advised me on so many things scholarly and otherwise.

Margot Canaday, Bob Lockhart, and the anonymous reviewers have been wonderful. Thank you.

I have been very lucky to have support and encouragement from family and friends during the years I've been writing this book. Thank you to the Abate Family, Trey Andrews, Megan Biddinger, Heather Edmands, Donna Foster, Rob Kleinman, Shan Lindstedt, Melanie MacBride, Max Martin, Rachel Mugg, Nancy Parnell, and the wives for being so fun. My parents, Paul and Michele Lefkovitz, are the best parents a daughter could ask for. Thank you so much. Steven Lefkovitz and M. K. Akers have been tremendous sources of support. Drew Endicott, Adriel Endicott, Malcolm and Minda Pownall, Manunya Nookong, aunts, uncles, the Neskers, and cousins have all cheered me on along the way. Dan and Betty Lyons and Sam and Sylvia Lefkovitz in many ways inspired this project on marriage.

And finally, I must thank my own household, Stephan Endicott and Indiana Lefkovitz. You have both brought me so much joy. I could not have done this without you, and I love you so much.